THE COLLAPSE OF ORTHODOXY

The Intellectual Ordeal of
George Frederick Holmes

THE
COLLAPSE OF ORTHODOXY

The Intellectual Ordeal of

George Frederick Holmes

Neal C. Gillespie

Georgia State University

The University Press of Virginia

Charlottesville

For Sherrie

Contents

Preface ix

I   Travels and Trials, 1820–1849   3

II   Enchantment and Disenchantment   40

III   The Rustication, 1849–1857   81

IV   The Philosophy of Faith   108

V   Auguste Comte and the Challenge of Positivism   123

VI   Revolt, Reform, and Reformers   151

VII   Defending Slavery   178

VIII   In the Groves of Academe, 1857–1897   199

IX   "Overwhelmed with Honest Doubts"   226

Select Bibliography   249

Index   269

Preface

INTEREST in the career of George Frederick Holmes, though still of modest dimensions, has been steadily growing. Though ignored for decades, he has now found his way into the pages of a number of books, among them Harvey Wish's *George Fitzhugh: Propagandist of the Old South*, Louis Hartz's *The Liberal Tradition in America*, Clinton Rossiter's *Conservatism in America*, Joseph Dorfman's *The Economic Mind in American Civilization*, Jay B. Hubbell's *The South in American Literature*, and Eugene Genovese's *The World the Slaveholders Made*. Holmes has also been the subject of a number of articles. But no biography has yet appeared; and, as a consequence, some of those who have written about Holmes have not always understood him.

One of the reasons Holmes has escaped a biographer for so long is that during his life he shunned the light, with the result that he became obscure to a later time. Contemporaries who knew him, however, had no doubt about the quality of his participation in the intellectual life of their age. One purpose of this book is to tell that story. It is a story that contains three intertwining themes. One is Holmes the southern critic of nineteenth-century civilization, defender of slavery and the established order. Another is Holmes the embattled Christian struggling to meet the challenges emerging from contemporary science and historical scholarship without sacrificing his faith or his intense love of learning. The third is Holmes the historian attempting to use the methods of science to discover the controlling laws of human society.

But there is another story as well. George Frederick Holmes is of interest as much (perhaps more) for what he was as for what he did. In fact, some who have written about Holmes have inflated his achievements unduly, which doubtlessly is what provoked Eugene Genovese recently to brand him an "overrated pedant." And, in truth, his accomplishments fell far short of his aspiration; in what he did he almost attained the oblivion he sometimes professed to seek. But if Holmes did not make history, he did live through it. Therein lies the importance of what he was. Like thousands of other intellectuals whose names are now forgotten and whose work has lost the vitality it once seemed to have, Holmes had to make his own personal accommodation to the forces of modernity. Historians have made certain that we are familiar with the lives and ideas of the leaders of the intellectual revolution which began in the last century. But for such a revolution to succeed it must also win converts among the lesser minds who follow. This biography has been conceived and written chiefly as a part of that larger story. In so far as it is possible to do so within the scope of one life, I have sought to depict some of the processes by which the mind of an age was changed.

In preparing this book I have incurred a large number of obligations. My first debt is to I. B. Holley, Jr., under whose guidance the work was begun as a dissertation at Duke University. Whatever blunders the book contains the reader may be sure have crept in since it left his supervision. Among the custodians of books and manuscripts, without whose help no scholar could work, I wish to select for special thanks Miss Mattie Russell and the staff at the Duke University Library. Thanks are also due to the staffs of the Library of Congress, the Swem Library at the College of William and Mary, Emory University Library, the University of Virginia Library, the South Caroliniana Library at the University of South Carolina, the Southern Historical Collection at the University of North Carolina, and not least of all, the staff of the Georgia State University Library. I am grateful to the editors of the *Journal of Mississippi History* and the *South Atlantic Quarterly* for permission to use parts of articles first published in their pages and to Duke University Library, the Library of Congress, the Swem Library at the College of William and Mary, Emory University Library, the University of Virginia Library, and the South Caroliniana Library for allowing me to quote from the collections in their care. I am also indebted to Georgia State University for a quarter's leave-of-absence to work on this book.

Special expressions of thanks to George Street of the University of Mississippi, to Joseph O. Baylen and my other colleagues at Georgia State University for their help and interest, to Miss Jane Hobson of the Georgia State University Library, and to the editor and contributors whose labor made possible the valuable *Holmes Family History*. I am above all grateful to N. Floyd Holmes, who made it possible for me to use this history, for his kind interest and very generous help over several years. Finally, my deepest debt is to my wife Sherrie who without complaint gave up countless hours of her time to read and type the many drafts of this book.

Atlanta, Georgia
June 1971

THE COLLAPSE OF ORTHODOXY

The Intellectual Ordeal of
George Frederick Holmes

I   Travels and Trials
1820-1849

O N A June day in 1837 the *Norfolk*, a merchantman bound for
Quebec, left its moorings at Berwick, England, and pulled out
into the channel of the Tweed. Among the *Norfolk*'s passengers was
a tall, spare lad of almost seventeen years. He knew that the voyage
was the beginning of an important period in his life, but he did not
know that he would never see England again.

No one knows for certain how George Frederick Holmes came to
be on the *Norfolk*. According to the earliest published account he
had gone into debt in order to buy an expensive gift of books for his
aunt and benefactress Elizabeth Pemberton. When Aunt Pemberton
discovered the circumstances of the purchase, she and her sister Maryanne Holmes, George's mother, had resolved to teach the erring boy
a lesson and temporarily exiled him from England thinking that a few
uncomfortable months at sea and in America would teach him respect
for the virtue of frugality.[1] Another version of this incident—and one
apparently coming from Holmes himself in his later years—reveals
that the gift was for his sister Annamaria, that his mother was very
cross with him over his violation of the moral code of their class ("I
consider it a necessary principle of *honesty not* to incur a debt without you can pay it" she wrote many years later to another son), and
it implies that George left England in high dudgeon, with his mother
pleading with him to stay.[2] Yet a third source would lead one to
believe that the exile was primarily the idea of Aunt Pemberton and
Dr. James Cowan, headmaster of The Grange School where George
had prepared himself for Durham University.[3] But whatever may

[1] John Robinson, "Sunderland Worthies, No. 3, George Frederick Holmes,
D. C. L.," *Library Circular: A Quarterly Guide and Catalogue for Readers at
Sunderland Public Library*, no. 5 (1900), p. 70. This version of Holmes's exile is
not documented but internal evidence suggests that its source may have been his
youngest daughter Isabel.

[2] N. Floyd Holmes, a grandson, in Mary Hull Buchanan, editor, *Holmes Family History* (published privately, 1960), p. 86. Maryanne Holmes to Edward A.
Holmes, December 11, 1854, *ibid.*, p. 52.

[3] James Cowan to G. F. Holmes, October 29, 1841, MS vol. 1808, George
Frederick Holmes Papers, Duke University Library, Durham, North Carolina;
hereinafter cited as Holmes papers, D.

have been the actual cause of his leaving England, that summer George found himself on the deck of the *Norfolk* bound for the New World under circumstances that were not too promising for the future.

The severity of George's punishment (if one accepts the earliest version of the story) is best explained as the result of fear on the part of Maryanne Holmes and Aunt Pemberton—and perhaps Dr. Cowan—that George would follow his late father into the snare of improvidence. Joseph Henry Hendon Holmes had not been a man of family or wealth, but he was ambitious. That Maryanne was the daughter of Stephen Pemberton, master of the estate of Bainbridge-Holme near Sunderland and head of a family prominent in the Northumbrian gentry, did not keep him from falling in love with her. Nor did the fact that he had to borrow a thousand pounds keep him from marrying her.[4] Apparently believing that a man of his circumstances could achieve success more surely in the colonies than in England, Henry went out to British Guiana, a relatively new imperial possession just won from the Dutch during the Napoleonic wars. Not long thereafter, in July 1817, he was admitted to the practice of law in the province of Demerara. Returning to England the same year, he married Maryanne in December and in January 1818 sailed with his bride on the *Clyde* from Liverpool.

At the time of their arrival, Georgetown, the capital of Demerara and metropolis of British Guiana, was an orderly, clean, and attractive town with wide, well-paved streets, well-kept houses, and a bustling business center.[5] In this environment Henry's rise was steady and swift, and the growing Holmes family enjoyed an affluence that, as it turned out, was quite beyond their means. Maryanne's notes on their life in Demerara reflect an attachment to a circle enjoying a casual, aristocratic life characterized by large houses, crowds of servants, and plenty of everything. In 1820 Henry received a coveted customs appointment. Four years later, when the new governor Major General Benjamin D'Urban arrived in Georgetown, Holmes was made judge advocate of the military forces in Demerara and in the neighboring province of Essequebo. At the time of his death in 1831, he was also senior proctor in the Court of Vice-Admiralty.[6] Domestic responsibilities kept pace with public ones. Annamaria, the first child, was born in March 1818 and George Frederick followed in August

    [4] Buchanan, *Holmes Family History*, p. 1.

    [5] Charles Waterton, *Wanderings in South America, the North-West of the United States, and the Antilles, In the Years 1812, 1816, 1820, and 1824*, new edition (London: Macmillan and Company, 1879), p. 174.

    [6] Buchanan, *Holmes Family History*, pp. 13, 18, 22–31.

1820. Others arrived to number eight before Henry's death: Henry Augustus in 1822, the twins Charlotte and Charles in 1824, Penelope in 1826, Edward in 1828, and Julia in 1830. Henry Augustus, Charles, Penelope, and Julia all died in infancy.

In 1822 Mrs. Holmes returned to England with Annamaria and George on the *Paragon*. After the custom of Englishmen living abroad, the children were left with relatives, Grandfather and Aunt Pemberton living at Bishop Wearmouth near Sunderland, to be properly educated. It was four years before George began his studies under Dr. Cowan at The Grange, but at that time he already had begun to read Greek and Latin and to give indications of his exceptional scholastic abilities. Young Holmes stayed at The Grange for ten years and left behind him a reputation for possessing "no ordinary degree of talent" as a classical scholar and mathematician. In the fall of 1836 George left Dr. Cowan's school and matriculated at nearby Durham University where he won a prize scholarship and praise from his examiner as "a gentleman of great ability."[7] Unfortunately, George's stay at Durham was cut short by the incident of the books.

Shortly after leaving Annamaria and George with the Pembertons, Maryanne returned to Demerara. Twice more she made the crossing before leaving British Guiana for the last time. In 1825 the entire family came to bring Charlotte to stay with Aunt Pemberton. Henry returned to South America the next year and Maryanne followed in 1827 after the birth of Penelope and her sudden death from measles (brought home by George from The Grange). Maryanne's final voyage was made with young Edward in 1830. She was in England, then, when she received the news from Demerara that her husband was dead.[8]

The shock of Henry's death was increased by the revelation that he had died bankrupt. In his will he left everything to Maryanne with the exception of a few minor bequests. He seems to have convinced himself and his wife that his debts were few and manageable. That Maryanne thought herself and her children well off may be inferred from the value of Henry's estate which, when liquidated, brought almost eleven thousand pounds. It was the unenviable responsibility of Henry's friend and executor of his estate, Dr. Peter Miller of Demerera, to tell the widow that after expenses and the payment of preferred claims her husband's estate was reduced to little more than a fourth of what it had been and that against this relatively small sum

[7] Robinson, "George Frederick Holmes," pp. 69–70. Testimonial letters of James Cowan, October 18, 1838 and Thomas W. Peile, October 18, 1838, Holmes papers, D.

[8] Buchanan, *Holmes Family History*, pp. 18–19.

there were claims in British Guiana alone totaling approximately sixty-four thousand pounds, to say nothing of the debts Henry had contracted in England. To further increase Maryanne's difficulties, her father also died in 1831 and, probably assuming that her prosperity was assured, left virtually everything to her brother George and to Elizabeth. As a result, Maryanne and her children were forced to accept the charity of Aunt Pemberton which, though ungrudgingly given, was galling to them.[9]

One does not wonder, then, at the alarm of Maryanne and Aunt Pemberton when George showed an aptitude for incurring debt. Actually, many other parallels may be drawn between George and his father, and, taken together, they raise the intriguing question of the extent of influence exercised over George's life by this seldom-seen man.

Certain details in the lives of the two men are curiously and strikingly analogous. Each was an exile forced by circumstances to make his way in a foreign land. Each practiced law as his profession, although Henry did so with much more success than George. Each married above himself socially while in a condition less than affluent and each to a woman who was four years his senior. Less superficial are the parallels of character and talent. Neither Holmes nor his father possessed a great deal of judgment where money was involved. Both were life-long chronic debtors, although in neither case was this the result of moral weakness so much as the consequence of a generosity that may have bordered on prodigality (George, fortunately, had less opportunity for indulgence in this direction than his father). In this regard Maryanne's comments are pointed. To her son Edward concerning his brother and father she wrote,

It would be of no use your staying in America, leaving us destitute, if it was not to save money, for making it (like dear George) is of no use if you do not *save* it. Every day must convince you more how much we suffer from poverty[.] (Your dear Father *made* enough, if he could only have been prevailed upon to *save* it! but he trusted to his youth and abilities, and postponed the necessity whilst it was in his power! and you know the consequences.)

Again, about George she said,

I hope you will strain every nerve to save what you make to obtain a little independence to *return* to retire in England with [;] *not* like dear George

_____

[9] *Ibid.*, pp. 13–14, 16–17. Peter Miller to Maryanne Holmes, December 28, 1832, *ibid.*, p. 15. Maryanne Holmes to Edward A. Holmes, February 28, 1854 and May 3, 1854, *ibid.*, pp. 50–51.

work *very hard* & spend it, be *cheated* out of it, or *let it slip* through his fingers without minding. He seems almost determined not to realize anything. If he had had a common share of prudence with his abilities, he would have been independent long since.[10]

In addition to an inability to avoid debt and a tendency to self-deception (seen in Henry by Miller and apparent in George to anyone who studies his papers), George and his father shared an ambition to excel in scholarship and letters. Here George outstripped Henry, for while the latter dabbled in poetry and translation and left behind a book on coal mining, his son became one of the Old South's most distinguished reviewers and essayists.[11]

Under the circumstances, George's boyhood must have been spent in the shadow of his father's memory which provided him with a contradictory model of both excellence and failure. After he grew up he was very much aware of the similarity between his career and Henry's. He was convinced that he, like his father, would die young. He looked on the year 1857 (when he would be the same age as Henry had been when he died) as his year of crisis.[12] Once 1857 had passed safely, Holmes felt that he could look forward to a long life. But could he rid himself of his father's legacy so easily? Or rather, did the futility and disappointment of Henry's career continue to be an incubus for the son which became more burdensome and disheartening as each frustrating year passed? That Holmes lived the greater part of his mature years in a condition of acute despair no student of his life will doubt. Was this entirely the result of his own experiences, or did he come to believe himself fated to repeat his father's blighted life? Did an overwhelming sense of hopelessness predispose him to a religious philosophy of existence? Such questions concerning the father's influence tantalize, but with the sparse evidence available they may only be posed, not answered. Yet in trying to understand Holmes's response to the intellectual and spiritual challenges of his age they should not be forgotten.

When George arrived in Quebec late in July 1837, he found the colony of Lower Canada in turmoil. The French Canadian population, racked by crop failures and economic depression, was moving toward open rebellion over the inequalities of the existing colonial administration. Holmes tarried in uneasy Canada for something over

[10] Maryanne Holmes to Edward A. Holmes, February 28, 1854 and November 13, 1854, *ibid.*, pp. 50–52.
[11] Miller to Maryanne Holmes, December 28, 1832. Buchanan, *Holmes Family History*, pp. 10–12, 16, 36.
[12] MS vol. 1791, August 21, 1857, Holmes papers, D.

a year seeking employment as a bookkeeper or tutor and working at whatever came to his hand. By the fall of 1838 he had decided to try his fortune in America. Consequently, in November of that year, he entered the United States, passed rapidly through New England and the middle Atlantic states, and temporarily came to rest in Virginia.[13] One is tempted to see in Holmes's flight through the northern states an expression of the aversion he later manifested for "Yankee" civilization. There is, unfortunately, little evidence to indicate that he intentionally sought out the social and intellectual world of the Old South, however much his class origins, education, and temperament were later to show him predisposed to fit it. More probably, he was pursuing opportunities for employment as a schoolmaster, which was at that time what he did best.

In Caroline County, Virginia, Holmes found a position teaching in a boarding school operated by John G. Lawrence. He must have constituted a large part of the faculty for he was credited with teaching Greek, Latin, French, Italian, mathematics, algebra, and, in addition to these, "all the English branches necessary for a useful and elegant education." While at Lawrence's school, he became friends with Benjamin B. Minor, later editor of the *Southern Literary Messenger* (1843–1847), who was then attending the University of Virginia, and also met William G. Minor, a lawyer who shared his interest in literature. But in spite of finding the two Minors and other friends congenial literary companions and impressing them all with his own "classic and general literary lore," Holmes was discontented. He certainly had no intention of remaining a provincial schoolmaster. In the fall of 1839 he decided to move farther south and try his luck in the greener fields of Georgia and South Carolina. He spent several months in Macon, Georgia, again teaching school to support himself and crowding in a few hours of legal studies when he could for he had now determined that the law would be his profession. But Holmes's new situation in Georgia proved no more satisfying than had the old one in Virginia. He moved restlessly around the state, settled briefly in Decatur, considered leaving for Missouri, and later even contemplated returning to England or emigrating to Russia. But none of this came to pass. In the summer of 1840 the young wanderer moved to

---

[13] The Canadian period of Holmes's life is obscure. Bits have been gathered from the following letters: Thomas Brown to Alexander Skakel, August 19, 1837; J. G. Pemberton to G. F. Holmes, December 9, 1837; Msgr. Jean Jacques Lartique to L. Dolittle, December 19, 1837, all in the Holmes papers, D. See also George Frederick Holmes, "A Day in the Woods of Lower Canada," *Magnolia*, II, n.s. (February 1843), passim. See also Holmes's declaration of his intention to become a citizen of the United States, dated September 4, 1846, Holmes papers, D.

South Carolina where he was to remain until shortly after his marriage five years later.[14]

Holmes's continuing unhappiness in the United States may be traced to two major problems (in addition, of course, simply to being away from England). The first of these was prejudice against him as an Englishman—or so he thought. But, in truth, the fact was that Holmes did not impress favorably everyone he met. Those not inclined to be overwhelmed by his precocious learning seem to have put him down as an arrogant, outspoken, young foreigner who had very little complimentary to say about things American. When he complained to his American friends they admitted the existence of some anti-British feeling, but suggested that Holmes might take the edge off of it by being a little less free with his criticism. It may be that he followed their advice, for soon after he went to South Carolina his fortunes did improve; but it should also be noted that one who knew him years later at Oxford, Mississippi, claimed to have found him still bristling with British prejudices.[15] One might easily suppose that this proud and censorious exterior which Holmes showed to Americans (actually common enough in even *secure* British visitors at the time) was partly his compensation for the loneliness he felt in an alien place and among alien people. It may also have been a compensation for the dubious circumstances under which he had left England. But whatever the sources, it did not smooth his path before him in America.

The second source of Holmes's discontent was his chosen profession, the law. It is more than probable that he did not really want to be a lawyer. His natural gifts favored a career as a writer or critic, but he bowed to the common opinion that there was no future in letters in America. Unfortunately, it was obvious to those who knew Holmes well that he would never be a successful lawyer. His manner was thought too refined, his temperament too "classic," to stand up to the pressures and verbal brawling of a courtroom in Jacksonian America and the mad scramble for fees that a career in law necessitated. Also,

[14] Testimonial letter of John G. Lawrence, September 18, 1839, undated copy, *ibid*. Benjamin B. Minor, "Some Further Notes Relating to Dr. G. F. Holmes; Munford's Homer, Etc., "*Alumni Bulletin of the University of Virginia*, V (November 1898), 74. William G. Minor to G. F. Holmes, September 22, 1839, Holmes papers, D. William G. Minor to G. F. Holmes, December 26, 1839; J. Loterington to G. F. Holmes, August 15, 1840, MS vol. 1808. Cowan to Holmes, October 29, 1841.

[15] John G. Lawrence to G. F. Holmes, January 18, 1840; Heman Mead to G. F. Holmes, April 7, 1840, *ibid*. James E. Pope, "Reminiscences of Dr. George Frederick Holmes," *University of Mississippi Magazine*, XX (December 1895), 4–5. As a student Pope had boarded in the home of President Holmes.

as William Minor pointed out, to be a success in the law one needed money and Holmes was a poor man. But Holmes was not to be discouraged. Throughout the early 1840s he persevered, telling himself that the courtroom was his proper environment, while mixing law and literature in such a way as to supplement his anemic professional income by his pen. Important as his legal career might be, however, Holmes could not bring himself to follow the advice given him when he first embarked on it: "Don't coquet with the law—she is a jealous vixen, and must have all your attention or none."[16]

Although not at the time an American citizen (and he never became one), he was licensed by the South Carolina Court of Appeals in 1842 to practice law. A budget of his time shows that he made a genuine effort in law but diluted his intention with a generous mixture of his real interests. It called for Greek and Latin before nine o'clock in the morning; "Law, Business, etc." from nine until four; "Spanish, German, or Italian" from four until seven; and "History, Miscellaneous etc." from seven until ten. His sole remaining case ledger indicates his success. It has only one page of entries, and the only entry in the receipts column records a loss of fees, costs, and commission: the plaintiff had died *"dead drunk."*[17] And, as if in conscious symbolism, the ledger is then given over to notes on theology and metaphysics. Despite his failure, Holmes continued to think of the law as his chosen career long after the question of his profession had been settled pragmatically by his return to teaching in 1846 at Richmond College in Virginia. It would have provided badly needed prestige and, if successful, much needed money. It was a dream that died hard.

Holmes first settled in Walterboro, a town of about five hundred inhabitants and the seat of Colleton District, located between Charleston and the state capital at Columbia. The surrounding countryside was for the most part made up of flat, monotonous marshes and given over to rice culture with some cotton raised in drained swamp land. Walterboro itself was located in one of the drier sandy areas scattered about the region and enjoyed a somewhat better climate than the surrounding district. Holmes had not yet been licensed to practice law, so he made his living by teaching in one of the two academies found in the town.[18]

---

[16] William G. Minor to G. F. Holmes, February 2, 1845, Holmes papers, D. Minor to Holmes, September 22, 1839.

[17] MS vols. 1842, 1840, *ibid.* When manuscript volumes are cited without pagination, the page is unnumbered.

[18] Testimonial letter of Adam Gilchrist, dated on reverse, February, 1843, *ibid.* William Gilmore Simms, *The Geography of South Carolina* (Charleston: Babcock and Company, 1843), pp. 64–66. Daniel Haskel and J. Calvin Smith, *Descrip-*

After lingering in Walterboro for a year or so, he moved to Orangeburg, a village of about the same size and some forty miles to the northwest. Orangeburg District was much like Colleton: to a large extent flat, reasonably fertile, and sickly with occasional stretches of elevated sandy soil which were healthy but less suited to cultivation. Cotton provided the economic foundation of the community although the productivity of the Orangeburg fields was somewhat below that of more fortunate districts. The town itself, as William Gilmore Simms's *Geography* described it, boasted "a handsome Court House, Jail, and several tasteful private habitations." One of Orangeburg's strong points was that it lay "in the great line of thoroughfare, between the sea board and interior," and so possessed a railroad. To the west about five miles was Poplar Springs, "a salubrious place of summer retreat" for the planters and their families who lived in the surrounding neighborhood.[19]

Simms noted "an increasing taste for letters" in Orangeburg District, and in this doubtlessly lay its special attractiveness for Holmes.[20] He went there to practice law with a man named Preston, but both professionally and financially Orangeburg was a disappointment. This was not so intellectually, however, for it was there that Holmes met David Flavel Jamison, who is best known today as the president of South Carolina's secession convention in 1860, but who in 1842 was a leader among those literary Orangeburg planters reported by Simms. Jamison had a great interest in history even though his writings on the subject were not extensive. During the period of close association with Holmes he produced no more than a handful of reviews.[21] His two volume biography, *The Life and Times of Bertrand Du Guesclin*, was a labor of many years and did not appear until shortly before his death in 1864. Between reviews he found time to be a successful cotton planter and a political leader in the state. Jamison's writings show him to have been familiar with the works of Guizot, Niebuhr,

---

tive and Statistical Gazeteer of the United States (New York: Sherman and Smith, 1844), p. 691.

[19] Simms, *Geography*, pp. 112–14. *Statistics of the United States of America as Collected and Returned by the Marshals of the Several Judicial Districts under the Thirteenth Section of the Act for Taking the Sixth Census; corrected at the Department of State.* (Washington: Blair and Rives, 1841), pp. 250–51.

[20] Simms, *Geography*, p. 115.

[21] "Progress of Civilization," *Southern Quarterly Review*, III (January 1843), 1–17, IV (October 1843), 157–78; "The French Revolution," *ibid.*, V (April 1844), 1–102; "Lamartine's Histoire des Girondins," *ibid.*, XVI (October 1849–50), 53–76. Two essays sometimes attributed to Jamison, "Herder's Philosophy of History," *ibid.*, VI (April 1844), 256–311 and "Rome and the Romans," *ibid.*, VI (October 1844), 296–306, were written by Holmes.

and Gibbon, keenly interested in the historical development of civilization, and well-read in the Greek and Latin classics, although they do not indicate that he possessed any striking originality of mind. Even so, Jamison first introduced Holmes to the philosophy of history and to the idea that history could be more than an opportunity for literary composition. Although Jamison was ten years Holmes's senior and (one would assume) considerably more blessed with what Maryanne would have called "prudence," their relationship was one of equals. Jamison did not patronize the young lawyer. He recognized his friend's talents and, on one occasion at least, would not submit an article to the *Southern Quarterly Review* until Holmes had gone over it "with pen in hand."[22]

His friendship with Jamison and his association with other Orangeburg planters doubtlessly strengthened Holmes's already genteel political and social attitudes as well as influencing his intellectual interests. One may be confident that from his Mother and Aunt he had acquired a strong respect for high social status. The surviving traces of his Canadian experiences more than hint at a strong aversion to the lower orders of society. During the years spent in South Carolina he had little difficulty adapting himself to the congenial attitudes and customs of the southern planter gentry and, although not indifferent to the welfare of common folk, easily came to share Jamison's distrust of a rapidly growing political and social democracy. In 1846, after Holmes had left Orangeburg to teach at Richmond College, Jamison wrote to him lamenting the results of a recent state election. The planter-historian had been returned to the legislature but he had lost his previous colleague, one McMichael. "I have to take—will you believe it—Lew Cooner. . . . Something of the sort nearly occurred in Barnwell District, Mr. Patterson was run at by a low fellow, because he was low, and was nearly run out by him. . . . I am affraid [*sic*] democracy is gaining on us too in So. Carolina, tho' I trust with the help of God we may choke it off for some time longer." Holmes could only agree.[23]

Inspired by the companionship of Jamison and by Simms with whom he corresponded regularly (and as the law—that jealous vixen—gave him time), Holmes devoted himself to his studies and to the advancement of his literary career. At first he experienced some hesi-

---

[22] G. F. Holmes to D. F. Jamison, February 7, 1846, Holmes papers, D. D. F. Jamison to G. F. Holmes, September 29, 1842, vol. I, George Frederick Holmes Papers, Library of Congress, Washington, D. C.; hereinafter cited as Holmes papers, LC.

[23] Holmes, "A Day in the Woods," p. 120. D. F. Jamison to G. F. Holmes, October 16, 1846, vol. I, Holmes papers, LC.

tation as to what branch of letters he should cultivate. Was his natural bent toward creative writing? Or could he better follow the path of criticism and concentrate on essays and reviews? Here again his activities more or less drifted into a pragmatic resolution. Just as a life of law gradually and without premeditation on Holmes's part, gave way to an academic career, so fiction was replaced by the commentaries on his times upon which his reputation was largely to rest.

An enthusiasm for learning is not surprising in one with Holmes's family and educational background. He grew up in a bookish environment. Both of his parents loved books and carefully fostered the boy's education. One might assume that during the unsettled early years of his exile Holmes did not find it at all easy to maintain the literary activities to which he had grown accustomed in England. Nevertheless, one way or another, in all of his wanderings, he did; and his enthusiasm was matched by seriousness. In a notebook begun in the spring of 1841, Holmes inscribed the following passage from Francis Bacon who was one of his earliest intellectual guides and whose works formed an important part of the foundations of his own thought. "But because it is but a counterfeit thing in knowledge to be pregnant and forward, except a man be deep and full, I hold the entry of commonplaces to be a matter of great use and essence in studying, as that which assureth copy of invention and contracteth judgement to a strength."[24] Holmes's activities and personality left no doubt in the minds of those who knew him that he was "pregnant and forward." And he did everything in his power to insure that he would also be "deep and full." Throughout his life, he kept notebooks in which he copied extracts from the books he read along with sometimes lengthy commentary on them. He was such a careful penman and wrote in so perfect a hand—as beautiful as "a page of choice Greek," an editor once remarked[25]—that merely writing must have given him a great deal of pleasure. In fact, one can hardly avoid the conclusion that sometimes the copying became an end in itself. In addition to this, Holmes habitually broke up each day into work periods carefully assigned to some particular intellectual occupation. Anyone who has ever done this may doubt whether the intention was always consummated in action; nevertheless, the intention was there. He kept reading lists of books which he had read and those he intended to read (sometimes even with the time he had spent reading them). In short, Holmes was a conscientious and dedicated intellectual. But his intellectual vitality could not content itself with the solitary existence of

[24] MS vol. 1792, Holmes papers, D.
[25] Daniel D. Whedon to G. F. Holmes, March 25, 1857, vol. I, Holmes papers, LC.

a closet scholar. Consequently, almost from the time he entered the United States, he began to contribute to the reviews.

Unfortunately, his early efforts as a reviewer were as financially unrewarding as his law practice, the reason being that if a reviewer is to prosper, the review for which he writes must prosper. The *Southern Quarterly Review*, for which Holmes wrote most of his articles during his South Carolina period, was potentially a good magazine, but it suffered from a mixed bag of editors and poor business practices. The *Review* was founded and edited for a large part of its life by a transplanted Yankee from Massachusetts, Daniel K. Whitaker. Whitaker came south in the 1820s to practice law, and in 1835 he began his editorial career with the ill-fated *Southern Literary Journal*. After two years he left the *Journal*, which seemed to be staggering to its grave in spite of the sponsorship of the Literary and Philosophical Society of South Carolina and, in 1842, began the *Review* at New Orleans, though the next year it was moved to Charleston where it remained until it ceased publication in 1857. Under the guidance of Whitaker and his successors (J. Milton Clapp, 1847–1849; William Gilmore Simms, 1849–1855; and the Rev. Dr. James H. Thornwell, 1856–1857) the *Review* was a persistent spokesman for the traditional southern doctrines of slavery, free-trade, and states' rights, in addition to promoting southern letters. Cornelius Mathews, a well-known New York editor, satirist, and novelist, who, like Holmes and Whitaker, had tried the law and then turned to letters, recognized the general quality of the *Review* as did Edward Everett and others. Early in its life, Mathews had assured Holmes that it "should and can push the North American to the wall: it has more honesty, more catholicity of feeling and really a higher standard of taste: although not white-sugared to quite the same point of nicety as its Boston rival." When the *Review* neared the end of its days, Everett told its editor that he had always thought it a "very able" periodical and that he had on his shelves "A complete Set of it from the beginning."[26]

The road traveled by southern periodicals generally was not an easy one and that of the *Southern Quarterly Review* was particularly

[26] Frank Luther Mott, *A History of American Magazines, 1741–1850* (New York: D. Appleton and Company, 1930), pp. 664–65, 721n. Cornelius Mathews to G. F. Holmes, November 15, 1844, MS vol. 1808. Edward Everett to James Henley Thornwell, February 7, 1856, James Henley Thornwell Papers, South Caroliniana Library, University of South Carolina, Columbia, South Carolina. The most comprehensive study of the *Southern Quarterly Review* is Frank Winkler Ryan, Jr., "The Southern Quarterly Review, 1842–1857, A Study in Thought and Opinion in the Old South" (Ph.D. dissertation, University of North Carolina, Chapel Hill, North Carolina, 1956).

rough. Most of these magazines were not able to gain the support given to their counterparts in the northern states. But in the case of the *Review* the problem was not a lack of subscribers as much as it was a lack of *paying* subscribers. In 1846 the *Review* had a circulation of two thousand, which was respectable for a southern periodical of its kind, but it also had arrears in subscription payments of ten thousand dollars.[27] Why? Subscribers complained that it was difficult to pay their bills or even to receive their copies because the *Review* had no efficient system of agents or dealers. Wrote one irate patron as the magazine passed away in 1857:

One of the most judicious gentlemen in the city of Charleston remarked to me one month back —"The fault of the Southern Quarterly is, and has been from its very start, that *it has no judicious system of agents.* It surely should be offered for sale at Russell's[,] Courtenay's[,] or McCarter's." I can assert upon the best accurate personal knowledge, that it cannot be obtained now, and could not have been for two years at what are termed "the respectable book-stores": and have heard more than one say, "he had not received his copy." The habits of our planters and of the Southern People generally are such, that an agent must call & collect dues. I, for instance, have been a subscriber ever since Dr. Thornwell has edited the Review, have been perfectly willing to pay down the money to the agent if I could find him without wasting a morning's valuable time, and have received but the first Copy April year, and cannot find the Review, though I have twice tried to do so at the four first book-stores in town. I know I am not the only case of this sort.[28]

In addition to poor circulation and collection practices, the *Review* (except for the last issue) carried no advertising as did the more successful *De Bow's Review* and the *Southern Literary Messenger.* The men of belles-lettres and the cloth who managed the quarterly more than proved their ineptitude as businessmen and were too frequently forced to rely on the subsidation of wealthy patrons who, unfortunately, were not always to be found.[29]

The rates offered Holmes and the other contributors by the *Review* —one to three dollars per printed page—were necessarily low, though still competitive with other magazines. But because the *Review* could

[27] Mott, *American Magazines*, pp. 380, 722. By 1849 subscriptions had fallen to 1700: W. G. Simms to Carey and Hart, April 12, [1849], Simms, *The Letters of William Gilmore Simms*, ed. by Mary C. S. Oliphant et al. (Columbia: University of South Carolina Press, 1952), II, 501.

[28] Benjamin R. Stuart to the Editor of the *Southern Quarterly Review*, June 4, 1857, Thornwell papers.

[29] G. F. Holmes to J. H. Thornwell, March 7, 1857, *ibid.* For an earlier rescue of the *Review* by patrons see W. G. Simms to N. B. Tucker, January 30 and May 18, [1850], Simms, *Letters*, III, 12, 39–40.

not pay its way, the difficulty for authors lay in trying to collect. Simms, who before he became editor was a fellow creditor of the *Review*, twice advised Holmes how to best handle this problem but, it would appear, to no purpose. One solution that he suggested was to demand payment in advance: "They will yield, *for they cannot well do without you.* There is no good reason why you should work for nothing." Simms also counseled sending in contributions one at a time rather than in bunches in the hope that this would stimulate more prompt payment. Even so, he feared the debt was hopeless, and in part it was.[30]

Not all of the trouble was the result of poor business methods. The *Review* also suffered from "hum-drum" writers who doubtlessly won toleration by not being too demanding about payment but who nevertheless served to lower the quality of the magazine. From December 1842 to June 1843 Holmes was associate editor of the *Review* and so had a firsthand knowledge of this problem. His reaction to one such contribution was vigorous: The *Review* accepted "a miserable essay on the Civil Law, by Judge Porter of Tuscaloosa, who knew nothing at all about the subject. [The article] was partly printed when I first saw it. I had to stop the press, while I corrected the most obvious blunders. . . . Porter was, and is a presumptuous blockhead, pretending to write on subjects of which he is totally ignorant." For this he blamed Whitaker who, he said, lacked the courage to rid the magazine of such writers.[31] But whoever was to blame, subscribers, contributors, or editors, the *Southern Quarterly Review* did not prosper nor did those who wrote for it. Holmes's literary activity in the 1840s brought him many rewards; some were intellectual, some personal, but few were financial. By the end of the decade he had the beginnings of a modest fame, but his prospects for economic solvency and security were as dim as they had ever been.

Holmes's earliest literary effort of which any record remains was a lengthy poem written in the style of Lord Byron and entitled, "The Brides of Venice." This work was, as he laconically remarks in his notebook where he had transcribed a stanza, "Written in England in May, 1837; Burnt at Quebec, 21 August of the same year." What mixed despair and resolution must have attended that action on his first birthday in exile! When he reached the United States, Holmes pub-

[30] Mott, *American Magazines*, pp. 505–07. W. G. Simms to G. F. Holmes, July 10, [1844], MS vol. 1808. W. G. Simms to G. F. Holmes, March 15 [1849], Simms, *Letters*, II, 494.

[31] MS vol. 1843, Holmes papers, D. G. F. Holmes to D. J. McCord, October 24, 1846, MS vol. 1808.

lished two "Persian" stories in the *Southern Literary Messenger*: "Amram, the Seeker of Oblivion" (November 1839) and "Abou Hassan, the Recluse of the Mountain: an Allegory" (November 1841). Even though he later dismissed "Amram" as a "flighty humbug," and tried to suppress "Abou Hassan" before it was printed, both pieces were well received. James Gordon Bennett, the controversial New York publisher, praised "Amram" in the pages of the *New York Herald* as "capital prose," which moved Holmes's friend William Minor to urge him to continue along that line. "You may do it," he wrote, "with great credit to yourself, for it has arrested the public's reading eye." Thomas White, the editor of the *Messenger*, wanted more stories like "Abou" but he did not get them.[32] Holmes's forte was not storytelling and only two more pieces of published fiction were ever to come from his pen: "Mr. Wintrysides—a Character" appeared in the *Messenger* for June 1848 (more of the adventures of this gentleman were promised but not delivered), and "Mr. Caxton's Review of 'My Novel' " a review in dialogue in the *Messenger* for May 1853.

Holmes began to write for the *Southern Quarterly Review* in 1842 with an article on Bulwer-Lytton's historical novel, *Zanoni*. Here he found his medium. Although Holmes at first had fancied himself to be a man of belles-lettres and had later projected a number of books on various topics which he never wrote, his natural mode of expression was the critical review-essay. A flood of these pieces followed "Zanoni" in rapid succession, essays on literary, historical, and philosophical subjects. As was so often the case in the nineteenth century, many of these were reviews in name only. In actuality, they were compositions in which Holmes used the book in question only as an excuse to set forth his own ideas on the subject at hand.

As in the case of his fiction, Holmes's essays were read in the northern states as well as in the South. The *National Intelligencer* favorably compared the young Englishman with some of Britain's leading scholars in his "intimate acquaintance with ancient literature." Mathews wrote to Holmes that his 1844 essay "Rome and the Romans" "has been well noticed here at the North." His series of essays, "The Present State of Letters" impressed the editor of the *Messenger*, Benjamin Minor, as containing "new & striking views;" and prompted Mathews to write to Simms, who passed it on, that in the opinion of his literary circle in and around New York, Holmes was "touching

---

[32] MS vol. 1843. W. Thomas White to G. F. Holmes, November 13, 1841, Holmes papers, D. *New York Herald*, November 22, 1839. Minor to Holmes, December 26, 1839.

chords which, though hidden, are vital; and that you can't do better than to go on probing the matter to the quick."[33]

Holmes's rise in the world of letters was complemented by an advance in the social world. While in South Carolina he met, courted, and married Eliza Lavalette Floyd, a daughter of Dr. John Floyd who had been a member of Congress and governor of Virginia from 1830 to 1834, and who died shortly after Holmes arrived in Canada. The Floyd family was wealthy and prominent. Lavalette's brother, John Buchanan Floyd, would, like his father, serve as governor of Virginia (1849–1852), and later as secretary of war in James Buchanan's cabinet. Another brother, George, was secretary of state for the Wisconsin Territory and a member of the Virginia legislature; of the two remaining brothers, Benjamin Rush Floyd was a lawyer and William Preston Floyd, a physician. Lavalette's two sisters, Letitia and Nicketti, had each married well-to-do landowners. Like his father before him Holmes was intimidated by neither the wealth nor the age of the lady (Lavalette was four years older) and pressed his suit with a disregard of his own meager circumstances. Miss Floyd owned land both in Fayette County, Virginia and near the family estate in Tazewell County, and had four Negro slaves, as well as a claim to a large portion of the remainder of her mother's dowery. (Her mother, Letitia Preston, was herself a member of a distinguished family.) In addition to this, she owned fifty head of cattle, sixty sheep, forty hogs, five horses, and her father's gold watch.[34]

It is possible that the unknown Preston who was Holmes's law partner in Orangeburg may have been the agency through whom George and Lavalette met—if he were, in fact, related to Letitia Preston. At any rate, the courtship took place at Millwood, the home of Colonel and Mrs. William S. Lewis near Orangeburg, where Lavalette was visiting. Mrs. Lewis ("Letty"), Lavalette's sister, was to be one of Holmes's firmest friends and champions. And he was to need a champion, for the marriage in February of 1845, while not unexpected by the Floyd family, did not meet with widespread approval. "I can but have fears about it," wrote John to his mother, and Mrs.

---

[33] *National Intelligencer*, February 27, 1843. Heman Mead to G. F. Holmes, April 20, 1843, MS vol. 1808. Mathews to Holmes, November 15, 1844. W. G. Simms to G. F. Holmes, May 14, [1844], Simms, *Letters*, I, 417.

[34] Charles H. Ambler, "Life of John Floyd," *John P. Branch Historical Papers of Randolph-Macon College*, V, no. 1 (June 1918), 77–78. Marriage settlement, Holmes papers, D. Shortly before their marriage Lavalette's property was given in trust to a friend, Henry Massey. Both she and Holmes could sell or exchange it at will but it could not be subject to Holmes's "debts, contracts, or engagements" which by this time were growing troublesome.

Floyd herself seems to have wished more for her daughter than a poor immigrant.[35]

Lavalette, of course, did not share her family's concern. Her impressions of her new husband and her hopes for their future together which she put into a letter to her sister Nicketti cannot be improved,

You must not expect to see a *beauty* for everyone says that he is *plain*[.] I differ in *opinion from the majority*. he is six feet high & about as *fat* as *Richard Matthews*, but with a fine forehead, hair a shade darker than mine, hasle eyes, over which he wares *specks*, as he is very neer sighted, (Which accounts for his fancy for me) & a *nose*, as *large for a nose as my head is for a head*. he is an English man by birth & education, or rather he was born of English parents in Domarara, and educated at Durham. Mr. Holmes is as poor in worldly goods, as he is in flesh, but he is sensible, morral, & industrious, so in the course of time I hope we will be as rich, *as you &* your husband, for I look upon you as *rich kin*. you have a house & home to invite your relations to, & it may be many a day before I have the happiness of being similarly situated.

She did not know how true a prophetess she was for it was to be not many days but many years before she had a permanent home of her husband's providing. Lavalette's enthusiasm was shared by Letty who also wrote to Nicketti praising the new in-law: "Lavalette could never have married better if she had tried 20 times[.] he is so tender, gallant & effectionate to her & is so perfectly moral & honorable & domestic in his turn. I have got to love him like a brother indeed." Holmes seems to have been aware of the anxiety of the other Floyds for, Letty went on, "He anticipates great pleasure in going to Va. and knowing his kin, tho he is dreadfully afraid, & fully persuaded that no one will like him." Letty did what she could to prepare his way before him. She continued, "I never told you what sort of looking man he was. I think him handsome & he is certainly *very* genteel looking. he is as thin as John G. Floyd & not unlike him in his character." In the end, Holmes was accepted with better grace than he expected though his diary contains hints of tensions suggesting that some of the male Floyds, at least, never completely lost their reservations.[36]

The match was scarcely better received in England. Whatever Maryanne might have thought about George taking a wife before he

[35] John Buchanan Floyd to Letitia Floyd, January 14, 1845 and H. Finch to Letitia Floyd, January 29, 1845, Johnston-McMullin Papers, Duke University Library, Durham, North Carolina; hereinafter cited as Johnston papers.

[36] Lavalette Holmes to Nicketti Johnston, April 11, 1845 and Letitia Preston Lewis to Nicketti Johnston, May 8, 1845, *ibid.* MS vol. 1791, February 13 and 19, 1856.

had made his fortune, her central fear was for his Protestant faith. Lavalette and her two sisters were Roman Catholics and apparently rather militant. In later years, Maryanne warned Edward Holmes of this danger again and again when he, in his turn, was seeking an American wife. But she became reconciled, especially when grandchildren began arriving, and before too many years she felt only "affection for poor Lavalette" if not for her religion. Holmes's sister Annamaria, on the other hand, was so disappointed in his choice that she put animadversions on her sister-in-law's faith into her will.[37]

The acceptance of the marriage by the two families, however, did not relieve Holmes's indigence. Even at first he was barely able to provide for his family. Later on, in the 1850s, he was forced to take them to live with his mother-in-law and to confess to himself that he could not independently support them. This burden of anxiety and shame only increased the bitterness of his other disappointments and frustrations.

The circumstances in which the new couple began their married life in Orangeburg were not auspicious, but were tolerable because these conditions were expected to be temporary. The couple lived at a boarding house and Holmes did what he could to scrape together a living by teaching at a local academy. Of course, he had no desire to remain in such an undesirable situation any longer than necessary. As early as 1841 he had tried to gain an appointment to a professorship at South Carolina College in Columbia but without success. He renewed the effort a year or so before his marriage when a new chair of Greek was created. He and Lavalette centered their hopes on this opportunity, but Holmes was resolute that if he was not elected this time they would leave South Carolina and join Lavalette's brother George in Wisconsin or try their luck in Missouri.[38] The law beckoned once again.

Knowing the prejudice that existed in South Carolina against the election of outsiders—Holmes, unfortunately, was not the catch Francis Lieber had been ten years earlier—to professorships in the

---

[37] Letitia Preston Lewis to Lavalette Floyd, June 20, 1842, Johnston papers. Maryanne Holmes to Edward A. Holmes, September 28, 1852; October 12, November 13, 1854; May 12, 1858; April 15, 1861, Buchanan, *Holmes Family History*, pp. 46, 52, 60, 62.

[38] Letitia Preston Lewis to Nicketti Johnston, May 8, 1845; Lavalette Holmes to Nicketti Johnston, April 11, 1845. James S. Rollins to William G. Minor, October 19, 1841, Holmes papers, D. W. G. Simms to G. F. Holmes, October 27, [1843], Simms, *Letters*, I, 379. G. F. Holmes to W. G. Minor, January 9, 1845, Holmes papers, D.

college, his expectations were not high.[39] But with an outside chance that he might be successful he was reluctant to leave for the west while the issue was still undecided. Meanwhile, to guard against probable failure in Columbia and to feed his family, he accepted an appointment as professor of ancient languages at Richmond College, a Baptist institution located in the Virginia capital. His anticipations about the balloting in South Carolina proved true. The post went to Professor Robert Henry of the college in compensation for being turned out of the presidency.[40]

If Holmes entered upon his new duties in Richmond with little enthusiasm his attitude is understandable. Not only was the college small and unpromising, but Lavalette, who was expecting their first child, had chosen to stay with her mother at Cavan, the Floyd estate in western Virginia, rather than go immediately to Richmond. As a result, Holmes was not only disappointed and bored but also lonely. At first he had hoped that Lavalette and the child might join him in the spring, but he was forced to tell her that renting a house would be beyond their means for at least two years, and, meanwhile, she would have to "put up with the annoyances of cramped room, and public diet" in a boarding house.[41] Lavalette thought not; her health was none too good anyway—she suffered from headaches—and in October, when the new school term began, she was still at home. There she stayed as long as her husband was at Richmond College.

Loneliness was not Holmes's only problem. He was still poor and his new position portended no change in his status. To his dismay, he soon discovered that Richmond College suffered from chronic and severe financial troubles as well as academic shortcomings. In July he complained to Lavalette:

To show you the value of my situation here, I will mention to you that some of the Trustees very coolly intimated to me that they had no expectation of being able to pay me my whole salary by the end of the year. They seemed to consider this almost as a matter of course. At the close of this session when I ought to receive altogether $700, if I have very great good luck I may possibly receive $200 or $300.

[39] Holmes to Minor, January 9, 1845. For Lieber see Frank Freidel, *Francis Lieber: Nineteenth-Century Liberal*. (Baton Rouge: Louisana State University Press, [1947], pp. 118–21.

[40] Daniel Walker Hollis, *University of South Carolina* (Columbia: University of South Carolina Press, 1951), I, 146–47.

[41] G. F. Holmes to Lavalette Holmes, February 3, 1846, Holmes papers, D. For the depressing effect of her absence on Holmes see Letitia Preston Lewis to Lavalette Holmes, March 16, 1846, typed copy in possession of N. Floyd Holmes.

Not surprisingly, Holmes was forced to increase his burden of debt during his stay, and it was no secret among the Trustees that he was looking about for a better position.[42]

Within a short time after he took up his duties he was writing to Jamison lamenting the intellectual sterility of Richmond. No one, he moaned, shared his literary tastes or his interests in the ancient classics. "And the philosophical study of history is, as you may suppose, a still more lonely stranger in these parts, being not only without admirers or advocates, but also utterly without acquaintances." In disgust, he concluded that the college was nothing but a high school and that Richmond was "a terribly dull place." By September 1846 he had had enough and was calling on his friends to support his bid for the professorship recently made vacant at the College of William and Mary by the death of Thomas R. Dew.[43]

The importance of getting Dew's chair was increased by the news Holmes received late in 1846 that yet another attempt at election to the faculty of South Carolina College—as professor of Roman literature—had failed. Jamison, who counseled him in the matter, had thought Holmes's chances would be improved if he allowed William C. Preston, the new president of the college and Lavalette's cousin, to mention his name to the Trustees as an informal candidate. Doubtlessly Jamison intended this move to keep the prospective election of a non-Carolinian from the public eye. Preston, he assured Holmes, would find this "a willing duty." But as the election drew near, Letty wrote that Preston was proving false. With this intelligence Holmes lost all hope of success. He heard the outcome in December. Jamison wrote regretfully that a former tutor of the college, who had been very active in his own cause and who also had the help of "not very scrupulous friends," had been named the new professor of Roman literature. Letty attributed the reversal to the pusillanimity of Preston and the Trustees who, knowing that Holmes was the best candidate, had given the position to a weaker man out of fear of the "public feeling" that a "foreigner's" claims should not out-weigh those of a "native." Simms, writing later, agreed. Holmes's friends, he said, had not put his name forward openly because of "public prejudice" and consequently he was given little support even though his qualifications were freely admitted.[44]

42 G. F. Holmes to Lavalette Holmes, June 15, July 11, October 22, 1846, Holmes papers, D.

43 Holmes to Jamison, February 7, 1846. G. F. Holmes to Lavalette Holmes, June 15, November 28, 1846, Holmes papers, D. Testimonial letter of James McDowell, September 26, 1846, *ibid*.

44 Jamison to Holmes, October 16, 1846. Letitia Preston Lewis to G. F. Holmes,

Holmes's anxieties about the events at Columbia were only increased by the postponement of the scheduled election of Dew's successor at Williamsburg in October 1846. Suspense, added to anticipations of failure, once more turned his mind to the west; and he and Lavalette began to make serious plans for going to Wisconsin the following spring or fall. While Holmes brushed up on his law between classes at Richmond, George, delighted at the prospect of their joining him, located a place for them to settle. Lavalette described it to her husband as "a small Farme near to Madison with a good house and well of water and some improvements that we could get if we have an idea of gowing to that countery to live." Fortunately for Holmes (in his strained financial condition) this removal was not necessary. Thanks to his Virginia friends who—as his brother-in-law sneered—did better by him than his "dear *cronies*" in South Carolina, his appointment to the faculty of William and Mary was accomplished.[45]

Prior to the election at Williamsburg testimonials favoring Holmes had poured in to the Board of Visitors. The president of Richmond College praised his ability as a teacher. Simms described him as "a graceful, free & impressive writer." Lieber, who at the time was professor of history and political economy at South Carolina College and one of Holmes's advocates there, told the Visitors that his writings showed "a manly intellect; and sound scholarship, as well as experience and true judgement." Others who supported his candidacy were Robert M. T. Hunter, congressman and trustee of the University of Virginia, Preston, who may not have wanted a "foreigner" like Holmes in Columbia but was glad enough to help him get on at William and Mary, South Carolina Chancellor William Harper, Whitaker, and, of course, Jamison. One enthusiast, William M. Peyton, went so far as to recommend Holmes for the presidency of the school which had also been made vacant by the death of Dew. But Holmes's most important champion and the man who prevailed in his election was former President John Tyler, a friend of the Floyds and acting Visitor of the college, who was able to bring considerable influence to bear in his behalf.[46]

November 21, 1846, Holmes papers, D. Holmes to Lavalette Holmes, November 28, 1846. D. F. Jamison to G. F. Holmes, December 13, 1846, vol. I, Holmes papers, LC. Letitia Preston Lewis to Nicketti Johnston, December 6, 1846, Johnston papers. W. G. Simms to G. F. Holmes, March 18, [1847], Simms, *Letters*, II, 283.

[45] G. F. Holmes to Lavalette Holmes, October 10, 1846; Lavalette Holmes to G. F. Holmes, October 19, 1846, Holmes papers, D. William P. Floyd to Lavalette Holmes, February 6, 1847, Johnston papers.

[46] Testimonial letter of Robert Ryland, February 1, 1847, George Frederick

Needless to say, Holmes was ecstatic over his good fortune. He happily wrote to Lavalette telling her of the response to his election in Richmond: "a glowing puff in this morning's Enquirer [*sic*], which would have admitted any other name than my own equally well." He went on:

Ritchie (Wm F) met me in the streets on Saturday and after congratulating me, expressed his joy that the election had fallen upon a man of the right stripe, whereupon I informed him that he was mistaken as I was of the Calhoun stripe—but he seemed satisfied with any Democrat. . . . Ought I not to attribute my success to your Mother's having kicked her shoe after me for good luck, when I left you in September.

He closed, very satisfied: "This Professorship has magnified me into something of a big fish."[47] And with good reason, for his acquisition of even a part of the redoubtable Dew's chair was the first real opportunity he had had since coming to America.

Dew, who at the time of his death had been professor of logic, belles-lettres, moral philosophy, metaphysics, history, and political economy, as well as the president of William and Mary, was a central figure in southern intellectual life. His *Review of the Debate in the Virginia Legislature of 1831 and 1832*, written to convince Virginians of the folly of changing the state's social and economic system, became a scripture for those defending slavery, while his tenure of almost twenty years at Williamsburg gave him the opportunity to mold the minds of his students in conformity with the regional doctrines of states' rights, slavery, and free trade. It was no small compliment to Holmes that he was thought capable of filling even one of the great man's shoes. But only one it was. The Visitors dissolved Dew's near monopoly on instruction and gave the new professor no more than ancient and modern history, political economy, and national law. Altogether they formed, in Holmes's estimate, "the most delightful and brilliant Professorship that could be devised." Holmes was, of course, aware of his responsibilities and promised Lieber faithfully to continue Dew's mission of preaching salvation through free trade

Holmes Papers, Swem Library, College of William and Mary, Williamsburg, Virginia; hereinafter cited as Holmes papers, WM. W. G. Simms to John B. Christian, October 15, [1846], Simms, *Letters*, II, 193. Testimonial letter of Francis Lieber, January 29, 1847, Holmes papers, D. Robert M. T. Hunter to Robert McCandlish, January 28, 1847, *ibid*. G. F. Holmes to Lavalette Holmes, October 22, 1846 and November 21, 1846, *ibid*. John Tyler to G. F. Holmes, October 20, 1846, vol. I, Holmes papers, LC. G. F. Holmes to Lavalette Holmes, February 24, 1847, Holmes papers, D.
47 G. F. Holmes to Lavalette Holmes, March 1, 1847, Holmes papers, D.

alone,[48] but he was more interested in the opportunity offered by the chair of history.

Since the early 1840s when Holmes first began to think about new approaches to the study of history, he and Jamison had agreed that "History was the amplest and noblest theatre now offered to the student," and thought "a Professorship of History and Political Economy in all respects the most desirable position that could be occupied in this age and country." Once he had accepted history as a major interest it stirred his ambition as well as his imagination. Before taking over his new appointment he again confided his hopes to Jamison as he must have many times before: "I have long indulged the wish of being able to reform the study of history and the branches immediately connected with it; and placing History on its true platform as a moral science. I am conscious of the vastness of the subject [but] . . . I may lay the foundations, if I cannot erect the edifice." Now, at Williamsburg, one of a growing number of American colleges beginning to teach history as such at this time, he at last had his chance. He told Jamison, "It will be my endeavor to map out my future course and to plan the labours of my life in my Inaugural Lecture, which I design writing with great care, and so as to produce a lasting impression." In partial realization of his goal he organized a comprehensive course of instruction that related the development of religion and literature to political events and prefaced the whole with a discussion of the nature of history and its prospects as a science. He did well if all of his associates were as impressed as President Robert Saunders who found him to have "a deeper and broader foundation for universal knowledge" than anyone he had ever known and believed him destined to "become one of the most learned men of this or any other country."[49]

Holmes was also optimistic over the more mundane aspects of his future. His annual salary was to be one thousand dollars plus twenty dollars "a head from every pupil." This enabled him to expect to be free of debt within two years.[50] He also hoped to be able to provide (at long last) a permanent home for his growing family which had

[48] *Ibid.* Francis Lieber to G. F. Holmes, March 14, 1847, vol. I, Holmes papers, LC. G. F. Holmes to Francis Lieber, April 14, 1847, Holmes papers, D.

[49] G. F. Holmes to D. F. Jamison, April 14, 1847, MS vol. 1808. MS vol. 1806, Holmes papers, D. Photocopy of a testimonial letter of Robert Saunders, June 16, 1848, William and Mary College Papers, Swem Library, College of William and Mary, Williamsburg, Virginia; hereinafter cited as WMCP. George H. Callcott, *History in the United States, 1800–1860: Its Practice and Purpose* (Baltimore: Johns Hopkins University Press, [1970]), pp. 59–61.

[50] Holmes to Lavalette Holmes, March 1, 1847.

again increased by the time he assumed his new duties in October 1847; a son, John Floyd Holmes, was born that spring only to die the following year just as his father's future at Williamsburg slipped away. The disappointment that had dogged Holmes like a curse since his arrival in the New World was still with him.

His difficulties began almost immediately. Not the least of these was his wife's troublesome reluctance to leave the mountains. Well toward the end of November, and several weeks after Holmes had begun teaching, she was still not in Williamsburg. To add anxiety to his irritation he did not know where she was. She had been delayed in leaving the family home in Burke's Garden by lack of money. Now she was long overdue and no letter had come to explain why. Lavalette was not much of a letter writer—everyone in her family complained about it—and she had the habit of stopping en route to visit with friends. By the last days of November, Holmes was so distracted with worry that he was preparing to leave the college and go westward searching for her.[51] She came in eventually (when or how is not known) for she was there in the spring. This was not to be Holmes's last experience with his wife's nonchalant ways.

Williamsburg in the 1840s still retained something of the charm of the colonial capital, though the marks of decay were evident. Holmes soon discovered that this deterioration had spread to the college. During his long tenure President Dew had improved the condition of the college and had it flourishing as in former times. When he died, however, evil days set in once more and within a few months after Holmes took up his duties the college was on the verge of dissolution.

The main reason for this sudden downward turn in the school's course was the election to the chair of moral philosophy of A. C. Peachy, a protegé of the late Dew, against the wishes of a significant portion of the faculty. Professor John Millington spoke for this faction:

After Dew's death we were all desirous that some man of acknowledged ability and reputation with the public, should be elected as his successor; the right of election being vested in the visitors; and not with ourselves. Candidates were advertised for, and many presented themselves, among whom were several names perfectly unexceptionable. But instead of taking any of them, Nepotism prevailed, and attempts were made to introduce persons no doubt of good character & attainments, but unknown to the public, and therefore not of the kind we required, or wished to have.

Professor Charles Minnigerode seconded his appraisal: "The injudicious action of the Visitors in forcing Mr. Peachy into the faculty,

---

51 G. F. Holmes to Lavalette Holmes, November 28, 1847, Holmes papers, D.

and his strange demeanor in raising points of personal variance with some of the Professors, have resulted in an entire dismemberment of the Faculty."[52] Peachy's "strange demeanor in raising points of personal variance with some of the Professors" must be, in part at least, a reference to an incident that to Holmes was the major scandal involved in the entire business: a challenge issued by Peachy to Saunders, professor of mathematics and briefly president of the college.

The affair began early in November 1847, when the Board of Visitors confirmed Saunders in the office that he had been filling as president pro tempore, and also elected Peachy to the chair of moral philosophy. Saunders promptly resigned both the presidency and his professorship of mathematics, but for the sake of the school agreed to remain until the end of the academic year. The Visitors were somewhat surprised by this, of course; but in itself his resignation was not serious for finding a new president would be more troublesome than difficult. Things took on a different color, however, when word began to go around that the cause of Saunder's resignation had been Peachy's election. Student meetings were held to agitate the issue and rumors spread over the state that a number of students and two professors had left the college in protest over Peachy's appointment.[53]

Peachy, who had not yet arrived in Williamsburg when the trouble started, learned of it by happening on a copy of a student resolution in the office of the *Enquirer* blaming his election for Saunders' resignation. He promptly demanded an explanation from Saunders. Saunders curtly refused to answer a demand. Peachy's challenge followed immediately and was as promptly accepted. At this point a mutual friend intervened and restored peace. Peachy agreed to withdraw his challenge with the understanding that Saunders would alter his reply to suggest that Peachy might request an explanation rather than demand one. Peachy then sent a second note stating that he originally had thought himself obliged to make a demand, but now that Saunders had admitted he was willing to give an explanation, he would accept it. Letters were exchanged, and that, ostensibly, was that.[54] But in reality the threat of a duel between the president and a newly elected professor only served to set loose the spirit of faction and the college was soon prostrated.

The reasons for the feeling against Peachy are not clear. Saunders probably had opposed his election openly and so could only look on

[52] John Millington to Joseph Henry, March 10, 1848; Charles Minnigerode to L. C. Garland, August 31, 1848, WMCP.

[53] *Richmond Enquirer*, November 12, 23, 1847.

[54] The correspondence was published by Peachy. *Enquirer*, December 10, 1847.

the Visitors' action as an affront and a vote of no confidence. But why did he oppose Peachy's appointment in the first place? Why did the faculty oppose him? From the letters of Millington and Minnigerode one might infer that Peachy was an unknown and a troublemaker; and it is entirely probable that as President Dew's favorite he had not endeared himself to the other professors while a student at William and Mary. The charge of nepotism made by Millington obviously included Peachy who had the support of the admirers of Dew on the Board of Visitors. But recall that Millington spoke of "persons" being forced on the college. Could Holmes have been one of these also? He admitted that he owed his election largely to the influence of Tyler,[55] and, although he could not be called a man unknown to the "public" if by that term we designate the relatively small circle of literary and academic people who knew him and his work, that is obviously not the meaning of "public" that Millington intended. The truth was that Holmes had little reputation with the "public"—and even less in Virginia than in South Carolina. At any rate and whatever faculty resentment there might have been, Holmes soon discovered that he had enemies on the Board where resentment of Tyler, who was only an acting Visitor (acting for the occasion of pressing the interests of Mrs. Floyd's son-in-law?), would have been keenest.

Holmes had been disturbed by the Saunders-Peachy affair, but when Judge John B. Christian, a Visitor whose son had been expelled from the college for bearing the challenge, began to talk of "the pernicious influence of these damned foreigners" he became alarmed. Holmes himself was not the immediate target of this remark but his English citizenship and his family's Catholicism made him an easy mark for an upsurge of nativism. He believed that Judge Christian was not (and never had been) his friend, so when the Judge began seriously to agitate the issue of "damned foreigners" in the college, Holmes anticipated events by resigning his chair.[56]

He had no trouble finding justifications for this step other than his fear of an impending nativist purge. Discontents had been building up for months and they poured out in his letter of resignation. The college was obviously in decline, he believed, and showed no sign of immediate revival; he was not a rich man and could not afford to wait for the recovery of its fortunes. He did not care to become identified in the public mind with a failing institution "against which the feelings of the whole state seem to be arrayed." Too, because of

[55] Holmes to Lavalette Holmes, February 24, 1847.

[56] G. F. Holmes to George Floyd, January 25, 1848, Johnston papers. See also John Tyler to G. F. Holmes, January 31, 1848, John Tyler Papers, Library of Congress, Washington, D. C.

shrinking enrollment, his income from student tuition had been much smaller than he had been led to expect. Worst of all, the strife among students, faculty, and Visitors made the college an impossible place for serious teaching and scholarship. Since he saw no way of living in peace with all factions, the only recourse, he felt, was to resign.[57]

Holmes looked on his move as a master stroke. He boasted to Judge Christian's face of his astuteness in heading him off and laughingly wrote to his brother-in-law George that the Judge felt "himself completely out-generalled." In addition, he told George,

> The result of my resignation has been to induce every Professor to explain to me his course, and exculpate himself—to excite universal regret; with the admission of all hands, (including Mr. Peachy) that throughout I have done exactly right—and am the only one connected with the College who has done so in the opinion of every one. . . . By this course I have attained a stronger hold in the public mind—and a higher reputation than I could have if I had remained in office as long as Mr. Dew.

Both Christian and Robert McCandlish, rector of the Board of Visitors, (whom Holmes thought to share Christian's aversion to him) went through the motions of expressing regret and asking him to reconsider, but he knew that actually they were "at heart glad enough to get rid of me." Apparently alone among the faculty, Nathaniel Beverly Tucker, professor of law, thought Holmes's action hasty, but Holmes dismissed this as being merely "in accordance with his intrigue with Judge Christian." All in all, his resignation seemed to be a great success and he expected it to have the effect of forcing the rest of the faculty to follow suit.[58] In March the Visitors met to do something about the deteriorating situation, and, as Holmes had predicted, called for the resignations of the entire faculty.

Following his resignation, Holmes was at his characteristic loose ends as to what to do next. He knew of a number of openings in schools, but, as he wrote to George, "I am getting somewhat tired of the insecurity of Colleges, and the improvidence, & faithlessness of Trustees." A more promising alternative at the time of his resignation in January was the oft-deferred prospect of going to Wisconsin and practicing law with George. But George seriously injured his back and, in February, returned to Virginia. Plans had to be changed once again.[59]

The Visitors came together at Williamsburg on March 2 for an arduous three day meeting to attempt to save the college. The result

[57] G. F. Holmes to Robert McCandlish, January 22, 1848, Holmes papers, D.
[58] Holmes to Floyd, January 25, 1848.
[59] *Ibid*. Letitia Floyd to G. F. Holmes, February 22, 1848, Holmes papers, D.

of the session was a determination to reorganize the college throughout. Accordingly, all of the faculty were required to resign their positions (Saunders and Holmes for the second time) effective at the end of the current term. In July the Board was to meet again and elect a new group of professors and a new president. The Visitors also issued a "short and spirited address" on the state of the college to reassure the public. A few weeks later, advertisements appeared in the newspapers soliciting candidates for the six chairs at the college.[60]

Jamison had been following the turmoil at William and Mary as best he could in the public press and with considerable anxiety for his friend because, as he wrote, "I know you are able to take sides, and that warmly." He need not have worried. Holmes carefully avoided unnecessarily antagonizing anyone. In fact, in early May, when Judge Christian tried to capitalize on Holmes's high local standing by making him an ally in a long-running dispute at the college over the Judge's morals and religious beliefs, he passed up this chance to make a friend of one known enemy at the cost of making enemies of an unknown number of possible friends and politely but firmly declined. When the Visitors met in July, Holmes was reelected to his chair despite the animosity of Christian and McCandlish (the degree or duration of which he may have misjudged), as were Judge Tucker, Millington, and Peachy. The other two chairs (mathematics and ancient languages) and the presidency were filled with new men. Holmes, who was summering in Burke's Garden, was notified of his reinstatement by the rector and urged to reply promptly. He dallied for several days as if waiting for something. And waiting he was, for he had determined sometime earlier to try for the presidency of the newly organized University of Mississippi. But he heard nothing and decided to accept reinstatement in spite of all that had gone before. He did so with little enthusiasm, however, and with the understanding that he was not obligated to stay or even to remain throughout the coming term.[61]

A week after he had mailed his acceptance, he received notification of his election in Mississippi. Dashing off a note telling McCandlish of this development, he promised a formal letter of resignation later. The same day he set to work on it and unburdened his soul. He declined to so much as even return to the college. "Nearly all the reasons

60 *Enquirer*, March 10, 28, 1848.
61 D. F. Jamison to G. F. Holmes, April 8, 1848, Holmes papers, D. G. F. Holmes to John B. Christian, May 10, 1848, *ibid. Enquirer*, July 18, 1848. Robert McCandlish to G. F. Holmes, July 25, 1848; John Millington to G. F. Holmes, July 29, 1848; G. F. Holmes to Robert McCandlish, August 7, 1848, Holmes papers, D.

alleged for my first resignation are applicable now," he began, "and are more than doubled in intensity." To that catalogue of wrongs he now added that he had received "nothing but loss and injury" from the Visitors, that he had not requested to be reinstated, that he deeply resented having been required to resign a second time when his resignation was already before the Board and after he had explained to them that his participation in the general resignation was unnecessary because he had held aloof from the factionalism that had provoked the mass resignation. He also resented having had his chair advertised as vacant while he still held it, he accused the Board of unforgivable delay in giving public notice that the resignations of March in no way reflected on the characters or abilities of the professors, and ended by saying that he would have resigned when the Saunders-Peachy challenge was originally given if it had not been for the interests of his family. He assured the rector that he intended no disrespect to the Board, but that he could only regard their conduct during the entire time as "injudicious, ordinarily reckless and negligent—and frequently unjust . . . but," he added diplomatically, "I do not think I have ever accused them in word or thought of intentional wrong." Having gotten this off his chest, he turned westward to what he hoped would be more rewarding days in Oxford, Mississippi. William and Mary continued to decline. The graduating class of 1849 was only 7, compared to 32 in 1848 and 47 in 1847. By August 1848, Judge Tucker and the tenacious Mr. Peachy were the only members of the old faculty still at Williamsburg.[62] But all this was of no concern to the new president. He had worries enough of his own.

The University of Mississippi was the product of the general movement throughout the South to provide safe education for southern youth in response to the increasing vigor of criticism of things southern in the North. The school was incorporated in 1844 and after a delay of several years owing to the mismanagement of its resources, it finally opened its doors in November 1848. The village of Oxford, where the new university was located, was the county seat of Lafayette County which had itself been created barely ten years earlier out of territory ceded by the Chickasaw Indians in 1832. At the inaugural ceremonies Jacob Thompson, who spoke in behalf of the Trustees, and the new president both warned Mississippians of the dangers of northern education. Thompson called it "a sin against our

[62] G. F. Holmes to Robert McCandlish, August 14, 1848, *ibid.* G. F. Holmes to Robert McCandlish, August 18, 1848, *ibid. History of the College of William and Mary from its Foundation, 1660 to 1874* (Richmond: Randolph and English, 1874), pp. 139–45. Minnigerode to Garland, August 31, 1848. See also Robert Saunders to G. F. Holmes, May 10, 1850, Holmes papers, D.

children" to subject them to the fanaticism of northern colleges. President Holmes hoped that southerners would "prefer to trust the education of their sons to a southern institution, [than] to the hazardous, expensive and humiliating experiment of sending them abroad, to imbibe at the North delusive views which will infect their minds during their whole life."[63]

Strife and ill feeling gathered around the new school even before Holmes appeared on the scene. It began when the Trustees convened in July 1848 to elect the faculty and to determine the curriculum. There were well over a hundred candidates for the teaching positions: seventeen of them for the presidency alone.[64] A popular favorite for the post of president—though an unofficial candidate—was Augustus Baldwin Longstreet, a Methodist clergyman who recently had been president of Emory College in Georgia.[65] His candidacy served to underscore the question of the role of religion in the school which had already set off quarrels among the Trustees. The leader of the anti-clerical faction was Judge E. C. Wilkinson. He and his associates objected to having ministers on the faculty and protested that if the conventional course in apologetics, "Evidences of Christianity," were included in the curriculum as proposed it could not be taught in a non-sectarian manner. Although the judge and his friends based their objection on the doctrine of the separation of church and state, two of them are said to have been so bold as to deliver attacks on the Christian religion and its ministry thereby exciting considerable public indignation. The Board overruled the dissenters on "Evidences" and on the principle of clergymen on the faculty; nonetheless, the Wilkinson group was able to prevent the election of Longstreet.[66] Leading

---

[63] James Allen Cabaniss, *A History of the University of Mississippi* (University, Mississippi: University of Mississippi, 1949), pp. 7-8. Jacob Thompson, *Address Delivered on Occasion of the Opening of the Universty of the State of Mississippi, in Behalf of the Board of Trustees, November 6, 1848* (Memphis, Tenn.: n. p., 1849), pp. 5-6. George Frederick Holmes, *Inaugural Address Delivered on Occasion of the Opening of the University of the State of Mississippi, November 6, 1848* (Memphis, Tenn.: n. p., 1849), p. 12.

[64] John N. Waddel, *Memorials of Academic Life* (Richmond: Presbyterian Committee of Publication, 1891), p. 252. Waddel was briefly a Trustee and was elected the first professor of languages.

[65] John Donald Wade, *Augustus Baldwin Longstreet* (New York: Macmillan and Company, 1924), p. 292.

[66] John Waddel's memory is the source of our knowledge of these events. He was at Oxford and, while no longer a member of the Board, remained in a good position to know what was going on. The minutes of the Trustees confirm the general content of his account but are discreetly silent about the details. They do show, however, that Wilkinson was willing to compromise by allowing the university to establish a chaplaincy to rotate among the various sects for the

the list of official candidates for president was Holmes, who was personally unknown to the Trustees but who had many "flattering testimonials of accomplished scholarship" in his support. He was given the position. But popular disapproval of the presence of infidels on the Board of Trustees was not mollified by the election of another man of the cloth, John Waddel, to the professorship of languages. The fracas over religion had given many Mississippians the impression that the university was a hot bed of infidelity.[67] The impression lingered and the resulting lack of public confidence did not make Holmes's task any easier.

The curriculum was good by contemporary standards. Holmes taught mental and moral philosophy, belles-lettres, international law, and political economy, in addition to struggling with the duties of president. Though "Evidences of Christianity" by custom fell to the president also, it was normally taught only to seniors and, as the highest class in 1848 was the sophomore,[68] it was not given that year, an omission that must have seemed appropriate to an "infidel" institution. Professor Millington, a fellow refugee from Williamsburg, offered chemistry, geology, mineralogy, botany, and natural philosophy. Albert T. Bledsoe, recruited from Miami University in Ohio, held classes in mathematics and astronomy. Professor Waddel taught languages.[69] The faculty was as able as their responsibilities were numerous, but the university itself was poorly prepared to begin instruction.

The location of colleges in rural areas in order to protect the health and morals of the students was not unusual in ante-bellum America, but this one was truly isolated. No railroad or main thoroughfare ran near it. The school opened without text books.[70] The campus was littered with stumps and tree limbs. Buildings were without their outer doors and stoops. "Scaffolding and scantling were scattered all about."[71] The university had no library, observatory, chapel, or auditorium, and the professor of natural philosophy was forced to

---

purpose of providing a minister to come twice a day and read prayers for the students. His motion to this effect was defeated. Waddel, *Memorials*, pp. 252–54; Minutes of the Board of Trustees, July 11, 12, 1848, Mississippi Collection, University of Mississippi, University, Mississippi; hereinafter cited as MBT.

[67] Waddel, *Memorials*, pp. 254, 266–67.

[68] *Ibid.*, pp. 267–68.

[69] Newspaper clipping announcing the opening of the university in Holmes papers, D.

[70] Waddel was able to relieve this situation somewhat by purchasing the supplies of a defunct academy nearby. Waddel, *Memorials*, p. 268.

[71] George Frederick Holmes, "Professor John Millington, M. D." *William and Mary Quarterly*, III, 2nd ser. (January 1923), 32.

use his personal scientific apparatus for classroom experiments.[72] But the most serious lack was an adequately prepared student body. Several years later Holmes was reminded of his Oxford days and wrote, "We are acquainted with one State University, and a class of Natural Philosophy, one of whose members, with concurrence of others, expressed an anxious desire that the Professor would perform 'a few more of them tricks'—thus designating the scientific experiments."[73] Indeed, the faculty spent many weary hours privately tutoring students to prepare them for college work. But the students were not to be blamed entirely for their lack. The hectic circumstances surrounding the opening of the university had caused many of them to arrive in Oxford not even knowing what they were expected to study.[74]

And yet the most vexing problem facing the authorities at the university was not an excess of ignorance but rather a lack of self-discipline among the students. Many years later, Professor Waddel remembered that "Very rarely, if ever, was an institution attended by a body of students so disorderly and turbulent." Most of the students of that first session, he added, "were idle, uncultivated, viciously disposed, and ungovernable." Waddel's memory did not play him false for at the end of the term his colleague Professor Bledsoe was moved to give a lecture on the significance for education of man's total depravity.[75]

To a large extent the collapse of order was the consequence of President Holmes's progressive notions about student discipline. What were they? One of Holmes's most vigorous statements of what they were *not* was made well after his disgrace when he was futilely trying to regain his position. Defending his course, he wrote to Trustee Wilkinson that he "was opposed to violence, harshness of action, espionage, and hasty procedure on suspicion without conclusive evidence, in the case of students.[76] In short, he was opposed to the way almost everyone else kept order in a college. President Holmes pro-

---

[72] Holmes, *Inaugural Address*, p. 12.

[73] [George Frederick Holmes], "Sir William Hamilton's Discussions," *Southern Quarterly Review*, VIII, n.s. (October 1853), 318n. Cabaniss tells the story but from another source, Cabaniss, *University of Mississippi*, p. 18. The authorship of anonymous articles attributed to Holmes has been verified in the relevant manuscript collections and in the bibliography of his writings in Herbert B. Adams, *Thomas Jefferson and the University of Virginia* (Washington: Government Printing Office, 1888).

[74] Cabaniss, *University of Mississippi*, p. 18.

[75] *Ibid.*, p. 19. Waddel, *Memorials*, p. 267.

[76] G. F. Holmes to E. C. Wilkinson, January 24, 1850, Holmes papers, D. See also [George Frederick Holmes], "Universities and Colleges," *Southern Literary Messenger*, XX (August 1854), 456–57.

posed to do it differently and made a public announcement of his new method in his inaugural address. At the end of his rather long speech and after pointing out the necessity of order and harmony in a college, he turned to the assembled young men and said,

Instead of adopting the inquisitional system of discipline adopted in most other Colleges, we appeal to your honor as Mississippians. The laws [of the University] will be made known to you before your admission, you will assent to them or not as you please. If you are unwilling to incur the obligations which they impose, you do not enter the University. . . . If you approve of the laws on the contrary, you pledge your honor as gentlemen that you will not willfully violate them. We then hold you by your own promise, and keep you on your word of honor during your connection with the University. If there should be reason to suspect any of you of any breach of discipline; of any violation of the laws, we do not hunt up evidence against you, but ask you privately on your honor as gentlemen, whether you are guilty or not of the offence.

Holmes apparently had not been able to get this liberal innovation approved by his colleagues and the Trustees without provoking some skepticism regarding its effectiveness, for he continued,

It has been suggested that we hold you by a weak tenure—we think not. We have remitted all of discipline that is harsh or oppressive—we make you feel as gentlemen and that you are under the responsibilities of gentlemen—and we will not harbor for one moment the suspicion that any Mississippian—that any young man of the South will deliberately tell—a lie. . . . Here we hope to build up a society of gentlemen—he who may have falsified his word and stained his honor, can have no place among gentlemen, and must go out from their midst.[77]

His hot-blooded young charges were "gentlemen" of another stamp than that Holmes had in mind, and the tenure proved weak indeed.

The new plan had been drawn up by the faculty and approved by the Board of Trustees on November 7, 1848. It had many of the features that one would find in any set of college regulations at the time: students were disarmed upon entering the university; they were required to attend class and religious services; their activities when not in class were closely supervised; drinking, dueling, gambling, and playing on musical instruments were forbidden. The guiding hand of President Holmes appeared not in the list of offenses but in the provisions for punishing them. Each entering student signed an oath that on his honor he would obey all the rules of the school. This was filed with his records and all offenses were permanently entered on it. When he broke the law the procedure was set in the by-laws:

[77] Holmes, *Inaugural Address*, p. 24.

When a student is suspected of having committed any offence, one of the Faculty shall be appointed to confer with him. If he admits it, or refuses to deny it the due penalty shall be enforced by resolution of the Faculty. If he denies it on his honor, he shall be acquitted, unless the evidence of its commission be so strong as to produce a *unanimous* conviction of his guilt in the minds of the Faculty. (Italics mine).

This lenient course of action was not always the rule. The by-laws also provided that, "When a Student commits an offence under the eye of a Professor, he shall not be questioned on his honor, but proceeded against." Should we not see in this exception the skepticism of those officers of the university who were less certain that Holmes of the gentlemanly character of the students? Perhaps. But, at any rate, their gentlemanly character was to be acknowledged: "No reproof shall be given by any Prof. in public except where the good order of the class requires it, and in all cases the feelings of the students shall be respected," and "No reprimand shall be given but by a resolution of the Faculty."[78]

The result of Holmes's rule for gentlemen was massive disorder. Some gentlemen, it appeared, would lie—and take advantage of trust as well. There was that saving loophole in the honor code, of course. If the evidence against the culprit were strong enough to compel (or justify) unanimous condemnation by the professors his word of honor might be disregarded. But Holmes's evident unwillingness to punish unfairly those who might be innocent probably more than once prevented this unanimity from occurring. At least one may so infer from Waddel's remembrance of his methods through which the scorn comes clearly even after the intervening years:

It was a practice to which the President habitually resorted, and upon which he seemed entirely to rely for success in his government of the student body, to make earnest appeals to the high-toned principles of true honor and gentlemanly manhood; and this he evidently deemed abundantly direct and effective in all cases of disorder and lawless outrage that might be prevalent in any student body.[79]

The chaos eventually became so great and public confidence in the institution so damaged that in July 1849 the Trustees were forced to undertake an investigation. They found that in spite of Holmes's leniency and exhortations by the end of the first session well over a fourth of the student body of eighty had been expelled, suspended,

[78] MBT, November 7, 1848.
[79] Waddel, *Memorials*, p. 270.

voluntarily withdrawn, or in some other way had departed from Oxford.[80]

Professor Bledsoe, not a man to tolerate foolishness, was made president pro tempore and the rules and regulations revised. The flavor of the new regime may be sampled by one quotation:

Sec. 6. It shall be the duty of some one member of the Faculty to visit the room of each student, daily at such times as he may deem proper.

Sec. 7. It shall be the privilege of any member of the Faculty, to enter the room of any student at pleasure.

Sec. 8. Each student when required shall open the door of his room to any member of the Faculty and on his refusal, the officer may break it open, and the expense of repairing shall be defrayed by the student, who shall also be punished for disobedience.[81]

That characteristic of the American college for which Holmes had so much contempt—espionage, spying on the students by the faculty—had come to the University of Mississippi.

But, as Bledsoe's appointment indicated, Holmes was not present in July to see the ignominious collapse of his experiment. Early in the year, when his daughter Mary Anne had become dangerously ill, she and Mrs. Holmes had returned to Virginia. By early March Holmes's concern over Mary Anne was so great that he left Oxford and started for Virginia on a six weeks leave of absence. The end of his leave came and went and Holmes did not return. His delay was apparently caused by his own serious illness which also prevented his communicating with the Trustees. But whatever the reason for his absence, it needs little imagination to think that there were those at the university who were glad enough to seize the opportunity to be rid of this strange Englishman and to elect in his place the frustrated favorite of the previous year. Accordingly, on July 10, 1849, the Trustees declared Holmes to have voluntarily abandoned his office and the next day unanimously elected Longstreet as his successor.[82]

[80] MBT, July 12, 1849.

[81] *Ibid.*

[82] MS vol. 1808, entry dated March 1, 1850; Letitia Floyd to Lavalette Holmes, February 22, 1849, Holmes papers, D. Waddel, *Memorials*, p. 271. John Millington to G. F. Holmes, April 19, 1849, Holmes papers, D. Charles Dabney to G. F. Holmes, October 26, 1849, *ibid.* MBT, July 10, 11, 1849. James E. Pope's account is the source for most versions of Holmes's dismissal, but it is demonstrably wrong at every point where it can be tested against the evidence. His story of Holmes returning to the University after his recovery and finding Longstreet in his place has much circumstantial evidence against it and is undoubtedly apocryphal. The only documentary support for it is a recorded salary payment

Holmes did not take his dismissal lying down. As soon as he was able, he wrote to Judge Wilkinson to ask reinstatement. He excused himself on the grounds that he had "fallen a sacrifice to accident, and illness, and untoward events." In truth, the period of his separation from the university had been a difficult time for, in addition to his illness, a developing cataract had cost him the sight of one eye. Holmes had heard that some of the Trustees charged him with a lack of "firmness and tact in the government of young men." A mere red herring! The real reason for his dismissal, he said, was his disagreement with the Board and some of the faculty over methods of discipline. He also suspected that more than one of his enemies had resented his efforts to raise the academic standards of the university. He asked Wilkinson to plead his case and prevail with the Trustees to reconsider.[83] If the judge complied, it was to no purpose. Holmes was not reinstated.

To add to his injury, when the Trustees took final action on his case in March 1850, they refused to pay him for the entire session. The Board, however, was generous enough to resolve "that in dissolving the connection between sd. President and the institution, the board did not design to cast any reflection on his character, as a man, or his reputation as a scholar." Such balm was not unwelcome, for it would seem that unflattering tales of his ordeal at Oxford had followed him eastward. His old friends in South Carolina were glad to have his assurances (and those of the Trustees which were duly communicated to him) that his conduct has been perfectly honorable.[84] But Holmes keenly felt his humiliation and was not one to forget. Many years later, in 1888, a graduate of the University of Mississippi saw Holmes (who since 1857 had been a distinguished professor of history and literature at the University of Virginia) at a Chautauqua meeting in Georgia and introduced himself as an alumnus of his old school. When the former president discovered the young man's connection, " 'he assumed the air of haughty indifference.' "[85]

So ended the first phase of Holmes's academic life. Into three years he had crowded more frustration and disappointment than many ex-

to Holmes on July 12, 1849, but this was a routine end-of-the term payment and did not require Holmes being there in person. Then, too, Holmes's returning on July 12 would be incompatible with Pope's statement that he first left at the end of the term, i.e., July 12. See Pope, "Reminiscences," p. 3. Waddel, of course, says explicitly that Holmes never returned.

[83] Dabney to Holmes, October 26, 1849. Holmes to Wilkinson, January 24, 1850.

[84] MBT, July 10, 1850. D. F. Jamison to G. F. Holmes, April 16, 1850, vol. I, Holmes papers, LC.

[85] Quoted in Cabaniss, *University of Mississippi*, pp. 22–23.

perience in a lifetime. Jamison perhaps eased his chagrin by congratulating him on his "near deliverance from the pitfall that was due for you in Mississippi," and expressing hope that Holmes would remember "not to seek again in a new state, what you will never find there, wealth with comfort or 'ease with dignity.' " Be that as it may, Holmes now retired to the Floyd home at Burke's Garden where he remained until called to the University of Virginia in 1857. He farmed and now and then applied for a position in a college, but, in general, he found himself with "nothing else to do, except to write articles."[86]

[86] Jamison to Holmes, April 16, 1850. G. F. Holmes to Lavalette Holmes, December 4, 1850, Holmes papers, D.

II   Enchantment and Disenchantment

Holmes's work in the early 1840s was almost bare of anything which would have indicated the religious crisis which was to haunt the remainder of his days. He was, in most respects, an enthusiastic and outspoken devotee of the Enlightenment. His confidence in the superiority of nineteenth-century civilization and in the promise of reason and science were virtually without limit. Addressing the Orangeburg Athenaeum in the summer of 1842, he proclaimed that "It should be a source of congratulations and delight to all that our lot has been cast in these ages of the world when the supremacy of Intellect is universally acknowledged and a preference for Intellectual pleasures everywhere manifested." This comfortable state of affairs was "the natural fruit of the Intellectual advancement and general cultivation of the country and the age."[1]

Such opinions, of course, were not novel at the time nor were they new with Holmes himself. Two years earlier, while musing in the privacy of his notebook, he had expounded at some length on the virtues of the modern era. Anyone who carefully studied the matter, he thought, would find that the modern world improved on the ancient in almost every realm of culture and human activity: modern history was more philosophical, modern poetry possessed more feeling and passion, modern knowledge of human nature was more complete. Through the influence of the Gospels the human mind had become more humble and cautious, and these qualities, in turn, had assisted the progress of knowledge by nurturing the spirit of science. As a result, the modern intellect was inductive and practical rather than deductive and speculative: "we have been taught to prefer the truly useful to that which is merely glittering, to found all our reasoning upon facts and to appeal unto facts for the correctness of our inferences." All in all, the modern age had lost nothing by an abandonment of ancient modes of thought except perhaps a felicity of art, but this loss easily could be repaired by "a constant recurrence to the *heroes* of the Greek & Latin Tongues as models of style." The new

---

[1] [George Frederick Holmes], MS "Introduction to a Sketch of the Intellectual Progress of Mankind," vol. II, Holmes papers, LC.

spirit of scientific inquiry, on the other hand, had "made such a vast addition to our stores of learning & knowledge that though we may grieve over what is gone, it were folly to desire to have it back at the price of its purchase."[2]

There were, he recognized, grumblers and faint-hearted persons who did not share Holmes's confidence in the merits of the nineteenth century. And he acknowledged that, superficially at least, there was some basis for their apprehension. In an 1842 review of William Whewell's pioneering volume, *History of the Inductive Sciences* (1837), he announced that "a new revolution is even now in progress, analogous to and in furtherance of that which was advancing from the times of Luther to Montaigne . . . a renovation not merely of one particular branch or department of knowledge, but of the whole domain of intellect. The signs and symptoms of this coming revolution are thick around us." What were these signs? They were obvious enough, he thought, and were frequently noted, though their true significance was seldom recognized. The foundations of social order were cracking and threatening to collapse; long accepted principles of government and religion were under attack; traditional axioms of politics, law, science, and learning were being called into question or denied outright; literature, having thrown off the restraints of classicism, was bound for who knew where. "In fact," the young revolutionary enthusiastically concluded, "all philosophy, speculative and practical. has been thrown into the furnace, and the ferment is now in progress, which will effect its transmutation."[3]

Holmes admitted the danger latent within the wave of intellectual innovation which he saw sweeping over the Western world. He recognized that the nineteenth century was marked, perhaps too much, by a "love of investigation," by "an anxious, restless, feverish spirit of inquiry." But this turbulence was the unavoidable characteristic of a revolutionary age. It was not a rashness to be feared but a hope to be embraced. The world stood on the brink of "a new philosophical era." There must be no holding back; he saw "no listlessness, no slumbering, among those who are producing this great mutation; every eye is open and on the alert to detect the course of the approaching change; every muscle braced, to seize and bear forward the torch in the race." The world was as if seized by a fever. "Intellect is claiming her throne, and though we live in the day of battle, we cannot doubt the issue of the contest."[4] Not too many years were to pass

---

[2] MS vol. 1782, p. 27.

[3] [George Frederick Holmes], "Whewell on the Inductive Sciences," *Southern Quarterly Review*, II (July 1842), 194.

[4] *Ibid.*, pp. 194–95.

before Holmes began to doubt the wisdom of such an uncritical faith in the spontaneous tendencies of the age, but in 1842 he was looking to the future, ignorant of the outcome of the present turmoil but filled with great expectations.

It is not surprising to find this optimistic, even aggressive belief in human progress united with a liberalism in religion which bordered on what the orthodox called infidelity. And yet, Holmes's religious training as a child has been conventional. He had been born into a moderately pious family and had been raised in the Church of England. One assumes that Dr. Cowan's school sowed no seeds of infidelity; nor is it likely that Durham University did so, for it was an institution of pronounced ecclesiastical tone and completely dominated by the "Old Warden," Archdeacon Charles Thorpe, a Highchurchman and a convinced traditionalist.[5] As far as anyone can tell, when Holmes left England he may well have been a model of piety and orthodoxy. But in time his omnivorous reading had its effect and in America his religious opinions changed drastically.

Indicative of these new attitudes was Holmes's mode of keeping the Sabbath. He ceased to attend church (a practice he apparently resumed only at Williamsburg and perhaps then only for appearances) and instead spent Sundays in study. From time to time he fell under the critical eye of certain "unco righteous" Sabbatarians who condemned his study of secular subjects on the Lord's day but who themselves, the young Englishman noted, thought nothing of spending their Sabbath "in the most idle and empty conversation." Holmes had no hesitation in using this leisure time to advance his "literary studies" though he did think it proper to abstain "from works whose tendency is too light for such a day."[6] This reverent qualification sprang from a basic piety which Holmes retained throughout his period of youthful freethinking. But this piety was intellectual and was not derived from a deep religious emotion. In fact, it is doubtful that he had any significant degree of religious faith at this time. On the contrary, the thrust of his mind was exceptionally critical. His enthusiasm for religious studies was generated not by a love for the Word but by the desire for a rational grasp of the essence of Christianity. Ironically, this tendency toward Christian rationalism, had he persisted in it, might have offered him a much less painful accomodation of his reli-

5 Joseph Thomas Fowler, *Durham University, Earlier Foundations and Present Colleges* (London: F. E. Robinson and Company, 1904), pp. 109–13, 248.

6 Adam Gilchrist to G. F. Holmes, May 24, 1842. Holmes papers, D. Testimonial letter of William S. Plumer, January 28, 1847, *ibid.* MS vol. 1840, budget of time dated January, 1848. MS vol. 1792, p. 33, *ibid.*

gious beliefs to the changing world view than he finally achieved, but this inclination was to be nipped in the bud by his orthodox reaction in the 1850s.

The skeptical turn of his mind may be seen in the notes he made while studying the Bible during the years 1839 to 1844. Later in his life, when he regretted the loose faith of those years, Holmes destroyed many of the notes lest his children be corrupted by their "impropriety and infidelity."[7] Yet he could not bear to destroy them all and preserved some for the "valuable observations" they contained —apparently willing to risk the salvation of his heirs to some extent. Fortunately, the "weeded crop" that he left behind him is sufficiently revealing of his attitude toward such orthodox doctrines as the plenary inspiration of the Bible and the authority of Scripture to enable us to gauge the degree of his departure from the reigning Protestant literalism.

Curiously enough, the guide that Holmes chose for his journey through the Old Testament was the well-known Anglican scholar Thomas Hartwell Horne, one of the most orthodox of English commentators and author of the immensely popular *Introduction to the Critical Study and Knowledge of the Holy Scriptures* (1818) which Holmes used. But no tourist ever paid less attention to his Baedeker. Insist and prove as Horne might that Moses wrote the entire Pentateuch and that the other books of the Old Testament were what tradition said they were, Holmes thought otherwise. A few examples of his commentary will illustrate this point. Of II Chron. 21:7 he wrote,

This verse is strongly at variance with the notion of any inspired author for this book. The reason assigned for the continuance of the kingdom is just such as we might expect from a weak man determined to account religiously for all things, yet wholly ignorant of any metaphorical or higher sense, beyond the mere significance of the terms literally interpreted.

Elsewhere,

From the manner in which the reigns of the Kings of Judah and Israel are mentioned in this and the other books of the Old Testament; I should infer that they are either copied verbatim from the Jewish pontifical annals, or abridged from them and the royal archives. . . . It would seem that the two Books of Samuel, the two Books of Kings, and the two of Chronicles, had a similar origin, perhaps from different sources, are all equally worthy of attention, and all equally uninspired.

[7] MS vol. 1803, p. 49, *ibid.*

He added somewhat irreverently, "compare the various series of monastic Chronicles [*sic*] in the Middle Ages."[8]

Holmes found that textual criticism raised a number of problems, among which was the sufficiency of the Scripture itself as a revelation. While studying 1 Kings he discovered a reference to " 'The Book of the Acts of Solomon,' " and asked,

If 1 Kings must be considered an inspired writing, it might be supposed that this allusion to another work would indicate that such work was of equal authority and inspiration also. But, as it is lost, one of two conclusions is inevitable,—either that the whole of the inspired writings are not necessary for us and that some were superfluous and have not been preserved: or that we have not now sufficient for our complete edification, and that the inspiration was wasted. But [he added cautiously] the whole subject of inspiration is a very perplexed and difficult one.

None the less, Holmes thought that a critical scrutiny of the historical books of the Old Testament justified doubting the direct inspiration of the Scriptures as a whole and his other studies convinced him that the internal unity of the Pentateuch as well as its Mosaic authorship could not be believed.[9]

Turning to the New Testament Holmes was hardly less skeptical. He agreed with Dr. Thomas Cooper, former president of South Carolina College and the South's best-known infidel, that all the essential doctrines of Christianity were contained in the four Gospels and that the remainder of the New Testament lacked independent authority. The writings of Paul were singled out for special criticism.

He out of Christianity formed Christianism and I think the change was attended with as much loss in a moral as gain in a political point of view. . . . It was he that drew from the declamations of the Apostles the groundwork of the new religion and by the addition of much of his own formed the outlines of that system which is now regarded by the nations of Europe and of the greater part of America as the sole standard of appeal.

But even as doubtful as he was about numerous points of doctrine, Holmes never became sufficiently disillusioned to give up the Christian religion entirely. Cooper's philosophical writings worried him a good deal but he declined to follow him into open skepticism. Nor should Holmes's theological liberalism be exaggerated. In spite of his objections to parts of the Old Testament, he accepted much of the early chapters of Genesis as history and even seemed to have a certain amount of sympathy with the Oxford Tractarians. Moreover, he was

[8] *Ibid.*, pp. 76, 79, passim.
[9] *Ibid.*, pp. 49–60, 65–80, 327–40.

sensitive to the opinions of those who were more conservative in their religious views. After writing in one of his notebooks a brief and sympathetic discussion of an essay on the true nature of the Lord's Supper by Ralph Cudworth, the seventeenth-century Cambridge Platonist, Holmes remarked, "NB Gen. Jamison disagrees with me in toto. Reconsider this opinion."[10] In brief, then, Holmes's religious beliefs during the early 1840s were caught in an ambivalence between a conventional faith and a rationalistic "infidelity" and he was the victim of more than one disquieting doubt. This is nowhere better seen than in his attitude toward organized Christianity.

In 1844 Holmes published an article attacking a recent review by the Rev. Dr. M. J. Spalding, a prominent Roman Catholic priest. Spalding's review had been a harsh indictment of the historical reliability of Jean Henri Merle d'Aubigné's popular *Histoire de la Reformation au XVI^{ieme} siècle* (1835–1853), a work which was becoming a favorite with Protestants because of D'Aubigné's sympathy with the Reformation. Holmes began by supporting Spalding in condemning the work as "weak, defective, injudicious, and ill-timed."[11] Privately he confided to editor Whitaker of the *Southern Quarterly Review* that Protestants thought highly of the work only because they were too ignorant of Reformation history to know any better.[12] Catholics, however, were able to take little comfort from this. Turning to Spalding's defense of Catholicism's past, Holmes sarcastically pretended admiration for "the singular logical dexterity which is displayed by the Roman Catholic champions in using or refusing a particular line of reasoning, according as it is employed by themselves or their adversaries." They would have us believe, he said, that the depravity of certain popes in no way detracts from the spiritual grandeur of the Church, but the "comparatively trivial offences" of the reformers "utterly defeated the possibility of any pure Protestant faith." Actually, he continued, the individualistic nature of Protestantism made the morals of its founders of little importance, while one might have expected more righteousness where "Christianity descends in *mortmain* through the successions of an ecclesiastical corporation." Spalding's contention that the spirit of the Reformation had had a baneful effect on "civil and religious liberty," and that its effects had been harmful "to literature, and to civilization" was particularly ab-

---

[10] MS vol. 1792, pp. 8–9, 12–13, 16. MS vol. 1782, p. 35, Holmes papers, D. [George Frederick Holmes], "Schlegel's Philosophy of History," *Southern Quarterly Review*, III (April 1843), 284–86. MS vol. 1789, Holmes papers, D.

[11] [George Frederick Holmes], "Spalding's Review of D'Aubigné," *Southern Quarterly Review*, VI (October 1844), 446–47.

[12] G. F. Holmes to D. K. Whitaker, September 14, 1844, MS vol. 1808.

surd: everyone knew—or should know—that the "Protestant States of Europe [are] decidedly superior, in all respects, to Catholic France and Italy."[13]

Holmes anticipated with relish the brief furor stirred up by this review. To Whitaker he wrote,

> You are afraid the Protestants may pounce upon me for my article. . . . I confidently anticipate a murderous onslaught from the Catholics. If both parties attack me I shall find myself in a dangerous predicament. . . . However, if I should find myself so uncomfortably placed, I shall retire quietly from the field, when the double fury is at its highest point, and I shall let the tiger leap into the jaws of the crocodile—hoping that; [*sic*] while one adversary is suffocated, the other may be strangled.[14]

His hopes were fulfilled and the review was attacked in the *United States Catholic Magazine* where an anonymous writer acknowledged Holmes to be "one of the ripest scholars and, withal, one of the most accomplished gentlemen of the chivalric Palmetto state," but nevertheless sought to refute him by the venerable polemical device of merely restating Spalding's points and accusing Holmes of misrepresentation.[15] The Protestants (represented by the Presbyterians with whom D'Aubigné was a great favorite) got in their licks in the *Christian Observer* ("a Presbyterian Paper of Knox-ious principles," Holmes remarked), and two eminent divines of that sect, James H. Thornwell and Robert J. Breckinridge (who was one of the most active religious controversialists of the day), threatened to combine their forces against Holmes's review. They failed to do so (to Holmes's disappointment), even though late the following year Thornwell was still encouraging Breckinridge to write a defense of D'Aubigné for the *Southern Quarterly Review*.[16]

In the same issue of the *Review* in which he had criticized D'Aubigné, Holmes published another attack on the Roman Church that, like the first, contained an oblique criticism of Protestantism. In "Rome and the Romans" he had these unwelcome remarks for the Protestants:

---

13 [Holmes], "Spalding's Review," pp. 448, 450–52.

14 Holmes to Whitaker, September 14, 1844.

15 "Southern Quarterly Review," *United States Catholic Magazine*, IV (February 1845), 105–08. The journal was the organ of the Archbishop of Baltimore and the Bishop of Richmond. Dr. Spalding was co-editor.

16 MS vol. 1843, pp. 400–01. J. H. Thornwell to R. J. Breckinridge, October 4, 1845, B. M. Palmer, *The Life and Letters of James Henley Thornwell, D.D., LL.D.* (Richmond, Va.: n.p., 1875), p. 269. For Holmes's anticipation of an encounter with Breckinridge, see Simms, *Letters*, II, 138–39.

The ordinary rant against Catholicism is ridiculous; it has its defects, and great and grievous in our estimation they are; but to the Papacy we owe the revivification of the world, and without it Protestantism itself would have been impossible. The Catholic church preserved for us Christianity; she cherished the early growth of our modern organization; she was the law to Europe, when Europe would have bent to no other law; she was the bulwark of Christendom against the Saracen; she saved the literature of antiquity and [preserved the Latin language]; while, at the same time; she furnished thereby the germ and model of our modern literature.

But, he charged, the papacy was "the most strict and permanent system of ecclesiastical tyranny, that ever cursed any portion of the human race."[17] Which accusation prompted the Catholic Bishop of Charleston to remark to a mutual friend that "Mr. Holmes, as a scholar, should have known better, and, as a man, should have felt better, than to have given utterance to such views." "Rome and the Romans" was subsequently attacked in the *United States Catholic Miscellany*, the voice of the Charleston diocese.[18]

At length, Holmes's sniping at sectarian religion, and at Catholicism in particularly, provoked an inquiry by Letty Lewis, his sister-in-law, who, like Lavalette, was a member of the Roman Church. In this correspondence Holmes again revealed—and more candidly—his antipathy for existing forms of Christianity. "You are a queer fish, brother Fred," Letty wrote. "You are so afraid that somebody will think you have a leaning to papism—that you write no article, but that you clean your skirts *in some form or other* of the unbecoming imputation." Here Letty probably unknowingly hit on one reason for Holmes's open hostility to Catholicism: the desire to ward off nativist prejudice. She, however, had another explanation. She accused him of being too proud intellectually and suggested that his dislike of Catholicism was in part a fear of emotional religious commitment—a fear that Catholicism, once it had seized him, would make him into something "unnatural and loathsome." Then Letty went right to the heart of his trouble. His reason, she said, offered him only two options in religion: Catholicism on the one hand and "ultra-protestantism or infidelity" (she identified the two) on the other.[19]

Holmes could only agree with Letty's analysis. But he could not become a Catholic: "my prejudices, if you will, and my judgment

17 [George Frederick Holmes], "Rome and the Romans," *Southern Quarterly Review*, VI (October 1844), 279, 306.
18 MS vol. 1843, p. 387. "The Southern Quarterly Review," *United States Catholic Miscellany*, October 19, 26, November 16, 1844, pp. 118–19, 126–27, 150.
19 Letitia Preston Lewis to G. F. Holmes, March 16, 1846, MS vol. 1808.

are both opposed to it." And, as far as Protestantism was concerned, he had to acknowledge the justice of the extreme polarization she suggested. "Protestantism does lead to infidelity, and I fear that even the Protestantism that I would now advocate would after a single generation become infidelity under a very thin disguise." What he would advocate, of course, was not practiced; and for Protestantism as practiced he had nothing but contempt. Anglicanism, the church in which he had been raised, was "a humbug as a religious institution," of some use politically but "its theory is an anomalous mass of inconsistencies." It was the mere "shell of religion . . . , it may excite sentiment but it has no soul." The creed of the Presbyterians was "Malignity, self-seeking, self-righteousness, under the name of Christianity." Methodists were "mystics. Each man's dreams are his God, his creed, his bible [*sic*]." Baptists were "a religious laity, whose main belief is in the necessity of the Hindoo practice of purification by bathing in 'much water' "; this was the extent of their religion—"the rest is ignorance and implicit credulity."[20] Not long after writing this Holmes found himself in Richmond in the midst of a Baptist revival. His flippant comments to a South Carolina friend, Colonel D. J. McCord, emphasized his disdain. "We have had, and still have Dr. Fuller labouring here most diligently in the holy work of exciting revivals. . . . Such is his wonderful gift of continuance, that he never runs down, and seems never to require winding up. He is a truly-going twelve-month clock. . . . Dr. Fuller is a new and modernized edition of the Apostle Paul." He confided to McCord that, to one who found himself "among the Baptist Brethren, there is nothing so refreshing to my monotonous existence, as the epistle of a South Carolina gentleman." In short, (as he wrote elsewhere) whatever merit may have existed in the original principles of the Reformation (and he, like Jamison, thought there was much), the Protestant churches of the nineteenth century had "perverted, misapplied and misunderstood" them. He admitted his dilemma ruefully to Letty: "I really feel myself in an unpleasant predicament. I admit all the inducements to religion—all the great points of Christianity, but deny every one of the avenues to it."[21]

The religious problem that Holmes faced during the 1840s was not so much one of belief as one of allegiance—Catholicism or "infidelity"? But before he could resolve this question he was faced with another

[20] G. F. Holmes to Letitia Preston Lewis, March 26, 1846, *ibid.*

[21] Holmes to McCord, October 24, 1846. George Frederick Holmes, "The Present State of Letters," *Southern Literary Messenger*, X (July 1844), 414. Holmes to Letitia Preston Lewis, March 26, 1846.

even more disturbing. The choice between the two forms of theism, one an orthodox form of Christianity, the other a liberal one, was at bottom only a question of the claims of Catholicism and what Holmes took to be the logical tendencies of Protestantism. The choice still assumed the underlying harmony of faith and reason, the traditional union of learning and religion that even in his periods of deepest skepticism he did not question. Yet it was exactly this harmony that the intellectual revolution of the nineteenth century would challenge; and not until near the end of the decade of the 1840s did Holmes encounter that challenge. Like Christians traditionally, he assumed that sacred and profane knowledge were complementary not contradictory. It is ironic that throughout this period of personal disappointment and religious confusion he was enthusiastically engaged in a quest for a new science of history that would eventually bring the challenge hard upon him.

During this same period Holmes's suspicion of organized Christianity was coupled with a philosophical attitude of extreme empiricism which, because of his subsequent intellectual development, may be called crypto-positivism.[22] He based his doctrine on the classic dictum *nihil est in intellectu quod non prius fuerit in sensu* (nothing in the mind that is not first in the senses) and supported his position by the authority of Bacon, Locke, Hume, and certain of the Scottish realists, although he followed none of these men consistently and frequently dissented from all of them. He firmly refused to speculate about what could not be empirically verified. Discussing the mind, he wrote:

Admitting that the doctrine of *nihil in intellectu quod non prius fuerat in sensu* [*sic*] is not sufficient to explain fully all the processes and peculiarities of the human mind, can we not quietly, and like reasonable beings, acknowledge our ignorance, and wait patiently until our means of knowl-

[22] Terminology is always a problem. What is meant here is the attitude of scientific empiricism, the search for facts and laws, that became so general in the nineteenth century and which is variously called scienticism, naturalism, or positivism. The attitude has affinities with Comtian Positivism but should not be equated with it. The "crypto" is applied in Holmes's case because he was unaware of the skeptical implications of his epistemology. For the semantic problem of "positivism," see W. M. Simon, *European Positivism in the Nineteenth Century* (Ithaca: Cornell University Press, [1963]), pp. 3–4. Professor Simon suggests that "positivism" be reserved exclusively for Comtism and that "scienticism" be used to describe a strict scientific empiricism. The suggestion, on its face, is a good one, but as "scienticism" is sometimes used by the enemies of that persuasion, the usage would be, I think, invidious. In this book, "Positivism" shall mean the philosophy of Comte and "positivism" the more general attitude.

edge may be enlarged, without veiling the former and impeding the latter, by inventing hypotheses to throw dust into the eyes of ourselves and our neighbors.

He believed that too often contemporary philosophical and scientific discussions were filled with meaningless verbalisms. Various popular and traditional psychologies with their intuitions, innate ideas, and deductions about the structure of the mind he considered to be "the most hollow, the emptiest, and most unsubstantial species of cant by which the generations of the world have ever yet been gulled." He had no more use for philosophical abstractions:

We have always indulged ourselves in [a] peculiar species of unbelief . . . when infinity, eternity, necessity, universality, absolute perfection or other abstract notions of this kind have been submitted to us; for these are conceptions which the human intellect can neither form nor comprehend and upon which, therefore, human reason ought not to argue.

"The facts are all we know," he wrote. And, in view of that, he was determined to "restrict our speculations to the phenomena, and when these cannot be explained without such hypotheses as innate ideas, spiritual essences, etc., we should leave them, as for the time, inexplicable."[23] Empiricism of this sort, the popular Baconianism devoted to "facts" and "laws" but scorning "hypotheses," was standard fare in American philosophy and science at the time and could not have struck Holmes's readers as extraordinary, nor would it merit special attention now except that it relates importantly to his religious development.[24]

The notable thing about Holmes's crypto-positivism was that he saw no contradiction between it and his religious views. True to his Baconian method, he demanded facts in all areas of knowledge with one exception—theology. Divine revelation (curtailed though it might be by his "infidelity") was called in to supply what the senses and the intellect could not.[25] Unfortunately for his later peace of mind, this device contained unresolved ambiquities arising from his failure to deal with the problem of establishing the validity of revealed religious knowledge as knowledge. Once he had encountered the speculations of Auguste Comte it was clear to him that a consistent empiricism could not but undermine belief in revealed dogmas when the latter were simply tacked onto the end of an empirical epistemological system. But it did not seem so in the early 1840s; the fact that this problem was not articulated by Holmes at that time shows that at this

---

23 [Holmes], "Inductive Sciences," pp. 216–18.

24 For Baconianism see George H. Daniels, *American Science in the Age of Jackson* (New York: Columbia University Press, 1968), especially chapter III.

25 MS vol. 1792, pp. 6–7.

point in his development he saw no challenge to religion in science and experienced no conflict between science and religious belief. None the less, his acceptance of a crypto-positivistic epistemology prepared him for a serious intellectual crisis later.

Another important aspect of his early empiricism was his low opinion of that type of thought conventionally dismissed as "metaphysics." Declaring himself "nearly as sceptical as Jefferson, Broussais or Dr. Cooper, of the utility of metaphysics," he went on to say that nothing had "debauched so many minds, and poisoned so many well-springs of knowledge as . . . Transcendental Metaphysics." "Truly," he lamented, "it would be well if human nature had a little more unbelief in its composition."[26] His special ire, though, was reserved for German idealist metaphysics, that bête noire of almost everyone in the tradition of British empiricism. An early attack on Kant in 1844[27] was renewed three years later and mixed with a broad denunciation of German writers. Holmes was reviewing an English translation of F. L. J. Thimm's *The Literature of Germany*, and he let fire.

German authors have, indeed, a language entirely their own—as distinctly and peculiarly theirs as the language of Balaam's ass was of that remarkably intelligent animal. They claim to utter oracles beneath that peculiar phraseology, in the same way that the Delphic Priestess could give no response unless drunk or crazy. . . . The speaking of Balaam's ass was a miracle; but unless the Germans . . . can prove a miracle in their case, we must class their language so entirely their own, along with that of Balaam's ass when uninspired.

In the same piece, he wrote of Kant specifically,

We must candidly declare, that to us [Kant's works] are the most incomprehensible farrago of hypermetaphysical reveries that we have met with even in Israel. The worthy Hudibras is a child in logical refinement to Kant; and until we can comprehend the essential universality and natural connection of the world and its archetype, deduced *a priori* by analogical ratiocination, we shall not pretend to consider Kant as readable.[28]

This hostility toward German idealism was never overcome in spite of Holmes's later doubts about the philosophical adequacies of empiricism. As a result he was cut off from the methods and inspiration of the German idealistic accommodation of Christianity to science and historical scholarship. At no time in his life did Holmes have more

[26] [Holmes], "Inductive Sciences," pp. 210, 213, 217.
[27] [George Frederick Holmes], "Herder's Philosophy of History," *Southern Quarterly Review*, V (April 1844), 276.
[28] [George Frederick Holmes], "Thimm's Book," *ibid.*, XI (January 1847), 95, 102. Holmes had begun to read Kant in a French translation in 1846.

than a casual knowledge (if that) of the theology of such men as De Wette and Schleiermacher, and even had he known more about it, for much of his career he could not have cared less. His own tradition of British empirical philosophy provided little basis for an accommodation that required the freeing of Christianity from both nature and history, and it forced him into an orthodox theological reaction when he finally recognized his religious dilemma.

When Holmes turned his general enthusiasm for modern knowledge to something definite, his companionship with Jamison and his interest in classical antiquity determined that the definite something should be history—a philosophically sound science of history. For inspiration he turned to the French historians Jules Michelet and F. P. G. Guizot and to the French philosopher Victor Cousin. Cousin may seem an odd choice in view of Holmes's denegration of the very psychology of which Cousin was an acknowledged high priest, but what interested him was not Cousin's metaphysical eccentricities but his ideas on the historical development of the human mind and the history of philosophy. For Cousin's philosophical system, Eclecticism, he had little sympathy; nor should it be thought that his admiration of the two historians was unalloyed.[29]

A search for the reasons leading Holmes to select these Frenchmen as his guides would not take one far. Actually it would have been difficult to avoid Cousin and Guizot, both of whom enjoyed a wide popularity in the United States. Americans went to France for both pleasure and education with as much enthusiasm as they went to England or Germany, and they returned home filled with French ideas about society, civilization, and history. Reflecting this, and in turn promoting it, was the long use of Guizot's *History of Civilization in Europe* and Cousin's *Course of the History of Modern Philosophy* as textbooks in many of the nation's colleges. Holmes' own study of Cousin began in 1840 and his acquaintance with the writings of Michelet and Guizot soon followed.[30]

But despite a considerable interest in French thought in America, the historical ideas of Michelet, Guizot, and Cousin appeared to be far from gaining a common acceptance. When Holmes began publishing his appeals for a new scientific history he found it necessary to scold his fellow intellectuals for their serious neglect of "the mod-

[29] G. F. Holmes to D. F. Jamison, April 2, 1846, MS vol. 1808. For a more extensive critique of Eclecticism see [George Frederick Holmes], "Morell's Philosophy of the Nineteenth Century," *Southern Literary Messenger*, XVI (July 1850), 385–96.

[30] For citations from Cousin and Guizot, see MS vol. 1842, passim. By 1842 Holmes had read Michelet, MS "Progress of Mankind."

ern Historical School of France." Instead of continuing to feed on the vaporous musings of extravagant German metaphysicians such as Johann Gottfried von Herder and Frederick von Schlegel, he said, English and American historical scholars should turn to France. A familiarity with the works of Guizot, Michelet, and Cousin would soon convince them that "there is no room for doubt that, in historical science, the Parisian school of the present day is far, very far in advance of any other people, and we would do well to have constant recurrance to their writings, in preference to any other sources of information, with which the most of us content ourselves."[31]

Michelet, of course, was the romantic historian par excellence, and it was this quality, with its enthusiasm for the pageantry and passion of human history, plus the chance discovery of his *Introduction à l'histoire universelle*, that won Holmes to him. Like many of his contemporaries, and despite his hard-nosed empiricism, young Holmes was unabashedly romantic in his literary tastes. In poetry Byron was his model, and even later, when he had sobered somewhat, the monastic chronicles and fairy tales of the Middle Ages still provided him with hours of leisure reading. His early historical essays reveal both his penchant for the romantic narrative and his youthful if somewhat extravagant style which he must have flattered himself was a passing imitation of Michelet.

It was in Michelet's *Introduction à l'histoire universelle*, however, the "most boldly and genuinely original" of his works, rather than in his literary style, that Holmes found a genuine provocation to embark on the quest for a new historical science. He had discovered Michelet's small volume on the course of world history in 1842 and by the next year had read it three times: "I was very much struck with it the first time I read it. The treatment of the subject was then novel to me, the views harmonized very nearly with my own, though mine had lain in my mind with the germes [*sic*] only feebly developed, until I read this work." Michelet was not free of error, of course, but in spite of his faults, Holmes believed his book to be "the most profound, comprehensive, and reflective of all the works on the Philosophy of History which I have yet met with."[32]

Holmes's attraction to the French historians was also influenced by Jamison's interest in them and Holmes's own facility with the French language. But more important were the congenial assumptions about

---

[31] [George Frederick Holmes], "History of Literature," *Southern Quarterly Review*, II (October 1842), 474. [Holmes], "Schlegel's Philosophy," p. 268. For American preference for German philosophers of history see Callcott, *History in the United States*, pp. 9–10.

[32] MS vol. 1789.

the course and nature of history that he found running through the work of Michelet, Guizot, and Cousin.[33] They shared a strong conviction that progress was the essence of the historical process and that to tell the story of human progress was the main business of the historian. They presented the historical process as bound by laws capable of being discovered and understood by the human mind. In addition, and this was a vital element in sustaining Holmes's early optimism, they taught that the historical development of the world had properly culminated in the diverse and turbulent civilization of contemporary Europe where a devotion to liberty and a faith in progress had bred the confident attitude toward innovation and change that Holmes shared with them.

The most striking thing about the direction taken by Holmes's historical interest is not, however, the presence of French influence. That is easily explained. What is most noticeable is the absence of a formative German influence. One cannot but wonder why Holmes did not sufficiently overcome his dislike for German thought to model his new science of history on German historiography which, of course, led the historical world in the nineteenth century. It is somewhat surprising that Holmes virtually ignored the heartland of history from whence his French masters themselves drew much of their own inspiration and many of their ideas. Cousin, for instance, incorporated the thought of both Kant and Hegel into his Eclectic Philosophy and was a major channel through which German idealism came to America.[34] It was through his urging that Michelet learned the German language and traveled east of the Rhine where he found that "Germany is the bread of life for strong minds. She made me greater by Luther and Beethoven, Kant, Herder and Grimm."[35] That Guizot entirely escaped these influences may be doubted.

This neglect would seem to convict young Holmes of both ignorance and naïveté. And, in truth, he cannot be completely exonerated

[33] My generalizations are based on the major works read by Holmes: Victor Cousin, *Cours de l'histoire de la philosophie: introduction à l'histoire de la philosophie*, nouvelle ed. (Paris: Didier, 1841); Jules Michelet, *Introduction à l'histoire universelle*, 2nd ed. (Paris: Librairie Classique, 1834); François Pierre Guillaume Guizot, *History of Civilization in Europe* (New York: American Publishers Corporation, n.d.). Such views, of course, were not restricted to these three writers.

[34] Irving H. Bartlett, "Bushnell, Cousin, and Comprehensive Christianity," *Journal of Religion*, XXXVII (April 1957), 101; Isaac Woodbridge Riley, *American Thought from Puritanism to Pragmatism and Beyond* (New York: Henry Holt, 1923), p. 389.

[35] Quoted in George Peabody Gooch, *History and Historians in the Nineteenth Century* (Boston: Beacon Press, [1959]), p. 169.

on either charge. But the severity of the case against him may be mitigated by remembering the slowness with which German learning
penetrated the Anglo-American world during the first half of the
century. Historical scholarship was particularly slow in its full impact.
Leopold von Ranke, who more than any other single individual
symbolized devotion to the new historiography, began his career in
1824 with the publication of his *Geschichte der romanischen und
germanischen Völker*, and by 1850 dominated German historical
studies from his chair at the University of Berlin. But English translations of Ranke's works did not begin to appear until the 1840s and his
full impact upon Anglo-American academic historiography was delayed even longer. Many, like Holmes, might have heard of Ranke
earlier but not until almost mid-century could they easily obtain and
read any of his books in their own tongue. In the United States it was
not until the 1870s and 1880s that the Rankian seminar and the methods
of the new German historical schools began to appear in the colleges
and universities in the wake of the collapsing classical curriculum.

This should not, of course, lead one to the conclusion that Americans were completely ignorant of German scholarship during the
earlier period. The nation's best known historians, George Bancroft,
William H. Prescott, and John L. Motley, shared an ardent enthusiasm
for German historical methods and cast their own work in the new
critical spirit. The writings of Arnold Heeren, pioneer of economic
history, and of Barthold Niebuhr, who rewrote the early history of
Rome, as well as Friedrich Karl von Savigny's work in legal history
were known and admired in America. And yet, in spite of all this,
American historical studies continued to be dominated by the man of
letters who saw history as more literature than science rather than
the professional academic historian until well past 1850.[36] Jared
Sparks, one of the few to occupy a chair of history in America before
the Civil War, might praise the interest shown by both "scholars and
politicians" in history, but this enthusiasm seldom went beyond a
desire to be entertained and a searching for confirmation of the popular belief in progress and America's providential mission.[37] Because
of this dearth of academic historians in ante-bellum America the first
battles over the new German critical scholarship were fought not in

[36] For discussions of the American literary historians see Callcott, *History in
the United States*, ch. IV and David Levin, *History as Romantic Art* (Stanford:
Stanford University Press, 1959).

[37] Sparks as quoted in L. L. Bernard and Jessie Bernard, *Origins of American
Sociology, the Social Science Movement in the United States* (New York:
Thomas Y. Crowell, [1943]), p. 722. Callcott, *History in the United States*, pp.
13–19, 25–26, 194–203.

the colleges and among historians but in the seminaries and among
the nation's theologians. The exhaustive Germanic textual criticism
first came to America as a part of biblical studies and only later was
it extended to provide a basis for scientific history in opposition to the
tradition of genteel literary history.[38]

The situation was much the same in England where history was
long a division of belles-lettres, where the greatest historians were
commonly acknowledged to have been Greeks and Romans, and
where historical scholarship generally lagged behind that of Germany
and France.[39] The anemic condition of British historiography was
reflected in America where there existed a general dependence on
British writers for what little was known of the history of other lands.

With the basic orientation of his fellow students of history in both
America and England being literary and classical, Holmes's neglect
of the new German scholarship is understandable. Besides, even if he
had known more of Ranke and his school, the latter's almost exclusive
concern with political and diplomatic history would doubtlessly have
struck Holmes as too narrow a basis for a truly revolutionized history.
The French were much better for that.

Even if Holmes's slight of German historiography can be partly
redeemed, can he be as easily excused for his failure to take into account the ruling historical philosopher of the age, Hegel? Here again,
Holmes was in the large company of his fellows. Actually, Hegel (or
any other German idealistic philosopher for that matter) was not
widely known in America until after 1850. Prior to mid-century a
growing number of American intellectuals, most of them New Eng-
landers, had learned something of Hegel as well as of Kant, Schelling,
and Schliermacher, but usually indirectly through the writings of
French, English, and American commentators who had a direct

[38] Jurgen Herbst, *The German Historical School in American Scholarship*
(Ithaca: Cornell University Press, [1965]), pp. 73–97. See also Jerry Wayne
Brown, *The Rise of Biblical Criticism in America, 1800–1870: the New England
Scholars* (Middletown: Wesleyan University Press, [1969]). It should be noted
that in the decade prior to the Civil War local historians in America began to
develop a new critical attitude in their work, and apparently free of European
influence. See David D. Van Tassel, *Recording America's Past: An Interpretation of the Development of Historical Studies in America 1607–1884* (Chicago:
University of Chicago Press, [1960]), pp. 121–34.

[39] James Westfall Thompson, *A History of Historical Writing* (New York:
Macmillan and Company, 1942), II, 280–81. For the interest shown by some in
England in German historians, especially Niebuhr, see Duncan Forbes, *The Lib-
eral Anglican Idea of History* (Cambridge: Cambridge University Press, 1952).
These, among them Arnold and Thirlwall, were, significantly, those whom
Holmes most admired.

knowledge from reading the Germans for themselves.[40] German immigrants, especially after 1848, were another source of German idealism.[41] But the effect of this philosophical invasion on the dominant Scottish realism reigning virtually unchallenged in close league with Christian orthodoxy in the colleges and Protestant churches of America and embodying the anti-metaphysical bias of British empiricism was slight. To the true believer, whether in pulpit or classroom, anything tinctured with German philosophy, be it home grown or imported, was identical with infidelity. Samuel Tyler, America's leading Baconian philosopher, denounced German idealism as productive of "neology, transcendentalism, pantheism, and all sorts of mystical nonsense." Francis Bowen of Harvard condemned it as "sheer midsummer madness;" while to the influential Unitarian divine, Andrews Norton, its theological forms were "moonshine and cobwebs." Many American colleges closed their doors against the subversive influence.[42]

The story was much the same in England. German idealism had little impact on the educated classes there until well past mid-century. Englishmen had been introduced to Kant as early as the 1790s and the Critical Philosophy was praised, in part at least, by as famous a Scottish realist as Sir William Hamilton himself, but there was no serious attempt to introduce German idealism into British philosophy until Hutchinson Sterling published his *Secret of Hegel* in 1865. The English romantics, of course, had been stimulated by contact with the Germans, but they, like the transcendentalists in America, had little impact on respectable philosophy. Both John Stuart Mill and Hamilton had denounced the supposed vagaries of idealism.[43]

We know that Holmes had at least heard of Hegel by 1846 for in

[40] J. H. Muirhead, "How Hegel Came to America," *Philosophical Review*, XXXVII (May 1928), 227, 233. Henry A. Pochmann, *German Culture in America, Philosophical and Literary Influences, 1600–1900* (Madison: University of Wisconsin Press, 1957), pp. 60–114.

[41] A recent study is Loyd D. Easton, *Hegel's First American Followers* ([Athens, Ohio]: Ohio University Press, 1966).

[42] Wilson Smith, *Professors and Public Ethics: Studies in Northern Moral Philosophers Before the Civil War* (Ithaca: Cornell University Press, [1956], pp. 190–91; Pochmann, *German Culture*, pp. 304–05; Muirhead, "Hegel," p. 234; Tyler is quoted in Daniels, *American Science*, p. 83; Brown in Herbst, *German Historical School*, p. 62; Norton in the same, p. 86.

[43] Otto Pfleiderer, *The Development of Theology in Germany Since Kant and Its Progress in Great Britain Since 1825* (London: Swan Sonnenschein, 1890), p. 307. Pochmann, *German Culture*, pp. 85–88; Arthur Kenyon Rogers, *English and American Philosophy since 1800* (New York: Macmillan and Company, 1928), p. 220. James Seth, *English Philosophies and Schools of Philosophy* (London: Dent and Son, 1925), p. 237.

that year, while pining away at Richmond College, he included the entry *"Philosophie des Geschichte"* with Hegel's name in a notebook bibliography of works dealing with the philosophy of history.[44] He could not have read it in German until much later, however, because of his poor knowledge of the language. By 1850 references to Hegel (but no more than that) were appearing in his work with some regularity although there is no definite evidence of his having read him until 1857 when the first English translation of *The Philosophy of History* appeared.[45] Like many of his contemporaries, most of what he knew of Hegel was drawn from the writings of Cousin, Coleridge, Carlyle, and from J. D. Morell's *Historical and Critical View of the Speculative Philosophy of Europe in the Nineteenth Century* (1846) which he reviewed for the *Southern Literary Messenger* in 1850.

And yet, in spite of this exposure (or, more likely, because of it), Holmes continued to hold aloof from German philosophy. His lack of German and his long standing bias against metaphysics, of course, had much to do with this; but there were other reasons as well. Michelet (who himself thought none too highly of Hegel's philosophy) spoke of Germany in his *Introduction* in what could have been taken as a disparaging manner by calling it the India of Europe because of its penchant for mystical idealism.[46] This would not have led Holmes to reconsider his opinion. Nor would his reading of Cousin, Coleridge, or Carlyle have done so. His attitude toward Coleridge as anything other than a poet was, at this time, one of almost casual indifference, his early notes revealing no interest in his philosophical and religious views.[47] Carlyle he thought eccentric. Cousin's own transcendental flights, of course, would have lent no support to anyone else's. It should be stressed, however, that his contempt for German idealism did not extend to all of German intellectual culture. Like everyone else, and despite his aversion to German thought generally, Holmes was overwhelmed with admiration for Heeren,

44 MS vol. 5959, Holmes papers, D.

45 This was the Sibree version published in London. See Holmes's reading list in MS vol. 1832, Holmes papers, D.

46 Michelet, *Introduction*, pp. 47–48. For Michelet's attitude toward Hegelianism see Oscar A. Haac, *Les Principes Inspirateurs de Michelet: Sensibilité et Philosophie de l'Histoire* (New Haven: Yale University Press, 1951), pp. 97–101 and Jeanlouis Cornuz, *Jules Michelet: Un Aspect de la Pensée Religîeuse au XIX Siècle* (Geneve: Librairie E. Droz, 1955), p. 123.

47 MS vol. 1842, pp. 1–2, 20, 83, 84–85, 87. G. F. Holmes to John McClintock, March 3, 1853, John McClintock Papers, Emory University Library, Atlanta, Georgia; hereinafter cited as McClintock papers. By the end of the 1850's, however, Holmes was praising Coleridge as "that wonderful genius" and crediting him with ideas on the writing of history similar to his own, MS vol. 1832, p. 71.

Niebuhr, Savigny, and others of Clio's band in Germany. But the background of these men, it should be noted, was philology not philosophy. There was for Holmes no transfer of homage from one to the other.

Of the influence of English historians on him before mid-century little need be said. Holmes read Gibbon, Hume, Palgrave, Macauley, Hallam, and others, sometimes with comment, more often without, absorbed what they had to offer in the way of learning, but failed to find in them the inspiration he sought. Indeed, to him their weaknesses were obvious. Gibbon was undeniably great but too clearly a real "infidel"; Mitford was a biased Tory and unreliable; he found Macauley popular and even trashy; Hallam was careless and superficial. In fact, the only contemporary English historians for whom he seems to have had respect in the 1840s were Arnold, Thirlwall, and, toward the end of the decade, Grote. Buckle's *History of Civilization in England*, a work that might have appealed to Holmes's interest in scientific history, was not published until 1857.

Though at this time Holmes possessed less originality in his quest for a science of history than he would show later, he did have considerable independence. Nothing illustrates this better than his very real dissatisfaction with the "French school" and especially with Michelet. When Holmes surveyed the historical work of the outstanding historians of his day—and he included in this number not only his French masters—he found himself very "sensible of their want of perfection. They give us glimpses into the very heart of a new science, but they have not mastered the science themselves, and they give us little more than glimpses." Even in Michelet and Guizot, "certainly the most profound of these historians," one was almost as conscious of error as of truth.[48] One of Michelet's most valuable contributions to the new science had been his revival of the work of the eighteenth-century Neapolitan philosopher Giambattista Vico (who also had a lasting effect on Holmes) but Holmes feared that Michelet's own development had been marred by too great an admiration for Vico.[49] There was always this danger in following a master, and in a lengthy critique of Michelet's *Introduction* Holmes showed that he intended to be no slavish disciple.

For all his undeniable merits, Holmes found the French historian unconvincing in his attempt to capture the unique spirit of each nation that had played a role in the development of civilization. More generally, Michelet had not sufficiently analyzed the relationship between

---

48 [Holmes], "Herder's Philosophy," pp. 266–67.
49 [Holmes], "Schlegel's Philosophy," pp. 280–81.

humanity and its material environment and so had failed to discover the social and historical laws governing that relation. Too, Michelet lacked a systematic rationale for the apparently artificial east-to-west sequence of nations around which he built his vision of world history as the progressive realization of human liberty. His evaluation of climate, race, and other factors as historical causes Holmes found weak. But if Michelet lacked systemization in these things, he had too much of it elsewhere; "in his attempt to establish a parallelism not merely of systems but of nations in the Oriental and Occidental worlds he has suffered the mania of a system to [distort] the phenomena." Lastly, Michelet was blinded by national vanity. He, like Guizot and other French writers, insisted on placing France at the center of European civilization, while everyone knew, the offended Englishman retorted, that France was at least a century and a half behind England politically.[50] But despite these strictures, the French historians served as Holmes's main guides in his quest for a scientific history.

The science of history which Holmes saw emerging from the groping efforts of European scholars was a major part of the intellectual revolution that he believed to be underway in the 1840s. History, like all other aspects of western culture, was "on the eve of a great reformation." But before the promise of a better history could be realized, there had to be a complete reform in historical method.[51] When Holmes began his task of educating Americans along this line, he looked upon it as an uphill struggle. He acknowledged that some attention had been given to the question of a new history in England and America. There was a commendable interest in getting away from the "Kings and Wars" approach. But, nevertheless, a truly scientific history still seemed to be far from the thoughts of most Anglo-American historians and reviewers. They had singularly failed to apprehend the spirit of the new era, and some maintained a stubborn aversion to the idea of history as social law. Therefore, it was most important that they be weaned from stale, conventional ideas about history as a "mirror of human nature in the abstract" or as a source of "political wisdom" and instead introduced to a new technique of increased scope and depth. So conceived, Holmes thought, history would be the noblest possible study. Such a history would show how each historically important nation had formed a necessary stage in the progress of humanity, how each of the various peoples had contributed some special quality that in turn had "impregnated and

50 MS vol. 1789.
51 [Holmes], "Herder's Philosophy," pp. 267–68.

civilized all succeeding ages," how civilizations as well as nations had risen and fallen in cycles of progress and regression.[52] In his vision of history, however, he rejected the popular metaphor which saw the course of nations as a repetition of the phases of human life: birth, youth, maturity, old age, and death. For this Holmes substituted the romantic idea—drawn from Michelet and Vico—of a quest for the historical laws governing an indefinite dialectical progression in which each stage in the progress of world civilization grew out of, and yet retained features of, those which had gone before.

The new history that Holmes celebrated was not really new, of course. In some respects it reached back into the eighteenth century to Vico's *New Science*, to Voltaire's *Essay on the Manners and Spirit of Nations* and his *Age of Louis XIV*, to Winckelmann's work on Greek art, to Herder. In other ways it anticipated the comprehensive study of past societies that would later in the century be associated with Jacob Burckhardt.[53] While it would not do to claim a large degree of originality for Holmes's views—his debts are too obvious and some of his views too characteristic of his time for that—it is to his great credit that he saw the importance of this variety of history and advocated its realization. His goal, as Michelet's, was "the resurrection of the life of the past as a whole."[54] His view of scientific history, however, did not include the idea so popular among historians later in the century that science and art were incompatible. For Holmes, as for many of his contemporaries, the documents never spoke for themselves; it required all the historian's literary art to bring out their story. The historian, through his art, was the active creator of the past, but—and this is important—he must be no mere teller of tales, no chronicler of the deeds of heroes. The past he sought to reveal was the progress of nations, the development of institutions; his opportunity was to discover the essence of these things, the historical law governing them. For Holmes scientific history and literary art were inseparable. Art enabled the historian to mediate between the past and the reader. Without art the act of knowing could not be completed.[55]

The primary unit of study in the new historical science was the civilization, which Holmes (like A. J. Toynbee later) saw as a discrete

[52] [Holmes], "Schlegel's Philosophy," pp. 264, 266–67. Callcott, *History in the United States*, pp. 20, 90–91, 101–02, 155–56, 219–23.

[53] Gooch, *History and Historians*, pp. 523–24.

[54] Michelet as quoted in *ibid.*, p. 171.

[55] For the popularity of this view, see Levin, *History as Romantic Art*, ch. II; Callcott, *History in the United States*, p. 139.

societal entity possessing unique cultural attributes which set it off from all others, but which still affiliated it with those preceding and following. The historian's task was to uncover within each civilization its "intellectual spirit." The literature, religion, art, and science of the culture as well as those customs and institutions which embodied unconscious values and latent creative energies were the keys to this.[56] Taking them together, the historian could lay bare the national character of each people. Once this had been done for all civilizations Holmes expected that a sophisticated philosophy of history could be erected on a sound scientific foundation.

With this second step, a comprehensive philosophy of history, Holmes abandoned cultural history as Burckhardt was later to conceive it, and instead closely approached Hegel, at least in spirit— though ignorant that he was doing so, of course. The ultimate task of the philosophy of history he saw as twofold: first, to discover the laws that governed the unfolding of the historical process; and second, to demonstrate purpose and rationality in the course of historical events. The assumption that history was governed by law Holmes thought to be a necessary prerequisite for its serious study. If history were the product of chance, without pattern or rule, its study would be a waste of time. To date, he admitted, no such laws had been found, but the study of history was only in its infancy, the work was yet to be done, and even the great Michelet had proved wanting in this part of the task. That history was guided by Providence Holmes thought equally certain. Men in their social revolutions and in the "gradual advancement of humanity," in their "struggles for private gratification or private interest," had been "the immediate though unwitting instruments of God's will . . . effectuating higher purposes for the civilization of the world, than any they contemplated themselves." A true philosophy of history would demonstrate this providential order. It would show why the civilization of Greece was "necessarily subsequent to India and the East, Rome to Greece, the middle ages to Rome,—and . . . how essential it was that the Hebrews, with the peculiar destiny assigned them, should 'dwell alone, and not be reckoned among the nations.' "[57] At bottom, then, Holmes's new history was a form of theodicy, for God as creator was the source of both law and purpose in history. If Holmes had been sufficiently familiar with Hegel's work at this time, he might well have closed his own discussion with the words of the great German:

---

[56] [Holmes], "Schlegel's Philosophy," pp. 295–97, 312–13.

[57] Unpublished inaugural lecure at the College of William and Mary, pp. 15–18, Holmes papers, D. [Holmes], "Schlegel's Philosophy," pp. 276, 293. [Holmes], "Herder's Philosophy," pp. 293–94.

That the History of the World, with all the changing scenes which its annals present, is this process of development and the realization of Spirit— this is the true *Theodicaea*, the justification of God in History. Only *this* insight can reconcile Spirit and the History of the World—viz., that what has happened, and is happening every day, is not only not "without God," but is essentially his Work.[58]

The primary reason why the new history had not been realized at the time Holmes wrote was, he thought, because of methodological errors in traditional historiography. Not only had history been cursed with narrow partisan biases and superficiality, but even the best of the historians who had attempted to write more than mere chronicles of kings and wars had regularly fallen into fatal mistakes of method. In attempting to correct this, Holmes selected for criticism two abuses which he considered to be most harmful. One of them, not surprisingly, was the metaphysical impulse, the other was monocausality. His assault on what has been styled "metahistory" was directed at the works of Schlegel and Herder, and as examples of monocausalists he selected Montesquieu and Vico.

The German philosopher Fichte well exemplified what Holmes found objectionable in metaphysical history when he wrote, "The philosopher follows the world-plan which is clear to him without any history; and if he makes use of history, it is not to prove anything, since his theses are already proved independently of all history."[59] Schlegel's "lame and barren sketch" of the world's development seemed based on just such a priorism. Holmes respected Schlegel as a literary historian and critic, but he was certain that the *Philosophy of History* had received much more attention in America than it deserved. Indeed, its very popularity was a serious threat to the new history. Vico might remain unknown, the better works of Guizot and Michelet might be available only in French editions, but everyone with the slightest interest in the subject had read a translation of Schlegel's lectures. What did Holmes find wrong with Schlegel? One should recall Byron's quip that Schlegel seemed always on the verge of meaning, "but 'lo! he goes down like a sunset, or melts like a rainbow, leaving a rather rich confusion." Novalis said it another way when he told the German critic that "Most of your writings . . . lead me into Cimmerian darkness."[60] To Holmes, the *Philosophy of History* was

[58] Georg Wilhelm Fredrich Hegel, *The Philosophy of History*, trans. by J. Sibree (New York: Dover Publications, Inc., [1956]), p. 457.

[59] Fichte as quoted in J. B. Bury, *The Idea of Progress: An Inquiry into Its Origin and Growth* (New York: Dover Publications, Inc., [1932], p. 253.

[60] [Holmes], "Inductive Sciences," p. 196. [Holmes], "Schlegel's Philosophy,"

vague, fantastical and unsatisfactory,—there is a constant straining towards some invisible end,—a continual groping amid fogs, and clouds, and darkness, for something which the writer supposes to be latent there, but which remains wholly untangible to him. He starts some wild dream about Providence and man, and, pursuing the shadow which he has evoked, gives utterance to the thick-thronging fancies with much more of the air of a rhapsodist than a philosopher.[61]

But Holmes went beyond a general denunciation. Schlegel's sins were quite specific. In his desire to read history as a morality play with the reconciliation of God and man as its theme, Schlegel appeared to assume that man's environment had no effect on his feelings and desires, that nations could be judged by the same morality as individuals, that one could apply the same psychology to individuals and nations, and most outrageous of all, that religious piety (which Schlegel identified with Christian orthodoxy) was the hallmark of advanced civilization! By this criterion, Holmes protested, the intellectual refinement of modern times would not be progress but regression! Obviously, nothing could be more absurd. The book was a mere metaphysical fantasy with very little to contribute to the scientific study of history or to the understanding of the development of mankind.[62]

Nor was the other popular German philosopher of history any improvement. Holmes had taken up Churchill's translation of Herder's *Outline of a Philosophy of the History of Man* eagerly because of its great reputation.[63] The conception and sweep of the work won his praise, but, he wrote, "I can honestly say that I never read any work of note less worthy of its reputation." The book was "a barren waste of . . . empty speculation" with "little history and less philosophy" in its pages. On the whole, it was "inane, sophistical and frequently ridiculous."[64] Herder took up the reader's time proving things no one would deny: "that man is adapted to the world . . . , that the species of created things are numerous . . . , that man is not a beast, and that an ass is not a vegetable." Holmes found the plight of the persistent reader truly piteous:

While Herder struts before us on his lofty *super-terrestial* stilts, we are compelled painfully to wade after him through a sea of unconnected,

---

p. 270. For Schlegel's interest in America and vice versa, see Harold von Hofe, "Frederick Schlegel and the New World," *PMLA*, LXXVI (March 1961), 63–67. Byron and Novalis as quoted in Victor Lang, "Frederick Schlegel's Literary Criticism," *Comparative Literature*, VII (Fall 1955), 289.

61 [Holmes], "Schlegel's Philosophy," pp. 268–69.
62 *Ibid.*, pp. 272–73.
63 Both Schlegel and Herder were read in English translations.
64 MS vol. 1789. [Holmes], "Herder's Philosophy," p. 269.

though continuous observations, now sinking in the quicksands of error into which he leads us, now plunging hopelessly amid rocks, and stones, and other senseless things, now plashing and floundering in the waves, straining our eyes the while, in the attempt to determine his motions as he staggers on with his head lost in the clouds.

The ablest part of Herder's work, in Holmes's judgment, was the section dealing with the effects of climate and other environmental influences on man, but even here Herder refused to "dismount from his hippogriff . . . [and] fanciful and unfounded imaginations still . . . meet us at every step."[65] Nevertheless anyone comparing Holmes's own work with Herder's *Outline* may doubt that he entirely escaped the German's influence.

Holmes's censures of Vico and Montesquieu were less harsh. This is understandable since he considered Vico one of the main architects of the new history and Montesquieu hardly less significant. And yet, they represented a tendency that, in its way, was just as harmful to the new history as were the vagaries of Schlegel and Herder. Vico, Montesquieu, and most other historians who had attempted interpretative histories made the fundamental error of elevating some one factor to an all-determining importance and seeing it alone as the causal agent in history. A true science of history, Holmes argued, would unite all causal factors in a "combined and harmonious action."[66]

To Holmes's mind, Vico was the greatest of all the philosophers of history and he owed much of his own doctrine to him. He found especially impressive Vico's observations that the history of the human race is essentially the creation of man and not the result of environmental factors, and that humanity in seeking its own ends really fulfills the goals of Providence. But the former of these discoveries led Vico astray. His emphasis on man making himself involved him in neglecting the true role of environmental factors. And even within the realm of human agency, Holmes discovered that Vico had slighted the effects of folk migrations and racial amalgamation and had neglected the entire question of cultural diffusion. Vico's famous doctrine of *corso* and *ricorso*, in which the various civilizations are seen attempting to realize an ideal history existing in the mind of God and forming an archetype for the development of human societies, was the particular object of Holmes's wrath. Only because Vico had ignored the "constant tendency toward change" in human history could he have thought of successive civilizations as monotonous and circuitous cycles of birth, growth, climax, and death. Such futilitarian

---

[65] [Holmes], "Herder's Philosophy," pp. 277, 283, 291.
[66] [Holmes], "Schlegel's Philosophy," p. 283.

doctrine was, of course, incompatible with Holmes's own belief in progress and had to be rejected. Ironically, when he came to correct Vico, Holmes suggested that a more apt metaphor for the course of the world's historical development would be a spiral rather than a circle: "there is similarity not sameness" in human events.[67]

Yet this was exactly what Vico had said; nor was this the only point at which Holmes misunderstood him. Holmes's work on Vico, as with the other writers he examined, often left much to be desired. While the hasty and superficial judgments to which he was much too prone reflected his youthful arrogance and ignorance, in this case he may be partly rescued from blame. He had no opportunity to study Vico directly and was forced to rely on Michelet's rather free translation of parts of the *New Science* and on Cousin's interpretations. It is probable that his misunderstanding of the *ricorso* doctrine derived from Cousin whom he seems to have read before he came across Michelet's translation and who made the same mistake.[68]

If Vico erred in making man too much the master of his own fate, Montesquieu, Holmes charged, mistakenly took the opposite extreme. Holmes was willing to grant the Frenchman that such things as climate, topography, the proximity of navigable rivers and the sea, the nature of the soil, and so forth did have an undeniable effect on the fortunes of nations. But environmental conditions alone, he argued, could not explain adequately the rise and decline of states. They especially could not account for changes in a nation's customs and institutions. Environmentalism also ignored that some conditions of society were more susceptible to the pressures of environment than others; primitive cultures, for instance, were easily dissolved by natural changes while civilized communities with a stronger protective crust of institutions and science were less susceptible.

But Montesquieu, who would not have seriously objected to much that Holmes said in his criticism, was actually only a stalking horse. Holmes's real concern was with any scheme of materialistic determinism and his objection was theological as well as historical. Environmentalism, or any other similar approach to history, he feared necessarily deprived men of their free will and reduced them to futile beings molded by external forces. Worst of all, he found such a view difficult to reconcile with the concept of a governing Providence without which he thought history was meaningless.[69] Holmes shared to its full the metaphysical terror of those Christian apologists who

---

[67] *Ibid.*, pp. 274–78.

[68] Cousin, *Cours de l'histoire de la philosophie*, pp. 342–45.

[69] [Holmes], "Schlegel's Philosophy," pp. 279–80, 310–11.

since the seventeenth century at least had quaked before the materialist's vision of a mindless mechanical universe remorselessly grinding its way to some grim and unknown destiny. His new history, with all of its scientific aspirations, was actually a surrogate religion. From it he received existential consolations which his lack of religious faith prevented his obtaining from conventional theology.

But Holmes was not content with merely calling for a new history. He wanted very much to write some of it himself. Simultaneously with his theoretical discussions he began a series of essays on the significant peoples of the ancient world and their distinctive national characters. Although the last of these pieces to appear, "Athens and the Athenians," was left unfinished, taken together they give a fairly clear idea of what he thought a reformed history should be.

His basic assumptions about historical inquiry were, of course, informed by his crypto-positivistic empiricism. The facts of history comparatively studied and interpreted without the benefit of chimerical a priori theories would yield to the perceptive mind the laws governing historical development. In essence, his approach represented a marriage of Bacon and Vico. Within this context he relied chiefly on four techniques.

The first of these was the comparative method. From his study of Vico and, to a lesser extent, from Michelet—and possibly from Niebuhr, a translation of whose important but formidable work on early Rome he finally succeeded in reading through to the end in 1843 after several false starts[70]—he drew a belief in the importance of the history of institutions. Central to this was the conviction that by studying the historical development of institutions comparatively the historian could discover analogies which would make possible not only more accurate generalization, but which also could be used to fill in the blanks when one ran out of evidence.[71] To illustrate, he used what he knew of American Indians to clear up points about the tribes of early Italy who were assumed to be at a similar stage of culture, drew parallels between the Roman Republic and the Roman Catholic Church, and compared the struggle between the patricians and plebians in Rome to that of the Lords and Commons in England finding, in the

[70] MS vol. 1792, p. 38.
[71] For Vico see [Holmes], "Schlegel's Philosophy," p. 276 et passim. For suggestive elements in Michelet see his *History of the Roman Republic*, trans. by William Hazlitt (New York: D. Appleton and Company, 1847), p. 13 et passim; for Niebuhr see Gooch, *History and Historians*, pp. 16, 19–20. Holmes may also have picked up something of this from the "conjectural history" of the Scottish Enlightenment. See J. W. Burrow, *Evolution and Society: A Study in Victorian Social Theory* (Cambridge: Cambridge University Press, 1968), pp. 10–16.

latter case, that "the principle contended for is the same, and the means adopted have been, in many respects, strikingly analogous." Suggestive as this technique might be, it assumed a rigid formula of uniform cultural evolution—an idea that has not worn well. Nonetheless, the analogical approach to the study of cultures would later form the basis of his most interesting historical work. Holmes was less venturesome when dealing with cultural diffusion as a factor in the growth of civilizations. Unlike some of his contemporaries, he hesitated to leap to the conclusion that similarities in, for example, the architecture of Egypt, Etruria, and pre-Columbian Mexico implied cultural contact. "It may be," he warned, "that in all three cases, people of like tendencies and with analogous wants devised, in the infancy of art, structures which bore upon them the marks of apparent imitation."[72] In this reluctance may be seen again the influence of Vico even though Holmes frankly thought the Neapolitan to have been overly cautious on this point.

He also made use of philology and the critical analysis of texts. In this he followed the example of Niebuhr and of Friedrich August Wolf, whose *Prolegomena to Homer* (1795) was available in Latin.[73]

From the much abused Schlegel he adopted the historical study of literature which formed his third technique. Literature, Holmes claimed, was a most important key to the intellectual progress of mankind. It could provide unique insights into the mental life of each era, and taken as a whole, gave an invaluable "chronicle of the successive triumphs of the human mind."[74] But his fourth method, the critical study of religion and myth, is of greater present interest for this, like his crypto-positivism, was filled with latent peril to his religious beliefs.

"The religion of nations," he declared, "whether false or true, is always the chief and most significant feature in their character, and the surest route to a certain knowledge of their own genius, and the spirit of their institutions." Apparently once more following Vico, he urged upon his readers the view that mythology was not to be dismissed as a primitive delusion, but rather studied as a stage in the development of human thought. When viewed in this light, he continued, myths "reveal to us the character of intellect in the day in which they were entertained; and their gradual changes indicate to

[72] [George Frederick Holmes], "Ante-Roman Races of Italy," *Southern Quarterly Review*, VII (April 1845), 276, 291, 297-98. [Holmes], "Rome and Romans," p. 281.
[73] [George Frederick Holmes], "Anthon's Classical Dictionary," *Southern Quarterly Review*, III (January 1843), 121.
[74] [Holmes], "History of Literature," pp. 472, 474-77.

us the gradual advancement of human intelligence."[75] In "Athens and the Athenians," he summed it up succinctly: the "religion of a people is invariably the reflex image of that people's feelings and fancies."[76]

Holmes's attention to myth, while not profound in its results, was somewhat precocious, for it was not until the latter part of the century when anthropologists began to add their wealth of information to the store already accumulated by students of classical archaeology and philology that the sophisticated study of myth began to throw real light on the history of human institutions and ideas. Regrettably, however, Holmes's sources were not always the latest. Here again, his ignorance of German concealed from him a firsthand knowledge of the work of such pioneers in the historical study of classical mythology as Creuzer, Lobeck, Voss, and Otfried Müller. Instead, he relied heavily on traditional Christian interpretations inherited from the seventeenth and eighteenth centuries as well as on Lord Bacon's *The Wisdom of the Ancients*. His knowledge of more recent writers was dependent on chance discovery. He knew the theories of Benjamin Constant de Rebecque (1767–1830), a French political pamphleteer and member of Madame de Staël's circle, whose five volume work, *De la religion considerée dans sa source, ses formes, et ses developments* (1825–31), attempted to reveal a permanent and elevated religious sensibility underlying the world's numerous cults. Holmes had encountered the interpretations of a scholar cited by him as Rosenmüller, who was probably Ernst F. K. Rosenmüller (1768–1835), a noted German Orientalist, some of whose work on the Old Testament would have been available to him in Latin. He also followed C. G. Heyne (1729–1812), for fifty years professor of Greek antiquities and philology at Göttingen, who also conveniently wrote in Latin. But at the time under discussion, Holmes's major source of mythological learning was *A Classical Dictionary* compiled and largely written by Charles Anthon, professor of Greek and Latin at Columbia College in New York. This valuable book, which went through several English as well as American editions, drew liberally on the most recent German scholarship and attempted to mediate with discretion between the various emerging schools and theories. Holmes found it a mine of information and the allusions to the theories of Creuzer and Müller found in his writing may doubtlessly be traced to it. But he did not depend entirely on the work of others. Though he was more than happy to have access to aids like Anthon's dictionary, he worked directly in the sources and sometimes, as in his discussion of

---

[75] [Holmes], "Classical Dictionary," pp. 129–30.
[76] [George Frederick Holmes], "Athens and the Athenians," *Southern Quarterly Review*, XI (April 1847), 314.

the rise and progress of the cult of Dionysus, felt entitled to claim some originality.[77]

Holmes, naturally, was concerned primarily with classical mythology since his historical interests centered on the classical world. Like Anthon, he tended to interpret some Greek myths as symbolic representations of the forces of nature, others as showing the influence of "oriental mysticism and philosophy," and yet others as masking historical events.[78] Although each religious system exhibited the indelible stamp of the people who had created it, the major mythological forms were similar for all races and, he suspected, derived ultimately and in a corrupted form from a single primitive revelation: "The tendency towards superstition is undoubtedly one of the essential characteristics of human nature; this feeling was directed into the due channel of religious belief, by the direct influence of God upon Adam and probably Noah: and as we follow back the stream of the various pagan creeds, they all obviously converge towards this common origin."[79] Such views were not uncommon in the early nineteenth century and certainly do not reveal an anticipation of modern interpretations of myth. Even though Holmes realized that myth could expand our historical knowledge when studied critically and saw that it was not merely a delusion to be exposed and cast aside, he did not grasp the importance of ritual and rites in understanding myth nor the sociological importance of religion in archaic societies. Of psychological interpretations of myth, of course, his writings were almost completely bare.

Anthon's book was very careful of Christian beliefs so the emerging science of mythology gave Holmes no religious difficulty until 1850 when, just two years after his reading of Comte had pointed out to him the implications of his empirical epistemology, David F. Strauss's *Das Leben Jesu* (1835; English translation, 1846) showed him how the study of myth could be used to destroy the historical reliability of the Gospel narratives. Even so, it was not until many years later that the implications of Strauss's work became clear.

In applying these various techniques to the ancient world Holmes tried to isolate the most notable features of the three peoples who had molded classical Mediterranean civilization: the mysterious Pelasgians, the Greeks, and the Romans. His object was to depict the national

[77] For references to these authorities see [Holmes], "Classical Dictionary," pp. 131n, 132–35, 136–42.

[78] [Holmes], "Classical Dictionary," pp. 132–35; [George Frederick Holmes], "The North American Indians," *Southern Quarterly Review*, V (January 1844), 147–48.

[79] [Holmes], "Ante-Roman Races," p. 284.

character of each of these nations as a prelude to tracing their respective influences in history. Although his use of the term "national character" was not rigidly systematic, he usually meant by it a group of biologically inherited traits which promoted the growth of distinctive attitudes and institutions in a population by providing it with an innate predisposition towards them. There was implicit in his conception what one might call a quasi-Darwinian notion of social natural selection, an interaction of heredity and environment, which operated to select and perpetuate certain values and to eliminate others. National character, then, was for Holmes largely genetic in origin; in time it became racially fixed and constituted the main counterpoise to environment in molding a society. Put more simply, the historical career of a people was the process whereby an ethnic personality was developed in response to the challenges of their experience freeing them from the complete domination of their natural environment.

Since the fundamental traits of a national character were biologically inherited and virtually immutable, adaptive change in it was necessarily slow. But nations were not totally dependent on genetic innovations from within the group. Among advanced nations such as the English, French, and Spanish, and presumably in the more progressive ones of the ancient world, new developments in the national character had followed an amalgamation with other peoples as a result of migration or conquest. Holmes believed that racial amalgamation, by enriching a people's heredity with the characteristics of other races, increased their options and so provided them with a greater flexibility with which to react to challenges in their historical experience and changes of physical environment. It was then no coincidence for him that those whom he took to be the most racially pure peoples, the American Indians, the Negroes, the Jews (always a special case, however), and perhaps the Chinese, he also found to be among the most unprogressive and therefore the most unsuccessful of the world's inhabitants.[80]

By stressing race in this way Holmes was following a prominent line of thought in the new historiography. Herder, Michelet, Niebuhr in dealing with early Rome, and Augustin Thierry in his work on the French nation had done the same. Despite this, he thought race had been neglected by historians as an important factor in the world's history. It was really a key element, for once the importance of racial or

---

[80] Holmes's views on national character have been systematized from remarks scattered through several essays, primarily "Herder's Philosophy," "Schlegel's Philosophy," "Ante-Roman Races," "Athens and Athenians," "Rome and Romans," and "North American Indians." For similar ideas in other writers see Callcott, *History in the United States*, pp. 166–73.

national character had been grasped, it became obvious that by isolating each example in its pure and original state and discovering its primary characteristics, one could follow its action on subsequent affiliated societies and perhaps even discover the laws of its operation.[81]

Of the Pelasgians Holmes could not say a great deal. Like Niebuhr and Michelet he found them a people of mystery, their character and specific accomplishments almost wholly obscured by the mists of time. They had inhabited the northern littoral of the Mediterranean from Asia Minor to Italy before the rise of Athens and Rome and were "the true fathers of Greek and Roman civilization, and hence of all modern advancement of the human race." The language, religion, and institutions of the Greeks, he believed, were Pelasgian in derivation; in their remote origins the Athenians were "pre-eminently" a Pelasgian people as were the Etruscans. The debt of Rome through Etruria to this race was great. In character they seemed to have been peaceful, hard-working agriculturalists. Their impressive creative genius, the like of which the world had little seen before their time, was passed on to their successors to become a valuable part of civilization's heritage.[82]

The Athenians, of course, were much less obscure. Holmes was thoroughly familiar with Greek literature and, in addition, had the guidance of Thirlwall's superior history. The article on Athens, though unfinished, explored the question of the source of the universally acknowledged uniqueness of Athenian culture. What was the essence of Athenian national character? History had favored Athens and had allowed her people and their institutions to mature slowly and (unlike the Romans) securely, safe from the ravages or interference of outsiders. The result was the development of a devotion to freedom unique in the world's experience. This was the secret of Athenian society. But the Greek love of freedom possessed all of the unrestrained and disordered excess of a first creation. It was a

riotous love of liberty, which raged with restless violence, and formed the very breath of Athenian existence. The liberty, however, of the Athenian's conception was in no respect what we should recognize as such; there was no homage paid to either the principles or practice of justice and propriety —no strict subjection to the dictates of law and order, without obedience to which freedom can never find its best form and only guarantee; but with him it was a wild frenzy of acknowledging no authority but such as he individually might constitute for himself, of following his own uncontrolled impulses alone, and giving a loose rein to the free play of either

[81] [Holmes], "Herders Philosophy," pp. 287–89; "Schlegel's Philosophy," p. 311.

[82] [Holmes], "Ante-Roman Races," pp. 289, 292–95, 299.

his passions or his caprices. The *summum bonum* of his imagination was the entire absence of restraint, and thus he gradually reduced his country to those Saturnalia of licence which she exhibited in her decay. [This] is the most deeply significant phenomenon of the history of Athens, and furnished the key note to the singularly commingled elements of the Athenian character. Everywhere we shall discover its regulating influence; it is equally discernible in morals, politics, legislation and the practice of the Courts; in literature, philosophy, science and art; in private life and social intercourse. Everywhere it was the moving spirit of Athenian life.

In the initial article Holmes was able to cover no more than Athenian morality, and here, unlike many of his contemporaries, he would not idealize the Greeks. A study of their myths showed that their morals had never been high and had become worse as time went on. Women were little more than slaves; "celebrated courtesans" alone were allowed the pleasure of male company. As a consequence, the uplifting influence of the wife and mother (of which the nineteenth century thought and expected so much) was almost totally absent. But worst of all "the degrading practice of paederasty was universal and sanctioned by law. The whole literature of the Greeks, and particularly the vaunted Dialogues of Plato, are filled with allusions to it, or illustrations drawn from it. And the familiarity, with which it is habitually mentioned, proves the shamelessness with which it was regularly regarded." Greek religion was sensual, completely devoid of any moral guidance. Athens was vice-ridden: sexual immorality, lying, political corruption, vanity, greed—an endless list. And yet, the Athenians were not vicious in their evil; rather, they were like children, simple and spontaneous. And from this simplicity came their excellence as well as their shortcomings. In the lack of restraint in their lives as in the amorality and spontaneity of their religion and in the sublime anthropomorphism of their art, which itself was "the deified incarnation of their own desires," one found an "all pervading spirit of love [which] was the breath of their existence, and the universal inspiration of their whole culture."[83] This distinctive characteristic—love of beauty and love of freedom—was the Athenian legacy to European civilization. Who could deny its subsequent and continuing operation?

The spirit of Roman civilization Holmes found to have been the spirit of law; in Rome the love of freedom that had been born in Greece received a necessary check. Roman culture lacked the spontaneous human naturalness of the Greeks, but none the less it achieved political greatness. The history of the city was a reflection of the essence of the Roman national character: selfishness. Just as all Roman

[83] [Holmes], "Athens and Athenians," pp. 285–88, 305–06, 308–09, 312–13, 318–19.

citizens were bent to the service of the state, so all other nations were bent to the service of Rome. "From his cradle to his grave, the Roman was a machine, acting for one definite purpose, and immolating all the softer features of humanity to the attainment of this one object,—the elevation of himself in connection with the advancement of the State." Rome was the archetype of the warfare state; this was a legacy of her own precarious birth and early threatened existence among the tribes of Latium. Unlike the Greeks, the early Romans were marked by "private purity and remarkable simplicity." This naïveté, and their conservative agricultural economy, determined that their own institutions early became objects of veneration. Their religion was a religion of institutions; its sole purpose being the promotion and conservation of the state. The "first great fact," then, informing "the national character of Rome [was] the union of the political and religious systems, and the strict subordination of the latter to the former." Borrowing her mythology from Greece, Rome carried polytheism to its limits, exhausted what religious content it had by debasing it with her own spiritual sterility, and prepared the way for the introduction of Christianity. Roman religion, like all of Roman life, was "an anomalous monster of state machinery . . . wholly devoid of any irradiation, any enthusiasm from above."

The Roman's virtues and ideals were practical. Such characteristics could be found "firmly developed and in colossal proportions," but "the tenderness of the heart,—the poetry of existence,—the soul of humanity,—was entirely wanting in Rome." Among the Romans one found

> none of that enthusiastic and chivalrous ardor for liberty, which we notice in Greece: a sound, a name, an idea, has no influence over them—they seek only the tangible. There is nothing abstract in the Roman mind: if they declaim about justice, it is *jus Romanum*; if about liberty, it is *jus civitatis*; if about honour, *honestum et utile* become convertible terms. What they aimed at was the precise, the perceptible, the real: hence the peculiar character and subsequent perfection of the Roman Law.[84]

This, then, was Rome's dubious legacy to the West: patriotism, a reverence for law, and Christianity on the one hand, and a collective devotion to the omnipotent state on the other. Like Greece, Rome contributed the various traits of her "national character" to the growing cultural mixture of Western civilization.

Originally, Holmes had intended the series of essays in the *Southern Quarterly Review* which began with his discussion of Schlegel's *Lec-*

----

[84] [Holmes], "Rome and Romans," pp. 273–75, 280, 282–84, 285, 292, 296, 303–05.

tures on the History of Literature and ended with "Athens and the Athenians" to be a sequence setting forth the theory of the new history and then applying it in specific studies. But his enthusiasm slackened as he wrote; he found "the vastness of the subject" alarming, and confessed in his notebook in 1846 that "the enterprise which I undertook in hope I now prosecute in despair."[85] The project was fated to die of neglect, for soon thereafter he encountered Comte's Positive Philosophy and turned his attention to more basic and more serious problems. His honeymoon with the nineteenth century was over.

In the new history Holmes was working with ideas that in the hands of others would constitute a profound challenge to the traditional Christian world view; a world view which basically he accepted, even though he questioned and rejected some aspects of the religion supporting it. But his enthusiasm prior to 1848 for these ideas as well as his agreement that true history was a positivistic quest for law shows that he had no more fear of empirical history than of an empirical philosophy. Crypto-positivism with its emphasis on facts and its search for law formed the epistemological foundation of his history just as it did of his philosophy and his view of science, and the implications of this orientation did not alarm Holmes until he read Comte. And yet, from about 1845 on he felt increasingly dissatisfied with it. In time he would come to the conclusion that an empirical philosophy of the sort he had advocated was incapable of solving the problems that the contemporary world was rapidly creating, nor could it provide the complementary union of religious belief and secular learning which he still accepted as their normal relationship.

Holmes's early optimism fell victim to a number of things. Closest to him, of course, was the personal failure that dogged him during the 1840s and culminated in the disappointments at Williamsburg and the University of Mississippi. Throughout this period his growing pessimism about the unfolding century fed on his personal frustration. The harassments suffered because of his wife's immaturity, the gradual realization that his daughter Minnie was hopelessly retarded, and the death of his son Floyd, were all added to his burden by the decade's end. His anxiety at his personal misfortune was increased by an apprehension over public affairs. As sectional strife increased, the future of the United States and the South in particular grew more vague and uncertain with each passing year. Looking at Europe, he saw the heartland of civilization once again on the verge of revolution—and who knew where it would lead this time? European and American

[85] MS vol. 1843, p. 207.

governments were struggling blindly and, for the most part, ineffectively with the problems of an urban and industrial civilization. Under the temptations of a flock of theorists the Western world seemed to him determined to cast off all of its traditional moral, spiritual, even intellectual moorings at a time when it had nothing but naïve hope to put in their place. Holmes pondered all of these things and gradually reached the conclusion that something was seriously, perhaps even fatally, wrong.

Not long after his review of Whewell's history of science in 1842 he had begun to suspect that there might be more in the present turmoil than he had believed when he had first announced the coming revolution and had advised his readers to put their trust in empirical science. In 1844 he reexplored the question more specifically and with less implicit approval of the chaotic events that seemed destined to occur. The reappraisal appeared as a series of essays, "The Present State of Letters," published in the *Southern Literary Messenger* and cast in the form of letters to his friend Simms.

In stating in the Whewell review that the world was entering a period of intellectual reformation Holmes was not a lonely prophet; rather, he was joining a rapidly swelling chorus. Emerson, to name only one, had several years earlier in "The American Scholar" pointed out the revolutionary character of the times and had seen signs of a new and emerging but still uncertain era in literature, art, philosophy, science, and in the institutions of the present world. Holmes's correspondence with other writers throughout the country showed that they too shared this general expectation.[86] But what specific indications did Holmes now see when in the letters to Simms he took a closer look? Believing that literature was "the most delicate and universal expression of [a society's] various thoughts and feelings," and—with unknowing irony—that science was generally "much later in receiving the permeating influences of a spirit of general innovation," Holmes naturally looked first to the world of letters.[87] There he found that although the age of the romantic poets was coming to an end, the skepticism, despair and uncertainty which had characterized that

[86] Ralph Waldo Emerson, "The American Scholar," *The Complete Works of Ralph Waldo Emerson* (Boston: Houghton Mifflin Company, n.d.) I, 109–10. George Frederick Holmes, "The Present Condition of Letters," *Southern Literary Messenger*, X (September 1844), 540. The series is entitled "The Present State of Letters" in the initial installment only, but for convenience the first title is used throughout in the text of this book. For a general study of the anticipation of a new era in America see Arthur Ekirch, Jr., *The Idea of Progress in America, 1815–1860* (New York: Columbia University Press, 1944).

[87] Holmes, "State of Letters," pp. 412–13.

time were still present. Byron had best represented the former state of mind: "He uttered the common but indistinct feelings of men of that day in their most beautiful and poetic form—the melancholy occasioned by the departure of a former system—the full intelligence of the discord and ruin around—and a sad despair of any better fruits, but only the fear of deeper and deeper degradation." Holmes's generation had continued to feel this despair, though less acutely, for a new dawn did seem to be breaking through the gloom. But gloom was still the prevailing characteristic of the age. When he turned to philosophy he could hear only the dying gasps of Scottish realism. The work of Mill, if anything, was only a preparation for a new era. Current philosophies generally were "in part the highest and ultimate expression of an effete system—in part the menstruum in which float about the timbers of an incipient structure; but to a still greater extent they are subversive of everything which preceded them." In natural science things were no better. Recent attempts at classifying and clarifying scientific doctrines and methods only indicated an increasing "consciousness of imperfection."[88] In public life, the "violent antagonisms of political opinions," the inability of governments to cope with the novel problems of the day, the dissensions tearing at the vitals of almost all ecclesiastical groups, suggested forcefully that everywhere an upheaval was eminent. It was clear that the creative energies of the Enlightenment were played out.[89]

Through his literary criticism Simms had been the catalyst which had moved Holmes to undertake his own appraisal of modern culture and at first, like Simms, he had moved forward in the current of revolution with confidence.[90] But his optimism, as we have seen, was soon mixed with a growing alarm, an anxiety about the future that could not be entirely assuaged by paeans to empirical science, even to science in the form of scientific history. Unlike Simms, Holmes grew increasingly uneasy as 1848—the year of revolution in Europe and of his shattering encounter with Comte's new order—approached. Before that eventful year, he was not able to pinpoint the source of his uneasiness; it was little more than a vague fear. For all his growing doubts, to turn against science was not even in his mind, not yet; but

[88] Doubtlessly Holmes was thinking of such works as Sir John Herschel's *Discourse on the Study of Natural Philosophy* (1830) and Andre-Marie Ampère's *Essai sur la philosophie des sciences* (1834–43).

[89] Holmes, "State of Letters," pp. 412–14.

[90] For Simms's influence see *ibid.*, p. 410. For Simms's career as a revolutionary and his own subsequent disillusionment, see William R. Taylor, *Cavalier and Yankee: The Old South and American National Character* (New York: Doubleday Anchor Books, [1963]), chapter VIII, and especially pp. 249–60.

whatever promise science held had to be realized through the agency of men, and there lay the problem.

For a time Holmes thought greater efforts at popular education would head off the disasters he anticipated. In the "Present State of Letters" he lamented the low quality of the popular press in America and attributed it to a growing tendency for all sorts of people to write and publish—or to try, at any rate. The press, he charged, generally pandered to public taste rather than attempting to improve it and this, in turn, had a corrupting effect on both writers and literature. To end this vicious circle the general public's intellectual level had to be raised.[91] In 1845, when he addressed the Beaufort District Society in South Carolina, he told the group, formed to promote education, that the increased industrialization of the economy of the Western world and the increase in population constituted a major threat to the future of civilization. The impatient masses had to be educated to understand the necessary and sometimes slow processes of social transformation; only in this way could violent revolution be avoided.[92] Science, which understood such things, could solve men's problems, but only if only men could be persuaded to follow.

By the end of 1848, however, Holmes's disenchantment was complete. He concluded that science, at any rate as presently constituted, could not save itself, much less society. First of all, contemporary science suffered from a dangerous imbalance that stressed physical science too much and neglected the social sciences. Consequently, in the present day, the

physical sciences have by their discoveries multiplied incalculably our powers, our resources, our knowledge, our comforts, and our wealth—they have rendered us independent of the elements, and have made us superior to the ordinary restrictions of time and space. But notwithstanding these proud achievements, there are urgent questions of the gravest importance, which no light from Physical science will enable us to solve.

Society was confronted with enigmas created by the fertile growth of physical science and technology but incapable of being solved by them. More delay in the fostering of social science, especially scientific history, could be fatal.

We have been imbibing and inhaling one only of the elements that constitute the atmosphere of knowledge—the other is ready to ignite and

91 Holmes, "Condition of Letters," pp. 540–41, 674–75, 677–78. G. F. Holmes to R. W. Singleton, September 13, 1844, MS vol. 1808.

92 [George Frederick Holmes], MS beaufort Society address, pp. 24–25, 28–29, Holmes papers, D. Published as George Frederick Holmes, *Address Delivered Before the Beaufort District Society* (Columbia, S. C.: A. S. Johnson, 1845).

explode. . . . We must restore the healthy combination of the constituent elements of our intellectual atmosphere, or perish by its disorganization. No speculations or discoveries in Natural science will enable us to do this—our sole therapeutics are contained in the Social sciences.[93]

Nor was the difficulty confined to this misplaced emphasis. There was also the danger of making too much of the powers of science. Holmes feared that even where social science flourished, its advocates were caught up in a pride of method and were more determined on using their science to establish an earthly utopia than in concerning themselves with the more limited task of discovering the laws of social development.[94] Unlike the physical scientists, who, he believed, were beginning to sense the limitations of their method,[95] the social scientists seemed overcome by an urge to dominate and remake the social creation. Science, then, was perhaps too frail a reed to lean on. At cross purposes and confused—or worse, deluded—about the sufficiency of its method, it, too, seemed headed for catastrophe.

This unwelcome conclusion was reenforced by his investigation of Comte's philosophy. During the course of his own studies Holmes had come to believe that of all the historians and philosophers of history then writing, Comte was most interested in the discovery of the true laws of history, and so his quest for a new history led him in the summer of 1848 to a close reading of the Positive Philosophy.[96] His encounter with Positivism convinced him that the chief intellectual error not only of contemporary science but of nineteenth-century civilization as a whole was an unjustified confidence in the self-sufficient powers of the human intellect; the central problem of the age, therefore, was to discover and, no less important, to accept the proper limitations of human knowledge.

Thus chastened in his admiration of science, Holmes turned with a new appreciation to the study of metaphysics and traditional formal logic. Kant was studied with a new seriousness for Holmes was willing to overlook his "farrago of hyper-metaphysical reveries" if the Königsberg philosopher could instruct him in the nature and limits of

[93] [George Frederick Holmes], "On the Importance of the Social Sciences in the Present Day," *Southern Literary Messenger*, XV (February 1849), 78.

[94] For this tendency see Bernard, *Origins of American Sociology*, pp. 51–52, 53, 386, 717–18.

[95] [Holmes], "Importance of Social Sciences," 78.

[96] See Holmes's inaugural lecture at the College of William and Mary, p. 22. He began reading the *Cours de philosophie positive* in the summer of 1848 and had finished it by the fall. See Floyd Nelson House, *Development of Sociology* (New York: McGraw-Hill, 1936), p. 219. House came into possession of Holmes's copy of the *Cours*. See also G. F. Holmes to Auguste Comte, October 30, 1852, MS vol. 1808.

knowledge. But the admission of Kant into his circle of masters did not extend to the more recent German idealists. Holmes's new orientation in philosophy was accompanied by an upsurge of religious orthodoxy in reaction to the threats to Christianity which he found in so much contemporary thought. Hegel and his followers with their strange heterodox theologies seemed to him more like infidels than ever before. Rather than German idealism, the philosophical tradition that Holmes now embraced was Aristotelianism.

In reality, his admiration of Aristotle was not new; he had long preferred him to his rival Plato.[97] But Aristotle, unfortunately, had taken metaphysics seriously and this had separated him from the hardheaded young empiricist. But when Holmes began to suspect that metaphysics, far from being contemptible, was actually what Aristotle had called it, the "First Philosophy," the most basic of human sciences, the foundation of all forms of knowledge—even science, then obviously it was a necessary prolegomenon to the study of both science and history. He then unavoidably faced the question of which system of metaphysics among the conflicting schools should he embrace? Certainly not the German variety for Holmes retained all his Anglo-American horror of "mysticism." Doubtlessly, he was attracted to Aristotle partly because of the latter's attacks on Platonic "mysticism." Actually, contemporary philosophers held little attraction for him; it was Aristotle who offered Holmes just the right mixture of science and metaphysics. Later, when his religious reaction had reached its height, he would find Aquinas's version of Aristotle's teaching in some ways even better than the original because of its incorporation of Christian theology. But much of this anticipates our story. His reevaluation of metaphysics and his growing appreciation of traditional Christianity were not fully developed until the 1850s, but the direction of his thought was already clear in the late 1840s, and was amply previewed in his inaugural address at the University of Mississippi.

In 1850 when Holmes settled into his mountain retreat and took stock of the intellectual world it was clear that he had come a long way since his enthusiastic manifesto of 1842. He was now very much aware of the conflict between faith and intellect inherent in the culture of the nineteenth century; a conflict of which he had been unaware eight years earlier. He was also more conservative in religion; the encounter with Comte had removed the scales from his eyes. During the next decade his intellectual life continued to flourish, but it did so under the tension of a growing spiritual estrangement from his age.

97 [Holmes], "Philosophy of Herder," p. 277n.

III   The Rustication
1849-1857

WHEN it became clear that he was not going to regain his position as president of the University of Mississippi, Holmes reconciled himself to what he hoped would be only a temporary retirement in the country. Unfortunately, the interruption of his academic career was to last almost a decade. Most of this time was spent in the isolation of Burke's Garden where he studied and wrote extensively, farmed after a fashion, and grieved over his prospects for the future. The years from the summer of 1849 to the autumn of 1857 were hard, often desperate years, filled with frustration, disappointment, and poverty. Added responsibilities and worries mounted with increases in his family and in his debts. Letitia ("Letty"), his second daughter, was born in 1850; the third—his favorite—Coralie, in 1852; and a fourth, Isabel, in 1856. His other two sons, Henry Hendon and Frederick Lawrence, were born in 1855 and 1858 respectively. Yet despite all the cares and distractions, the years spent in Burke's Garden were among his best intellectually. It was there that he produced some of his finest work and won recognition in England and France as well as in the United States.

Burke's Garden was located in Tazewell County, a mountainous, somewhat isolated, but modestly prosperous area. In 1850 the census listed population of almost 9,000 free whites, 75 free Negroes, and 1,060 Negro slaves. The majority of its inhabitants were farmers who raised wheat, corn, potatoes, and livestock. The religious life of the county was expressed in an evangelical frontier Protestantism of which the Methodists were the most numerous sect. Several one-room schools enrolled a total of over six hundred pupils, although almost fifteen hundred of the white adults were illiterate. Interest in education grew in the county during the 1850s, but even so there was no college, nor even an academy or a public library. While in many ways probably a pleasant enough rural southern community, Tazewell County was not the sort of place in which Holmes would have freely chosen to spend eight years of his life.[1]

[1] William C. Pendleton, *History of Tazewell County and Southwest Virginia, 1748-1920* (Richmond: n.p., 1920), pp. 542-43. Richard S. Fisher, *Statistical Gazetteer of the United States* (New York: J. H. Colton and Company, 1857),

Burke's Garden itself was as fertile an area as any in the county, though something of a geological oddity. It was not a valley in the usual sense of the word but rather a sort of basin or cup surrounded by a range of high mountains. It ran ten miles from northeast to southwest and five miles across, and had only one natural entrance: an opening cut in the mountain range, known as "the Gap," and bordering Wolf Creek, a stream that had its source in the Garden. Situated at an elevation of 3200 feet above sea level, the Garden had lower temperatures than the rest of the county. Spring came later, summers were milder, winters more severe. It was good pasture land. The house at Cavan, where Holmes and his family lived with Lavalette's mother, was pleasantly located in a grove of sugar trees and commanded an estate of some three thousand acres.[2]

In the fall of 1850 the needs of his family and his own pride forced Holmes to leave Letitia Floyd's house and go to Richmond looking for work. He met with an opportunity to serve as clerk for a legislative committee but was warned away by his brother-in-law Governor Floyd on the grounds that his accepting a political appointment might cause him embarrassment later in his life. He found nothing else. He had hoped he might secure a teaching position at Emory and Henry College or at the University of Virginia, but these faint hopes were unrealized. He did some writing to save his stay in Richmond from complete failure, bought a new desk to make the labor more agreeable, and took lessons in German from a Hanoverian refugee.[3]

The next year Holmes returned to Burke's Garden as he had little enough to keep him in Richmond. At Lavalette's insistence, the family moved to Jeffersonville, the Tazewell County seat, where he purchased and tried his hand at editing a small newspaper, the *South-Western Advocate*.[4] This venture proved as fruitless as his Richmond excursion. Jamison sent his regrets that his unlucky friend had been so reduced; he was certain that Holmes could only find the work tiresome, unrewarding, and a corrupting influence on his literary style, and was sure that he would "cut it" as soon as he could. Like sentiments came from England where Maryanne Holmes expressed dismay that her son had come "down the ladder so as to Edit an American N.P. for a place of 500 persons!" Why, she exclaimed, "the village of Acomb [the smallest town in her direct experience] was

---

p. 836. United States Census Office, *Seventh Census of the United States, 1850* (Washington, D. C.: n.p., 1853), pp. 257–92.

[2] Pendleton, *Tazewell County*, pp. 501–03, 505, 536–38.

[3] Holmes to Lavalette Holmes, December 4, 1850.

[4] No copies of this newspaper from the time of Holmes's editorship have been located.

800." Although this was not to be his last fling with an "N.P."—he edited the *Richmond Examiner* briefly in the summer of 1853—Holmes agreed with the evaluation of Jamison and his mother, tired of the "petty cares" of a country editor's life, and after a few months gave up his newspaper and moved his family to Tanglewood, a large uncleared farm belonging to the Floyds located high on the side of Buck Horn Mountain about five miles east of Jeffersonville.[5]

The construction of a log house on the Tanglewood property got underway in the fall of 1852, but in spite of help from his brother Ed, who had arrived from England earlier in the year, progress on the house was slow. Labor was indifferent and had to be bossed every step of the way. As winter came on Holmes found himself and his family moving into "an unfinished house [in] the heart of an uncleared forest." The hardships of that winter are not difficult to imagine. Not surprisingly, February found them back at Cavan where they could at least keep warm. Although abandoned as a permanent home, Tanglewood continued to be one of Holmes's many harassments. During the next several years he tried renting it, then he persuaded Ed to farm it for a short time, and then, after he had gone to the University of Virginia, he even thought of selling it.[6] In the end, Tanglewood remained a combined financial burden and mountain retreat for the rest of his days.

The period from his return to the Floyd place in 1853 to 1856 is an obscure one. The details of his life that can be gleaned from letters and occasional notes indicate that he occupied his time much as he had in Richmond writing articles, worrying, and now and then trying for a professorship. But in January 1856 this changed. He added agri-

[5] D. F. Jamison to G. F. Holmes, May 26, 1852, vol. I, Holmes papers, LC. Buchanan, *Holmes Family History*, pp. 83, 86. Maryanne Holmes to Edward A. Holmes, June 3, 1852, *ibid.*, p. 42. G. F. Holmes to N. H. Massie, August 27, 1853, George Frederick Holmes Papers, University of Virginia Library, Charlottesville, Virginia; hereinafter cited as Holmes papers, V. MS vol. 1792. G. F. Holmes to John McClintock, November 8, 1852, McClintock papers; Buchanan (p. 86) gives the size of Tanglewood as 1,000 acres. The property passed to Lavalette when her mother died in December, 1852.

A check of the *Enquirer* during the 1850s and of the *Examiner* during Holmes's editorship failed to turn up any contributions which can be identified with certainty. Accordingly, no possible attributions have been used as sources for this book. It is doubtful, moreover, that his newspaper writings departed significantly from his opinions expressed elsewhere. That he did not preserve a record of them indicates that he placed no great value on them.

[6] Maryanne Holmes to Edward A. Holmes, November 13 and 22, 1852, July 19, 1859, December 12, 1860, Buchanan, *Holmes Family History*, pp. 45, 61, 62. G. F. Holmes to John McClintock, October 1, 1852, MS vol. 1808, and November 8, 1852. MS vol. 1791, August 26 and 28, 1856, November 14, 1856 et passim.

culture to his other occupations, and, as a consequence, the record of his activities improved. Like Jamison and other successful farmers of his acquaintance, he began keeping an agricultural log or journal, which, fortunately, he also used as a diary. Holmes had dabbled at farming for years (his letters from Richmond and Williamsburg in the 1840s had been full of advice for Lavalette) but he nevertheless considered himself "a mere tyro." When he began his log he frankly admitted that a rural life was contrary to both his "habits and anticipations," but, as he was determined to be optimistic, he acknowledged that he really disliked cities and that country life did have many charms to compensate for its isolation. And so, finding himself possessed of a small but adequate stock and supplies, he began the new year "with hopefulness." His hope was matched by his evident seriousness, for while only one farmer in ten in America subscribed to even one agricultural journal in the 1850s Holmes took two of them.[7]

He soon discovered that reading about farming and practicing it were different things. His ineptitude was compounded by bad luck. Debts continued to accumulate; frost, bad weather, and insects destroyed his crops; careless help killed and maimed his livestock; winters were frequently so cold he could not even work on his writing, but found it necessary "to bend over the fire" the entire day (once a stray spark almost set the house afire in near zero weather); the burden of work in the fields was so great that even he—to say nothing of Lavalette and the children—was forced sometimes to chop weeds in the garden; he and his family were frequently sick. Scarcely a page of his journal is free of some catastrophe—even such a minor one as his cabbages coming up radishes.[8]

Needless to say, these trials were not conducive to literary creation. He tried to reserve his mornings for writing, but too frequently found that it was "utterly impossible to continue my literary labours in consequence of distractions and interruption." Even when uninterrupted, his work was often "irksome" and the effort made to do it "very much against the grain." It frequently seemed no more than "daily literary drudgery for bread."[9]

Although the traditional hazards of farming and the tedium of a professional writer's life plagued his existence, Holmes's chief worry was debt. His growing family, his agricultural fiascos, and his need

[7] MS vol. 1791, pp. 1, 10. Paul Gates, *The Farmer's Age: Agriculture, 1815–1860* (New York: Holt, Rinehart and Winston, [1960]), p. 343.

[8] MS vol. 1791, passim. G. F. Holmes to James H. Thornwell, [January 21, 1857], Thornwell papers.

[9] MS vol. 1802, p. 251, Holmes papers, D. MS vol. 1791, January 15, June 23 and 27, November 26, 1856.

for books were all sources of indebtedness that at times forced him into real poverty. At one point he calculated that the comfortable support of his family, including slaves and white help as well as his wife and five children (a total of twenty persons), would require three dollars a day. This alone would have been manageable even in his circumstances, but when farm expenses and payments on already existing debts were added, his requirements came to more than three thousand dollars a year! This was an almost impossible sum for one with his sad resources. Even so, economy might have helped if economy had been one of his virtues. But it was not. He could spend over seventy-five dollars on a single purchase of books and repeatedly consider borrowing to buy other farms for several thousand dollars each at a time when he could not even pay his grocery bill.[10] The absurdity of his situation was not lost on him. In contrasting his poverty with his growing literary fame, he wrote "Got a letter from Mr. John D. Sterrett of Lexington asking about my articles on Comte—they are slowly making an impression. To descend from grave to matters so trivial in comparison apparently to be almost ludicrous—We are out of bacon and I cannot afford to buy it."[11] Maryanne found it hard to attribute her son's penury to anything but his own folly. "I fear he is very soft," she wrote to Ed,

& either is very much cheated or cajoled, & lets his money be sifted and frittered away, by his (over kind and Pretended) friends. It is impossible with his abilities and industry, and living off the produce of his own farm & servants, without the opportunity of incurring expense in society, dress, public amusements, luxuries, or any thing, but that he must have accumulated some capital in numerous years, (if he had not been bambooseled [*sic*] out of it in one way or another!) instead of being over-whelmed with rapacious debts.

Nor was George's situation redeemed in her eyes by his high position in Virginia's "literary world." "I consider that almost valueless," she wrote, for it "is not enough to enable him to live, without . . . drugery . . . or able even to pay his way!" Maryanne's strictures were not exaggerated. When Holmes left Burke's Garden in 1857 for his new appointment at the University of Virginia he was forced to settle his local medical bill by parting with some of his books, while still owing other creditors (his mother among them) a total of ten thousand dollars.[12]

[10] MS vol. 1791, May 12, July 29 et passim, 1856.
[11] *Ibid.*, June 5, 1856.
[12] Maryanne Holmes to Edward A. Holmes, May 1, 1856, Buchanan, *Holmes Family History*, p. 56; Maryanne Holmes to Edward A. Holmes, July 19, 1859. MS vol. 1791, September 16 and 19, 1857.

The one bright spot that appeared briefly in Holmes's monotonous financial situation was Ed's desire to free his brother of his debts and help him to return to England. In April 1856, Ed ended a visit in Burke's Garden to return to Minnesota where he had gone two years before to make his fortune. Holmes rejoiced, "He is determined to . . . purchase my debts, and thus relieve me from the heavy load which has been pressing on me since I came to America, and growing more and more heavy every day." Ed did well in the West as a civil engineer (among other things laying out a plan for the city of Duluth) but Holmes's hopes were blasted. The following February he wrote sadly, "Ed is on a matrimonial hunt; and is, I fear, disposed to throw me overboard for a wife." Maryanne thought as little of Ed's western amours as did Holmes. "You astonish me," she had written her younger son during his first stay in Minnesota, "by saying you have some idea of taking an American wife. You give the young lady many *necessary* qualifications but still she is American, and seems to have no fortune, & you have not yet made yours. Her speaking 'Weimebago' so well, I would think was not a very necessary accomplishment."[13] As it turned out, Ed did not marry in Minnesota, but neither did he redeem his brother's debts. Fortunately Holmes, by this time, was no stranger to disappointment.

While his journal shows him at times energetic, hopeful, and anxious to succeed, at others—and more frequently—it reveals him dejected and despondent over his affairs, as in January 1856, when he wrote, "I think I may yet do well; but my spirits are nearly broken by the events of the last two years." Misfortune, however, had mellowed rather than embittered him. In 1853 the newly arrived Ed had reported to Maryanne how patient his brother was with him, which prompted her to remark "what a violent change must have taken place in his constitution!" Yet she knew the cause: "I fear misfortunes & disappointments must have broken his spirits." Several years later she added, "My poor dear George. Nobody knows what he suffers. Life is blasted in him and he feels he is not in the sphere he ought to shine in."[14]

Holmes was very much aware that he was out of his sphere, but for awhile at least he did his best to put a good face on a bad condition. In 1850 he represented himself to Saunders as happy and content in

[13] Buchanan, *Holmes Family History*, pp. 52, 64. MS vol. 1791, April 10, 1856, February 4, 1857. Maryanne Holmes to Edward A. Holmes, October 8, 1855, Buchanan, *Holmes Family History*, p. 55.

[14] MS vol. 1791, January 25, 1856. Maryanne Holmes to Edward A. Holmes, March 9, 1853, Buchanan, *Holmes Family History*, p. 48. Maryanne Holmes to Edward A. Holmes, October 8, 1855.

his rustic seclusion. Two years later, he told Comte that he actually valued his isolation because it provided him with quiet surroundings in which to mature his thoughts. In the same year he was almost ecstatic in a letter to John McClintock. He had no wish for fame or fortune; he wrote only because he could not resist the temptation (and the duty) of "shooting error as it flies." Rather, "my only wish for myself is the hush and quiet of a country retreat and the salubrious airs, the pellucid waters, the green valleys, and the tranquillizing scenery of this lovely portion of the Virginia mountains . . . mingling the active pursuits of country life with the healthy action of the mind."[15] But before too much time had passed the role of forest sage began to chafe. He wrote to McClintock to be on the lookout for an academic or literary position "within striking distance of New York." He had to get closer to the materials needed for his work. Living in the woods was too expensive and the mails were too slow for a scholar who had to rely on them for his books. Worst of all, he found that it took a ride of twenty-five miles on horseback before he could hope to find anyone capable of carrying on a literary conversation.[16] And yet the solitude of Burke's Garden was not the only source of his discontent. The land of his exile, no less than himself, was outside "the sphere he ought to shine in." Once, while reviewing a collection of essays by Sir William Hamilton, Holmes declined to go into the philosophical writings in any depth, excusing himself with the acid remark, "how could we hope to find an apology ample enough to palliate our offence, if we were to re-open such inquiries in the midst of a community which understands little and cares less about these abstract and tantalizing investigations?"[17] His frustration was well summed up in a despairing remark jotted down in one of his notebooks during this period:

I am only too much afraid that there is some propriety in applying to myself the following remark of Niebuhr. . . .
"There, too, has a fine character been rendered almost useless by the force of circumstances: there was more in the heart of the tree than ever appeared in its foliage and blossoms." . . . Strike out the word "fine" and it is appropriate, especially the latter member of the sentence.[18]

From time to time, when defeat became almost unbearable, Holmes took refuge in his old intention of going west to practice law. By

[15] Robert Saunders to G. F. Holmes, May 10, 1850; G. F. Holmes to Auguste Comte, July 8, 1852, Holmes papers, D. Holmes to McClintock, October 1, 1852.
[16] G. F. Holmes to John McClintock, February 17, 1853, McClintock papers.
[17] [Holmes], "Hamilton's Discussions," p. 297.
[18] MS vol. 1802.

now this threatened intention, which doubtlessly began in complete sincerity, had become little more than a device for protecting his hurt ego. It was as if Holmes were saying to himself, "I do not have to endure these humiliations. I can leave anytime I really want to go." Jamison had warned him when he left South Carolina that he would not be appreciated in Virginia, and true enough the present lot and future prospects of his family and himself seemed to be little more than "disgrace, infamy, quarrels, heart-burning, and embarrassments." But with the prospect of a new life as a western lawyer to solace him, he could withstand the buffets upon his thwarted ambitions. His projects for a western migration, though, never got beyond the talking stage. Practice law again he might, perhaps in Wheeling, Virginia —not too far away—and this his mother anxiously encouraged, but to attempt a legal career as far away as Minnesota was quite another matter. She knew, as he must have known, that scholars with refined classic temperaments do not make good pioneers. She confessed to having no knowledge of Minnesota other than its being "more outlandish than even Virginia" and full of wild Indians, but that Ed had been forced to walk one hundred fifty miles with a fifty pound pack on his back through "dangerous forest and swamp" convinced her it was no place for her older son. "You say you make a first-rate pioneer," she wrote to Ed, but added, "I am sure George would not."[19]

A more realistic plan of escape from Burke's Garden presented itself in his attempts to reenter academic life. Holmes seems to have taken this avenue of deliverance more seriously than his project of joining Ed in the West, at least he worked harder at it. In 1850, three years before he appealed to McClintock to help him find something near New York, he had solicited assistance from his old associate Simms in hopes of gaining some sort of teaching position in New England. Simms, however, replied that as he had "no influence in that quarter" he feared he could not be of much help, which, in view of the results, must have been a fair evaluation. Holmes also mulled over the prospect of returning to Richmond College if and when the school was reorganized and put on its feet financially. But that contingency he thought distant, and probably, unlikely. In the winter of 1855–56, Dr. Henry, who had been elected professor of Greek over Holmes at South Carolina College back in 1845, died leaving the chair vacant once more. Holmes's loyal friends, with Jamison at their head, again

19 MS vol. 1791. February 9 and March 13, 1856. G. F. Holmes to Richard Vincent, January 15, 1851, vol. I, Holmes papers, LC. Maryanne Holmes to Edward A. Holmes, September 28, 1852. Maryanne Holmes to Edward A. Holmes, May 29, 1855, Buchanan, *Holmes Family History*, p. 54. His reading lists and work schedules for the fifties show no legal studies.

put up his name for the position. Holmes, however, was not too keen about going to Columbia: "I feel very indifferent on the subject," he wrote in his diary. "The disadvantages of the move would be almost a full counterpoise for the advantages." More to his liking was an expected vacancy at Charlottesville and, best of all, there was a chance (disappointed as it turned out) that he might be named Virginia State librarian. So, when Jamison sent the doubtlessly anticipated news that the outlook for his replacing Henry was not good, Holmes was not upset. South Carolina College, he consoled himself, was "completely prostrate and disorganized" anyway. Later in the year he was offered a professorship at the Richmond Female Institute teaching classical and English literature, rhetoric, and history. He declined, pleading his poor aptitude for "instructing young ladies."[20] Actually a much better position was in prospect.

The chair of history and general literature at Charlottesville which Holmes was finally to occupy had been sanctioned by the Virginia legislature in March 1856, and was established the following May by the Board of Visitors.[21] At that time the Board had also divided the chair of ancient languages and raised Greek to the dignity of a separate professorship. This gave Holmes two opportunities and greatly increased his chances of receiving a position. A friend from Mississippi days, Bledsoe, who was now on the faculty at Charlottesville, advised Holmes that he should apply for both chairs, perhaps thinking that the Visitors would be greatly impressed by such a confident display of erudition.[22]

The elections were to be held in the summer. Near the middle of June, Holmes, who had labored furiously for the previous month writing to all his friends, patrons, and associates asking for testimonials, laid down his pen in the knowledge that the decision was now out of his hands and declared himself "tranquil" regardless of the outcome. Of course, he was not, and as the election drew near, he became less so. Preparing for the inevitable failure, he resolved that if he did not succeed now he would give up academic life forever. But,

[20] W. G. Simms to G. F. Holmes, August 2, [1850], Simms, *Letters*, III, 55. Holmes to Massie, August 27, 1853. MS vol. 1791, February 20, March 7, 1856. D. F. Jamison to G. F. Holmes, February 27, 1856, Holmes papers, D. Basil Manly, Jr. to G. F. Holmes, September 9, 1856, G. F. Holmes to Basil Manly, Jr., September 15, 1856, Holmes papers, D. For the unsettled condition of South Carolina College at this time see Hollis, *University of South Carolina*, I, 194f.

[21] Philip Alexander Bruce, *History of the University of Virginia, 1819–1919* (New York: Macmillan and Company, 1921), III, 33; Board of Visitors Minutes, May 26, 1856, University of Virginia Library, Charlottesville, Virginia; hereinafter cited as BVM.

[22] A. T. Bledsoe to G. F. Holmes, May 13, 1856, Holmes papers, D.

as so often happened, the elections were postponed: the decision on the chair of Greek was to be made in September, that on the chair of history and general literature sometime the following year. When the September election took place (and notwithstanding the enthusiastic support of the *Charlottesville Advocate*) Holmes lost the Greek chair to Basil Gildersleeve, a native of Richmond. After the Civil War, Gildersleeve was to be appointed to the faculty of the new Johns Hopkins University and to become one of the nation's most distinguished classicists. Holmes's friends, however, had thought earlier that his chances for the other post were good and he was not discouraged. As he wrote to Thornwell, "there seems to be an entire unanimity amongst my friends and the public in designating me by preference for that position."[23]

Nonetheless, as election day drew near Holmes once more began to worry. His chances improved when his most serious rival, Professor Washington of Williamsburg, withdrew because of poor health. James C. Welling, the literary editor of the *National Intelligencer*, who was backed by an influential member of the Board of Visitors, was still in the race and could be held a definite threat. Some of the Visitors may have been disturbed by the debacle in Mississippi for they questioned Bledsoe closely before voting. Some, perhaps Welling's partisans, whispered against Holmes as a Swedenborgian and others (less confused) opposed him as a Roman Catholic, but such attacks proved futile. His undeniable qualifications and the "very wide . . . and very powerful" Floyd influence prevailed. When the Board of Visitors met in February Holmes was unanimously elected, his appointment to begin July 1, 1857. Former Governor Floyd sent his congratulations and hinted at his brother-in-law's obligation. "I had good reasons," he confided "to believe for some time past that it would take place; but" he added, "I felt so much solicitude about it that I could not help but entertain a feeling of doubt."[24] His doubts, fortunately, were groundless.

Holmes's joy was somewhat dampened when he discovered that his appointment was only for a year, "an old rule being revived for my benefit, requiring my confirmation at the expiration of the year." Having become quite touchy during his long neglect, he took excep-

[23] MS vol. 1791, June 18 and June 28, July 8, 1856. *Enquirer*, July 18, 1856. BVM, September 8, 1856. *Charlottesville Advocate* quoted in *Enquirer*, February 27, 1857. G. F. Holmes to James H. Thornwell, September 16, 1856, Palmer, *Thornwell*, p. 403.

[24] A. T. Bledsoe to G. F. Holmes, February 14, 1857, MS vol. 1808. MS vol. 1791, January 27, 1857. T. V. Moore to G. F. Holmes, May 14, 1856, MS vol. 1808. BVM, February 14, 1857. John B. Floyd to G. F. Holmes, February 18, 1857, MS vol. 1808.

tion to this special consideration, but since the ruling had actually been made the previous summer and not because of his election, he was easily mollified and accepted the appointment unconditionally. He was, however, somewhat puzzled by the nature of his new chair: "What," he wrote to Thornwell, "is General Literature?"[25]

The *Charlottesville Advocate* acknowledged itself well pleased by the Board's selection: "Mr. Holmes's varied and profound scholarship, his recognized ability as an essayist and historian, eminently qualify him as the first professor of the school of History and General Literature, upon whose genius . . . will rest the success or failure of the new course of studies."[26] The task to which Holmes had been elected was not an easy one, and in its performance he would need the qualities so generously credited to him by the *Advocate*.

The resolution of the Board of Visitors that established the chair also outlined the new professor's duties. He would be required to teach the "true objects and best methods of the Study of History; the general course of human affairs" emphasizing those developments having the most influence on the course of human history and tracing the effects of religion and law on human culture. He was to teach his students the principles of historical criticism and give them a knowledge of "the most authentic sources and best authorities" for the study of "the various branches of History, Ethnology, and the principles of Chronology." He was to show the influences of race and climate upon man, and discuss "whatever pertains to the history of the general progress of human civilization." As professor of general literature he was to teach "the history of the rise and progress of general literature," its stages of development, and the influence of the great writers in this process, with special attention to English literature.[27] When Holmes left the mountains for Charlottesville, then, he possessed a charge worthy of his talents.

The one agreeable thing about Holmes's forced retirement was that it had given him plenty of time for thinking and writing. During the Burke's Garden years he continued and expanded the function he had earlier assigned himself of awakening Americans to the intellectual opportunities and challenges that were crowding fast upon each other into the nineteenth century. Holmes never became a citizen of the United States, and though he aligned himself with the South he did not consider himself an American and actually took relatively

[25] MS vol. 1791, February 24, 1857. G. F. Holmes to R. T. W. Duke, March 14, 1857, MS vol. 1808. Holmes to Thornwell, March 7, 1857.

[26] Quoted in *Enquirer*, February 27, 1857.

[27] BVM, May 26, 1856. The resolution was printed in the *Enquirer*, June 3, 1856.

little interest in American books or American ideas.[28] Instead, he was a cosmopolitan interpreter, a conductor and filter for European ideas, one who carefully separated what he thought to be sound and profitable from what he considered dangerous. The contents of these categories differed as his own ideas changed. As we have seen, in the early 1840s he promoted the empirical study of society and warned against the delusions and fantasies of transcendental metaphysics. In the 1850s, on the other hand, the danger was the anti-metaphysical bias of positivism and the other forms of what he considered to be modern infidelity. Also, in the late 1840s, a new emphasis on social questions appeared in his writing. Socialism, various reform movements, abolitionism, laissez faire economics, all were analyzed and their combined threat to established society and to the necessary and desirable scientific reform of admitted abuses pointed out. But underlying this concern with growing social tensions was a continuing preoccupation with the developing intellectual crises of the modern world, with the "new instauration" that he had heralded at the start of his career. Whatever the question about which he wrote at any given time, his purpose always was the same: to reach "right-minded but unreflecting men"[29] and persuade them of the perils that lay in an uncritical acceptance of contemporary civilization.

In line with his mission Holmes's writing in the 1850s continued the broad scope of the previous decade's work. It ranged from the philosophies of Comte and Hamilton to contemporary reform movements, and from the arcana of political economy and the thought of Herbert Spencer to recent German poetry. Occasionally he allowed himself the pleasure of a classical essay such as "Cimon and Pericles" or "The Athenian Orators"—contributions which editor Simms of the *Southern Quarterly Review*, at least, preferred to all others from him;[30] but his pleasures came second. His primary purpose was to sound a warning, to be a guide for the unsophisticated reader, to encourage the more knowledgeable in the preservation of sound philosophy and true religion.

[28] For his not thinking of himself as an American, see G. F. Holmes to Samuel Tyler, August 25, 1854, MS vol. 1808. Aside from the books which he read for review, his reading lists for the 1850s show only a handful of American writers and those are poets and novelists: Longfellow, Hawthorne, Mrs. Stowe. There is no mention of Emerson or, oddly enough, even of his friend Simms. It is quite possible that not everything he read was entered on these lists but Holmes seems to have intended to place on them everything he thought to be of interest and value. See MS vols. 1792, 1802, 1803, 1832.

[29] [George Frederick Holmes], "Greeley on Reforms," *Southern Literary Messenger*, XVII (May 1851), 259.

[30] W. G. Simms to G. F. Holmes, April 25, [1851], Simms, *Letters*, III, 112.

Holmes wrote some sixty-six articles while rusticating in Tazewell County and was able to expand his outlets to include *De Bow's Review*, the *Quarterly Review of the Methodist Episcopal Church, South*, and the *Methodist Quarterly Review* (New York)[31] as well as continuing to publish in the old standbys the *Southern Quarterly Review* and the *Southern Literary Messenger*. Nonetheless, he found his efforts almost as financially unrewarding as they had been earlier. Occasionally he allowed himself a little optimism, but his multiplying needs (and, he feared, inflation) more than canceled out his rise in income which, itself, was not great.[32] As earlier, editors were seldom able to pay more than a dollar or two per printed page and even this was not always collectable. On one occasion he stopped work on a piece for the *Messenger* because of the editor's "inability to meet his engagements;" another time he wrote in his diary, "Received a letter from De Bow inclosing $15.00—it should have been $19—but I must content myself with what I can get;" and in 1857 the *Southern Quarterly Review* died owing him over three hundred dollars. All in all, over a seven year period Holmes received from the *Methodist Quarterly Review* the grand sum of $508.40. From 1855 to 1857 *De Bow's Review* paid him $165, and the *Quarterly Review of the Methodist Episcopal Church, South* paid $315.[33] When one remembers that these amounts represent a fairly large portion of his cash income and recalls the size of his family, Holmes's debts are not too surprising. From time to time his meager income was supplemented by public lectures, although he gave these more in hope of gaining publicity that would be helpful in obtaining a college position. A history of the governors of Virginia, which might have repaid him handsomely, was begun with hopes of considerable profit in 1853; but Holmes had little taste for archival research in "dull" Richmond and a very few months' labor converted the effort into a tedious chore which was quietly abandoned.[34]

Anything, then, that improved the prospects of a journal for which

[31] These last two journals should not be confused as they sometimes are. The former was informally known as the "Methodist Quarterly Review" and both were sometimes called simply the "Methodist Review." Here *Methodist Quarterly Review* will always mean the New York publication while the other will be given its full title.

[32] Holmes to Massie, August 27, 1853.

[33] MS vol. 1792. MS vol. 1791, May 13, 1856. Comment following a letter of J. H. Thornwell to Holmes, January 8, 1856, MS vol. 1808. MS vol 1781, passim, Holmes papers, D.

[34] G. F. Holmes to Nicketti Johnston, November 10, 1853, Johnston papers. Holmes to Massie, August 27, 1853. G. F. Holmes to W. G. Simms, October 1, 1853, Simms, *Letters*, III, 319n.

he wrote was good news. Accordingly, Holmes was greatly pleased when, in January 1856, he received a letter from Thornwell, who was at that time president of the Presbyterian theological seminary at Columbia, S. C., telling him that he was taking over the editorship of the faltering *Southern Quarterly Review* and asking Holmes to continue contributing to it. "Dr. Thornwell," Holmes wrote in his diary, "is one of the few real scholars in the South, one of the few competent to conduct a review creditably."[35] Unfortunately, a scholar was not what the *Review* needed; a business manager would have been more in order. Simms had been editor of the journal from 1849 until 1855 at a salary of $1,000 a year, but had quit in despair. Holmes himself had turned down an offer to relieve Simms in 1853.[36] When the thankless task devolved on Thornwell he undertook it with determination.

"If," Thornwell told Holmes, "the *Review* cannot be made a first-rate journal, we had better let it linger out and die." By the end of the year, it looked as if that was exactly what it was going to do. In addition to public apathy, Thornwell had been plagued by the usual corps of bad writers: "I have a drawer full of essays," he wrote to Holmes in June, "which the kindness of friends has sent to me, but which no blindness of friendship can induce me to accept." He had gone out of his way to avoid any hint of controversy or unpleasantness among the contributors (which was perhaps unfortunate for a little excitement might have helped circulation) and, while retaining the ban on advertising and failing to revamp the inefficient distribution system, had sought to save the *Review* by forming a company and soliciting contributions of one hundred dollars each from a hundred public spirited patrons.[37] But all to no avail.

Holmes watched the death of the *Review* with considerable sorrow. He did all he could to save it: "whatever my remote position in this retreat may permit," and thought it better for South Carolina to lose half of her cotton crop than the *Review*. But after a year as editor, Thornwell, like Simms before him, was threatening to quit.[38] The prognosis for the *Review* worsened as the last weeks passed. Praise, be it ever so warm, Thornwell sadly remarked, paid "neither printer, editor, nor contributors." Holmes grasped eagerly at the desperate idea of private subsidy, for the end of the *Review* was more to him

[35] Thornwell to Holmes, January 8, 1856. MS vol. 1791, January 22, 1856.

[36] D. F. Jamison to G. F. Holmes, March 26, 1853 and notation on envelope in Holmes's hand, vol. I, Holmes papers, LC.

[37] Thornwell to Holmes, January 8, June 17, 1856, February 28, 1857, Palmer, *Thornwell*, pp. 398, 408; July 30, 1856, MS vol. 1808.

[38] G. F. Holmes to J. H. Thornwell, December 1, 1856, Thornwell papers. Part of this letter is given in Palmer, *Thornwell*, p. 407. Holmes to Thornwell, January 17, 1857, *ibid.*, p. 408.

than the loss of income; the journal had great sentimental value as well. The *Review* had "exercised and promulgated my earliest specu-lations, it gave me my first reputation, it has been instrumental in securing my present appointment [i.e., at Charlottesville]."[39] But his protests were unable to prevent the *Review*'s failure. Its last number appeared in the spring of 1857. And Holmes had more reason than sentiment to mour its going: it owed him money.

As it turned out, the passing of the *Southern Quarterly Review* was not the "crushing disaster" that Holmes earlier had feared it would be.[40] By the time it was gone he had secured his appointment at the University of Virginia and had long since established another major channel as an outlet for his ideas. This was the *Methodist Quar-terly Review* of New York, one of the nation's best-known theological journals.

The magazine that in time became the *Methodist Quarterly Review* had been founded in 1818 by the General Conference of the Meth-odist Episcopal Church and had limped along under a series of undis-tinguished editors and a variety of purposes until 1848 when John McClintock, then professor of classics at Dickinson College in Penn-sylvania, assumed its editorship and determined to turn it into a quality theological magazine—though not without some protest from the brethren, both clerical and lay. McClintock established new depart-ments devoted to important current trends in both American and European theology and literature, greatly expanded the short book review section to cover more works, particularly the latest publica-tions of European scholars, and solicited the most able writers he could find in America to contribute articles on theology, philosophy, biblical criticism, philology, and social questions of especial interest. In spite of complaints that the magazine was not "popular," ("a *little* too much solid matter in [*sic*] for my readers," he wrote to one contributor)[41] he refused to compromise on quality and his successor, the Rev. Daniel D. Whedon, who replaced him in 1856, carried the journal to even greater heights.[42]

[39] Thornwell to Holmes, February 28, 1857. Holmes to Thornwell, March 7, 1857.
[40] MS vol. 1791, January 17, 1857.
[41] John McClintock to James O'Connell, October 18, 1854, McClintock papers. In 1855 McClintock defended his policies in an open letter to his fellow Metho-dists. To the charge that the *Review* had become too erudite, he replied that he intended it for erudite readers. He admitted that subscriptions had fallen off, but argued that this was the price exacted by quality. Vol. 33, *ibid.*
[42] George Richard Crooke, *Life and Letters of the Rev. John McClintock* (New York: Nelson and Phillips, 1876), pp. 197, 208–12, 254–44. Mott, *American Magazines*, pp. 299–301.

Holmes's relationship with the *Review* began in 1851 with the publication of "Philosophy and Faith," the initial statement of his solution to the problem of religious faith in his time and an introduction to his extensive criticism of Comte's Postive Philosophy which appeared in various numbers through 1854. In addition to his work on Comte, McClintock asked Holmes to write articles on other subjects, among them the philosophy of Hamilton.[43] He soon became one of the *Review's* most valuable contributors and this, in turn, was of no little assistance to the growth of his own reputation. In 1852 McClintock wrote to him

I feel honored in being made the medium of bringing your intelligent and thoughtful criticisms before the public. You may not perhaps be aware that our Review has twice as many subscribers as any other in America, and that it finds its way to most of the literary men of the country. What you publish with us then is diffused—as far as such writings need to be diffused.[44]

Holmes's relations with McClintock's successor were less placid. The peppery Whedon found it intolerable that a man of Holmes's parts should be a defender of slavery. And so, in due time, Holmes received a "very intemperate and coarse letter"[45] from his editor, a letter than began with four lines of ordinary business matter and then launched into a diatribe against the South that ran on for eleven pages. In the course of his indignant explosion Whedon blamed the aggressions of the "Slave Power" for the present national crisis, pronounced the South to be "without faith, honesty, or honor," stated that "No Southerner ought to feel that he can step into Europe without a stigma upon his honor as a gentleman," and called the governor of Virginia—Henry A. Wise—"Henry A. Fool" and a "madman & a fool" who was supported by "the race of Southern Fools." After threatening Holmes and the South generally with blood and destruction, Whedon pleaded with Holmes to use his gifts to bring the South to its senses, not to worsen matters by defending slavery. He closed with, "you may become my enemy because I tell you the truth. I am not yours." Contrary to his expectations, Holmes did not become his enemy. Indeed, after his initial indignation had passed, he shrugged off the attack. At any rate, by May Whedon had cooled off and was writing again, in a different vein if not with a change of heart. He was glad, he said, that Holmes had not taken his letter as a blanket indictment of all

[43] John McClintock to G. F. Holmes, December 17, 1851, Holmes papers, D. G. F. Holmes to J. H. Thornwell, August 8, 1856, Palmer, *Thornwell*, p. 400.

[44] John McClintock to G. F. Holmes, June 29, 1852, MS vol. 1808.

[45] MS vol. 1791, April 3, 1857.

southerners. "I abjure you as a Pro-slavery Man," he wrote, but, "I admire you as a man of genius, I am amazed at your erudition, I feel the genuine amiableness of your nature. I still desire you as a contributor."[46] The connection was too valuable to both parties to allow a difference of opinion over slavery to ruin it.

Even so, Holmes's appearances in the pages of the *Methodist Quarterly Review* ceased after 1858. The cause would seem to have been not disagreement over the slavery question, but rather his removal to the University of Virginia. Once he was in Charlottesville he had little leisure and, with one exception, published nothing more anywhere until 1866. After the Civil War, he attempted to renew his connection with the *Review* but failed. Why is not clear. He remained on good terms with both McClintock and Whedon,[47] producing forty-six articles for the former's religious encyclopedia,[48] but nothing by him ever again appeared in the *Methodist Quarterly Review*. Yet while it lasted the connection was one of his most valuable. It not only put his views before the intellectual community, but McClintock fostered his career in other ways. He saw New York publishers about issuing a book on Comte (which Holmes never got around to writing),[49] and, more importantly, it was through McClintock's efforts that Holmes came to the attention of Comte himself. He also assisted Holmes in making a brief contact with the British reviews.

Encouraged by both McClintock and Ed, Holmes made several attempts to publish in England. His reasons were practical enough: the British reviews paid more than the American, they had much more prestige both in England and in America, and Holmes, like Maryanne, felt that England was his proper sphere. If his work proved popular there he might even be able to return home. His first try was made in 1852 shortly before Ed's arrival but was ill-starred from the beginning. He approached the editors of the *Westminster Review* hoping that they would publish a piece on Comte, but McClintock sent Holmes's letter of application to John Stuart Mill in the mistaken idea that he was the editor. Mill passed the letter on to the *Review* and promised to forward the specimen article when he received it, but for some reason did not.[50] Consequently the editors were not able

46 Whedon to Holmes, March 25, 1857; May 19, 1857, MS vol. 1808.

47 G. F. Holmes to John McClintock, November 17, 1865, January 19, 1866, McClintock papers.

48 John McClintock and James Strong, eds., *Cyclopaedia of Biblical, Theological, and Ecclesiastical Literature*, 12 vols. (New York: Harper and Brothers, 1868–1891).

49 G. F. Holmes to John McClintock, February 18, 1854, MS vol. 1808.

50 *Ibid.*, June 21, 1852, McClintock papers. John Stuart Mill to G. F. Holmes, April 29, 1852; G. F. Holmes to John Stuart Mill, June 21, 1852, MS vol. 1808.

to see a sample of Holmes's work. Not that it mattered, for the editors' reply was a curt letter informing Holmes that it was their policy not to receive unsolicited contributions from America "as it must frequently have no other issue than disappointment to the writer and loss of time to ourselves." But Holmes was too anxious to be put off by rudeness. He replied that he interpreted their refusal as discouraging rather than prohibitive and would send them any articles he might write that he thought worthy of their pages. If he did, no record of it survives; nor did a second set of articles on Comte dispatched by McClintock make a better impression.[51] The *Westminster Review* simply was not interested.

The *North British Review* was more receptive, possibly because by 1854 interest in Positivism was beginning noticeably to stir in England.[52] At any rate, in 1854 "Auguste Comte and Positivism" appeared in that journal and Holmes received twenty-five pounds even though there was some question about the freshness of the piece—the editor of the *North British Review* was perhaps familiar with the London edition of McClintock's *Review*. Holmes, who had never before received so much for an article, leaped at this new opportunity. He immediately requested permission to review a new edition of Francis Bacon's works and projected some eighteen articles which he thought suitable for English readers. He confessed to the editor, Alexander Campbell Fraser, that his main desire in seeking a connection with the British reviews arose from the hope that it might allow him to return to England: "Poverty rendered me an exile—and still delays my return."[53] But no more was heard from Great Britain. In 1856 Holmes sent Fraser a puzzling and eccentric piece on Hume's philosophy. It was rejected and its author was advised that the *North British Review* would not be able to accept anymore of his contributions.[54] That was the end of Holmes's efforts to break into his "proper" sphere.

Holmes's inability to gain a place in the English reviews was not indicative of the reception given his work in the United States. In addition to the enthusiasm with which McClintock and Whedon responded to his writing, his articles on Comte brought him new correspondents and helped to increase the sale of the French philos-

[51] Editors, *Westminster Review* to G. F. Holmes, May 26, 1852; G. F. Holmes to Editors, June 21, 1852, MS vol. 1808. Holmes to McClintock, June 21, 1852.

[52] See Simon, *European Positivism*, Chapters VII and VIII. Harriet Martineau's English translation of Comte's *Cours de philosophie positive* appeared in 1853.

[53] G. F. Holmes to Alexander Campbell Fraser, July 29, 1854, MS vol. 1808. MS vol. 1802, pp. 393-94.

[54] MS vol. 1791, February 5 and August 28, 1856.

opher's works in America. His pieces on the Scottish philosophy were studied in several colleges.[55] He insisted on writing anonymously when editorial policy allowed it and this doubtlessly served to retard the spread of his reputation; even so, a surprising number of readers managed to find out who he was and wrote to him. But these minor plaudits for relatively minor accomplishments must have grated him as much as they gratified. One suspects that his own verdict on his erratic career was similar to his mother's. She warned Ed against the promise of success in America that like a "Willey the Wisp [*sic*]" and an "Ignus fatuous [*sic*]" had lured George on from year to year; his writings were "a waste of his abilities" for they brought him no "reputation and fortune" and never would except in England. She acknowledged that his work was "far above my capacity," but nevertheless made clear that his critique of Comte was only too typical of his efforts:

a complete waste of words and learning; sifting the subject to prove a mad atheistical visionary was wrong in his theory, when it did not need two lines of common sense to do it! and he wrote a treatise sufficient to bother anybody, which one could hardly understand what he was driving at; such criticisms may do to show learning, but they do no moral good to the world, and will never pay. I wish he would turn his education and abilities to some better use.[56]

That his talents would never pay (in Maryanne's sense) Holmes could not deny, but they could reward him in other ways if he were only allowed the time and the resources to present to the world what he knew was in him. Much of his unhappiness in the 1850s was caused by his continued frustration as a scholar and this in turn played no small role in promoting his intellectual and religious revulsion against his age.

In the 1840s Holmes had intended eventually to write a history of civilization that would relate the main events of universal history to the laws that governed their development; it would be, in his words, "the only complete and valid philosophy of history."[57] After laying

[55] J. H. Thornwell to G. F. Holmes, July 7, 1857, Palmer, *Thornwell*, p. 410. Whedon to Holmes, May 19, 1857. John Lord to C. Collins, April 12, 1857, Holmes papers, D. G. F. Holmes to Auguste Comte, September 21, 1853, Richard Laurin Hawkins, *Auguste Comte and the United States, 1816–1853* (Cambridge: Harvard University Press, 1936), pp. 135–36.

[56] Maryanne Holmes to Edward A. Holmes, June 3 and November 13, 1852; March 9, 1853. Maryanne Holmes to Edward A. Holmes, October 18, 1859, Buchanan, *Holmes Family History*, p. 61.

[57] The following summary of Holmes's reflections on his career is based on passages in MS vol. 1802, passim. The passage quoted throughout is dated March

down a few basic principles and applications in his work of 1842–1847, he began his studies in earnest in February of 1848, only to have them "arrested" when they had hardly begun by his encounter with Comte. Before he had time to absorb fully and to evaluate Comte's achievement, various "misfortunes and difficulties" intervened and prevented the resumption of his own project. The ensuing "years of fruitless hope and disappointed toil" compelled him to drop his original ambitions, "or at any rate so far to dwarf and modify them as almost to change their character." He then restricted himself to the study of the Middle Ages which he thought to be "the most neglected and the least known portion of history." Naturally, this unrealistic goal was also frustrated by his isolated situation which, even in the sunniest of times, would have prevented the amassing of the necessary materials for an enterprise of that scope. By 1853 he again narrowed his interests, this time to the smaller theatre of northern Italy during the medieval period. "This limited task," he ventured, "I may perhaps be able to accomplish."

Holmes knew that he was tempting the gods with even this humble scheme: "I have so deeply, so keenly, so frequently experienced the frustrations of all my intellectual hopes." Much depended on his mental tranquility, health, leisure and money, and these were so uncertain. "The map of the whole subject lies clearly traced in my brain," he wrote impatiently and with a metaphor that symbolized his desperation:

If by any machinery divine or human, the implicit consequences of unrecognized principles, the symmetrical evolution of vital germs, could be impressed upon paper, or if, like Minerva starting full-armed from the head of Jove, the embryo of thought could spring into material being in its contemplated maturity; then all that is essential . . . might at once be exhibited by subjecting my brain and its present contents to the pressure of the printing press. But it is far otherwise;—and the future lies dim, obscure, and shrouded with clouds before me. Will life pass away from me without vouchsafing one glimpse of its sunshine?

His frequent disappointments not only eroded his optimism but also took their toll of his self-confidence. His notebooks show that he needed the continuous ego reenforcement gained from the practice of copying down passages from the works of famous people—Comte, Niebuhr, Hamilton—in which they agreed with his own opinions, and pointing out that he had thought or expressed such ideas before he read their work.[58] His unhappiness, however, did not completely

18, 1853, *ibid.*, pp. 299–302. For the neglect of medieval history in America see Callcott, *History in the United States*, p. 95.

58 MS vol. 1802, passim.

destroy his ambitions. Even while he was sorrowfully restricting his intellectual designs, he was still anxious to

lay down the conditions and phenomena of human association, reduce them to their normal laws, discover the dependence of man and society upon a Supreme power, reconcile the pretensions of reason with the demands of religious faith; and show how religion is the vital breath of human organization; and the essential corrective of human speculation.[59]

These grandiose plans had seen little realization in 1857 when Holmes left the mountains for Charlottesville and what he hoped was a greater opportunity. "Four years of want, penury, struggle, almost of contempt and despair" had intervened;[60] but, even so, they had not been idle years. Holmes had used conscientiously what time and resources he had. The field was plowed and sown. He now hoped for a bountiful harvest. Unfortunately, the dashed hopes of these years were not easily to be shrugged off. His thwarted ambition, the self-deception that ran through his unrealistic projects and the lack of self-acceptance as an essayist and reviewer which they reflected, had marked him. The pessimism that they inspired became a permanent part of his character as well as a powerful formative and sustaining element in his philosophy.

This growing pessimism is nowhere more apparent than in his religious life which flourished in response to his failures. He began to show a new interest in a life of piety and faith as well as in the traditional dogmas of Christianity. Holmes did not believe the ascetic doctrine that worldly knowledge is mere vanity and the fame that sometimes accompanies it a delusion; his goal was a careful balance between piety and learning, even though he admitted that if the choice had to be made, a life of simple though ignorant faith was preferable to one infected with the skepticism of the nineteenth century.[61] In pursuing an ideal of Christian scholarship he combined his religious reaction and his new interest in traditional philosophy into a single intellectual and spiritual defiance of the increasing secularization of life.

Holmes laid no claim to being a philosopher, but thought of himself as a student of history and the science of society. In the course of a long philosophical correspondence with Samuel Tyler, a Baconian philosopher and legal scholar, he remarked that his work in philosophy had been forced upon him by a conviction that the religious, social, political, and intellectual errors of their time had originated in "un-

---

[59] *Ibid.*, pp. 301–02.
[60] *Ibid.*, postscript dated February 20, 1857, p. 302.
[61] *Ibid.*, p. 211.

sound philosophy and inadequate logic."[62] He freely admitted that there was much of value in modern thought. Overcoming his theological conservatism, he broadmindedly praised Strauss's *Das Leben Jesu* as "fully and profoundly" developing the function of myth in religion[63] and was second to few in his admiration of Comte. Nonetheless, he found too much in contemporary thought that was sheer fancy. As he wrote to McClintock, "In the present age it is indeed difficult to steer safely through the intricate variety of specious theories, all involving a small modicum of novel truth, but burying it below an endless mass of error and crude fantasy." Each of the modern heresies, he thought, had its own peculiar dangerous appeal. "Sirens are all around us," he warned. "I am endeavouring to perform the arduous experiment of Ulysses: to see, to hear, to estimate, without suffering myself to be allured within the influence of the vortex."[64]

But for all his recognition of the merit of contemporary philosophy and scholarship Holmes's main goal remained the same: the defense of traditional Christianity. Even more than he admired the acute heretics themselves, he admired attacks upon them, such as Thornwell's essay on miracles which appeared in the *Southern Quarterly Review* in 1856 and was intended to oppose "the prevailing tone of speculation imported from Germany on that whole subject." It became evident to him that contemporary minds needed a guide who was free of the errors so common in the intellectual world of the nineteenth century. Holmes had decided that that guide was Aristotle. "The more I study Aristotle," he wrote to Thornwell, "the less necessity do I discover for any other philosophy than modernized and Christianized Peripateticism. Aristotle is still, as in the thirteenth century, '*il maestro di che chi sanno.*' "[65]

Holmes's enthusiasm for Aristotelian philosophy was paralled by a strong leaning toward Roman Catholicism. This striking reversal of his earlier attitude is not too surprising when one considers the factors combining to bring it about. There was, of course, the constant example of his Catholic family and friends; add to this his growing sympathy for traditional Christianity, his increased social conservatism and pessimism, and the inclination toward the Peripatetic school already mentioned (a persuasion shared with Thomists), and it is not extraordinary that he found Catholicism a congenial faith. What is

---

62 Holmes to Tyler, August 25, 1854.

63 MS vol. 1802, p. 4. MS vol. 1792.

64 G. F. Holmes to John McClintock, April 8, 1852, McClintock papers.

65 Thornwell to Holmes, July 30, 1856. G. F. Holmes to J. H. Thornwell, August 25, 1856, Palmer, *Thornwell*, pp. 399–401. Holmes to Thornwell, September 16, 1856.

remarkable is that he did not become a Catholic when he became a more convinced Christian.

There can be no doubt about the intensity of Holmes's reaction against the religious "infidelity" of his youth. A work schedule for 1851 had him studying a chapter of the Bible first thing everyday; on Sunday he read in the Greek testament, studied ten chapters of the English Bible, and the Hebrew language, all of which was topped off by three hours of metaphysics. He began to experience flights of mysticism: premonitions and "prophetic instincts" that were sometimes strangely realized. In 1855 he began the regular practice of "diligent and beseeching prayer, and anxious meditation upon life, death, the grave, and immortality." In addition to other causes, this new spiritual life was in no little degree a response to the "dull, aimless, desponding agony" of his life following the death of his son Floyd in 1848. It was this tragedy that removed "some of the greatest difficulties of Christianity" from his mind and apparently set in serious motion his spiritual pilgrimage. By the early 1850s his notebooks reveal an attitude increasingly critical of Protestant doctrine. This tendency was re-enforced by a preference for Catholic authors. His reading lists from 1853 on reflected a growing interest in Catholic thought with the religious readings for 1856 and 1857 given over entirely to Catholic writers.[66]

Even before his religious opinions began to turn toward Catholicism Holmes had had some second thoughts about his pet subject, the philosophy of history, which, when developed, pushed him toward Rome. As his confidence in inevitable progress was shaken he became open to a more pessimistic interpretation of the past. In commenting in a notebook on his earlier review of Schlegel's philosophy of history, he wrote "In this article . . . I have not done justice to Schlegel, and have overpraised Michelet. Were it now to be written over again both the censure and the praise would be very much modified. I have most unpardonably neglected to take any notice of the Catholic view of history which Schlegel develops throughout his work."[67] Holmes did not abandon his belief in historical law but he grew much less confident about the destiny of the race. The age-old Christian view of history as a grim and sin-filled tale dominated by corrupt human nature became a tacit assumption of his thoughts. He also came to share the romantic Catholic vision of the medieval period as a golden age and immersed himself in the works of Chateaubriand, Joseph de

---

[66] MS vol. 1792. MS vol. 1802, p. 211. MS vol. 1791, August 21, 1857; April 18, 1862; March 9, 1864. For his criticism of Protestantism, see MS vol. 1792 and MS vol. 1803, p. 19. For his reading lists, see MS vols. 1792, 1802 and 1803, passim.

[67] MS vol. 1843, p. 207.

Maistre, and Frederic Ozanam, all of whom were proponents of the post-Napoleonic Catholic reaction in France. Holmes found the writings of Ozanam and Lacordaire particularly powerful attractions to Catholicism.[68]

But it was in the Thomistic philosophy of the Catholic Church that Holmes felt the strongest allurement toward Rome. He first showed an interest in the philosophy of Thomas Aquinas in 1853, but a serious study of it did not begin until the following year when the family priest from Wythville brought him the first two volumes of the *Summa Theologica*. "From a hasty glance over some of the chapters," Holmes noted, "I find my opinions on many important and disputed topics of theology fully confirmed and admirably illustrated by him."[69] When he began to read in earnest, he did not always like what he found, for Aquinas' thought was sometimes bewildering, inadequate, or illogical.[70] But by 1856, all faults aside, the saint's victory was complete. Holmes declared that the *Summa* was "an amazing work—amazing in this age by its perspicuity, its cogency, its depth, its acumen, its logical precision. I must master it thoroughly," he resolved, "as the groundwork of my future studies."[71] But however great his interest, neither Aquinas nor anyone else was able to convert him to the Catholic faith. His religious opinions remained unsettled, and he remained a proselyte at the gate until in later years his interest lessened. In reality, his flirtation with Catholicism was only a symptom of the profound reorientation in his intellectual and religious life that occurred during these years.

In some ways his essay on Hume's philosophy, with which Holmes risked and lost his connection with the *North British Review*, best illustrates this religious reorientation.[72] Nowhere in his writings, not even in the long series on Positivism, can one find a stronger rejection of skepticism; nowhere is there a more emphatic repudiation of the spirit of his youthful philosophy, or a more determined demonstration of his "will-to-believe." As did so many of his evangelical contemporaries, Holmes attacked Hume as the father of lies and as the source of the philosophical errors and infidelity of the modern world. "Is not,"

[68] MS vol. 1791, August 15, 1856.

[69] MS vol. 1803, p. 47.

[70] MS vol. 1802, p. 387. MS vol, 1791, August 24, 1856.

[71] MS vol. 1791, October 7, 1856.

[72] Though written in 1856 the article was slightly revised and published in 1872, [George Frederick Holmes], "Hume's Philosophy," *Southern Review*, XI (July and October 1872), 92–120, 309–36. For the date of composition, see MS vol. 1793, May 8, 1872, Holmes papers, D.

he asked, " 'the trail of the serpent'—the slime of Hume's slippery cavilling—over all subsequent speculations?"[73] For Holmes Hume stood at the head of modern metaphysics both logically and chronologically. The sound metaphysics that he knew the modern world needed could only follow the destruction of Hume and his diseased descendants.[74]

To Holmes, Hume was a flagrant sophist and he found it somewhat difficult to account for his impact on subsequent thought. "We do not participate," he wrote, "in the common estimate of either his perspicacity or his logical precision, but think that he usually bewilders himself and his readers by the confident employment of loose and undefined assumptions, by verbal fallacies, and by sophistries." And more than being illogical, he was insincere. Hume's one guiding purpose through his entire philosophy was to "overthrow Revelation." He sought to subvert "faith, reverence, and the sense of moral responsibility." But what could Hume offer in the place of these things, Holmes asked, what moral standards, what hope? Nothing, he answered, but "A void—an aching void." Holmes could tolerate and forgive honest error, but "what toleration can be granted to that Mephistophilean temper, which unsettles belief for no purpose, and destroys conviction to leave nothing but dismay and bewilderment behind?"[75] He would allow Comte his madness to excuse his errors, but aside from sheer malignancy, Hume had no justification whatever for seeking to destroy the Christian paradigm that provided men with their only reliable meaning for life. Clearly, Hume, more than any other modern writer, provoked a shattering existential terror in Holmes.

The essay itself is a curious thing. In places it would appear to have been written by a man who had never read a line of Hume. Its subject was the Hume of orthodox legend, the arch-infidel who reduced the world to an irrational chaos by denying the reality of cause and effect and who sought to destroy religion by demonstrating the physical impossibility of miracles. Yet Holmes's reading lists and notebooks show that he did read Hume,[76] so one can only conclude that his religious reaction had so biased his mind that he either could not see what was before his eyes or was afraid to read too closely. In his review the legendary Hume was subtly substituted for the real philos-

---

[73] [Holmes], "Hume's Philosophy," p. 96.

[74] *Ibid.*, pp., 92–93.

[75] *Ibid.*, pp. 97–98, 320, 334.

[76] Four volumes of Hume's essays were read as recently as 1855. See MS vol. 1802, p. 411.

opher and his essay suffered accordingly. No doubt this was the reason for its rejection by the editor of the *North British Review* and for his decision not to continue his relationship with Holmes.

The article abounds in misstatements of Hume's meaning. In his essay on miracles, Hume did not write to demonstrate the impossibility of what are called miraculous events but rather to examine the credibility of varieties of testimony to the miraculous. And yet Holmes, while attempting to deal with the issue of credibility, went to great lengths to refute his adversary on the possibility of miracles.[77] Elsewhere he repeatedly charged Hume with denying the occurrence of cause and effect when Hume's only concern was to inquire into the psychological origin of the idea and to examine whether it could be demonstrated by a priori reasoning.[78] His condensed versions of Hume's positions were without exception far from their true meaning, and on occasion he had the impertinence to refute Hume with Hume's own conclusions.[79] Nor could Holmes keep his own arguments any straighter. In one place he magnified the importance of the essay on miracles by asserting that it was consecrated to Hume's central purpose of "overthrowing revelation," on the next page he denigrated the piece as an "after thought."[80] On one page he insisted that the truth of religion was independent of miracles, on another, that the authority of revelation rests on miracles.[81] But why go on? The essay on Hume—from which Holmes expected so much—is without a doubt among his most unsatisfactory pieces, but that he took it so seriously amply demonstrates its importance as an indication of the domination of orthodox Christianity over his mind. The essay on Hume also points up a danger implicit in that dominance, the danger of an obscurantism growing out of religious fervor. Holmes here approached it, but fortunately he never fell totally under the influence of that prevalent form of opposition to nineteenth-century skepticism. That this did not happen was primarily because of the ambivalent nature of his own religious response.

The intensity of Holmes's religious reaction was mitigated by his loyalty to the life of the mind—a loyalty as great as his belief in the Christian religion. It is true that during the fifties his personal faith deepened. He ceased his youthful questioning, his rationalistic search for weaknesses in Christianity, and turned, instead, to a vigorous

77 [Holmes], "Hume's Philosophy," pp. 320–34.
78 *Ibid.*, pp. 104, 113, 114. Compare with his earlier view in "Inductive Sciences," p. 226.
79 For instance, [Holmes], "Hume's Philosophy," pp. 333, 334.
80 *Ibid.*, pp. 320, 321.
81 *Ibid.*, pp. 332, 333.

assault on all enemies of the faith. But this counterattack was not carried out in the mindless way that so often disgraced the church of his time. Holmes wanted no pious anti-intellectualism, but a true philosophical accommodation of Christianity and the new science, criticism, and philosophy, an accommodation that would defend the traditional faith from skepticism and. at the same time, promote the increase of secular learning. It was to this difficult problem that he had turned his attention just prior to his going to Oxford and it continued to occupy him during the years of his rustication.

IV   The Philosophy of Faith

T HOSE who had gathered at Oxford, Mississippi, in the fall of 1848 to open the new state university almost certainly had not expected to hear that their future security depended on the discovery of a true metaphysics. That was, however, the message that the young president had for them. Holmes's study of Positivism during the summer just passed had led him to the conclusion that the basic intellectual dilemma facing Western society was the problem of the validity of human knowledge and the extent of the powers of human reason. It was this that lay at the heart of the growing conflict between science and religion. Holmes had become convinced that the difficulties surrounding the problem of knowledge were an integral part of the neglected and abused discipline of metaphysics, and this conclusion was instrumental in his own revaluation of the importance of metaphysics and assured it the place he now gave it as the foundation of both science and philosophy.

In his Oxford address Holmes had been concerned to leave no doubt in the minds of his audience about the significance of metaphysics or the risk involved in continued indifference to it. The self-confident progress of the age, of which the new university itself could be taken as both consequence and symbol, he called an illusion. Closer inspection would reveal that the times were "sorely diseased," that a revolutionary spirit was raging in the civilized world, that all society was infected by it. Nor was the danger solely a foreign problem as provincial southrons might be tempted to imagine. "In the Northern States of the Confederacy" he warned, Americans already were experiencing in their midst "Socialism, Mormonism, Fanny Wrightism, and [were] rapidly naturalising St. Simonism, Fourierism, and the other diversified forms of Agrarianism." Meanwhile, he explained further, moral philosophy (in America, at least), which should guide public policy and head off these movements by resolving the dislocations that produced them, was corrupted by the reigning maxims of a "beggarly Benthamism, which is the meanest form of Utilitarianism—itself always mean." Political economy, which was to many of his contemporaries the quintessence of modern wisdom, had failed to solve the problems created by a rapidly developing capitalism and had produced nothing but rival and contending schools. Science, instead of providing man with a unitary vision of the creation, had degenerated into little more than a petty concern with practical technology and monetary profit. All of these various ills, which to the superficial might seem unrelated, were at bottom intellectual problems and were all rooted in false philosophy. "If we would discover a remedy for these evils . . . ," he claimed, "we must detect the intellectual aberration from which they have sprung—and that aberration must be found in the domain and by the aid of metaphysical science." Unfortunately, most contemporary thinking along this line was of little help:

the idealism of the transcendentalists, the materialism of the positive school; the eclecticism of Cousin, the mysticism of the Germans, and the empiricism of the Scotch. —Which of these is right?—or are they all wrong. As yet they have been prolific of little but wranglings and disputes—the foundations of our knowledge remain as indistinct and obscure as they were in the Brahminic age of the Sankhya and Nyaya philosophies.

No, the only way in which catastrophe could be avoided was a complete reconstruction of metaphysics and, hand in hand with that, a revival of the study of logic which Holmes thought lay prostrate after four centuries of neglect.[1]

In 1850, writing in the *Southern Literary Messenger*, Holmes enlarged on his Oxford critique. A neglect of logic was not the only shortcoming of contemporary philosophy. He detected in the work of virtually all modern thinkers a "lamentable, but almost universal inclination, to speak of the Philosophy of the Nineteenth Century as something novel and peculiarly excellent." Such "vulgar adulation and self-idolatry" he saw as symptomatic of the age's complete confidence in the powers of the human intellect. It should surprise no one that the end result was widespread infidelity. Among the philosophers of his homeland Holmes found striking illustrations of this zealous overconfidence. Their supercilious scorn for the metaphysical and logical studies of medieval philosophy helped to conceal from them the true nature of the modern problem. Bacon had rightly saved natural science from the misuse of the deductive method by the Schoolmen but his British disciples had since gone too far and had developed a "contemptuous disregard" for their sounder logical achievements as well. The time was coming, Holmes prophesied, when such cavalier ignorance would not be found among serious scholars. Even learned opinion now was beginning to seek in the philosophy of the Middle Ages guidance to lead it through the "universal anarchy of the times."

[1] Holmes, *Inaugural Address*, pp. 19–21.

To this end he conceded that even German metaphysics might have its uses.[2]

The popularity of Cousin's Eclecticism revealed to Holmes even more clearly the bankrupt condition of modern thought. Any age, he wrote, that turned to eclecticism in philosophy was only revealing its own inner despair of further philosophical progress; syncretism was a tacit abandonment of original thinking. Cousin's special brand, borrowing as it did from other modern philosophies, was no more than "a diligent brooding upon addled eggs in the hope of a living progeny." Yet, despite his censures, Holmes acknowledged that Cousin and his followers were engaged in a commendable battle against skeptics such as Comte and Strauss, fighting a holding action until a better philosophy could appear "to expose the fallacies of those arch-infidels, and wrest the victory from their grasp." Equally important in his view was the Eclectics' dedication to the historical study of philosophy which at least kept men aware that more creative minds than theirs had once existed. But the history of philosophy, he warned an historically minded age, was not a substitute for philosophy itself.[3]

Holmes's disappointment with contemporary philosophy was softened somewhat by his belief that there were signs of an approaching eclipse of Eclecticism and other modern systems by a philosophy "more generous, more elevating, and more rational" than any yet produced in the nineteenth century.[4] He was under no delusion that he was the one to found the new system of thought, but he was more than willing to oppose the ideas that prevented its realization. To this end he wrote in 1849 and published two years later a short inquiry into the principles of human knowledge.[5] Holmes claimed no great originality for his effort—and, in fact, it possessed very little. It was written primarily to put before the Christian community the precise nature of the challenge that it faced. "Philosophy and Faith," as he entitled his essay, was the prologue to his extensive critique of Comte's Positive Philosophy and formed the philosophical base of that critique.

Holmes admitted that there had always existed a certain amount of tension between science and philosophy on the one hand and religious

---

[2] [Holmes], "Morell's Philosophy," pp. 385–387, 393.

[3] *Ibid.*, pp. 388–89.

[4] *Ibid.*, p. 385.

[5] George Frederick Holmes, "Philosophy and Faith," *Methodist Quarterly Review*, III (April 1851), 185–218. The presence of citations of the English version of Strauss's *Life of Jesus* (p. 208n) indicates that the article was modified in or after 1850 when Holmes first read the book. For the date of initial composition see G. F. Holmes to Auguste Comte, October 26, 1852, MS vol. 1808.

faith on the other. But even in the "infidel age" not too long passed it had been possible for such a thoroughgoing skeptic as Pierre Bayle to anticipate their eventual reconciliation. He was not at all sure that in the nineteenth century this expectation was any longer plausible. The rupture had grown so wide that many intellectuals were openly questioning the very reasonableness of Bayle's hope. On one side there was Comte openly declaring science and theology to be irreconcilable; on the other, one found Strauss and the Hegelians trying to save Christianity by philosophical reinterpretation but in such a way that necessarily destroyed the dogmatic and historical foundations of the faith and conceded virtually every contested point of doctrine to modern skepticism. Equally alarming was the fact that in previous generations the controversy had been confined almost entirely to the educated classes, but now the common people were beginning to become aware of the discrepancy between modern knowledge and their traditional faith. For the first time since the founding of Christianity it seemed that the Western world was on the verge of a genuine and complete apostasy. The present duty of Christians was clear to Holmes. Everyone "who is unwilling to renounce his Christian convictions . . . must strain every nerve" to achieve the very reconciliation that Comte deemed impossible. If this could not be done, then the task was to find the errors in modern thought (which Holmes always assumed to be at fault) that prevented reconciliation.[6]

Holmes had no doubt that the conflict could be traced to a mistaken conception of knowledge. What Comte had made explicit in the uncompromising empiricism of the Positive Philosophy was implicit in the thought of many moderns: that human knowledge in all its aspects must be based entirely on perceptions of the phenomenal world, that a science resting on a reasoned appeal to evidence and a theology based on revelation and faith cannot both be epistemologically valid. Obviously, Holmes concluded, part of the blame for this widespread doubt about religious knowledge should be put at the door of contemporary science and philosophy, but not all. Much of the trouble had resulted from a "narrow-minded theology which generates an hostility between science and religion, by utterly denying the independent validity of scientific reasoning." Holmes interpreted Comte's position as being, to an extent, a reaction against this Christian obscurantism.[7] But in saying this he was not advocating a modernizing of Christian dogma; he wanted no "fantastic" remodeling of "the

---

[6] Holmes, "Philosophy and Faith," pp. 186–87.
[7] [George Frederick Holmes], "Faith and Science—Comte's Positive Philosophy," *Methodist Quarterly Review*, IV (January 1852), 33.

doctrines or prescriptions of Christianity."[8] Instead, he was proposing that a new and more valid theory of knowledge should be large enough to accommodate the ways of knowing of both science and religion.

Any true reconciliation of science and faith, then, had to be preceded by an inquiry into the question of human knowledge.[9] And this, in turn, would involve a reappraisal of the discipline of metaphysics—the *prima philosophia* of Bacon, the science of method and the basic principles of knowledge—that had attracted Holmes as early as 1843. Then as now, almost a decade later, the certainty of human knowledge was the "ultimate problem of metaphysics."[10] Holmes retained his old skepticism about the utility of such extravagant metaphysical systems as the Germans were so adept at producing; nevertheless, he was sure that a logically valid method of investigating metaphysical questions would be of determining value in the present crisis.[11]

In Holmes's judgment almost all contemporary philosophers were guilty of the same error, though in varying forms. They either refused to recognize the limitations of thought and confidently included what was really unknowable in their systems, or they excluded the unknowable as nonexistent because unknowable. The root of their failure he found in a tacit acceptance of "the old sophism of Protagoras—the assumption that the human mind is the measure of the universe, and not merely the measure of that fragmentary knowledge of the universe of which it is capable." These imperfect systems, which were the unavoidable result of such an oversimplification of reality, had "paved the way" for modern secularism: they had poisoned "the whole organism of society and . . . produced a daily-spreading belief that religion must be rejected as inconsistent with science" and had "fearfully sapped all the foundations of faith." The damage could only be undone by reformed philosophy and a truer metaphysics: "We must fight fire with fire."[12]

But if contemporary philosophers were too confused to be reliable, where should one turn? To Aristotle, of course, who had originated the basic quest for philosophical method that came to be called metaphysics, and was still the best guide to it. But Holmes was not suggesting that Aristotle be elevated by the modern world to the exalted position he had occupied during the Middle Ages. No, Aristotle's

8 [George Frederick Holmes], "Instauratio Nova-Auguste Comte," *Methodist Quarterly Review*, (July 1852), 340.
9 Holmes, "Philosophy and Faith," p. 187.
10 *Ibid.*, p. 188. For Holmes's earlier interest see MS vol. 1792, p. 22.
11 Holmes, "Philosophy and Faith," pp. 216–17.
12 *Ibid.*, pp. 204, 215–16.

usefulness lay primarily in the example of his restraint in making claims for the scope of human understanding, in his careful avoidance of Teutonic-like system-building, in his emphasis on methodology. While his doctrines in their totality could not be embraced by a modern philosopher, it was inescapable that if the modern world "would retain its belief in Christianity and the sanctity of religion, [it must] plant itself on similar ground."[13]

Among later thinkers Holmes put most reliance on the work of Bacon and Kant. Indeed, he believed that a careful examination of Aristotle's metaphysics would show it to have been the prototype of what was sound in these more recent philosophers.[14] Holmes's admiration of Bacon, of course, was as old as his interest in philosophy, but his appreciation of the importance of Kant was more recent. Not until Holmes had become concerned with the same problems that had brought forth the *Critique of Pure Reason* could he learn from it or from Kant's other writings, but once he had undertaken a study of the foundations of human knowledge a sympathetic reading of Kant was a foregone conclusion. Although he rejected much of the Critical Philosophy as typical Germanic moonshine, Holmes accepted the *Critique of Pure Reason* as "imperatively the *primer*" for all future speculation dealing with "imperfections and limitations of the human reason, and their causes." In fact, his final article on Comte implied that Kant was virtually the last sound philosopher to write on these questions.[15]

The uncertainty of human knowledge had been a basic problem for as long as men had been interested in philosophy. When Holmes took it up he found it as obscure as ever. Although he drew some encouragement from the work of Kant, he had no idea that anyone could solve the dilemma in any final sense. In "Philosophy and Faith" he was satisfied with an argument (derived largely from Scottish realism and Kant) which demonstrated the limitations of the human mind and suggested a realm of experience in which the intellect could not operate. The data upon which the mind worked he saw as received through the senses from the external world or from a consciousness of psychological changes within. These data were analyzed, classified, and organized by the mind according to the constitution of the mind. It followed that all of human knowledge of the phenomenal world—both internal and external—was relative to the conditions

---

[13] *Ibid.*, pp. 190–91.
[14] *Ibid.*, p. 190.
[15] [Holmes], "Instauratio Nova," p. 338n. Italics in original. [George Frederick Holmes], "Auguste Comte and Positivism," *North British Review*, XXI (May 1854), 133.

prescribed by the mind. Men had no way of determining the ultimate truth of this knowledge; yet, at the same time, they could not doubt it. They believed, whether they would or no, in the reality of a world apart from their own consciousness, in the truth of their perceptions of that world, in the existence of mind and matter, in the legitimacy of the conviction of certainty that attended the mental process and sanctioned its results. All of these things were beyond proof but were universally accepted by sane men. They formed the primary unquestioned foundation on which men rested their science, their philosophy, and othr varieties of particular knowledge.[16]

Holmes cautioned, however, that the conviction of certainty which attended the knowing process did not justify men in concluding that all of their assumed knowledge was thereby made certain. This would open the door to "all the vague reveries of dreamers and mystics, founded upon any assumption or conjecture from which they might be pleased to set out." Beliefs about the phenomenal world must always be subject to logic and the methods of science. But it was equally wrong to assume that because science and philosophy could not reach beyond the phenomenal that our idea of knowledge should be limited to that. This "would negative everything that might not be capable of strict logical proof from directly observed facts, while at the same time it would render that logic itself invalid" by depriving it of its ultimate basis in unquestioning belief. This was the mistake of Positivism.

A true analysis of human knowledge would recognize that it combined two distinct elements: the demonstrable and the indemonstrable, the comprehensible and incomprehensible, the certain in the sense of being probable and the certain in the sense of depending on irresistable conviction.[17] Holmes stressed that his analysis of knowledge in no way endangered the authority of science when it operated within its true province which was the phenomenal world. But the central problem of the nineteenth century, he urged, was exactly to recognize what were the proper limitations of science, to draw carefully a distinction between knowledge that derived its persuasiveness from logical demonstration and knowledge that was the product of irresistable faith.[18] Any adequate idea of knowledge must contain places for both and allow each of them to be sovereign in its own area.

"It would appear, then," Holmes clinched his argument, "that faith, belief, conviction—call it by any of these names, but a principle

16 Holmes, "Philosophy and Faith," pp. 192–201.
17 *Ibid.*, pp. 201–04.
18 *Ibid.*, p. 205.

which is 'the evidence of things not seen'—lies at the very foundation of all reasoning, and is necessarily presupposed in all reasoning, which without it would be impossible." All metaphysics, all systems of ethics could be traced back to this faith. It was the "remote foundation of all scientific knowledge." In our everyday lives we had no thought, contemplated no action that was not predicated upon it.

If this were true, Holmes went on, then religion—Christianity in particular—was justified in appealing to faith as the foundation of belief in revelation. Just as men believed in the reality of the external world through faith, so religious faith existed as a faculty of the mind ready to respond to divine revelation. Two important conclusions followed from this. First, it showed that belief in the dogmas of Christianity was no less rational than the activities of science or philosophy which the apostate world so admired. Second, religion, being epistemologically autonomous, was not a proper area for the exercise of the "plastic manipulations of human speculation."[19] It was immune to the threat of rationalistic criticism. A failure to recognize the independence of religion had led too many modern thinkers to slice away at the traditional theological edifice of the faith in order that revealed truth might correspond to the theories of contemporary science and philosophy. This could have no result but infidelity.[20]

Holmes's attempted solution of the religious problem of his time with a separate but equal theory of knowledge was not, of course, unique. It had been a common answer to the dilemma at least as far back as Bacon and was still popular in the nineteenth century. Unhappily, Holmes's form of this argument, which he called the Philosophy of Faith, was not among the more acute of its kind and eventually it failed him. The reason is not far to seek for its inherent weakness is plain. His basic assumption that the faith of science is identical with the faith of religion was an error growing out of a confusion of two different meanings of the word "faith." The faith of science is faith in experience: "animal faith" to borrow a term from Santayana. It is a naïve and spontaneous affirmative reaction of the mind to the stimuli of its environment. This primary faith does not involve an act of decision. It is not voluntary in the sense of choosing nor does it involve the intellectual acceptance of propositions about reality. Religious faith, as Holmes understood it (and he adds to the confusion by using the term so that it has two different implied definitions), necessarily at some point involves belief in the truth of a given set of theological propositions such as were em-

---

[19] *Ibid.*, pp. 206–08. See also [George Frederick Holmes], "Philosophy of Sir William Hamilton," *Methodist Quarterly Review*, IX (April 1857), 197.
[20] Holmes, "Philosophy and Faith," p. 213n.

bodied in traditional Christianity. If it does not, it cannot be articulated as a creed. One cannot merely "sense" the divine and be a
Christian in Holmes's sense of the word; one must believe in God
the Father with all that the phrase implies. This type of faith is an
act of decision, an act of will. It involves the conscious affirmation of
certain propositions about reality, about the world, about history.
Such affirmation was inseparable from the then conventional idea
of Christian revelation. Even if faith had its origin in a mental "faculty," as creedal theological belief it was not spontaneous and could
not be viewed as analogous to the primary faith arising out of sensory
experience. Religious faith of the sort defended by Holmes, then, is
totally different in kind from the spontaneous "animal faith" of the
mind. Accordingly, his attempt to defend Christianity by claiming
for its doctrines the same immediate conviction as characterized
"animal faith" in the truth of the sensory experience had to collapse.

This criticism would not apply, of course, to a mystical religious
faith born of a direct experience of grace or of deity and devoid of
intellectual content—and sometimes Holmes's usage implied this second definition. Faith of this kind would be of the same spontaneous
sort as "animal faith." But Holmes denied himself this weapon (indeed, he seemed unconscious that it was his) by contemning all forms
of mysticism as the vagaries of personal fantasy.

There was an additional serious and equally important difficulty
with the Philosophy of Faith. Holmes was a Christian and Christianity
was a religion revealed in history through certain sacred events. This
raised a basic question which for years Holmes never faced. What
happened when the Bible or the Church made certain statements about
history which secular learning denied? When both of these separate
but equal modes of knowing dealt with the same question (Noah's
flood, for instance) and gave different answers—one the product of
revelation, the other of science—which one was authoritative? To be
sure, Holmes was not alone with this dilemma. It was a common one.
But most intellectuals who were adjusting their religious views at the
time were content to assume that revelation (properly understood)
could not contradict the established results of science and scholarship, and when the two did disagree revelation was quietly brought
into accord with science. Holmes would have none of this. But then,
these others were not as a rule favored with a systematic epistemology
of faith. Holmes, one might think, would have had a better answer.
But he did not. As it was, one might well wonder whether "Philosophy and Faith" clarified the issue for Holmes or only obscured it.
Did his continuing preoccupation with the problem of knowledge

only blind him to the very real threat to religious faith embodied in the theories of historical sciences and biblical criticism? Quite possibly. It is ironic that the historical achievements of the century—and one must include in this the discoveries of geology and other sciences, biblical criticism, and mythology, as well as the more traditional forms of history, for they are all part of the same reorientation in thinking—which Holmes so carefully fostered should have been the chief danger to his religion, but it is even more ironic that he did not see it immediately.

One explanation of Holmes's failure to detect in this new historical activity the main challenge to Christianity is that his own mind continued to examine the question of belief in the abstract, nonhistorical manner characteristic of so many of eighteenth-century religious controversialists. In the Anglo-American world, at least, both believers and skeptics during the Enlightenment usually tested the claims of Christianity by means of a simple formula: it was either conscious fraud or genuine revelation. When free thinkers spoke of the corrupting of primitive Christianity (which they saw as being originally a form of exalted moral teaching) by the church they did not have in mind the introduction of the creations of the mythopoeic mind into the church's faith and practice (as would Strauss and others in the nineteenth century) but instead referred to lies and deceptions contrived by ambitious priests to delude the people. Similarly when believers defended the historical reliability of biblical testimony they (as did Holmes in meeting Hume's attack on the credibility of testimony to miracles) commonly assumed that the authors of scripture were, in outlook at least, eighteenth-century rationalists like themselves and governed by the same standards of objectivity, rectitude, and aversion to what the age called "enthusiasm." Neither side attempted to think historically, to see the documents of faith through the eyes of the faithful who created them. Both assumed a universal human nature and a changeless human mentality unaffected by successive and differing world views.

The bent of Holmes's thinking about Christianity and skepticism was analogous to this. Like the apologists of the previous century he sought to meet the challenge of religious skepticism by examining the question of the reasonableness of belief in terms which were foreign to the historical dimension of the contemporary problem.[21] For him the difficulties did not arise from discoveries about the past which

---

[21] A not uncommon problem: for a discussion of ahistorical apologetics in Holmes's contemporary, the Harvard Unitarian Andrews Norton, see Brown, *Rise of Biblical Criticism*, pp. 80–81, 144–45.

were contrary to the teaching of Christianity; such discoveries he either ignored or dismissed as illegitimate intrusions into an area reserved for faith. Rather, he insisted that the major danger to contempory Christianity came from fallacious thinking—and not only by its enemies who made mistakes in epistemology, but by its friends as well whom he thought frequently confused about how best to defend the faith. Bad logic, however, was not the real problem, and the defense which Holmes built on the assumption that it was, was built on sand.

His attack on the improper defense of Christianity consisted specifically in a radical critique of natural theology, an ancient defense that for the last two centuries had been a particularly important weapon in the arsenal of Christian apologetics. This misguided attempt to provide rational proofs of the truth of Christianity, Holmes warned, played right into the hands of the infidels. In "Philosophy and Faith" he asserted flatly that all intellectual proofs of the existence of God were logically fallacious since each of them contained a *petitio principii* (the premises inevitably implying the existence of a god) and approvingly quoted Comte to the effect that natural theology was the beginning of atheism. In 1854 he planned an article (which was never written) to be entitled "Evidences of Christianity—Modern Fallacies" for an English review.[22] He did, however, publish an extensive examination of the weakness of natural theology in an essay on Joseph Butler's classic work of apologetics, *The Analogy of Religion, Natural and Revealed, to the Constitution and Course of Nature*. In this he attacked the ever-popular "Watchmaker" argument of William Paley, which stressed alleged design in nature as evidence of divine activity, as a "logical see-saw . . . the equipose of correlative or tautological terms." The most such arguments could prove even if stated in a logically sound form was that the world was the product of an intelligent cause, but this was hardly adequate to argue the truth of Christianity and, besides, Holmes seemed to doubt that such arguments could be logically presented.[23] He found equally serious weaknesses in the traditional apologetics of his contemporaries.[24]

All of this pointed out two lessons. The first was that traditional apologetics was actually a danger to Christianity since it could be easily overturned by any astute unbeliever. The unsophisticated might

[22] Holmes, "Philosophy and Faith," pp. 210–11. MS vol. 1802, pp. 393–94.
[23] [George Frederick Holmes], "Butler's Analogy," *Quarterly Review of the Methodist Episcopal Church, South*, VIII (April 1854), pp. 235–37.
[24] G. F. Holmes to John McClintock, January 23, 1854, MS vol. 1808. Holmes to Tyler, August 25, 1854. Holmes to Thornwell, August 25, 1856.

then think that the infidel, in doing this, had discredited Christianity itself. Second, by stressing the ability of reason to prove the truth of theological beliefs advocates of natural theology implied an equality between reason and revelation. In some forms, for example in those which defended revealed religion by appeals to its reasonableness, revelation even seemed to depend on reason for its justification; and this, charged Holmes, made revelation and faith seem unnecessary and fed the already too great enthusiasm of the century for the self-sufficiency of the human intellect. Paradoxically, he concluded, natural theology served to promote infidelity rather than to combat it. This was not to say that natural theology did not have its uses. It could, if properly employed, confirm the teachings of revelation already accepted through faith, but it could not prove them and, on the whole, Holmes thought, such Christian rationalism did more harm than good.[25]

Holmes's war on the logical shortcomings of natural theology demonstrates again that his loyalty to intellect was no less strong than his loyalty to faith, and this double commitment found expression in the Philosophy of Faith. Significantly, however, it was only in an open acknowledgment of the complete impotence of intellect in matters of religion that Holmes could find a defense of Christianity. This was tantamount to saying that Christianity was beyond rational defense;—a conclusion to which Holmes was driven but which he must have found uncomfortable, for it created a profound tension between religious belief and intellect.

He saw that while faith could make belief possible it could not provide a reasoned defense of belief. If doctrines held by faith were beyond the reach of rationalistic criticism they must also be beyond rationalistic justification. "The subject matter of belief," he wrote, "transcends the range and comprehension of the human mind, but not the orbit of the human heart. It invites belief, but does not admit of rigid proof."[26] This was comforting when one was faced with rationalistic unbelief; unfortunately, it opened the way for the very excesses of religious mysticism that Holmes despised. Once reason ceased to exercise any restraint over belief what check could there be? The only answer was the prescriptive authority of revealed scripture and the dogmas that rested upon it.

The authority of the Bible, however, was exactly the great question raised by the higher criticism, and in meeting this challenge Holmes was less than convincing. He could escape the dilemma created by a

---

[25] [Holmes], "Butler's Analogy," pp. 219, 227, 228–29, 238.
[26] *Ibid.*, pp. 218–19.

confrontation of historical criticism and revelation only by retreating into subjectivism.

> You cannot satisfy Strauss of [the Bible's] consistency, or Tom Paine of its probability. The divergence of opinions is not attributable to a difference of conclusions so much as to a primitive and inherent discrepance of sentiments. In such a case demonstration is of no use, there are no common premises to reason from, no agreement in the manner in which the same propositions are accepted. . . . The subjects transcend the mere intellect, and are beyond the forms of thought.[27]

In his Philosophy of Faith Holmes had been concerned not with proving dogmas but with establishing a way of knowing religious truths, that is, validating religious faith as a human experience. He specifically refused to enter into the question of the content of faith for to have produced a philosophic theology would have contradicted his argument on the limitations of reason.[28] Revelation would provide the flesh for his epistemological bones. But when the question of the truth of definite religious beliefs about the past was forced upon him, when Strauss or Paine or anyone else raised the issue of the historical credibility of biblical narratives and so attempted to bring intellect to bear on questions of history which were legitimately its province by Holmes's own doctrine, then he evaded the problem by reducing these unwelcome challenges to no more than vagaries of individual minds. In doing so, he failed to notice that this type of reductionism called into question the very possibility of a rational systematic history or science. If men's ideas about the explication of a biblical text were the result of a "primitive and inherent discrepance of sentiments," the same could be said of the interpretation of any historical document or of any process of nature. No, it should have been clear whenever Holmes came within even the periphery of the historical challenge that the Philosophy of Faith would not do so long as he continued to hold historical scholarship and science to be of equal epistemological value with religious faith. And yet, it was in the Philosophy of Faith (or something like it) that he saw Christianity's only hope of survival in the modern world.

To be sure, there were other alternatives. One could, like "many of our orthodox evangelical divines," accept Christianity while rejecting science as folly and wickedness. Or, one could, like certain German theologians, pursue the "hazardous course" of retaining a renovated form of Christianity by founding it on Hegel rather than on the Bible. Holmes observed wryly that Christianity in the nine-

---

[27] *Ibid.*, pp. 230–31.
[28] Holmes, "Philosophy and Faith," p. 208.

teenth century showed "most aptitude for credence" where it had been transformed into a "transcendental dream," a "spurious and reductive idealism." Or, one could ignore the problem: Holmes had least patience of all with those men of science, particularly prevalent in England and America, who held an exclusively phenomenalistic theory of knowledge and yet were naïvely undisturbed in their religious beliefs.[29] None of these was acceptable to Holmes. The first offended his admiration of science and was opposed to intellectual progress; the second offended his piety; the third, his reason. The Philosophy of Faith was the only way out. Only a scheme that recognized two exclusive but equally valid spheres of knowledge could meet the present challenge and permit Christianity to remain "within the circle of our accredited truths." If the widely acknowledged dissonance between science and scholarship on the one hand and religion on the other could not be removed then there was no doubt in his mind about the outcome. Infidelity would triumph.[30]

Like many other troubled Christians, then, Holmes vaguely sensed that Christianity in some way had to be freed from its traditional relation to science and history—a relationship which for centuries had been one of mutual support—if it were to continue as a vital part of the modern world view, for it was from these former allies that the most telling attacks were now coming. Christianity needed a realm of truth in which it alone was sovereign. But Holmes was not willing to gain security for his faith by surrendering articles of belief about the past and the world which conflicted with modern knowledge. Unlike certain German theologian-philosophers and their followers, he would not reduce the biblical history of Christianity to a mythical symbolization of philosophical or psychological truths. But, in reality, this was virtually all that the Philosophy of Faith was capable of doing. It could plausibly defend a transcendent religion which had no essential involvement in either nature or history. But with it Holmes could not credibly maintain dogma in the face of scientific evidence to the contrary, nor could he reject the scientific inferences that opposed religious teaching, without violating the very theory of separate but equal means of knowledge on which the Philosophy of Faith rested. For many years, however, he continued to accept in theory the idea of separate areas of knowledge and avoided a real confrontation with the historical challenge. But the Philosophy of Faith was to prove a delusion; and, in practice, Holmes followed the example of the "orthodox evangelical divines" and rec-

[29] *Ibid.*, pp. 208–09. [Holmes], "Faith and Science," p. 187. [Holmes], "Instauratio Nova," pp. 341–43.
[30] Holmes, "Philosophy and Faith," pp. 207–08.

ognized no area in which science was allowed successfully to contradict revelation. It was with these weapons of wood that he advanced to attack the man whom he thought to be the major infidel of the age, Auguste Comte, whose Positive Philosophy had first aroused him from his own dogmatic slumbers.

V   Auguste Comte and
the Challenge of Positivism

Aᴜɢᴜsᴛᴇ Cᴏᴍᴛᴇ (1798–1857) was born into a French Roman Catholic Royalist family and raised in the conservative traditions of his class, but his student days at the École Polytechnique in Paris were marked by a growing radicalism. His philosophical career began when he was barred from further study because of his revolutionary sympathies. He then became the admirer and disciple of the utopian socialist, Henri de Saint-Simon. Although Comte broke with him in 1824, the four years spent as Saint-Simon's secretary were influential in his later intellectual development, though hardly more so than the writings of the Catholic romantic, Joseph de Maistre.

Comte wrote his *Cours de philosophie positive* between 1830 and 1842. This obscure, forbidding multivolume work presented his scheme of a hierarchy of sciences, his law of the three stages of the progress of the human mind, and introduced a new science: sociology. In the *Systéme de politique positive*, which appeared in the years 1851 to 1854, he applied his theories to the construction of a "positive" or completely scientific social order in which common people led happy lives carefully supervised by an elite of intellectuals and businessmen.

Positivism was slow in coming to America. Neglected even in France, Comte was little read in the United States before the appearance of Harriet Martineau's English translation and condensation of the *Cours* in 1853, and was known mainly through superficial and usually hostile commentaries in the reviews and by his reputation as a notorious atheistic philosopher. What little Americans did know about Positivism was gleaned primarily from British reviews and brief treatments in British books such as Mill's *A System of Logic* (1843) and George Henry Lewes's *Biographical History of Philosophy* (1845–1846).[1] The Positive Philosophy itself was noticed first in America by members of the New England intelligentsia. From 1844 on, William Henry Channing, Theodore Parker, George Ripley, and Orestes A. Brownson read and discussed Comte's books as they came from the press. In 1847 an English translation of Emile Littré's

---

[1] Richard Laurin Hawkins, *Positivism in the United States, 1853–1861* (Cambridge: Harvard University Press, 1938), pp. 3–5, 26.

popularizing essay, *De la philosophie positive*, appeared in the *United States Magazine and Democratic Review*, but the American public had no direct taste of Comte's work until 1851 when Professor William Mitchell Gillespie translated and published the first volume of the *Cours* under the title *The Philosophy of Mathematics*. The first creditable American review of Comte's thought was published that same year by Joseph Henry Allen, a Unitarian minister, in the March number of the *Christian Examiner*. Clerical denunciation of Positivism had appeared before, but Allen's appraisal was unusual in its fair-mindedness.[2] It was in this atmosphere of dawning interest that Holmes began to publish his articles on Positivism which he hoped would help to bring Comte's valuable scientific and social observations to the attention of educated people in the United States. "We shall censure as strongly as any one, the fallacies and sophistries of [Positivism's] infidelity, and the errors which we deem its author to have committed; but, on the whole, we regard it as the great and most valuable legacy which the first half of the nineteenth century has bequeathed to posterity."[3]

Holmes's own writings on the study of human society show that as early as 1842 he was moving in the general direction of the Positive Philosophy.[4] This being true it is not surprising that Comte's book acted as a great catalyst on his mind. Like many other intellectuals, Holmes saw in Positivism what seemed at first glimpse to be a systematic organization of his own inchoate notions. Consequently, his reading of the *Cours* in the summer of 1848 not only offered him a profound challenge but also gave form to his loose-floating discontent with the developing course of the contemporary world.

He found much in the system that was congenial to his own views. Both he and Comte were in search of a scientific history. They also shared a deep conviction that contemporary social and political disorder was rooted in an intellectual anarchy that could be removed only by a complete philosophic reform—although they disagreed as to what this reform should be. They shared dislikes: economic individualism, popular democracy, natural theology, the unsatisfactory state of contemporary science, Protestantism, introspective psychology, Strauss's *Das Leben Jesu*, socialism, and natural rights political philosophy. Equally binding were the things they both admired: the organicism of Aristotelian political theory, the security and discipline of Roman Catholicism (Comte, like Letty, saw only two alter-

2 Hawkins, *Auguste Comte*, pp. 14–16, 18–26, 38.

3 [Holmes], "Faith and Science," p. 23.

4 MS vol. 1789. Holmes to Comte, July 8, 1852. Holmes, "State of Letters," p. 414. [Holmes], "Importance of Social Sciences," p. 79n.

natives: Catholicism or infidelity; ironically, this aspect of Positivism probably helped to increase the fervor of Holmes's flirtation with Rome during these years), the socio-religious unity of the Middle Ages, the promise of social science, and the Baconian doctrine that knowledge is power. But despite his sympathy with Comte, Holmes saw the Positivist's war on theology and metaphysics as embodying one of the most serious challenges Christianity faced in the nineteenth century.

Comte's "atheism," that is, his denial of any significance to theological and metaphysical thought, then, was Holmes's chief objection to the new scientific philosophy and the one the Philosophy of Faith was intended to correct. He found other faults in Positivism, but these were secondary to the question of the validity of religious knowledge. Even though Holmes's opposition to Comte was inspired by his fear for the future of Christianity (his carefully prepared index for the *Cours* contains a special entry for "infidel tendencies,")[5] his method of attack was philosophical and historical. He knew that the Comtian party could not be scattered by theological thunder. Accordingly, his assault on Positivism was directed at its "fundamental principles and method" and at its purported place in history in the hope that if these were discredited the obnoxious parts of the structure would collapse.[6] But a total refutation was not Holmes's goal. While it was imperative to protect Christianity against the corrosive skepticism of the system, he was equally concerned to secure public acceptance of Comte's important contributions to the study of society.

Holmes agreed with Comte that the nineteenth century urgently required "a general intellectual regeneration," but he was apprehensive of the errors one might fall into while essaying the task of rehabilitation. He wrote to the editor of the *Southern Literary Messenger* that

Comte, . . . has so nearly unveiled the mysteries of the great social problems, that it is wonderful that he has missed their solution. . . . But though it is easy to discover his aberration from this truth, and his near attainment of it;—it is not easy to adminster the true correction to his errors, and to do what he has barely failed to achieve.[7]

Holmes gladly supported Comte's opinion that the Western world was marred by a spirit of rebellion against all kinds of authority, by "false and petty aims" put in the place of duty, by the prostitution

---

[5] MS vol. 1792.
[6] [Holmes], "Faith and Science," p. 183.
[7] G. F. Holmes to J. R. Thompson, November 30, 1850, Holmes papers, D.

of science to money-making, and by a spirit engaged in "a self-glorifying, self-stultifying" worship of intellect; but he found that his agreement with Comte stopped almost as soon as the problem had been formulated. His own sense of the immediate crisis was "irradiated by a very different spirit from that which breathes through the creed of M. Comte."[8]

Holmes began his criticism of Positivism inauspiciously by committing a blunder. Comte's Hierarchy of the Sciences was intended to show the historical evolution of scientific method through stages represented by six basic sciences and to reveal how they formed a chain culminating in sociology. Mathematics was the product of pure deduction, astronomy added observation, physics experimentation, chemistry systematic nomenclature, biology the comparative method, and sociology the historical method. Although each science utilized the methods of those below it on the scale, Comte denied that any given science could be reduced to the data and methods of another. The subject matter of each had unique features that required unique methods. He did believe, however, that all of the sciences shared the common purpose of describing the phenomenal world in terms of law. When the sciences were arranged in ascending order according to the increasing complexity of the phenomena which they reduced to laws, the series reflected the progressive development of the positive spirit and showed that the growth of science depended upon the continuing ascent of that spirit toward universal dominion. Initially, Holmes missed this important aspect of the Hierarchy of the Sciences and saw Comte's arrangement as no more than a superior logical classification. In fact, he seems to have considered it of little direct importance in the basic scheme of the Positive Philosophy.[9] Later, when challenged on this, he admitted his error, but still maintained that the Hierarchy of the Sciences was only a corollary of the Law of the Three Stages that, for Comte, governed the development of the intellect.[10] This oversight, while of little importance in itself, suggests that from the beginning Holmes was pre-occupied with the challenge to faith embodied in the Law of the Three Stages and in the Positivistic theory of knowledge.

Unlike Holmes's own speculations on the theory of knowledge which derived from the subtile refinements of British empiricism and the Kantian tradition, Comte's ideas were based on a naïve realism. When Comte spoke of observation and experiment he meant these terms in their everyday sense and not in a way that involved any ques-

8 [Holmes], "Faith and Science," pp. 20–22.
9 *Ibid.*, p. 14.
10 G. F. Holmes to the Editor, *ibid.*, VI (July 1854), 448–49.

tion of the validity of sensory perception.[11] Indeed, he ridiculed the psychology of Cousin and others, then so fashionable in France and England, as an absurd attempt by the mind to observe itself which could only give rise to illusions. Comte based his own epistemology on the collective development of the human intellect in history rather than on a study of the workings of the minds of individuals. His investigations convinced him that the positive or scientific method was the only reliable way to obtain knowledge. Any problems or areas of inquiry not open to this method were simply abandoned.

Holmes believed that Comte's refusal to credit any but scientific knowledge would work only to the disadvantage of humanity and of science itself. He had no argument with Comte's delineation of the province of science, but he firmly rejected his limitation of human knowledge to that alone. For Holmes, life and reason alike rested upon the "vague, undefined, unsystematized knowledge," the elemental "faith" on which day to day existence depended and out of which science itself had grown. He granted that this knowledge, "half-reason, half instinct," which had guided human beings since the very earliest times would gradually be replaced in many ways by the methods of science, but its "younger, but more showy and disciplined sister" could never replace it entirely. To do so would destroy the foundations of rational life and scientific progress. By ignoring this "faith" Comte had not only excluded "metaphysical" speculations from the realm of knowledge, but also had confined science itself to a utilitarianism. The free play of the mind, science for its own sake, was forbidden in the Positivist utopia. Holmes was certain that this restricted conception of knowledge would cut off the mind from the necessary stimulation of impulse, instinct, and fancy, and could only end by drying up the springs of civilization.[12]

Comte's rejection of faith and metaphysical speculation was expressed most completely and forcefully in his Law of the Three Stages. This law, which revealed the historical process by which the mind had matured and reached its culmination in the Positive Philosophy, was the overarching concept of the new system. The first (and most natural) mode of thought was the theological. Men sought to explain natural phenomena by attributing their causes to the activity of the arbitrary wills of spirits or gods. Comte held that theological thought was spontaneous in men and consisted of anthropomorphic projections of human agency into the processes of nature. The second stage, the metaphysical, formed a transition between the theological

---

[11] H. B. Acton, "Comte's Positivism and the Science of Society," *Philosophy*, XXVI (October 1951), 294–96.

[12] [Holmes], "Faith and Science," pp. 25–27.

and the positive. It sought to explain phenomena as resulting from the activity of occult entities such as "souls" or "vital principles" while at the same time pooh-poohing the anthropomorphic superstitions of the theological phase. Hence the metaphysical stage was mainly critical and its chief effect was to dissolve the power of theological thinking. Because of its anticipations of positivism—the last and final stage—the metaphysical way of thinking was inherently unstable and its reign temporary. Once it had trained the mind to see regularity in nature and to abandon the idea of divine caprice, its work was done and it gave way to the positive stage which was to be the permanent and normal method of thought and which broke with its predecessors by abandoning the search for causes and contented itself with describing the phenomenal world in terms of law. Its task was not to explain the world but to use it.

These three modes as sketched above were set forth by Comte only as schematic types. He knew that in reality the three had coexisted in all ages and could still be found even in the best minds of the nineteenth century; nevertheless, there was no doubt that the gradual emergence of positivism, which had actually begun with the astronomical observations of priests during the theological era, would in time drive out the other two with which it was fundamentally incompatible.

Comte's condemnation of theological and metaphysical inquiries and systems, then, derived not from epistemological inquiries (which he considered unavoidably metaphysical and illusory) but from the historical development of the mind. Positive science searched only for the laws governing the relations of phenomena and did not concern itself with unsolvable questions of their recondite causes. The fully developed intellect could only think positively and simply could not study problems formulated in the terms of the two other modes. Science, therefore, could not answer questions of a theological or metaphysical nature and so did not ask them. Problems of this kind were simply to be ignored and in time concern with them would disappear. "These spontaneous beliefs," Comte wrote, "have gradually fallen into disuse, not because they have been disproved, but because mankind has become more enlightened as to its wants and the scope of its powers, and has gradually given an entirely new direction to its speculative efforts."[13]

Holmes rejected the Law of the Three Stages as being both arbitrary in its terms and artificial in its application to history. Fur-

[13] Auguste Comte, *A General View of Positivism*, trans. by J. H. Bridges (London: Truebner and Company, 1865), pp. 49–50.

thermore, Comte was wrong in assuming that merely because one historical epoch was dominated by a certain mode of thought and a different epoch by another mode that the two ways of thinking were of differing worth. Holmes had to acknowledge that Comte recognized the historical coexistence of all three kinds of thought, but he charged that he did so only in a way which emphasized their alleged incompatibility. Quite in opposition to Comte's position, Holmes reasoned that the admitted universal operation of these mental processes was strong evidence that they were all permanently useful and valid methods of investigation and speculation.[14] Comte's use of the terms "theological" and "metaphysical" was simply "a piece of philosophical legerdemain, designed to excite prejudices for an ulterior purpose." What was involved in the so-called theological age, Holmes said, was not theology at all, but rather a primitive form of religion that had developed out of fear. It was not true that the retreat of this crude religion from many areas of intellectual life as a result of the rise of metaphysics and science meant that "theology" was being destroyed. Actually, religion, the domain of faith, was only being forced to discover and confine itself to its proper realm. Similarly, what Comte called metaphysics was actually a form of philosophical realism and not the equivalent of metaphysics as such.[15]

But in quibbling over names Holmes only obscured Comte's point. Comte did not intend that the present-day disciplines of theology and metaphysics be identified inflexibly with the two stages in history bearing those names. He acknowledged that both disciplines, as currently practiced, contained elements of all three modes of thinking. Comte certainly did not expect to find the sophisticated theology of the nineteenth century in the early stages of what he called "fetishism" at the dawn of human history. But the fact remained that both theology and metaphysics (even in Holmes's more precise sense) asked questions that could not be answered by positive methods. From Comte's viewpoint there was more similarity between "fetishism" and the *Summa* of Aquinas than Holmes cared to recognize.

As a part of his criticism of the Law of the Three Stages, Holmes wrote a lengthy defense of metaphysics. The necessity of this arose from the extreme importance of metaphysics to any resolution of the contemporary intellectual crisis. There were few errors of Posi-

---

[14] [Holmes], "Faith and Science," pp. 30–31, 169. Comte had a different explanation for the survival of theological beliefs and one similar to that offered later by Freud. When asked by an admirer to account for this persistent tendency in men, he replied, "Que voulez-vous, monsieur? Anormalité cérebrale." Hawkins, *Auguste Comte*, p. 60.

[15] [Holmes], "Faith and Science," pp. 30, 36–37.

tivism more serious in Holmes's eyes than Comte's contempt for this enterprise. Comte had leveled a broad fronted attack denouncing metaphysics as essentially a revival of theology in another form; as being, at best, a means of destroying even more delusive systems but still merely a transitional phase in the development of the mind, a phase that had been barren of significant results for two thousand years and which was itself too often no more than a "patchwork of imperfectly comprehended metaphors mistaken for reasoning." Metaphysics was simply incapable of being treated scientifically because of its inability to deal with external facts and not be simultaneously led astray by internal vagaries. Holmes admitted that these changes constituted a strong indictment. "We will not affect to disguise it," he wrote, "and they contain much truth in them, but they have been alleged [before] by . . . metaphysicians, not as destructive of this branch of knowledge . . . but as evidence of the inherent difficulty of the subject, and of the necessity for cautious and careful reconstruction."

In his defense of metaphysics (which again shows Kant's influence) Holmes passed over without comment Comte's charge that metaphysics was merely a revival of theology—probably because he believed the Positivist was wrong in describing the pre-metaphysical phase as theological. There was no need to take seriously the accusation that metaphysics was an attempt to revive theology in a disguised form when true theology presupposed metaphysics. To the charge that metaphysics had only negative value and was useful only in the criticism of other systems, Holmes replied that the real task of metaphysics was to analyze and define fundamental philosophical ideas. "At the very foundation of all reasoning," he said, "and especially of all science, lie primitive and abstract ideas, such as matter, substance, being, property, cause, effect, change, nature, time, space, relation, number, quantity, quality, accident, etc., which must be defined and explained." For Comte, of course, such ideas—when they were deemed to have any meaning at all—were given in experience and were assumed by the positive method. They could scarcely be investigated by it or by any other method which could provide real knowledge.

Holmes also denied that metaphysics was merely a transitional thought form characteristic of periods of intellectual crisis and destined sooner or later to fall away before the advance of positive science. He cited the flourishing of metaphysics hand in hand with religion among the Greeks, the Hindus, and the medieval Christians as evidence that it was not necessarily a product of crisis nor always destructive of "theology." He also pointed out its creative importance in the development of Positivism itself, as in the philosophy of Descartes whom Comte regarded as one of his precursors. In spite of his denial that all metaphysics was not transitional, however, Holmes did grant to Comte that all transitional states were necessarily metaphysical: those being times when the principles of theology and science were unsettled and men of necessity turned to the criticism of accepted systems and to a reappraisal of first principles. It was for this reason that metaphysics was not barren of results. If at first glance metaphysics did not seem very productive, Holmes went on, that was only because it did not pile up obvious conquests as did natural science. Metaphysics had not "invented a new motive power, nor analyzed soils, nor discovered another planet. . . . But it has discovered the conceptions, and invented and defined their appropriate terms, by which our science, our philosophy, and all our higher speculations are carried on." The perennial battles of metaphysical schools, then, were not "merely a silly recurrence of identically the same doctrines," but represented a continuing process of precision and refinement. Admittedly, metaphysics had had its stagnant periods —the present day was one—but it might become more vigorous at a future date as it had in the past; and, at any rate, its present confused condition did not justify its complete rejection.

Holmes conceded that metaphysics had often been damaged by loose metaphorical language, as Comte claimed, but the use of metaphor was, unhappily, a necessary evil. The two chief dangers involved in the use of metaphor in metaphysical speculation were that the metaphors might become hypostatized and cease to be only symbols, and that vagueness or misapplication might mislead and produce illusions. But, again, this objection was justification only for the exercise of caution, not for the rejection of metaphysics as such. That metaphysics could never become a strict science Holmes acknowledged, but he did believe that it could take on a more "positive complexion" than had usually characterized it. If it did—and there were signs that this was happening—it would not be the result of Comte's scolding but because of the more substantial work of Hume and Brown.[16]

Holmes rested his case on the proposition that metaphysics was a legitimate exercise of the mind because "it is spontaneous, inevitable, indestructible, and subserves purposes not otherwise to be effected." Its importance to science as well as philosophy, was clear. "All our reasoning and science depend upon first principles, which lie within the domain of Metaphysics," he declared, and, "if these [principles]

16 *Ibid.*, pp. 171–79.

be seriously incorrect, science will ultimately suffer its share of the penalty; and before the science can be reformed, the Metaphysics must be amended."[17] It was obvious to Holmes that there was no legitimate basis for Comte's rejection of nonscientific knowledge. Society would follow the lead of Positivism at its peril.

Comte's failure to achieve in Positivism an adequate individual and social philosophy was proved to Holmes by his promulgation of the elaborate secular religious cult, the Religion of Humanity, of which Comte proclaimed himself the high priest. Holmes was among that "nine-tenths of all readers" of Comte for whom, as Mill remarked, "to have no religion, though scandalous enough, is an idea they are partly used to: but to have no God, and to talk of religion, is to their feelings at once an absurdity and an impiety."[18] He interpreted the new religion, which rivaled (and imitated) Catholicism in its elaborate cultus and advocated the worship of humanity itself as the only true supreme being, to be but a futile attempt by Comte to give his spirit-denying philosophy a viable social embodiment.[19] Like many of Comte's own followers, he mistakenly believed that the social order built around the Religion of Humanity was a departure from the principles of the Positive Philosophy. For Comte however, the Positive Philosophy was but a prologue to the Positive Polity; it was only the intellectual foundation for a more complete social reform.[20] Nonetheless, Holmes wrote to McClintock that the new order was

a manifest abandonment of the exclusive scientific ground assumed by the Positive Philosophy; . . . [Comte's] recognition of the validity of instinct in reasoning is virtually the admission of the necessity of faith. . . . [The] manufacture of a Divinity [is] essentially a confession of the invalidity of the philosophical scheme, in that very respect in which I pointed out its peculiar deficiency.[21]

He was certain that if other critics should note these concessions to "theology" the credibility of Positivism would be seriously compromised.

[17] *Ibid.*, pp. 177–78.

[18] John Stuart Mill, *The Positive Philosophy of Auguste Comte* (New York: Henry Holt and Company, 1887), p. 132.

[19] [George Frederick Holmes], "The Positive Religion; or Religion of Humanity," *Methodist Quarterly Review*, VI (July 1854), 330–31, 359.

[20] For the consistency of the Positive Philosophy with the Positive Polity see Frank E. Manuel, *The Prophets of Paris* (Cambridge: Harvard University Press, 1962), pp. 265–66, 267 and Lucien Levy-Bruhl, *The Philosophy of Auguste Comte*, trans. by Kathleen de Beaumont-Klein (New York: G. P. Putnam's Sons, 1903), p. 11.

[21] G. F. Holmes to John McClintock, November 1, 1852, MS vol. 1808.

But the exposure of inconsistencies in Comte's system and philosophical refutations of his assumptions was not enough. It was not enough for Holmes nor did he think it enough for his contemporaries. In an age determined to find laws of historical development for everything, that Comte was wrong had also to be the verdict delivered by a study of history.

In the 1850s, then, Holmes turned again to the study of civilizations which he had begun ten years earlier. But this was only partly a response to Positivism, a testing of Comte's claims in the court of history. It was also a continuation of his role as cosmopolitan interpreter of the modern age for American orthodoxy. In this capacity Holmes now searched the history of past civilizations looking for a sign that would justify some hope for the future of Christianity. He again employed the comparative method that he had learned from Vico and the others; this time, however, the results were more sophisticated, the analogies less crude. There was a further difference between his earlier work and his present concern. The units of study on which he now centered his interest were not civilizations as such but periods of intellectual revival. What he wanted to understand now was not "national character" but the conditions that made possible an era of intellectual renascence, specifically the historical laws that could be expected to govern the birth of the instauration or cultural revival which both he and Comte hoped to see in the immediate future.

History showed Holmes that every past time of crisis similar to the present one had produced a longing for a great man who would usher in a new golden age; now, despite the errors of his philosophy—or because of them—many were hailing Comte as the deliverer of the nineteenth century. Was he? This was no idle question, for if he were, the world should at once submit to his authority; but if his pretensions were unwarranted, then the "blighting delusion" of his philosophy should be exposed before he could gather about him a large group of fanatical followers to delay and perhaps frustrate the fulfillment of the true renewal when it did appear.[22]

All of this assumed, of course, that a revival of civilization actually was in prospect. Holmes had no real doubt about this for the nineteenth century was filled with numerous harbingers and signs of it. He was no longer quite as sure as he had once been that the present century was the anteroom of heaven rather than hell, but a comparative study of past periods of cultural renewal might provide clues that would enable an acute observer to forecast the destiny of the

---

[22] [Holmes], "Instauratio Nova," pp. 329–30.

contemporary world. And so Holmes undertook a comparative study of the eras that he thought were analogous to his own time and to each other in being characterized by an exceptional vitality in their intellectual life. These, he believed, were the ages of Socrates and Aristotle, of Peter Abelard, and of Francis Bacon.[23] During each of these epochs, as in the nineteenth century, new intellectual systems had been created and the foundations of thought reexamined and reconstituted.[24]

Holmes saw the innovations of Socrates and Aristotle as being the earliest reform of the modes of thinking. It was in Greece that the first developments of speculative philosophy emerged from a background of myth and religion. The early philosophers of Ionia attempted to explain the uniformity of natural processes by means of a loose empiricism. But the poor state of logic caused these pioneers to experience great difficulty in deriving valid general principles from observed facts; and, being unable to detect the fallacies in their reasoning because of their inadequate logic, they were not able to discover the real source of their difficulty. The thought of the Eleatics also was weakened by logical fallacies. The philosophical paradoxes of this school, moreover, were so contrary to common sense that they provoked "a violent reaction," and a vigorous defense became necessary. Zeno of Elea attempted this by attacking rival philosophies with the *reductio ad absurdum.* Holmes interpreted this move as the first advance toward a real science of logic. And yet Zeno, by putting reason and experience in opposition through logical paradoxes, began a cynical vogue for sophistry that reduced all questions of truth to mere manipulations of words. The era of the Sophists had been inaugurated: a time analogous to the nineteenth century in its "mental disorganization" and "intellectual confusion." Though predominantly negative and destructive, the Sophists performed the essential function of clearing away the older forms of thought and so prepared the way for the first instauration in history.

While the Sophists were destroying the older philosophy, Socrates began his skillful reform of logic and ethics: logic because false reasoning was the chief cause of the intellectual anarchy he opposed; ethics because he realized the necessity of belief in moral principles and respect for religion and lawful authority.[25] Like the Sophists,

23 *Ibid.,* pp. 335–36.

24 What follows is based on Holmes's discussion of these three eras in "The Bacon of the Nineteenth Century," *ibid.,* V (July and October 1853), 329–54, 489–513.

25 It is interesting to note that Holmes's view of Socrates was much closer to that of Hegel who saw him as a moral reformer than it was to the conventional

though in a less negative way, Socrates freed the Greek mind from the delusions contained in the older systems and cleared the way for philosophies marked by an improved mental discipline. The first of these to appear was Platonism.

Although he was regrettably vague about the actual details of the relationship, Holmes believed that in each of the eras under examination the work of intellectual reformers and the various attempts to relieve contemporary social problems were organically related. It was a central feature of each of these epochs that the intellectual reforms were undertaken "more or less consciously" to correct the disordered state of society and that they were all initiated by a re-examination of the principles of logic and a rejection of hitherto conventional but erroneous modes of reasoning. The chief interest of Plato's philosophy to Holmes was the indication which it provided of an intellectual reaction to the growing social and political crisis of fourth-century Greece. In Plato's works he found "the first manifestation of that scheme of socialism to which the recurrence of similar contingencies has given such prominence . . . in our own day." Yet Holmes did not linger over Plato who, like his master Socrates, had made only tentative motions in the direction of a rehabilitation of logic. The central figure of the Greek instauration was Plato's pupil and critic, Aristotle.

For Holmes, Aristotle was the greatest of the ancient reformers. Independent of mind and exclusively bound to no already existing form of philosophy he was able to explore objectively the full range and methods of human reasoning and to create the science of logic. Since a lack of sound logic had been the main weakness of all earlier Greek thought, Aristotle's logic was the most important of his contributions and the foundation of everything else that he accomplished.

Holmes decided, however, that the Greek instauration had been largely abortive in spite of Aristotle's efforts. The loss of Greek independence to Alexander and subsequently to Rome brought political degradation accompanied by a parallel decline in the powers of the Greek intellect. Foreign domination denied an opportunity for the social application of the intellectual reform instituted by Socrates and Aristotle, and so the instauration remained almost entirely theoretical, having little effect on ancient society.

After the rise of Christianity and the transformation of the Roman Empire into separate successor states the little that remained of the

English interpretation, found in Mill and Grote, that he was a rationalist and a martyr for the cause of civil liberty. See Albert W. Levi, "The Idea of Socrates; The Philosophic Hero in the Nineteenth Century," *Journal of the History of Ideas*, XVII (January 1956), 89–108.

brilliant Greek instauration was swallowed up in theological disputes. A "lifeless orthodoxy" appeared supported by the "narrow and fallacious philosophy" of realism. Those who attempted philosophical studies under the inspiration of realism often lost themselves in pantheism as had the Eleatics before them. Others in rebelling against this approach produced a nominalism in which most philosophical disputes were reduced to battles about words. So, Holmes believed, the intellectual world in which Abelard began his career was analogous to that of the Greeks just before the beginning of the Socratic reform.

Although Holmes recognized Abelard as the inaugurator of the second of the three great instaurations, the medieval reform did not exactly parallel the others, for Abelard made no striking innovations in the science of logic. Rather his importance lay in his revival of the Aristotelian logical reform and in his promotion of a renewed interest in the functions of logic and in the investigation of the basic principles of knowledge. Abelard concurred in the increasingly popular notion that all knowledge comprised the province of logic, and from this confidence in the powers of dialectic sprang the "artificial and intricate logic of the schoolmen" and the general "expansion of intellectual progress" that came in the years after Abelard's death.

Just as the Greek instauration had accompanied a period of social dislocation in the ancient world, Abelard's attempted reform coincided with a crisis in the civilization of the Middle Ages. It was a time when new states were being established, the papal power was extended and consolidated, the new towns were growing, and heresy was beginning to spread. Holmes was not surprised to find that once again quasi-socialistic movements appeared, this time in the form of communistic religious sects. But Abelard's reform, like Aristotle's earlier, failed. The cause this time was not conquest and a decline of intellect, but rather a too great enthusiasm for deductive logic. The basic tool of the revival lost its effectiveness and had its edge dulled by being put to improper uses.

Of the three renovations the Baconian was the most significant for its author specifically intended it to bring about a "moral, political, and social amelioration as the consequence of an improved logical method." The *New Organon*, "the great axis" upon which Bacon's whole philosophy revolved, was to the seventeenth century what Aristotle's logic had been to the ancient world. In both cases, a reorganization of the intellectual world was accomplished by introducing "a more methodic, a better regulated, and a more comprehensive scheme of logic than had prevailed before." A large part of the merit of Bacon's reform of logic lay in the fact that (like Aristotle before him) he emphasized empirical science (because the Schoolmen had left it "diseased and . . . inefficient") without slighting or denigrating other realms of knowledge.[26] Holmes pointed out that much of the intellectual confusion which had developed since the third instauration was the consequence of Bacon's followers misunderstanding his reform and ridiculing deductive logic in general because of its ineptitude in scientific investigation. The result of this was a subsequent neglect of syllogistic logic which, in turn, had brought about the decline of theology and metaphysics which he so lamented.

The heart of his analysis, of course, was the parallels which Holmes found in each of the three instaurations. He knew that each period was unique with its own set of peculiarities and that the differences between the eras were far more numerous than the similarities. The analogies, however, were not any the less important for being relatively few.[27] On the contrary, he was convinced that they held a clue to the future course of civilization.

The pivot upon which each of the instaurations turned was a reform of logic. Holmes had picked up the idea that intellectual change must precede social and political change from many sources: Mill, Comte, even Bacon to name only a few. But to settle on recurrent reforms of logic as the essence of the process of intellectual reformation and to study eras marked by important developments in logic was apparently largely his own idea born of his concern with the condition of logic in his own time—although he may have also owed something here to Bacon's concept of the Great Instauration that was to follow the proper employment of induction.[28] Holmes's study of history proved to him that what he had concluded about his own time was universally true: that in all of the major instaurations intellectual and social activity were intimately related and that any reform of social or political problems was futile unless it began with a reform of the reigning modes of thought and communication.

This was, to be sure, the ground taken by Comte in his proposed intellectual reform. But when Holmes tested Comte's work against the measure of his historical analysis it became obvious that the founder of Positivism was not the expected savior of the nineteenth

[26] Holmes, "Philosophy and Faith," p. 190n.

[27] See his remarks on historical parallels in [George Frederick Holmes], "Louis Napoleon and Augustus Caesar," *Southern Quarterly Review*, X, n.s. (July 1854), 2–3.

[28] The germ of Holmes's theory of the importance of innovations in logic may have derived in part from Sir William Hamilton's prophecy that a rebirth of logical science was near in the nineteenth century. See John Passmore, *A Hundred Years of Philosophy* (London: Gerald Duckworth and Company, [1957]), p. 123.

century. While Positivism intended to end the growing social chaos of the time through a moral and intellectual reformation, and by its positive method to restore the confused Western mind to health, it was marred by many serious flaws. It shared the prevalent overestimation of the human intellect, refused to consider religious revelation as even possibly being knowledge, and lacked any transcendentally sanctioned moral standards. Comte's Religion of Humanity was no more than a species of self-worship: "an ingenious but revolting travesty of the Christian faith." But, worst of all, his contempt for the study of formal logic and his rejection of metaphysics as a worthwhile intellectual occupation made it impossible for Positivism to bring about the necessary reform in the necessary way. The instaurations of Aristotle, Abelard, and Bacon had begun with a reappraisal of the first principles of knowledge, but Comte had made no attempt to reform the foundations of thought generally. He had limited himself to improving the inductive methods of science, and in so doing, had, in Holmes's eyes, shut himself off from even a knowledge of what remedial action was needed. One might wonder if Comte's abandonment of pure logic in favor of an applied logic learned through the practice of a science could be considered a reform in Holmes's sense. Holmes apparently thought not. He ranked Comte as an important precursor, but refused to believe that Positivism was the wave of the future.

Comte, then, was a false prophet. But Holmes was none the less hopeful that his age was on the threshold of a fourth instauration. Modern civilization was tumbling pell-mell into a state of confusion very similar to that which historical investigation seemed to show always preceded an instauration of major proportions. One who knew the secret could detect the telltale signs that another renascence was already underway. He found hope for a revival of religion and morality in the spiritualist excitement which was sweeping over the United States; it was a delusion of course, but at least it was not scientific materialism.[29] Similarly, there lurked in the turbulent currents of contemporary philosophy a new interest in metaphysics and logic: subjects which would have to be restored to their primary dignity before an intellectual reform could occur.[30] To Holmes, the speculations of the last major spokesman of Scottish common sense realism, Sir William Hamilton, seemed to foreshadow the reformed philosophy of the future. Hamilton, almost alone among contempo-

---

[29] [George Frederick Holmes], "Revival of the Black Arts," *Methodist Quarterly Review* VI (April 1854), passim.

[30] [Holmes], "Instauratio Nova," pp. 347, 350–51. See also [Holmes], "Morell's Philosophy," p. 389.

rary philosophers, was motivated by "the pure love of truth" and was "seduced by no new-fangled theories, and misled by no deceptive lures of sudden reputation or popular favor; but [patiently pursued] the vanishing footsteps of sound philosophy."[31]

It is ironic that despite Holmes's emphasis on a revival of logic and his admiration of Hamilton's thought, he objected strongly to Hamilton's innovations in logic; nor did he care much for the novelty of Augustus De Morgan's *Formal Logic* (1849). "If . . . De Morgan understands his own Formal Logic," he wrote, ". . . it is more than we have been able to do." And he seems to have been completely ignorant of the advance toward symbolic logic launched by George Boole only a few years earlier in 1847.[32] But despite a general approval of the increasing activity in logical studies and occasional kind words for Mill's *Logic* and for Hegel's work, the truth was that Holmes did not really want a new logic but simply a revival of the old.[33] This was unconscious wisdom on his part for when new logical studies developed in the late nineteenth and twentieth centuries the work of certain philosophers, those associated with pragmatism and Logical Positivism for instance, turned out to be but another solvent on metaphysical and theological knowledge.

But prospective changes in religion and philosophy were not the only grounds for his hope. Contemporary poetry, especially Tennyson's, seemed "irradiated throughout with the sentiment . . . of coming change." In recent attempts to criticize and classify the sciences, Holmes saw an indication that new principles and revised ideas about the nature and validity of scientific knowledge might soon appear.[34] The intellectual vitality shown in the proliferation of philosophical systems and schemes of social reform during the past several decades also encouraged him in spite of the qualms he felt about the content of these offerings. He was confident that the great minds of the century: Strauss, Schelling, Fourier, Leroux, Proudhon, and, not least among them, Comte, were "the first swallows of coming spring."[35] The nineteenth century, as he never tired of pointing out, was unlike any of its predecessors in being dominated by an especially "riotous license of reason" and a lack of proper moral authority; and because

---

[31] [Holmes], "Hamilton's Discussions," pp. 295, 296–97.

[32] [Holmes], "Philosophy of Hamilton," p. 181. [George Frederick Holmes], "Remains of Sir William Hamilton," *ibid.*, IX (January 1857), 26. [Holmes], "Instauratio Nova," pp. 351–52.

[33] [Holmes], "Philosophy of Hamilton," pp. 180, 184–85. [Holmes], "Morell's Philosophy," p. 386. [Holmes], "Insuauratio Nova," p. 350–51.

[34] [Holmes], "Instauratio Nova," pp. 353, 356–60.

[35] *Ibid.*, pp. 330–331.

of this, Holmes did not feel able to predict with certainty the course the future instauration would take. Nor did he believe that history could be reduced completely to the laws of parallels which he sketched in his three instaurations. Sometimes God intervened directly, suddenly and unpredictably. The birth and career of Jesus and the Reformation had been instances of this sort. The present no less than the past, was subject to these spectacular breaks in the customary course of history and no historian could predict them. His time was not without signs of such providential acts and Holmes dared to hope. The rage of spiritualism, he thought, might be a "breathing-spell" graciously granted humanity to halt the tide of atheism while men came to their senses. Similarly, the sudden gold strikes in various parts of the world might quite soon improve economic conditions and reverse the tide of revolution.[36] But, whatever came to pass, he believed that "the mental throes and the social anguish which characterize the nineteenth century, much more significantly than its boasted intellect, may yet eventuate in the greatest instauration of all time."[37]

But Holmes was not so naïve as to think that the probable debacle of Positivism as reform would mean the end of its threat to Christianity. On the contrary, he expected the influence of the *Cours* particularly to be great among "a large, ingenious, and learned party" in the battle between science and religion which he was certain would dominate the intellectual life of the remainder of the century. Comte's influence would be seminal not because his philosophy was true but because it was in sympathy with the intellectual "instincts and appetites of the day."[38] There would be no peace between Christianity and Positivism. "Your philosophy," he wrote to Comte, "is not simply positive in the conditions of scientific development, but it also necessitates the absolute negation—not the segregation—of all revealed religion. It excludes revelation not only from the field of discussion, but from all influence on our conceptions and the modes of their development."[39] The issue was clear. If men took the direction pointed out by Positivism, there could be no religion beyond the mimicry of Christianity offered by the Religion of Humanity. Without a divine paradigm relativism would spread through human affairs making knowledge "illusory," and men's lives "vain and unsubstantial." Posi-

[36] *Ibid.*, pp. 336–37. [Holmes], "Black Arts," pp. 197–99. [George Frederick Holmes], "Effects of the Increase of Gold Throughout the World," *De Bow's Review*, XXI (August 1856), 111, 120.

[37] [Holmes], "Bacon of the Nineteenth Century," pp. 351–52.

[38] [Holmes], "Faith and Science," p. 10.

[39] Holmes to Comte, October 30, 1852.

tivism would reduce human life to an absurd and meaningless shadow-show.[40]

Despite the sharpness of his attack, Holmes exchanged polite and admiring letters with Comte during 1852–1854. For his part, Comte was flattered by the attention of his American critic, and even hoped to convert Holmes to the Positive religion. Holmes was no less flattered at being treated as almost an equal by the great man. Recognition such as this was precious balm indeed to the backwoods scholar. The exchange of letters began when Comte wrote to McClintock praising the article "Faith and Science—Comte's Positive Philosophy" as "a conscientious appreciation of my basic work by an eminent adversary."[41] Editor John R. Thompson of the *Southern Literary Messenger* had tried to interest Comte in Holmes's work earlier in 1851 but had failed.[42] Holmes now took advantage of this kinder reception to write to Comte and to suggest that they correspond.[43]

Quite aside from basic conflicts, Holmes could readily sympathize with Comte's material privations and, poor though he himself was, sent the French philosopher a small contribution (fifty francs) towards his support.

Like yourself, Monsieur, I am poor, and have often been almost destitute of the means of a sufficient daily support. I have had scarcely fewer persecutions or less grievous difficulties to contend against than yourself; but, having suffered from the abnormal condition of modern society and intel-

[40] [Holmes], "Auguste Comte and Positivism," p. 137.

[41] Auguste Comte to John McClintock, February 4, 1852, MS vol. 1808. My translation.

[42] Hawkins, *Auguste Comte*, p. 67n.

[43] G. F. Holmes to Auguste Comte, March 22, 1852, Hawkins, *Auguste Comte*, pp. 99–100. The complete correspondence is in the Holmes letterbook (MS vol. 1808). Three of Comte's letters and all of Holmes's are published in Hawkins. The remaining Comte letters have been published in Neal C. Gillespie and Gerald H. Davis, "Auguste Comte: Four Lost Letters to America," *Journal of the History of Philosophy*, VIII (January 1970), 49–63. The versions of the Holmes letters in the letterbook occasionally depart from the text published by Hawkins and apparently were altered by Holmes in copying. Hawkins's versions are from the originals in the archives of the *Société Positiviste* in Paris. The alterations are minor for the most part being only stylistic changes though with an occasional word substitution of interest. For example, in Holmes's letter of March 22, 1852 he wrote "I am ready to sympathize . . . with those whose intellectual claims are infinitely higher than my own." In the letterbook he substituted "much higher" for "infinitely." (Hawkins, p. 100). In the same letter Holmes wrote of Comte as "one whom . . . I venerate as the loftiest intellect of the nineteenth century," and in the letterbook, "regard" for "venerate." (Hawkins, p. 102). Some of the changes could have resulted from copying into the letterbook from a rough draft but the toning down of Holmes's adulation is too systematic to be accidental.

lect, I am ready to sympathize in sentiment and in act with those whose intellectual claims are infinitely higher than my own, and whose afflictions have sprung from similar causes. And this I shall cheerfully do without regarding the congruence or diversity of my views with theirs.[44]

Holmes also admired Comte for devoting his life to "the subversion of that false social system which is built upon the sandy foundations of pecuniary interest and unlicensed passions, and the substitution, in their place, of an homogeneous, compact, and interdependent scheme of society founded upon the solid basis of imperative duty." Since he agreed "almost entirely" with Comte's critique of modern society, in spite of the difference in their assumptions and goals, he found it easy to believe that in time the world would recognize Comte's valuable services and honor him as he deserved.[45]

Comte, who smarted from neglect even more than his American correspondent, eagerly grasped at Holmes's admiration. "I am more and more touched with the high philosophical position which your noble candour has been pleased to assign to me, and which is so decisive on the part of an adversary," he wrote, and added with unusual modesty that "[no one else] has ever ventured to compare me with Aristotle."

If those who here defend Positivism, brought to the task as much zeal, or even simply as much fidelity, as your attack testifies toward me, we would not now see, by a strange anomaly, the new philosophy more known and better appreciated in the United States, or perhaps in Russia also, than it is in Paris.[46]

Comte hoped that his American admirer might be converted to Positivism and he lost no time in suggesting this possibility. He was certain that if Holmes applied himself he would soon realize the superiority of the Positive religion over Christianity. There was, he claimed, nothing "noble or tender" in human emotions that was not to be found in the Religion of Humanity.[47] Comte assured Holmes that "the future is the prize of that doctrine which may be able to surmount this universal revolt of minds and to reconstruct suitably the discipline of men." The old, worn-out theological creeds, of course, were impotent to carry out this task. A true understanding of science and a proper utilization of scientific knowledge was the only way out of the present difficulty; any religion that could not

[44] Holmes to Comte, March 22, 1852.

[45] *Ibid.*

[46] Auguste Comte to G. F. Holmes, September 18, 1852, MS vol. 1808. All translations of Comte's letters are by Holmes unless otherwise noted.

[47] Comte to Holmes, April 19, 1852, MS vol. 1808.

be integrated with science and provide a moral direction for its energies must be cast aside as useless. The Religion of Humanity really was the only choice. After urging Holmes to reconsider his Christian beliefs in the light of the Positivist analysis of the current crisis, Comte confidently predicted that careful study and honest reflection would make Holmes a Positivist within three years.[48]

The prospect of his conversion was not one which Holmes anticipated with pleasure. He not only found Positivism "too narrow for the requirements of the moral nature of man, and . . . too limited for his speculative capacities,"[49] but it would have given him "much pain" to part with his religious beliefs.

I started with the repudiation of Christianity, [he wrote] recognizing only the operation of the laws of nature, the sequences and reciprocal relations of the various parts of the phenomenal universe, and the binding authority of the regulated instincts of humanity. Such religious negation—such infidelity of the reason[—] was the conviction of my youth: all this . . . I have gradually outgrown, from a thorough conviction of its logical fallacy and its moral inaptitude for man. There may be apparent presumption in the metaphor, though used in all humility, but I can look back . . . to the creed you are endeavouring . . . to establish as to an arid and thirsty waste which I long since traversed.[50]

He warned Comte that the social reformation they both desired could only rest upon a revival of Christian sentiments; and for that the Positivist religion could never provide a serviceable substitute.[51]

When Holmes rejected Positivism as a religion he boldly differed with Comte on other things, among them that Vico would make a better choice than Condorcet as Comte's precursor, and expressed satisfaction at the remarkable resemblance between his own ideas and those of his correspondent. Comte's reply was an outraged tongue lashing that could have easily ended their relationship had Holmes wished it. Comte condemned the younger man for having the arrogance to write to him as his equal and blamed his insolence on Holmes's "Protestant spirit" which made him ungovernable and impatient of authority.[52] Comte had supposed that his intellectual superiority as well as his age ("I am old enough to be your father," he

---

[48] Comte to Holmes, September 18, 1852, MS vol. 1808.

[49] Holmes to Comte, July 8, 1852, MS vol. 1808.

[50] Holmes to Comte, October 30, 1852, MS vol. 1808. There is no surviving evidence that Holmes's early views were so extreme.

[51] *Ibid.*

[52] Comte leveled the same charge against John Stuart Mill attributing Mill's refusal to follow him to his "Protestant origin and revolutionary habits." Simon, *European Positivism*, p. 189.

complained) would have moved Holmes to be more respectful. He was frankly amazed that "conceit and frivolity" could reach such a point that a young man of thirty-one years would presume to tell him that he did not know who was his own precursor. He made a point of censuring Holmes for his reference in "Faith and Science" to Comte's earlier insanity as the cause of his "sweeping and impassive atheism:" a "typically Christian" mode of polemic Comte thought. The high priest of the new religion finished by renouncing any hope of Holmes's conversion: his lack of mathematics was an insurmountable barrier to his enlightenment.[53]

Deeply shaken by this tirade, Holmes was quick to save the correspondence by expressing "surprise and pain" at Comte's attack. He pleaded that he had been misunderstood, that his views were offered only as suggestions to be considered and "not in any spirit of rivalry or ambition."[54] Though abjectly conceding to Comte almost all of the specific points to which the latter had taken exception, Holmes explained Comte's flare-up to editor McClintock in derisive terms which belied his contrition. It was, he said, the result of a "morbid irritation of his vanity" caused by the growing criticisms of "the regenerate men by whom he declares himself to be surrounded [in Paris]. When Balaam is mounted on his ass, and the Moabites are gathered round him, it is no wonder that he should be betrayed into cursing instead of blessing."[55]

When the mollified Comte wrote again, it was to advise Holmes about his future conduct in view of his refusal to accept the Positivist system. In the present Positivist era, he said, theological thought could only promote anarchy and decadence. It was too effete to restore its own rule, and its activity would only delay the realization of a new and better order. Those who, like Holmes, insisted on taking Christianity seriously should withdraw from public life and cease troubling the world with their pretensions. He warned Holmes that it was very important that he decide whether or not he would spend his life fighting against progress—a battle he could only lose.[56]

Holmes declined to be silenced. He maintained (somewhat disingenuously) that he had never spoken out in a spirit of obstruction, but only to help discover the truth. Originally he had written to call attention to Comte's philosophy which he considered the best of its

[53] Auguste Comte to G. F. Holmes, November 28, 1852, MS vol. 1808. [Holmes], "Faith and Science," p. 18.
[54] G. F. Holmes to Auguste Comte, February 5, 1853, Hawkins, *Auguste Comte*, pp. 125–27.
[55] G. F. Holmes to John McClintock, March 31, 1853, McClintock papers.
[56] Auguste Comte to G. F. Holmes, March 10, 1853, MS vol. 1808.

kind; but he could not stop a work only half completed. He owed it no less to Comte than to those who had read his previous articles to finish his criticism of the Positive system. Urging Comte to believe that he had no ambition to advance his own name or to denigrate Comte, he concluded by hoping that Comte would remember their common aims and preserve their cordial relationship.[57] Comte answered by expressing his appreciation for at least the honesty of Holmes's reply.[58]

Obviously an impasse had been reached: Comte was satisfied that he was not going to gain a disciple, and Holmes became increasingly contemptuous of the Positivist's messianic pretensions. As early as the spring of 1852 Holmes had ridiculed Comte in a letter to McClintock as "a regular Schaman [*sic*]" and "the Grand Lama of his own revelation" driven by the inadequacies of his philosophy to spreading a "monkey type of divinity."[59] By 1854 he had begun to wonder whether Comte did not "still retain some touch of his former insanity in the monomania of his religious egotism," and to speculate whether the founder of Positivism would end his days in a monastery or in a madhouse.[60] Little question remained in his own mind that Positivism as its originator conceived it was rapidly passing into "the curious archives" of forgotten philosophies.[61]

Comte was not the only adversary Holmes faced in his bout with Positivism. Two of the Frenchman's followers in America were also troublesome. Each of them proved to Holmes, in different ways, that the dangers of Positivism did not cease with Comte's work. James O'Connell, the first of them, is an historical enigma about whom almost nothing is known, not even the dates of his birth and death. A free lance writer who divided his time between New York and Europe with Paris as his favorite overseas headquarters, O'Connell was brilliant, arrogant, not a little grasping in money matters, and certainly skillful with his pen. An intellectual dilettante who grew impatient with those less ready than himself to abandon the comforting but erroneous beliefs of yesterday, he was an aggressive freethinker in the manner typical of the early nineteenth century. All taken together, the man was a worthy foe for such a defender of the faith as Holmes.[62]

---

[57] G. F. Holmes to Auguste Comte, June 20, 1853, Hawkins, *Auguste Comte*, pp. 132–33.
[58] Auguste Comte to G. F. Holmes, August 4, 1853, MS vol. 1808.
[59] Holmes to McClintock, April 8, 1852.
[60] *Ibid*., February 18, 1852.
[61] *Ibid*. See also [Holmes], "Auguste Comte and Positivism," pp. 129, 153.
[62] John McClintock to James O'Connell, December 3, 1852 and January 30,

O'Connell's book, *Vestiges of Civilization*, came to Holmes's attention through McClintock who persuaded him to review it for the *Methodist Quarterly Review*.[63] The book has usually been dismissed by historians as an imitation of Comte but a closer reading indicates that this evaluation is a little unfair, as Holmes recognized and as O'Connell never tired of claiming. O'Connell admitted Comte's inspiration for the version of the Law of the Three Stages found in *Vestiges* and, to a lesser extent, for his classification of sciences (which does bear a faint resemblance to Comte's), but his use of these ideas was so different from full-blown Positivism that his protests of originality must be granted some merit.[64] None the less, O'Connell wrote in the spirit of the Positivist Philosophy and was accepted as an advocate of it by Holmes.

The contents of *Vestiges* are not of central importance here and may be summed up quickly. O'Connell intended his book to open up the possibility of an historical science of man just as he thought Robert Chamber's controversial *Vestiges of the Natural History of Creation* (which title he consciously imitated) had provided one for the natural world.[65] For O'Connell the goal of historians was to establish a system of historical laws so thorough that a definitive scale for the classification of civilization could be constructed. This developmental scale would enable an historian to reconstruct an entire society from a single artifact. O'Connell made no claim that he could provide such a scale but he was confident that his separation of human history into three unique phases: the mythological (from the beginning of history to the Christian era), the metaphysical (from the Christian era to the seventeenth century), and the scientific (the seventeenth century to the present), and his division of each civilization into three elements: the aesthetic, the political, and the scientific, was a beginning.[66]

O'Connell's was an insolent book filled with ironic irreverence and

---

1855, McClintock papers. James O'Connell to John McClintock, dated Paris, 1853, MS vol. 1808.

[63] [James O'Connell], *Vestiges of Civilization: or, the Aetiology of History, Religious, Aesthetical, Political, and Philosophical* (New York: H. Bailliere, 1851).

[64] Bernard, *Origins of American Sociology*, p. 238. Hawkins, *Auguste Comte*, pp. 42–43. Holmes to McClintock, February 18, 1854. G. F. Holmes to Auguste Comte, January 14, 1854, MS vol. 1808. James O'Connell to Auguste Comte, September 25, 1853, Hawkins, *ibid.*, pp. 45–47. [O'Connell], *Vestiges*, pp. 169f, 180.

[65] [O'Connell], *Vestiges*, p. 30.

[66] *Ibid.*, pp. 11, 25–26, 30, 190–91.

abuse of proprieties. He heaped scorn on the heads of theologians, philosophers, and historians impartially and denounced the Bible as "a farrago of nursery tales, imagined two or three thousand years ago by a handful of scrofulous barbarians . . . ," containing "indecencies which would be thought too disgusting, by a voluptuary of any refinement, to insert in a book of obscenity."[67] This, needless to say, did not recommend his work to Holmes. There was, however, much that did. He shared Holmes's admiration for Aristotle and for modern French historians as well as his contempt for the bulk of the Scottish philosophy, the average run of Anglo-American intellectuals, German pedantry, and Cousin's psychology.[68]

Holmes found a review of *Vestiges* hard to write. "It has been," he wrote to McClintock as he neared its completion, "the most arduous task I have ever undertaken." He found profundity and fantasy almost inextricably mixed together. "The genius of the author," he concluded, "lies in his singular skill in fusing together the gold and the rubbish: his weakness in not being able himself to discriminate between the two."[69] Holmes put down his pen very much dissatisfied with his work. But his dissatisfaction was nothing compared with O'Connell's.

Vestiges had been thrown together in two months time during the summer of 1849,[70] and Holmes felt it bore too obviously the marks of the circumstances of its origin. The book was undeniably vigorous and witty, but it was also confused and eccentric. He speculated that the formulation of O'Connell's theories had been as hasty as his composition of the book. All in all, Holmes concluded that the book was poorly reasoned, shallow, and fanciful. Admittedly there was much in it that was suggestive, but it was hopelessly muddled and wrongheaded. To complete his demolition, he corrected O'Connell's grammar and his spelling.[71]

O'Connell's reply was a furious letter to McClintock. In the way typical of wounded authors, he charged that Holmes had not touched anything essential nor even understood the argument of *Vestiges*.

---

[67] *Ibid.*, pp. 352–53.

[68] *Ibid.*, pp. 12–15, 21–23, 35f, 101.

[69] Holmes to McClintock, October 1, 1852.

[70] [O'Connell], *Vestiges*, pp. 28–29.

[71] [George Frederick Holmes], "Vestiges of Civilization," *Methodist Quarterly Review*, V (April 1853), 213, 215–17, 230. A shorter review of *Vestiges* entitled "Positive Science," *ibid.*, IV (January 1852), 136–43, has been attributed to Holmes but was written by someone else, possibly McClintock. Holmes did not see *Vestiges* until the summer of 1852. See Holmes to McClintock, April 8, 1852 and February 17, 1853.

Furthermore, he did not even understand Positivism, on which "he has been legislating for you these three years back." O'Connell pointed out that Emile Littré, one of the leading French Positivists, had seen both the book and the review and had pronounced O'Connell the winner. "Why," he concluded, "Mr. H. himself admits that he has only attacked 'the outworks'—you see from the above with what success. He says, indeed, he deemed it idle, after that, to reduce 'the citadel'—which shows him as good a *general* as critic."[72] Holmes countered that he would rely on Comte's opinion of his criticism as a test of his understanding of Positivism and expressed full willingness to level O'Connell's citadel anytime.[73] But the opportunity never arose as McClintock did not arrange a re-match.

Comte, for his part, sided with Holmes. O'Connell, he wrote, had sent him a copy of his book but he had not read it. Instead, he had given it to a disciple to read and, apparently on the basis of an unfavorable report, agreed with Holmes's evaluation. Besides, O'Connell had been very rude. When in Paris he had never visited him—because he could not speak French, he said—and had later written Comte a letter filled with "revolutionary antipathy" and archaic eighteenth-century rationalism in which he rejected the Positive Polity and the Religion of Humanity as a humbug. Comte, needless to say, did not respond.[74]

O'Connell's refusal to embrace the Religion of Humanity was of great significance to Holmes. O'Connell's error was not in following Comte—Holmes himself would do that up to a point—but in following him into skepticism and infidelity. The tasteless attack on religion in *Vestiges* proved to Holmes what he had already concluded: that the principles and assumptions of Positivism in the hands of lesser men than Comte could too easily lead not to the Religion of Humanity but to a materialism that was impenetrable to the slightest religious sensitivity or impulse.

But there was yet another side to the Positivist challenge. Was it possible that Comte's philosophy could be used to create a new form of Christianity, one better able to survive in a scientific cosmos? This question was raised by Horace Benney Wallace, a more devoted Positivist than O'Connell, who rushed to defend Comte from Holmes's criticism.

Wallace, who committed suicide in Paris in 1852 at the age of

---

[72] O'Connell to McClintock, dated Paris, 1853.

[73] G. F. Holmes to John McClintock, no date, MS vol. 1808.

[74] Auguste Comte to G. F. Holmes, March 23, 1854, *ibid.* For O'Connell's letter to Comte see Hawkins, *Auguste Comte*, pp. 44–47.

thirty-five, was Comte's chief hope for American Positivism.[75] He looked upon this promising young legal scholar and man of letters as a second Jefferson who combined heart, mind, and character in a way that would have made him the ideal Positivist leader.[76] Before he left America for the last time in November, 1852, Wallace wrote out an extensive criticism of Holmes's evaluation of the Positive Philosophy which was found among his papers after his death and published by McClintock as part of his obituary.[77]

Wallace's major criticism was that Holmes had failed to realize the importance of the Hierarchy of the Sciences as a statement of the law of the progressive development of scientific method. In his reply, Holmes admitted the justice of the correction but dismissed Wallace's other criticisms as the result of his having seen only the first part of "Faith and Science."[78] What really interested Holmes about Wallace's piece was not the strictures on his review, but his critic's conviction that Positivism was not only perfectly compatible with Christianity in that the theological, metaphysical, and scientific modes of thinking could and should coexist, but that it would in time actually become the main intellectual support of the church. Positivism, Wallace had written, "is destined to furnish the demonstration of the Christian truth, and thereby to convert the world."[79]

Holmes thought not. Wallace had done what many Christian intellectuals easily might do unless they were wary. Carried away by an enthusiasm for science and an admiration of Comte's undeniable gifts, he had failed to see the implications of Comte's phenomenalism and had read into the Positive Philosophy his own religious faith. In Holmes's opinion, Comte was the best judge of the infidelity of his own system: "M. Comte continually repeats that science and theology, Positivism and Christianity, are absolutely incompatible. And he is entirely right: a system of pure and exclusive phenomenalism necessitates the repudiation of revelation, and cannot be logically

[75] For a discussion of Wallace's relations with Comte see Hawkins, *ibid.*, pp. 48–60.

[76] John McClintock, "Horace Binney Wallace," *Methodist Quarterly Review*, VI (January 1854), 132.

[77] *Ibid.*, pp. 136–42.

[78] Holmes to editor, July, 1854, pp. 447–53.

[79] McClintock, "Wallace," p. 142. In the last paragraph of his essay (which was omitted in the *Methodist Quarterly Review*) Wallace cautioned that Positivism should be kept from the common people until a reconciliation with Christianity could be worked out. See Horace Binney Wallace, "Comte's Philosophy," in *Art, Scenery, and Philosophy in Europe* (Philadelphia: H. Hooker, 1855), p. 345.

combined with Christianity."[80] Holmes would not allow Wallace or anyone else to do what he thought could have no result but delusion and the mutilation of the true faith. To reconcile Christianity to antagonistic philosophies and in the process abandon the faith piecemeal was no better than an open and complete rejection of it.

[80] Holmes to editor, July 1854, p. 453.

VI Revolt, Reform, and Reformers

HOLMES's ambivalence toward nineteenth-century civilization was not confined to a tense and anomalous loyalty to both religion and science. This was accompanied by a paradoxical attraction and repulsion toward the impressive social and economic transformations which his age hopefully called progress. In this he shared a growing apprehension about the future of America and Europe which, despite a surface optimism, had become widespread on both continents by mid-century.[1] Much of his writing on social problems in the 1850s expressed this anxiety. In it he spoke for a South which, although frequently among the loudest in boasting of the excellences of the New World and the modern age, was deeply frightened by its growing isolation over slavery; and for a bourgeoisie which, for all its affluence, feared revolution from below while at the same time burdened with the knowledge of the failure of its own ideals of freedom and prosperity for all men.

But voicing the self-interested fears found among stand-pat slaveholders and businessmen did not exhaust his concern. The study of history had taught him the folly of inflexible resistance to change or indifference to the need for reform. And, unlike many of those for whom he spoke, Holmes did not imagine that history could be stopped or thrown into reverse. "It is undeniable," he wrote in the mid-fifties, ". . . that a general system of social reform is almost universally felt to be a necessity. This is no longer the dogma of a heresy, or the watchword of a revolutionary party; it is the profound conviction of the most reflecting men, the instinctive requirement of the multitude."[2] What alarmed him was not the prospect of innovations but the probable mode of their accomplishment. Too many of those enlisted in the party of change he found guilty, to a greater or lesser

---

[1] Regarding this period of national self-doubt, see Fred Somkin, *Unquiet Eagle: Memory and Desire in the Idea of American Freedom, 1815–1860* (Ithaca: Cornell University Press, [1967]. Also Marvin Meyers, *The Jacksonian Persuasion: Politics and Belief* (Palo Alto: Stanford University Press, 1957) and Taylor, *Cavalier and Yankee.*

[2] [George Frederick Holmes], "Speculation and Trade," *Southern Quarterly Review*, II, n.s. (November 1856), 26.

degree, of the same excesses which he condemned in the renovative proposals of Auguste Comte. To change society as they wished he thought would necessarily require fundamentally altering the traditional Judeo-Christian world view. It would involve nothing less than apostasy from the Christian faith and a complete secularization of life. For Holmes the social crisis which fascinated and preoccupied so many of his contemporaries and consumed so much of their mental energy was but another form of the more basic religious crisis. The 1850s, then, saw his final alienation from his youthful enthusiasm for the culture of his time. As his religious reaction deepened, what had through the 1840s been little more than a vague but growing disquiet began to focus on two increasingly noteworthy and revealing manifestations of the nineteenth-century spirit. Intellectual pride and material greed—debased forms of science and capitalism—came to summarize for him the century's revolt against traditional moral and spiritual sanctions and authority.

Revolt, however, was not intrinsically evil. Holmes had learned from Michelet that it was a necessary part of human experience which had played a central role in creating human history. Revolt was the fire through which the race had passed to achieve liberty and a realization of man's possibilities as a rational and moral being. It was through revolt that first the tyranny of nature over the human spirit had been broken, and then the tyranny of political dominance. This drive toward freedom had culminated in the Protestant Reformation which Holmes identified as the seedtime of modern revolt. Though religious in origin, the rebellion against the Church of Rome had been quickly transformed into a more general attack on the traditional impediments to freedom of thought and action. "If we would know what the Reformation really was," he wrote in 1843, ". . . we must look at the fruits which it produced in every department of knowledge. . . . Revolt everywhere. . . . In letters, in science, in politics, in religion, the same opposition to tyranny over the mind manifested itself."[3]

By the 1850s, however, Holmes had detected a change in the spirit of revolt. Although the rebels of his own time might appear to be in direct descent from those who had laid the foundations of modern liberty, it was not so. Somewhere along the way the legacy of the Reformation had been perverted. It was during the eighteenth century, he decided, that the legitimate revolt of earlier years had become a rebellion against all restraint, that the quest for liberty had been

3 Michelet, *Introduction*, pp. 9–10. [Holmes], "Schlegel's Philosophy," pp. 305–09. See also D. F. Jamison to G. F. Holmes, April 23, 1846, vol. I, Holmes papers, LC.

replaced by a demand for indulgence, and the revolution against ecclesiastical repression transformed into religious skepticism.[4] This last, of course, was the critical factor. Opposition to theological autocracy, once it had begun, had proved so exhilarating that it had been continued long after the battle was won, had become an assault on Christianity and theologically sanctioned principles of social and political order, and had brought on all the current evils. "Today," Holmes wrote, "the world lies in danger of worse conditions than that which it sustained under the oppression of theological dogmatism."[5]

During the Enlightenment the defection from the principles of true liberty had been confined to a relatively small group of intellectuals. But the French Revolution had ignited the fire among the masses of the people; and this, with the addition of the problems created by industrialization and an expanding population, by mid-nineteenth century had made revolt chronic throughout the Western world. Of course, it was most serious in Europe, the birth place of the revolt in both of its phases, and Holmes, like most Americans, was anxious to have the New World profit from the agonies of the Old. Fortunately, the United States as yet was experiencing only initial shocks, but the time would come when it would face the same turmoil that was now tearing Europe apart. It should prepare against that day. In the meantime, Holmes found the outlook in Europe grim.

The prevalence of permanent, deep-seated, and extensive causes of excitement [he prophesied] . . . must produce a distracted and unsettled state of society throughout Europe, and eventuate in repeated and successive shocks to all her institutions. . . . Thus, the revolutionary movement may be expected to reveal itself, ultimately, in utter anarchy . . . and the anarchy to be prolonged into complete disorganization and decay.[6]

When Holmes attempted to break down contemporary revolt into its various parts, he settled on three distinct but related characteristics as containing its essence. First was the "anarchical character" of the nineteenth-century mind: an "anarchy of thought, sentiment, and action" that cast aside the promptings of conscience and the commandments of God as well as the inhibitions of sound science and philosophy. It was a "miserable arrogance of superficial knowledge" which believed all reality to lie within its understanding and which

---

[4] [Holmes], "Black Arts," pp. 198–99. [George Frederick Holmes], "The Wandering Jew," *Southern Quarterly Review*, IX (January 1846), 77.

[5] [Holmes], "Black Arts," pp. 198–99.

[6] [George Frederick Holmes], "California Gold and European Revolution," *Southern Quarterly Review*, I, n.s. (July 1850), 295. [George Frederick Holmes], "Latter-Day Pamphlets," *Southern Quarterly Review*, II (November 1850), 336.

never hesitated to construct a new theory to explain what an old one could not.[7] That such false intellectualism should have a leaning toward infidelity went without saying; but even if it continued to call itself Christian, it could do so only by dissolving the faith into undisciplined reveries.

The second constituent of modern revolt was a false democracy. Holmes was not an enemy of the humane ideals of democracy, and had never been as unreconciled a foe of its political expression as some of his South Carolina friends. Though he might have passed for a Tory almost anywhere else, in Charleston circles his ideas caused him to be thought too liberal. "Do not make your papers too democratic," editor Simms cautioned with mock seriousness, "We are all aristocrats here. Your article on Cymon & Pericles . . . has lost us some subscribers." Holmes enthusiastically recommended Tennyson to the American public not only as a poet but as a spokesman of the coming age of the common man.[8] But, even so, democracy had serious flaws: demagoguery, mediocrity, anti-intellectualism, all feeding the inflated opinion which the human mind currently had of itself.[9]

The third element was the development of capitalism as the economic base of modern society. This had not only caused serious maladjustments in society but had produced detrimental psychological effects in individuals. Capitalistic enterprise had promoted an adventuresome and self-confident individualism that was steadily eroding the traditional bonds of community feeling. Society was being divided into two antagonistic classes: one owning, the other laboring. A passion for gain was becoming the sole motivation to human activity. During recent centuries, Holmes feared, restraining customs had been discarded one by one under the influence of growing wealth until finally "the faith of men has dwindled into the commercial credit of tradesmen and hucksters." Those who would succeed in the society that was rapidly being fashioned had no choice but to "prey upon all who came within . . . reach, and to devour each other, like pikes in a fish pond."[10]

---

7 [Holmes], "Latter-Day Pamphlets," pp. 334–35. [Holmes], "Instauratio Nova," pp. 337–38. [Holmes], "Black Arts," p. 197. [George Frederick Holmes], "Spiritual Manifestations," *Southern Literary Messenger*, XIX (July 1853), 387–88.

8 W. G. Simms to G. F. Holmes, June 17, [1851]. Simms, *Letters*, III, 132. [George Frederick Holmes], "Tennyson's Poems," *Southern Literary Messenger*, XIX (November 1853), 657–58.

9 [Holmes], "Latter-Day Pamphlets," pp. 316–17, 338–40.

10 [Holmes], "California Gold," pp. 277–80, 282–83, 289. [Holmes], "Speculation," pp. 21–24. [Holmes], "Greeley on Reforms," p. 262. [George Frederick

These three fundamental changes in Western attitudes, working in concert, had created class strife, had set man against man, had promoted a widespread rejection of the moral and religious ideas which had developed so slowly over the centuries, and now threatened to dissolve what little social order remained. The modern world, it seemed, was hastening to repeat the experience of the ancient: Rome had fallen because the conquests of the Republic had brought about a sudden influx of wealth from Asia to which Roman society had not been able to adjust; Europe had been undergoing an analogous feverish economic excitement since the sixteenth century when the treasure fleets from Spanish America had begun to pour their golden cargoes into the centers of developing capitalism thereby dissolving the incrustations of custom and putting a premium on individualism and avarice. But it seemed to Holmes that too few of his contemporaries were taking alarm. "It has been the fashion," he observed, "to represent luxury, avarice, and inordinate wealth as the canker of ancient societies, but the preservation of modern communities." Both, in reality, suffered from the same disease: "a rabid fury to make money, as the sole end of life." Such hectic stimulation could only end in an attack of "social apoplexy."[11]

There was an outside chance that this would not happen. The recent providential gold strikes in the American West and in Australia offered a possibility that the precious metal which had been the cause of the current woes might also be the means of their solution. Holmes thought that an increased supply of money would create a more general prosperity and make possible emigration from Europe to less settled areas of the globe to equalize the distribution of population. This would remove much of the pressure underlying the present tension and achieve by a natural means the ends now being sought through revolution. When wealth was more common, he hoped, "it will cease to be an object of inordinate and exclusive desire . . . when money and money's worth lose something of their prestige . . . man and man's worth will resume a juster place in the estimation of society."[12]

But Holmes was sufficiently realistic to anticipate that humanity

---

Holmes], "The Nineteenth Century," *Southern Literary Messenger*, XVII (August 1851), 464.

[11] George Frederick Holmes, "Chastel on Charity," *Quarterly Review of the Methodist Episcopal Church, South*, X (January 1856), 34–36. [Holmes], "California Gold," pp. 277–80. [George Frederick Holmes], "Spencer's Social Statics," *Quarterly Review of the Methodist Episcopal Church, South*, X (April 1856), 216–17.

[12] [Holmes], "Effects of Increase of Gold," pp. 111–16.

would not accept the offered reprieve. Rapacity and greed, once in control, could not be easily overcome; nor did the counter tendency of concentrating wealth in the hands of monopolistic corporations (which he regretfully noticed to be well advanced) augur well for a deflection of the historical processes underway.[13] Then too, those who had placed themselves in charge of ameliorating the crisis did not always appreciate the significance of cheaper money. Comte, when Holmes asked his opinion of the economic importance of the new stores of gold, replied sarcastically that the surplus bullion might be useful in gilding the iron rails of the railroads which he expected to be much more important.[14]

The prospect, then, for a sharp reversal of the century's course by means of an extensive acceptance of providential bounty was not good. But if capitalists were not inclined to want less money because more was available, reformers were likewise not made more moderate by an increasing popular acceptance of the need for drastic changes in the constitution of society. Indeed, the democratic and intellectual impulses of the sort Holmes condemned seemed to be rapidly pushing all moderate proposals aside, dazzling the public mind with extravagant schemes of reform, and generally leaving the impression that these represented the only alternative to continuing things as they were. Holmes would hardly have shown enthusiasm for the scope of reform put forth by Ralph Waldo Emerson in his 1841 address, *Man the Reformer*:

We are to revise the whole of our social structure, the state, the school, religion, marriage, trade, science, and explore their foundations in our own nature; we are to see that the world not only fitted the former men, but fits us, and to clear ourselves of every usage which has not its roots in our own mind. What is a man born for but to be a Reformer . . . ?[15]

Such proposals were too much, too radical, too ambitious. On the other hand, they were equally wrong "whose only idea of amelioration is a return to the usages of feudalism and the thirteenth century;" nor could Holmes accept "that imprudent temporizing with incipient perils which canonizes the present and leaves time and accident to heal, prevent, or aggravate the imminent calamities of the future."[16] The only real cure was to be found in social science; in the use of the true Baconian method applied with patience and objectivity to the

---

13 *Ibid.*, pp. 112-13, 118-19.
14 Comte to Holmes, March 23, 1854.
15 Emerson, "Man the Reformer," *Works*, I, 247-48.
16 [Holmes], "Speculation," p. 31.

study of past and present society. Such application would not be easy; at times Holmes despaired of its accomplishment.[17] But he saw it as the only certain way out.

But the very mentality of his age seemed set against a solution through social science. Popular ignorance, of course, was a formidable (though not an insurmountable) obstacle. People could be educated; and the democratic spread of schools made it likely that eventually they would be. Much more serious was the growing *trahison des clercs* (to Holmes an impressively prolific and varied activity) which made their proper education increasingly unlikely. Reforming intellectuals, he found, had a weakness for hasty schemes spun out of their own brains with little attention to the challenge of facts.

It is not the least significant symptom of the disease and disorder of our times, that every scribbler, who, by painful diligence and long mechanic practice, has learnt to string words together into an intelligible, or apparently intelligible sentence, deems himself specially called upon to re-organize society—to remodel the laws imposed by the Creator upon humanity—and to re-arrange and improve the whole order of social and political experience.

The typical reformer, he complained, scorned to waste his time in study. Once he had gleaned enough learning to lend plausibility to his proposals and to gain them a public hearing, he rushed into print: his efforts almost always marked by "exuberant speculation," "hot haste," "rash conjecture," "disregard of immutable facts," "renunciation of all study," "abnegation of patient thought," "arrogant dogmatism," and "wretched incompetence."[18] This was not uniformly so, of course. There were exceptions: Comte was one; Pierre-Joseph Proudhon, the French anarchist, was another; and there were others; but, to Holmes reform writing generally was a great waste land of unrelieved mediocrity. The tendency to settle for an overly simple analysis and to launch an ill-considered crusade aimed at achieving a fore-doomed reform seemed depressingly well established. Holmes set himself the task of searching out these chimeras and destroying them.

He did not content himself merely with demolishing the peddlers of social nostrums. That would have been too easy. Writing in the agrarian tradition of the Old South and the English squirarchy, Holmes turned his criticism on the twin supports of the Anglo-

---

[17] [Holmes], "Latter-Day Pamphlets," pp. 329–31.
[18] [Holmes], "Greeley on Reforms," p. 257.

American laissez-faire capitalist ideology: the science of political economy and the individualistic philosophy of that soon-to-be *stupor mundi*, Herbert Spencer.

At first, one might wonder how Holmes could group the work of political economists with the reform literature that he lampooned so mercilessly, but their concern to discover and publicize the normative structure of capitalistic society made it necessary to view the dismal science as a covert reform. The natural interrelations of the economy carried with them an imperative: they were natural laws to be obeyed, and the economists were their prophets. This, taken with the fact that most writers on political economy were not dismissed by the educated public as ignorant and deluded social messiahs but had great influence, made their science, for all its respectability, just as dangerous as "wild-eyed" reform. Political economy as usually practiced was, in Holmes's view, a perversion of social science. Too many middle class intellectuals considered it to be the sole analytical tool and they employed it in a way that was at the same time too narrow in scope, too sectarian in content, and too imprecise in form to support a true science of society. Holmes hit at all three failings. He also feared that its popularity came more from its usefulness in providing a philosophical sanction for the existing capitalist order than on its scientific reputation, great as that was, and that this utility led its enthusiasts to overlook its methodological shortcomings. Contemporary political economy was dangerous because it was too frequently merely an intellectualization of the acquisitiveness that dominated the mind of the century.

The narrowness of scope was basically a narrowness of method, a mistaking of what was only a part of the scientific study of society for the whole of it. Holmes freely admitted this might have some utility as a methodological fiction provided it was recognized to be such,[19] but too often the study of a society's economic life alone was equated with the study of the whole. He also accused political economists of tending to gather themselves into dogmatic cliques, each of them teaching as a decalogue of settled doctrine what was necessarily only a "provisional systematization, more or less true, of a vast body of facts and inductions."[20] They were, he complained, "as bigoted in their exaction of orthodoxy, and in the asseveration of the absolute orthodoxy of the canons of their church, as any theocracy that ever attained dominion." Undeniably, there were "liberal minds" among

[19] George Frederick Holmes, "Fitzhugh's Sociology for the South," *Quarterly Review of the Methodist Episcopal Church, South,* (April 1855), 192.
[20] [Holmes], "Hamilton's Discussions," pp. 327–28.

them, but this did not prevent "the manifestation of a contrary spirit by the school whenever an occasion occurs to provoke it."[21] Nor did he find in their work the precision one might expect in such a respected science. Definitions of key terms, such as capital, labor, value, and so forth, he charged, were vague, tautological, and even "metaphysical" and differed from one school to another.[22] The continuing search for "the conditions of a permanent equilibrium" between economic factors seemed futile to him when all that science could hope to discover was the laws governing their respective "oscillations."[23] Years later, when he discovered German historical economics with its emphasis on historical growth and the operation of historical law, Holmes must have regretted that it had escaped his attention for so long.

His second criticism, that political economy owed its appeal as much to its convenience as a justification of capitalistic enterprise and the existing order of things as to its prestige as a science, was less technical but no less serious. In the United States particularly, he thought, a laissez faire economic theory fitted in neatly with a laissez faire view of government.[24] In this circumstance, the theories of the economists tended to become a theory of government. But political economy was not and never could be "a canon for the government of nations" and an attempt to put it to this use would be "fatal." This was particularly so in the present crisis where "the faineant procedure" could "only prolong the distress, to entail a heavier arrear of disasters when the storm finally bursts." Political economy, dealing as it did with "the lowest, meanest, most trivial, and selfish of the purposes of human association," could never provide an adequate theory of society as a basis for reform or anything else.[25] To identify the rules of the marketplace with the true conduct of life was folly.

And yet, Holmes was not an enemy of political economy. His criticisms were those of a friend who desired its improvement, not those of an opponent seeking its overthrow.[26] Within proper limits, it had its use. But when he pondered the profound effects of its principles on the social morality of the middle class, he was forced to

[21] George Frederick Holmes, "Capital and Labor," *De Bow's Review*, XXII (March 1857), pp. 249–50.
[22] *Ibid.*, passim. MS vol. 1803.
[23] George Frederick Holmes, "Population and Capital," *De Bow's Review*, XXI (September 1856), pp. 217–18.
[24] [Holmes], "Hamilton's Discussions," p. 327.
[25] Holmes, "Fitzhugh's Sociology," pp. 191–92. [Holmes], "Latter-Day Pamphlets," pp. 328–29.
[26] Holmes, "Capital and Labor," p. 250.

conclude that "they generate a monomania which must eventuate in social suicide."[27] "Its wisdom," he wrote, "is too frequently the wisdom of the ant, of which Lord Bacon says, 'an ant is a wise creature for itself, but it is a shrewd thing in an orchard or garden; and, certainly men, that are great lovers of themselves waste the public.' " It was a point which he could not overstress that "as the grand catholicon of social evils," political economy meant "ruin, to body and soul." It was then "the false prophet, which attests its mission by miracles . . . the Gospel according to Mammon, . . . the philosopher's stone of the rich man to the poor; the Oriental talisman which petrifies his bread. By its magic aid, capitalists fatten, and 'from him that hath nothing shall be taken away even that which he hath.' "[28]

Holmes's attacks on political economy apparently led to no canceled subscriptions as had his "democratic" pieces, but they did provoke a reply from the Charleston bluestocking Louisa Cheves McCord, who was a friend of economist Francis Lieber, translator of Frederic Bastiat's *Sophisms of the Protective Policy*, and outspoken defender of the dismal science. Her charges against Holmes were equally varied and severe. While admiring his ability as a classical scholar, she could only regret the "Quixotte [*sic*] valor" that had led him to "throw down the gauntlet" to the entire science. She wrote in specific rebuttal of his article "Slavery and Freedom," which appeared in the *Southern Quarterly Review* in April, 1856, and in which she thought Holmes had been particularly offensive in suggesting that political economy and abolitionism were in alliance against the South. To her mind he was biased, "a tyro" in the science, confused about its true character and limitations, an unwitting friend of revolution in finding capital and labor to be antagonistic, and much too much under the influence of Proudhon and other socialist writers.[29]

It took Mrs. McCord something less than two months after Holmes's article appeared to finish her reply and to set about making a fair copy for the *Southern Quarterly Review*, but tired eyes forced her to stop half way through her copying. Not to be daunted by the weakness of nature, she sent the completed half to editor Thornwell telling him that she expected him to refuse it, but that she was sending it to him first rather than be suspected of making a "discourteous attack" in another journal on one of his contributors. De Bow, she said, would be glad to have it.[30] Thornwell did as she expected, not caring

27 [Holmes], "Speculation," p. 24.
28 [Holmes], "Latter-Day Pamphlets," pp. 344–45, 354.
29 [Louisa McCord], "Slavery and Political Economy," *De Bow's Review*, XXI (October and November 1856), passim.
30 Louisa McCord to J. H. Thornwell, [July 1856], Thornwell papers.

to use controversy to help revive the languishing *Review* and looked upon the whole business as somewhat indelicate.[31] Holmes, who probably dreaded such an unnatural encounter as arguing economics with a female, was relieved that his editor thought no rebuttal from him necessary. His only regret was that some readers might interpret his silence as a confession that his antagonist's arguments were unanswerable.[32]

But whatever may have been the reaction of the public to Mrs. McCord's points of difference with Holmes, it may be safely assumed that the general response to his strictures of political economy, at least in the South, was favorable. The relevance of Holmes's emphasis on the shortcomings of the discipline as a science probably escaped most of his readers, but this was surely not true of his jeremiads against greed. In that he took up a favorite theme among the southern gentry whose scheme of values gave a prominent place to the idea that they all possessed a genteel aversion to making money. This was one of the insignia belonging to the true cavalier which in the minds of the planters set the South off from the rest of Christendom. Holmes willingly promoted this peculiaristic mode of thought in the South, and a full understanding of his attacks on political economy, laissez faire individualism, and other apparently determining ideas of his time requires some examination of his relation to it: a relation which was no more free of ambivalence than his enthusiasm for nineteenth-century culture itself.

Whether the aristocratic planter-cavalier ideal corresponded to any reality in the Old South has long been a subject of debate among historians and shows little sign of declining. During the earlier years of this century when Charles Beard set the pace of historical interpretation, scholars tended to take the Old South at its own estimate and commonly agreed that the Civil War had been the result of a deep and unavoidable antagonism between two incompatible civilizations: one agriculturally based and non-capitalistic, the other capitalistic and industrial. Within this analysis, the agrarian South itself was the subject of two contrary interpretations. Some saw it as a region whose social and political life as well as its economy was firmly controlled by the wealthy planter class. Others, reacting against this view, argued that the South had been the heartland of Jeffersonian agrarianism, a yeoman democracy, in which the large planter was merely allowed to lead—if, indeed, he led at all. This view of a South "different" from the remainder of the nation, was, in turn, attacked by those

[31] Thornwell to Holmes, July 30, 1856. Palmer, *Thornwell*, p. 399, omits the passage cited; see MS vol. 1808.
[32] Holmes to Thornwell, December 1, 1856.

who thought that, whatever might appear to be the case, the planters had been every bit as capitalistic in their outlook and in their activities as their counterparts in northern commerce and industry. The traditionally distinctive features of southern civilization, they said, were superficial window dressing: the hard-cash reality of the South was much like that of the rest of the country. Recently, the argument has taken a turn back toward the idea of a genuinely peculiar South. Eugene Genovese has argued forcefully that the Old South actually was a distinctive culture, a pre-capitalistic society resting on an archaic mode of production with an ideology uniquely its own, a society grounded in the master-slave relationship and, while equally as avaricious as the Yankee North, one in which land, slaves and the other honorific signs of cavalier aristocracy counted for more than did the monied success valued by the northern businessman. David Bertelson, another scholar who has challenged the idea of southern adherence to a national uniformity, believes that the patriarchal plantation was the generative center of the civilization of the Old South just as the planter-cavalier ideal claimed, but far from promoting a sense of community the plantation actually had retarded it and that, paradoxically, the South was not a less but a more laissez faire society than the North.[33]

It is neither possible nor necessary to decide between these views here. Whether the planter-cavalier ideal revealed or concealed the essential nature of the Old South, it is safe to say that the ideal existed and that it influenced—to whatever degree—the direction of southern aspiration. What, then, was the extent of Holmes's commitment to it? Surprisingly, while he wrote in the South and (on social questions, at least) for the South, his work contains very little about the South as such. There are no extensive analyses of southern life, no lengthy boastful assertions of southern superiority. Instead, there is only an occasional remark drawing the readers attention to the South's preferable situation in regard to some particular issue.[34] There are two reasons for this. First, the sectional quarrel over slavery was for him part of a larger question. The slavery issue was contained in

[33] The three interpretations of the Old South are briefly reviewed by David Potter, "Depletion and Renewal in Southern History," in Edgar T. Thompson, ed. *Perspectives on the South: Agenda for Research* (Durham: Duke University Press, 1967), pp. 84–86. Eugene D. Genovese, *The Political Economy of Slavery* (New York: Pantheon Books, [1967]) and *The World the Slaveholders Made* (New York: Pantheon Books, [1969]). David Bertelson, *The Lazy South* (New York: Oxford University Press, 1967).

[34] See, for example, [George Frederick Holmes], "A Key to *Uncle Tom's Cabin*," *Southern Literary Messenger*, XIX (June 1853), 323, 326, [Holmes], "Speculation," p. 34 and [Holmes], "Greeley on Reforms," p. 273.

the growing dilemma of the use and rewards of labor, free or slave; and the labor problem was, in turn, part of the more extensive social crisis. Secondly, one suspects that the absence of extensive writing extolling the South was owing to Holmes's quietly including the region in his general indictment of modern society. His experience told him that intellectual anarchy, false democracy, and avarice were not absent from the South. The South differed from the rest of the world only in that it was less sick. In slavery and agriculture, which together he freely admitted had retarded the region's economic and hence its social development, the South had the means of averting the catastrophe which lay in store for more advanced societies. But Holmes had doubts that the South possessed the wisdom to properly use her advantage. There was an increasingly vocal group of southerners who wanted to urbanize and industrialize the southern states. This would not, he thought, make them independent of northern economic exploitation as was hoped, but would only succeed in leading them farther into the common disaster.[35] There can be little doubt that Holmes subscribed to the prominent features of the planter-cavalier ideal: a cultivated and landed gentry benignly presiding over an hierarchical society economically and socially stable, careful of tradition, respectful of established institutions, reverent in religion, not venturesome in philosophy;[36] but his devotion to the South, like his defense of its labor system, was not uncritical.[37] He kept ever in mind the much larger problem in which he was so desperately involved and never allowed this to shrink to the dimensions of a merely sectional interest. He was, and remained, at a deep level of his being, an outsider. Nonetheless, for Holmes, as for Genovese's planter, the fate of the Old South "was the fate of everything worthwhile in Western civilization."[38] This concern led him to join the spirited attack on the foundations of modern libertarian political theory then underway in the South and in Europe.

The extreme political and economic individualism preached in

[35] [George Frederick Holmes], "Slavery and Freedom," *Southern Quarterly Review*, I, n.s. (April 1856), 72–74. [George Frederick Holmes], "Failure of Free Societies," *Southern Literary Messenger*, XXI (March 1855), 132–33. [Holmes], "Speculation," pp. 21–22.

[36] For a perceptive review of the planter-cavalier mind see William Henry Longton, "Some Aspects of Intellectual Activity in Ante-Bellum South Carolina, 1830–1860: An Introductory Study," Unpublished dissertation, University of North Carolina, Chapel Hill, 1969.

[37] See his vigorous attack on the South's neglect of her writers, [George Frederick Holmes], "Uncle Tom's Cabin," *Southern Literary Messenger*, XVIII (December 1852), 724–25.

[38] Genovese, *Political Economy*, p. 36.

Herbert Spencer's *Social Statics*, which appeared in 1850, revealed to Holmes with unmistakable clarity the dangers which were latent not only in some of the tenets of political economy, but in the commonly accepted assumptions of modern democratic political philosophy. The latter, no less than the former, he held to be partly responsible for the development of the egoism that was disturbing the world. Contemporary political economy, as he pointed out, flattered the middle class in their distinctiveness and stimulated their avarice. But the effects of the popular notions of natural rights and human equality were no less baneful. The emphasis on inalienable natural rights, which had become axiomatic since the American and French Revolutions, was now leading men to resist the prior rights of society. At the same time, the doctrine hampered the proper functioning of government by demanding that an "absolute canon of right" be applied in politics and denouncing as wicked the necessarily pragmatic operation of the state. "It must be obvious to every sober mind," Holmes thought, "that the greater part of political questions turn upon matters not of pure right, but of expediency; that the science of politics treats of civil prudence as well as of civil and social justice."[39] The idea that it could be otherwise he found hopelessly utopian.

Equally so was the principle that all men are born free and equal. While Holmes found it "in great measure, just and true" as a matter of abstract political philosophy, it was openly "an undiluted and pernicious fallacy" when applied to human societies as they actually existed.[40] No less false was the equal freedom of action advocated by Spencer and other laissez-faire liberals. Just as the Jeffersonian idea of human equality in rights must necessarily be modified in practice by a social hierarchy of privileges, so it was necessary to deny men an unrestrained opportunity to exploit their natural abilities. Any other practice, Holmes stated, "must result in the absolute dominion of the cunning, the dishonest, the fortunate, and the powerful. This wild pretence of liberty eventuates . . . in irremediable oppression."[41]

At this point one might ask that if the contemporary ideas of natural rights and egalitarianism were so at odds with present and past social practice, how did Holmes account for their popularity? There were two explanations. First, political individualism, the category in which he classified the abuse of both natural rights and equality, owed its success in part to skillful mimicry. It was easily confused, for instance, with "the natural and proper instinct of every man to

---

39 [Holmes], "Social Statics," pp. 194–96. See also MS vol. 1802, pp. 37, 43.
40 [Holmes], "Slavery and Freedom," pp. 75–76.
41 [Holmes], "Social Statics," pp. 199–200, 202–03, 207–08.

resist unnecessary control, and to prevent the undue infringement of his personal liberty." Such points of resemblance enabled political individualism to pose as the fulfillment of legitimate aspirations for freedom while actually subverting them. "Lofty maxims," he wrote, when directed to false ends, "serve as the vanguard of noxious immorality"; the unwary were in this way tricked into pursuing goals which contradicted their own values. Political individualism also counterfeited Christianity. At first glance it seemed to be inspired by the humane ethic of the Golden Rule but in reality the egoistic principle at its core worked only for the destruction "of all order and religion." Secondly, there was the persuasive argument of historical inevitability. The prestige of political individualism owed not a little to the popular belief that an historical tendency was in itself an adequate justification. Whether one based his confidence in the course of history on the idea of progress, a "Mahometan fatalism," or the conviction that "the instincts of the masses" possessed "a degree of rectitude and sagacity denied to the reflections and experience of sages and statesmen" the result was the same: "a reference to the tendencies of society" was considered "sufficient answer to all objections" from political doubting Thomases.

While Holmes never thought to deny that a marked and demonstrated tendency in the course of history demanded the utmost respect and attention, he believed it manifest folly to ignore the always complex structure of these movements. They were never simple. Like a river in flood, the main current of true, progressive historical change was always accompanied by peripheral eddies of delusion. The anabaptist sects had been the eddies of the Reformation just as the radical democratic ideologists of the nineteenth century constituted the eddies in the democratizing influences which were flowing into the channels cut by the American and French revolutions. While Holmes agreed that the direction taken by history seemed to favor the eventual achievement of a greater degree of human freedom, this did not sanction all types of emancipation. Some would realize good ends, but others would only promote moral anarchy and social dissolution. To advocate more political and economic egoism as a remedy for the present crisis was but to "cast out devils in the name of Beelzebub, the prince of devils."[42]

Individualistic philosophies, such as Spencer's, which lauded the private man at the expense of public interests had, in Holmes's view, obvious affinities to the nineteenth century's misguided revolt. To

[42] George Frederick Holmes, "Theory of Political Individualism," *De Bow's Review*, XXII (February 1857), pp. 138, 144–47. [Holmes], "Social Statics," pp. 211–12.

him their authors were invariably utopian in their goals, confidently deductive rather than cautiously empirical in their study of society, undisciplined and self-indulgent in their codes of behavior; Holmes thought them with equal obviousness not suitable guides for reform. But the danger they represented came not so much from the fallacies in their theories or from the impracticality of their schemes; Holmes was much more worried about the harm their very popularity could do to the unwary before these weaknesses led them to a well deserved oblivion. The optimistic ("always a mark of intellectual imbecility,"[43] he observed), aggressive, entrepreneural ethic advocated by the laissez-faire liberals and the individualistic values of contemporary democracy were combining to woo the citizen from his duty by undermining his respect for authority and suggesting to him that institutions long and painfully created might be renovated in the twinkling of an eye.[44] It was not given to man to work such miracles.

But it was not in the lopsided science of the political economists nor in the increasingly popular philosophy of political individualism that Holmes found the most acute analysis of the contemporary social crisis. That distinction went to socialism. Even though by the 1850s he had begun to suspect that the socialists were being pressed hard in the contest for men's minds by the oncoming advocates of increased personal liberty and were in danger of falling behind the times,[45] they had been the first to undertake a serious critique of the modern social order and, in many ways, Holmes felt their commentary was still the most penetrating. St. Simon had been the first to identify intellectual and moral anarchy as the primary problem; Comte had elaborated on this beginning; and others—socialists and non-socialists —had followed in turn some emphasizing one thing, some another.[46] But the socialists had probed the material as well as the psychological "wounds of society" deeper than anyone else and Holmes prophesied (with greater accuracy than he usually achieved) that when the *New Organon* of social philosophy appeared it would be written "by some heresiarch of their School."[47] Who were the socialists? Holmes cast a wide net and caught disparate fish in it. There were, of course, St. Simon and Comte; but also Robert Owen, Charles Fourier, Etienne Cabet, and Pierre-Joseph Proudhon whom he admired most of all. Proudhon, he wrote, was "unlike most modern philosophers" in also

---

43 [Holmes], "Social Statics," p. 205.
44 Holmes, "Political Individualism," pp. 143-44.
45 *Ibid.*, p. 138.
46 [Holmes], "Instauratio Nova," p. 339.
47 [Holmes], "Greeley on Reforms," p. 261.

being a logician.[48] The analyses of the socialists were marred, of course, by flaws that could not be ignored—impatient and hasty theories which only confused matters, simplistic and harmful notions of class struggle which divided rather than healed society, and (too often) a lack of religious faith—and to put their programs into practice would be preposterous, but the world should listen with respect just the same. All of their ideas were not silly and their existence was itself a reproach to society as it was. Few others had as keen an awareness of the importance of the relations of capital and labor and of the overriding necessity of universal social harmony.[49]

Closely associated with socialism in Holmes's mind and allied with it in spirit if not always in doctrine was the vast and energetic American reform movement. Holmes made no fine distinctions here. Nor was he as impressed by the domestic product as he was by the European import. He took Horace Greeley, the crusading editor of the *New York Tribune*, as the representative American reformer and unfairly assimilated all others to the type. Though he admitted to finding Greeley's ideas "by no means so ultra" as he had anticipated when he undertook to review the newspaperman's *Hints Toward Reforms*, Holmes was no admirer. He found Greeley "neither a great man nor the shadow of a great man," but "one of those presumptuous unfortunates, who, like the silly Malvolio, have had greatness thrust upon him by the blind accidents of life."[50] Holmes had hoped that American reformers would refrain from enlarging the flood of fatuous radical literature which was drowning Europe. His hope, he confessed, had not been large, but he had been disappointed in it even as modest as it was. "It requires no great effort of intellect," he scolded, "to evoke from the imagination conjectural reforms of the social state." Greeley's schemes, like those of most reformers, were "incomplete and distorted; and his dreams of the future regeneration of humanity are founded upon a most erroneous and Utopian estimate of men and society." In this he was typical, for American reformers with their one-sided cures—Women's Rights, Free Love, Teetotalism—dwelled amid the "shadows of a phantom land" and

---

[48] [George Frederick Holmes], "Alchemy and the Alchemists," *Methodist Quarterly Review*, VIII (July 1856), 468n. See also [Holmes], "Social Statics," p. 187; George Frederick Holmes, "Gold and Silver Mines," *De Bow's Review*, XXI (July 1856), 31; Holmes, "Population and Capital," p. 219.

[49] [Holmes], "Instauratio Nova," p. 345. [Holmes], "Greeley on Reforms," pp. 260–62. [George Frederick Holmes], "History of the Working Classes," *Southern Literary Messenger*, XXI (April 1855), 196–99, 201. Holmes to Thompson, November 30, 1850.

[50] Holmes to Thompson, *ibid*. [Holmes], "Slavery and Freedom," p. 67.

were uniformly reckless in both means and ends. Ignorant of the laws
which governed social institutions and reluctant to forego reforming
until such laws could be discovered, each pursued his own delusion.
Some hoped to completely transform society; others naïvely thought
one particular evil could be removed without disturbing any other
function of the social process.[51] "Shoals of reformers" were springing
to life throughout the land, "like weeds after a shower, each with his
own infallible panacea." Such people, Holmes charged, had no
knowledge of the complexities of current problems or of the evil
that premature or ill considered reform could work.[52] Like Spencer
with his political individualism, reformers of the Greeley variety
were obvious embodiments of modern revolt. Also like Spencer,
their success was no mystery to Holmes. "There is something infec-
tious," he reluctantly admitted to the editor of the *Southern Literary
Messenger*, "in this visionary and sanguine estimation of the capabil-
ities and possibilities of Humanity."[53] Its appeal was like that of religion; and that, of course, was precisely the trouble.

Given his analyses, it is not surprising that Holmes reached the
conclusion that the new era of reform, the New Instauration, was not
to be achieved by any of the methods or philosophies so enthusiastically hawked by his contemporaries: not by giving capitalistic development its head as the political economists seemed to want; not by
collectivizing society according to the gospel of socialism; not by
atomizing it in accordance with the principles of Herbert Spencer;
nor by "reforming" it after the ideals of Horace Greeley and his like.
No, true reform would only be accomplished through science carefully and properly applied.

In his refutation of Positivism Holmes had brushed in the image
of his ideal reformer: he would be intellectually modest, pious,
reverent toward the past, a model of scientific probity.[54] Elsewhere,
he elaborated on this sketch. The bona fide man of reform would in
addition be elitist in his view of society, cautious in remedies, judicious
in his decisions about the "rightness" of institutions, and, of course,
learned in science, history, and philosophy. Reform there had to be,
Holmes agreed, but it had to be reform of the right sort.

The reformer of Holmes's conception would not suddenly "attempt
to divorce the world from all its familiar modes of reasoning, action,
and belief." Even if an important belief or custom were wrong, "so
critical, so vital, so all-pervading" an error had to be handled gently.

---

[51] [Holmes], "Greeley on Reforms," pp. 257, 259, 260, 275.
[52] Holmes, "Political Individualism," pp. 135–36.
[53] Holmes to Thompson, November 30, 1850.
[54] [Holmes], "Bacon of the Nineteenth Century," pp. 496–97.

"The reformer," he advised, "must bend himself to times and occasions; he must patiently endure the more harmless delusions, until, by their aid, he has crushed the more formidable." He should disclose his "naked arguments" only to those able to understand them. The "ignorant and the prejudiced" must be themselves reformed before society could be bettered and this could be done best by high-minded leadership rather than by open opposition and bitter argument. The reformer should have ever foremost in his mind solid and clear ultimate goals, but he should be always an opportunist in means. Whenever possible, existing custom should be employed to achieve his purposes. He should avoid the error of reformers who seem to think that one part of society may be drastically changed without altering the rest of it.[55] He would take as a basic principle that "the amelioration of society proceeds by the gradual and constant substitution of what is demanded by present necessities for what has ceased to satisfy them; and by the cautious modification of what is no longer sufficient, and its careful adaptation to the altered condition of society."[56]

The ideal reformer would always remember that historical forms of society are the only legitimate subjects for his study, and would avoid a priori speculation about man and society.[57] He would constantly be on his guard against rash conjectures, the neglect of important facts, or the misinterpretation of some complex social phenomenon. Above all, he would keep his "eye steadily fixed on the polar star of historical science."[58] He would apply to the study of society the maxim given by Bacon for the study of nature: " 'Man, as the minister and interpreter of nature, does and understands as much, as his observations on the order of nature, either with regard to things or the mind, will permit him, and neither knows nor is capable of more.' "[59]

Lastly, he would continually be aware that "the merit of all social institutions must be tested by the experience of their effects, and in the same way must be estimated the validity of those theories of society by which each social system is maintained."[60] He would never forget that

the constitution of society is at all times pre-eminently relative, and varies, and must vary with the changes of the intellectual, moral, and material

[55] [Holmes], "Greeley on Reforms," pp. 275, 318–20.
[56] [Holmes], "Social Statics," pp. 193–94.
[57] *Ibid.*, p. 215.
[58] [Holmes], "Effects of Increase of Gold," p. 117.
[59] [Holmes], "Latter-Day Pamphlets," p. 329.
[60] Holmes, "Fitzhugh's Sociology," p. 198.

condition of every people and of every age. There is no mold of fashion or glass of form for communities; they are launched upon a sea of incessant mutation; what is best at one time is not best at another, nor is there any term where repose awaits them; nor could rest be perfection, for it would be paralysis. In order, that any such perfect social organization might exist, it would be necessary that human nature undergo a great change, that the tendencies of society should be uniformly progressive, and uniform in direction; and that the evil which corrodes the heart of man and corrupts the vitality of nations, should disappear before the advancing footsteps of humanity.[61]

Holmes was certain of one thing: a perfect social order could never be achieved. The ideal could be of use to the reformer only as a goal toward which he might lead mankind, a myth that stimulated but never satisfied human yearning, but it should never be thought to be more than this or it would betray those who sought it.

But for all of his awareness of the need to study social problems scientifically, Holmes discovered no body of social laws which could be applied to the solution of the current crisis; nor did anyone else. Reform on his terms was not possible. This, however, did not prohibit his speculating about it, and, in the course of his denunciations of premature reform, he offered several suggestions about desirable changes. A higher standard of living for the lower classes was imperative to remove the certainty of revolution and would probably require an "orderly modification of the laws of property." What did he mean by this vague phrase? Well, there might be a ban against land speculation, or a limitation placed on the amount of land one man might own, or perhaps even laws passed to "encourage" the wider distribution of capital. The great power which landed wealth and the money interests enjoyed over the political machinery of society should be lessened, and talents other than the ability to make money given a greater voice in government. The state should be made more capable of genuine public spirited action rather than merely continuing to serve the rich. Furthermore, if necessary, the state should not hesitate to coerce the propertied classes to make them more conscious of their duty.[62] Lest this sound too radical for his readers, Holmes assured them that he was "far from desiring to see the bulwarks of organized society surrendered into the hands of St. Simonians, Fourierites, Cabetists, Proudhonists and anti-renters"; although, he warned, this might well be the result unless men found a way to substitute a sense of social duty for the vigorous sense of

---

[61] [Holmes], "Social Statics," p. 196.
[62] [Holmes], "Greeley on Reforms," pp. 263, 269. [Holmes], "Latter-Day Pamphlets," pp. 347–48.

personal rights that dominated the century, among which rights not the least shrill in its clamor was the sanctity of private property.[63]

Even though Holmes felt he had sufficient justification for the generality and imprecision of his reflections—the infant state of social science—it remains that his discussions of social problems generally lacked proposals of specific remedies for specific problems. And here arises a difficulty analogous to his failure to see the central issue in the modern religious problem. Just as a preoccupation with the problem of knowledge caused him to fail to come to grips with the historical challenge facing Christianity, so an insistence on scientific reform sometime in the future lessened the plausibility of making proposals for reform now, and particularly for that reform which southerners dreaded most of all: the abolition of Negro slavery. Paradoxically, and for all his argument that reform was necessary, Holmes's belief that all social change must be slow if it is to be beneficial,[64] his faith in the merits of prudently following the inexorable tendencies manifested in history[65] (despite his condemnation of this attitude in others), and his paralyzing organic view of society which seemed to say that all must be changed or nothing can be changed, brought him in the end to much the same position on reform as that taken by Herbert Spencer and other laissez faire advocates. Like them he had little faith in the ability of the present generation to consciously shape the destiny of society. The best policy was to cling to the present, endure its evils, hope for improvement, and avoid creating future woes by ignorant tinkering with the social machinery. Holmes was not a reactionary, a regretter of the past; to see him as a convert to Tory socialism and a worshipper of Disraeli, as attempting a "reactionary Enlightenment," as weeping "over the death of feudalism," is to badly misread him.[66] Few men were ever more

63 [Holmes], "Latter-Day Pamphlets," p. 331.

64 [George Frederick Holmes], "Roman History," *Southern Literary Messenger*, XII (August 1846), 512; see also [Holmes], "Effects of Increase of Gold," p. 117.

65 [Holmes], "Working Classes," p. 196. [Holmes], "Social Statics," p. 204.

66 As does Louis Hartz in his *The Liberal Tradition in America* (New York: Harcourt, Brace & World, Inc., [1955]), p. 174, 179. Joseph Dorfman similarly misunderstands Holmes, *The Economic Mind in American Civilization, 1606–1865* (New York: Viking Press, 1946), II, 920–28. Dorfman's account contains a number of errors and should be used critically. Among the most noticeable: Calhoun, Lieber, Beverly Tucker and Carlyle were not the major influences on Holmes's thinking (p. 921), there is no reason to think that the "Life and Times of Pericles," *Southern Literary Messenger*, XVI (February 1850), 65–82, is a veiled defense of Calhoun (p. 927), "Maury on South American and Amazonia," *Southern Quarterly Review*, XXIV (October 1853), 412–49, on which Dorfman bases part of his analysis, was not written by Holmes but by M. C. M. Hammond

aware of the imperatives of the future. Consequently, his attitude toward the future was one of expectancy. But it was an anxious expectancy rather than an optimistic hope. Ultimately, his advocacy of reform was little more than a gesture made by a man who knew too much to believe that nothing was wrong with the modern world, but who was too wedded to the present and too frightened by the portents of the future to take or even to advocate effective action. To say this is not to indict Holmes's sincerity in his pleas for scientific reform, nor to imply that his position on reform had nothing in its favor. It did, of course. And though he may have deceived himself about the nature of his concern with reform, he worked hard to show that the scientific approach could illuminate current problems even though it might not be able to solve them. This much could be done right away although actual changes would have to wait, as he said, on the discovery of social law.

Holmes did, however, have one opportunity to join a group of intellectuals embarked on the practical task of reform. It began in September 1854, when George Fitzhugh, who was soon to publish his famous proslavery tract *Sociology for the South* (1854) and become one of slavery's foremost apologists, wrote to Holmes answering his inquiry about the forthcoming treatise and asking him to review it when it appeared. Holmes was personally unknown to Fitzhugh, but he had read his publications and had detected a kinship of mind in them. Holmes's letter had confirmed this. Briefly, he outlined for the English scholar the thesis of his book:

Its leading idea is this. Man is social, helpless, associative, gregarious. Like the bee and the ant he is born the member and slave of society. The Social Contract is false, because society and man are congenital. He does not form society. Laissez-faire or political economy proposes to benefit mankind by a general competition, even in which the few strong are benefited, the many weak ruined. Protection is the object of society and protection involves the necessity of slavery.

Wives, children, all dependents, he went on to say, were, in effect, slaves. He condemned political economy as a "Philosophy of pure selfishness," and its ethics as "worse than its economics." Socialism,

----

(see Simms, *Letters*, III, 246n), Holmes certainly did not look to "the restoration of an authoritative order of gentlemen" as a panacea for the social ills of his time (p. 928). These mistakes of fact and interpretation in Dorfman's and Hartz's books do not, of course, call into question the over-all merits of their work; although the section, "The Feudal Dream of the South," in Hartz's volume must be the most dubious part of that stimulating and important study.

he ended, had been generated by the suffering of the masses in free societies and was "slavery under a new name." There was enough here to interest Holmes. He encouraged Fitzhugh to continue.[67]

Holmes's favorable reviews of *Sociology for the South* in the *Southern Literary Messenger* ("kind and very able" said Fitzhugh), in the *Quarterly Review of the Methodist Episcopal Church, South* ("rather more close and critical . . . but so much the better for me, it teaches me how to improve next time") and in the *Southern Quarterly Review* pleased Fitzhugh in a number of ways.[68] He gave Holmes's essays a great part of the credit for the successful impact of *Sociology*: "the review [in the *Messenger*] far surpassed the work reviewed," he wrote, and the articles together had helped "revolutionize public opinion at the South on the subject of Slavery." But more important personally, Holmes's appreciations and the response of the public had convinced him that he might be capable of writing "a serious work on Social Science." Fitzhugh had had doubts about this. He was all too aware of his shortcomings as a scholar. He admitted to having had no idea that he was boldly attacking the entire body of modern ideology until Holmes told him so; and was somewhat chagrined to discover that others had originated many of his principles; Aristotle, for one. After reading the *Politics*, Fitzhugh confessed that he was "in a fix. If I admit I never read Aristotle, why I am no scholar. If I did read him, I am a plagiarist." But he vowed that if he wrote again, he would "make a clean breast, and acknowledge my pseudo-learning is all gathered from Reviews. I never read a Socialist author treating the subject philosophically in my life. Newspapers, Novels, Reviews, are the sources of my information." "I used to think," he reflected, "I was a little paradoxical, I now fear I am a mere retailer of truisms and common-places."[69]

Fitzhugh, of course, confirmed Holmes's analysis of the modern

[67] George Fitzhugh to G. F. Holmes, September 22, and October 12, 1854, MS vol. 1808. Holmes's letters to Fitzhugh have not survived; his initial letter is mentioned by Fitzhugh in the preface of his *Cannibals All! or Slaves Without Masters* (Richmond: A. Morris, 1857). The standard biography of Fitzhugh is Harvey Wish, *George Fitzhugh, Propagandist of the Old South* (Baton Rouge: Louisiana States University Press, 1943). The best analysis of Fitzhugh's thought is Genovese, *World Slaveholders Made*, Part Two: "The Logical Outcome of the Slave Holders' Philosophy."

[68] George Fitzhugh to G. F. Holmes, March 27, 1855, and undated letter written after April 1855, MS vol. 1808. The reviews were "Fitzhugh's Sociology," pp. 180–201; "Free Societies," pp. 129–141; "Slavery and Freedom," pp. 62–95. For Holmes's opinion of Fitzhugh's work see chapter VII of this book.

[69] George Fitzhugh to G. F. Holmes, April 11, 1855, MS vol. 1808. Fitzhugh to Holmes, March 27, 1855; undated letter *post* April 1855.

crisis. When he returned from his debate with the abolitionist Wendell Phillips in New Haven, he reported his alarm:

The prevalence of infidelity and of anarchical doctrines at the North, is far greater than described in my book. . . . Every one of the real Abolitionists, all the liberty party are socialists of the deepest dye—Woman's Rights, anti-marriage, anti-chastity and Maine Liquor Law men. Indeed, Sir, half the North is partially insane, worse than France during the Reign of Terror. Political Abolitionism, its most dangerous type, is almost universal.[70]

But his experience in the North had only confirmed him in what he already knew. To help check the apparently advanced dissolution of northern society, Fitzhugh had earlier urged Holmes to write to utopian reformer and abolitionist Steven Pearl Andrews, who, in league with anarchist Josiah Warren and the American Comtist, Henry Edgar, was hoping to reform the northern states, and who had suggested to Fitzhugh that he, Fitzhugh, Holmes and a few others meet in Richmond to found a "New School of Philosophy" for the purpose of promoting reform and sectional conciliation:

A new philosophy, [Andrews wrote] *our* new philosophy, broad enough to cover North and South, to neutralize factious demagoguism against the institutions of one section, to enlighten and liberalize all sections, to quicken lagging conservatism of the South into reform in its own way and adopted to its own wants, and to give the reformers of the North quite enough to attend to at home.

Two more unlikely yokefellows could not be imagined, but Andrews, like Holmes, was in search of scientific reform. One of his books, *Cost the Limit of Price*, said Fitzhugh, was "profound and true" in its criticism of the current capitalist system.[71]

Holmes would later take Andrews to task along with Herbert Spencer in his critique of individualism, but not for now. In 1855, he was willing to give Fitzhugh's enthusiasm some indulgence even if it meant writing letters to the notorious founder of the "Free Love Institute of New York."[72] Two weeks after Fitzhugh's urging,

[70] Fitzhugh to Holmes, March 27, 1855.
[71] George Fitzhugh to G. F. Holmes, February 5, 1855, MS vol. 1808. S. P. Andrews to George Fitzhugh, January 19 and January 21, 1855, *ibid*. The most recent work on Andrews is Madeleine B. Stern, *The Pantarch: A Biography of Stephen Pearl Andrews* (Austin: University of Texas Press, [1968]). Stern, however, omits reference to this episode of collaboration between abolitionist and slavery apologist. More pertinent in this regard is Harvey Wish, "Steven Pearl Andrews, American Pioneer Sociologist," *Social Forces*, XIX (May 1941), 477–482.
[72] [Holmes], "Slavery and Freedom," p. 65. Stern mentions no Free Love

Holmes despatched a long criticism of his *Science of Society* (1851) to Andrews. "The principles laid down and developed by you," he wrote, "are not principles . . . deduced scientifically from existing facts . . . but . . . ideal aims toward which humanity ought to tend. How," he asked, "have you arrived at them?" Unfortunately, by merely theorizing. Andrews had not discovered "the practical truths of social science" but the "ends toward which science should aspire." He had inverted the entire scientific approach and "set the pyramid on its point." Archimedes, Holmes went on, boasted that he could move the world if given a fulcrum outside it for his lever. "A similar necessity exists in the moral and social order to move the world of man. The ideal aim—the final cause—is such a fulcrum—but it cannot be the lever also. Where then is your lever? You have taken the fulcrum for the lever. Will it answer the purpose?" Holmes thought not: a science of society could not be built on the ideals of an earthly utopia; nor, did he think, could even an authentic social science achieve such a condition of bliss as Andrews and his fellows had in mind.[73] Andrews accepted these censures in good spirit and told Fitzhugh when the two met in New York that Holmes's letter was "the best critique of his book that has ever been written";[74] but Holmes could only conclude that his northern correspondent was no scientist. Alas, he was not even a philosopher.[75]

Holmes's interest in Fitzhugh, though greater than his curiosity about Andrews, seems to have declined, or, at least, cooled, as time passed. He knew the Port Royal writer only through his writings and letters and what his brother-in-law, Rush Floyd, told him after meeting Fitzhugh in Washington, D. C. in 1857: "a great egotist; a monomaniac on the subject of slavery, and an intolerable bore—an old Virginia gentleman however—good natured and familiar."[76] When Fitzhugh neared the publication date of his second exposé of free society, *Cannibals All! or, Slaves Without Masters* (1857) he sent Holmes a copy of his preface in which he acknowledged his intellectual debt to his "corresponding acquaintance and friend, Professor H. of Virginia." Holmes was pleased at the notice but irritated by the exposure to public view: "I dislike notoriety and publicity," he grumbled. Imagine his reaction to the nine-page excerpt from his *Messenger* review of *Sociology for the South* reprinted in the book

---

Institute. Holmes might have been referring to the Grand Order of Recreation which was accused of being "a nest of free lovers." See Stern, *Pantarch*, p. 90.

[73] G. F. Holmes to S. P. Andrews, February 20, 1855, MS vol. 1808.

[74] Fitzhugh to Holmes, March 27, 1855.

[75] [Holmes], "Slavery and Freedom," p. 66.

[76] MS vol. 1791, April 15, 1857.

itself which denied Holmes even the slight anonymity of an initial![77]
In February he read the new work and found it generally superior
to the *Sociology*. But Fitzhugh, in his preface, had feared that "Mr. H
. . . would dissent from many of its details, from the unrestricted
latitude of its positions, and from its want of precise definition." The
reality was worse: Holmes found himself compelled to dissent from
"many of its principles" and to regard the work, on a whole, as
"incendiary and dangerous." The *Southern Literary Messenger*
wanted a review, but Holmes failed to provide one.[78] The omission
became obvious after the public support Holmes had given *Sociology
for the South*: in July, Fitzhugh wrote again to cajole Holmes into
speaking for him once more. The doctrines of *Cannibals*, he told
Holmes, are yours as well as mine. "You owe it to yourself . . . to
enforce and establish them in a review."[79] But no review of the new
work appeared.[80]

The reasons for this abandonment of Fitzhugh are not clear, but
possibilities may be suggested. Holmes was, of course, busy preparing
for his new appointment at Charlottesville and soon found his leisure
greatly reduced; moreover, he was entering that long period in which
he published nothing. Perhaps, to suggest another, he felt that silence
was the better part if he could not give at least the same degree of
qualified praise as earlier to the South's best-known champion. And
it is doubtful that he could give such praise in this case. Despite his
over-all approval, he had had reservations even about *Sociology for
the South* and, while recommending it to "every Southern man—
planter, lawyer, mechanic, merchant and politician," had thought it
too full of "wild fantasies" to be put into the hands of students.[81]
But what was there about *Cannibals All!* that provoked Holmes to
brand it "incendiary and dangerous?" Its defense of slavery and its
attack on free society were no more extreme than before. Was it
the timing of publication which he thought unfortunate coinciding
as it did with "Bleeding Kansas" and rising sectional tempers? Perhaps. Had he come to fear that Fitzhugh's immoderate views would
gain such notoriety abroad and in the North as to be accepted as the
South's views and so make impossible the serious debate on slavery

[77] Fitzhugh, *Cannibals All!*, preface, pp. 120–29. MS vol. 1791, August 9, 1856.

[78] MS vol. 1791, February 21, 1857.

[79] George Fitzhugh to G. F. Holmes, July 27, 1857, MS vol. 1808.

[80] Harvey Wish attributes an unsigned review to Holmes: "Cannibals All! or
Slaves Without Masters," *University Literary Magazine*, I (May 1857), 193–99.
The authorship is possible, of course; but there is nothing in the Holmes papers
to support the attribution and the style of the piece makes it improbable. Wish,
Fitzhugh, pp. 194–95.

[81] [Holmes], "Free Societies," pp. 129–30.

which Holmes hoped to foster? If so, his fear was well-grounded.[82] But there may have been more. Fitzhugh's unconcealed contempt for intellectual labor voiced in both books, his somewhat boastful revelation in *Cannibals All!* that he was no scholar, his ethnocentric provincialism, would all have repelled Holmes; a repulsion not lessened by the fact that Fitzhugh's errors were frequently but extreme forms of his own doctrines.[83] Indeed, they may have suggested to him the paradox that the sage of Port Royal, the outspoken enemy of the contemporary gospel of freedom, was himself infected by that very intellectual anarchy which Holmes and Comte considered a primary affliction of the age.

Holmes could not accept the extravagances of either friend or foe, of Fitzhugh or Andrews. A good cause was never well-served by ill means whatever the apparent pragmatic gains to be obtained. The scientific reform of society would not be accomplished by such enthusiasts as the prospective membership of the "New School of Philosophy" and Holmes held aloof until such time as he should find less eccentric collaborators.

But even while exploring such possibilities as Fitzhugh and Andrews offered, Holmes had turned to his own consideration of the slavery question in the hope that a calm, scientific investigation might help prepare the world to accept a suitable solution when one finally became possible.

[82] Wish, *Fitzhugh*, pp. 213, 280–81.
[83] Fitzhugh, *Sociology*, pp. 118, 183; *Cannibals All!*, pp. 58–59, 67, 130–36.

VII   Defending Slavery

FROM Holmes's view point, the urgent need for an historical study of slavery had been created largely by the movement for the immediate abolition of the peculiar institution which had been gaining strength steadily since the early thirties.[1] He considered this new phase of abolitionism the most dangerous form of contemporary revolt. In their demand that slavery be ended regardless of the consequences to southern civilization, the immediate abolitionists represented irresponsible reform at its worst. Supposedly dedicated to legitimate human freedom, their campaign more than any other reform movement seemed to press forward the modern rebellion against traditional social, moral and religious restraints on the individual. To Holmes, abolitionism was not a quest for freedom but a perversion of freedom; it was a true child of the nineteenth century. He found combined in it all the cynical and hypocritical exploitations of capitalism, all the disrespect for traditional usages and institutions, all the irresponsible and irreverent rationalism, all the illogical dogmatism that in lesser degree and in varying form infected the multitude of schemes which he spent his efforts opposing. In his analysis, false intellectualism provided its philosophy, false democracy its sentiment, and avarice its motivation. Just as the peasantry of Europe had been freed from villeinage because the landed classes found free labor to mean higher profits and the act afterward was rationalized as a deed of political enlightenment, so now "the clamour for universal freedom," the "outcry against African slavery," found popular support in the runaway enthusiasm for personal liberty characteristic of the century. It was, however, actually inspired by the hypocritical desire of northern and European capitalists to distract the attention of their victimized workers and postpone the day of reckoning. "The Pharisees of Northern Abolitionism," Holmes sneered, "are taught a pleasant escape from the consciousness of their own inequities and domestic disorders by magnifying the supposed guilt of their neighbors," while "the titled lords of the soil and greedy capitalists of

[1] For a perceptive analysis of immediatism, see David Brion Davis, "The Emergence of Immediatism in British and American Antislavery Thought," *Mississippi Valley Historical Review*, XLIX (September 1962), 209–30.

England, after . . . wringing profits or selfish gratifications from the agonies of famished labor . . . thank Heaven that they are not as Southern men are."[2] Abolitionism, then, brought the social crisis home to America as no other reform had. It represented a challenge not only to the South, which was its most obvious target, but to the nation as a whole. Domestic disruption, however, was not the only evil in prospect; Holmes warned that the turmoil stirred up by the crusade against Negro slavery could permanently frustrate what most Americans, north and south, took to be the historical mission of the United States: the extending by expansion or by example or both her beneficent democratic institutions to other peoples.[3]

Like many others at mid-century Holmes foresaw a time when the expanding empires of Russia and America would come into conflict. While the United States worked out her manifest destiny in the New World, Europe, her immediate rival, would become more and more decadent and eventually would be swallowed up by the giant Slavic state. Then, perhaps after a "lapse of centuries," history would "bring the two conflicting systems face to face, and prepare the great and final contest" for possession of the earth.[4] In the meantime, it was the historical opportunity and duty of America to expand her power throughout the Western hemisphere. The Latin lands to the south were clearly "reserved for the heritage of the Anglo-Saxon race, and for the energetic development of the American people."[5] Not only was the future well-being of the United States involved in this but "the propagation and amplification of modern civilization" required it. Any other course would be "reversing the order of human evolution."[6] This was the role that Providence had assigned to America; and yet, it could all be lost so easily if the American people allowed themselves to be turned aside by delusive domestic reforms and fraternal strife. The choice was clear to Holmes. America could turn from self-destruction and pursue her grand imperial destiny or she could yield to "a world-wide fanaticism, of no limited or transient origin—the creature of political ignorance, of religious bigotry, of sectional jealousy and of the frenzy of innovation" and so require Providence to achieve its purpose through the agency of

[2] [Holmes], "Slavery and Freedom," p. 81.

[3] For an informative discussion of conflicting American attitudes on the historical destiny of the United States see Frederick Merk, *Manifest Destiny and Mission in American History* (New York: A. Knopf, 1963).

[4] [Holmes], "California Gold," p. 303.

[5] George Frederick Holmes, "The Races of Europe," *Quarterly Review of the Methodist Episcopal Church, South*, IX (October 1855), 524.

[6] George Frederick Holmes, "Relations of the Old and the New Worlds," *De Bow's Review*, XX (May 1856), 528–31.

another people.[7] But if Holmes thought to divert the national attention from slavery by jingoistic appeals to empire, he chose an unfortunate tactic. Slavery was an issue in this as in virtually all else in the fifties: new territories must be either slave or free and the problem lost nothing in virulence by being exported.

Abolitionism was not an abstract threat for Holmes but a very personal one. He was no less a patriotic southron for being an adopted one and he felt keenly every abusive barb hurled from the North. Through Lavalette's property he was also a slaveholder, albeit a small one. Even so, he was no fire-eater. Despite his adherence to the positive good school of proslavery thought, his support of the peculiar institution was not unqualified. He recognized that the interests of his own economic group should not be allowed to take precedence over those of the community as a whole and favored emancipation if this should ever occur.[8] And, when the verdict of arms and the thirteenth amendment freed the slaves in 1865, he quietly resigned himself to the unavoidable.[9] Nor is it probable that he suffered many assaults of conscience over slavery. His inherited attitudes were, as in the case of social classes, conservative, genteel, and pro-slavery. His father had been a slaveholder and Maryanne must have instilled in him the feelings of superiority toward the blacks which are reflected in her notes on life in Demerara.[10] Slavery as he knew it in western Virginia seems to have presented him with little moral challenge to provoke reconsideration of his beliefs. In Tazewell County in 1860 whites outnumbered blacks approximately eight to one and small holdings of Negroes seems to have been the rule.[11]

I am assured [he wrote to the anti-slavery John McClintock in the fall of 1852] that slavery, as it exists here, will not disturb your conscience, when you witness it yourself. It may be a distressing sight on the large plantations—tobacco, cotton, rice or sugar—but where only a few slaves are on each farm, you would rather wonder at our patience in being troubled with them, than at their satisfaction with their condition.[12]

[7] George Frederick Holmes, "The Virginia Colony, or the Relation of the English Colonial Settlements in America to the General History of the Civilized World," *Virginia Historical Reporter*, II (1860), pt. 1.

[8] MS vol. 1802, p. 43.

[9] The discussion of slavery in his *Science of Society* (Charlottesville: Miller School Press, 1883) shows, however, that he had not changed his mind on its theoretical justification: see chapter XVII, section 4–13.

[10] Buchanan, *Holmes Family History*, pp. 13, 23–31.

[11] United States Census Office. *Eighth Census of the United States: 1860. Population*. (Washington: Government Printing Office, 1864), pp. 505, 513. Pendleton, *Tazewell County*, p. 606.

[12] Holmes to McClintock, October 1, 1852.

But given all this, his relationship to slavery contained elements of ambiguity and hesitation. The conventional cheerfulness and confidence in the institution which he expressed to others, and particularly to outsiders such as McClintock, was sometimes contradicted by his actions when he was not thinking about slavery and by his private thoughts. To illustrate, only a few months after he had written to McClintock in 1853 asking him to help him find a situation near New York, he had written to Samuel Tyler that he was thinking of moving to Maryland but would do so only if the laws would "allow me to bring my servants with me—for I would not part with them till they desire to part from me."[13] Very paternalistic; but he could have taken no "servants" to New York, of course .The idyllic picture of slavery given in his letter to McClintock (cited above) in which he tried to persuade the New Yorker to buy himself a "Sabine farm" in the Virginia mountains is in stark contrast to his diary entry of a few years later: "Heard that Israel had made incendiary remarks. I attach little credit to the rumour; but must inquire into it. The negroes in this county are depraved and dangerous."[14] Distress over slavery was apparently not confined to large plantations. It should also be noted that by 1860 Maryanne seems to have become opposed to the institution. She expressed to Ed her hope that he would "prefer the free states" if the threatened breakup of the Union came to pass. This could only have increased Holmes's ambivalence though it does not seem to have influenced his intellectual commitment.[15]

But to point out the two contrary images of slavery in Holmes's mind is not to imply that his defense of it was hypocritical. The study of history told him that no social institution was perfect and he was fully aware of the flaws in this one. Unlike some proslavery writers, he seldom made a special effort to conceal the brutalities which attended slavery. Indeed, George Fitzhugh was moved by one of Holmes's letters to confess soon after appearance of his *Sociology for the South*: "I assure you, Sir, I see great evils in Slavery, but in a controversial work I ought not to admit them."[16] Holmes disagreed. The South had nothing to gain by deception, particularly when it was unnecessary. And it was unnecessary. It was to argue that the

---

[13] Holmes to Tyler, August 25, 1854.

[14] MS vol. 1791, February 14, 1857.

[15] Maryanne Holmes to Edward A. Holmes, November 13, 1860, Buchanan, *Holmes Family History*, p. 62.

[16] Fitzhugh to Holmes, April 11, 1855. Fitzhugh's work was more candid than his theory. For admissions of faults in American slavery see George Fitzhugh, *Sociology for the South or the Failure of Free Society* (Richmond: A. Morris, 1854), pp. 95, 171, 211, and 250.

mere presence of evils in a social institution did not justify or require its destruction that Holmes added his voice to the growing clamor engaged in proslavery polemics during the fifties.

When "Southron," who had supported Holmes's bid for a place at the University of Virginia, published his endorsement in the *Enquirer*, he contrasted the "accurate and extensive learning" and the "profound, bold and original thought" of his favorite with that of the traditional (and, by 1856, somewhat dated) "apologists for slavery" who were, in his opinion, the South's "worst enemies." Better to have even a "Red Republican" or a "Radical Abolitionist" in the chair of history and general literature, he thought, than some "silly old fogy of the South, who admits that northern institutions are better than ours, but [who] begs the North to let us alone, or to give us time to get rid of slavery, because it would be dangerous to set all the negroes free at once." The South, wrote "Southron," must cease to fill places of public responsibility with "half-way abolitionists" who admit slavery is wrong in principle but who defend it on pragmatic grounds. Professor Holmes, who believed Negro slavery to be right in principle, would train not "apologists" for the South but "champions" who would take the war to the enemy.[17] Actually, the professor's version of the positive good argument then so popular in the South was not quite as extreme a rejection of the "old fogy" defenses of slavery as "Southron" thought. Holmes never endorsed slavery as fully as some. But, as far as intentions went, "Southron" had picked his man well, for Holmes's purpose was, as his advocate said, to convert his fellow Southerners from "apologists" for slavery into "champions" of it. In 1850, when he published his first serious piece on the question, he wrote in the conviction that his "time cannot be more profitably employed than in a calm and philosophic investigation of the causes which originate, the circumstances which perpetuate, the influences which modify, and the reasons which justify" slavery. Then, as later, he felt the urgency to combat the "malignity, hypocrisy, fraud, fanaticism, false philanthropy, and imbecility" of the abolitionists before their version of slavery became so established in the public mind that effective reply was impossible. At the same time, a necessary part of this effort was to remove the remaining "scruples and doubts of the weak or the unreflecting" among those old fogies—and young ones too—in the South.[18]

17 *Enquirer*, June 4, 1856.
18 [George Frederick Holmes], "Observations on a Passage in the Politics of Aristotle Relative to Slavery," *Southern Literary Messenger*, XVI (April 1850), 193. An earlier short piece indicates a dissatisfaction with the "necessary evil"

When Holmes entered the fray with his 1850 article on Aristotle's *Politics* the basic lines of the defence of slavery had already been laid down. Since the thirties the argument had shifted from the "necessary evil" approach inherited from the Founding Fathers and so execrated by "Southron" to the position that slavery was "a good—a positive good," to use the words of Calhoun.[19] During the fifties, this would be expanded into the claim that slave society was not only good in itself but superior to the rival free systems which existed in the northern states and in Europe. In its classic formulation the positive good argument was virtually a creation of South Carolina and, in the hands of men such as John C. Calhoun, Chancellor William Harper, James H. Hammond, and William Gilmore Simms, reached its point of most vigorous development at the same time that Holmes was attaching himself to the ideological world of the planters. The ingredients of the positive good defense—historical, racial, theological, and scientific justifications of Negro bondage—may be traced back to colonial times, but they had floated about in the Southern mind mixed with incompatible notions of natural rights and equality during the last decades of the eighteenth and much of the early part of the nineteenth century. As pressures increased, however, Southerners became increasingly of one mind. What was needed was a time of crisis to give cohesion to the argument and also to accomplish the expulsion of contrary ideas left over from the Revolution. This happened during the 1830s. The rise of a more aggressive abolitionism, the evident failure of the attempt to colonize freed blacks and the consequent realization by whites that emancipation meant a racially mixed society in the South, an increased uneasiness about possible slave revolts in imitation of Nat Turner's rebellion, a steady rise in sectional tensions, all combined to galvanize southern intellectuals. Spurred on by the South Carolinians and inspired by Virginian Thomas Dew's scholarly critique of the colonization scheme and other emancipationist ideas, few southern controversialists during the late forties and the fifties cared to maintain the earlier position. Holmes was no exception.[20]

position. See [George Frederick Holmes], "On Slavery and Christianity;" *Southern Quarterly Review*, III (January 1843), 252–56.

[19] Speech in the U. S. Senate February 6, 1837 quoted in Eric L. McKitrick, ed. *Slavery Defended: the Views of the Old South* (Englewood Cliffs: Prentice-Hall), p. 13.

[20] The fullest account of the proslavery argument is still William Sumner Jenkins, *Pro-Slavery Thought in the Old South* (Chapel Hill: University of North Carolina Press, 1935): for origins of the positive good theory in the colonial and early national periods see chapters 1 and 2. See also Winthrop D. Jordan, *White Over Black, American Attitudes Toward the Negro, 1550–1812*

Holmes had followed the controversy since the early 1840s and had read everything he could obtain dealing with the "feracious subject."[21] Even so, he felt forced to apologize to his readers for his failure to always use the sources they might expect. His isolation and poverty limited him, he explained, to what chance enabled him to consult or copy.[22] Holmes was not a literary brawler and despite an occasional outburst of caustic condemnation was able to maintain a high and impersonal tone in his writings. Although admitting that popular prejudice in the North and in Europe was opposed to slavery, Holmes rejected the contention of John Stuart Mill (and, by association, that of fellow southerners such as Chancellor William Harper) that reflective minds outside the South were also made up on the issue, and insisted that, on the contrary, the world was just turning to a serious and scientific examination of the question.[23] Unlike most of the South, Holmes believed that his section had much to gain by a free and open exchange of ideas. But public opinion, he realized, was a capricious thing, slow in basic change and almost unconscious in its processes.[24] No one could predict its course. Yet whatever the true situation, the South could not afford to assume that the battle was already lost.

Holmes was not interested only in controversy. Slavery deserved scientific study in its own right as an institution. It was "one of the principal and most enduring arrangements of humanity" whatever might be the right or wrong of it.[25] Happily, the defense of the South

---

(Chapel Hill: University of North Carolina Press, [1968]), pp. 304-11. For pro-slavery thought from antiquity on see David Brion Davis, *The Problem of Slavery in Western Culture* (Ithaca: Cornell University Press, [1966]). For the development of the positive good argument in South Carolina see, in addition to Jenkins, *supra*, Clement Eaton, *The Growth of Southern Civilization, 1790–1860* (New York: Harper and Brothers, [1961]), p. 304 and William W. Freehling, *Prelude to Civil War: The Nullification Controversy in South Carolina, 1816–1836* (Harper & Row, [1966]), pp. 79–82, 328–29. The reference is to Dew's *Review of the Debate in the Virginia Legislature of 1831 and 1832* (Richmond: T. W. W. White, 1832).

[21] George Frederick Holmes, "Bledsoe on Liberty and Slavery," *De Bow's Review*, XXI (August 1856), 142.

[22] [Holmes], "Observations," p. 205.

[23] [George Frederick Holmes], "Uncle Tom's Cabin," *Southern Literary Messenger*, XVIII (December 1852), 724-25. [Holmes], "Slavery and Freedom," p. 75. Chancellor Harper based his pessimism on the outside world's ignoring Thomas Dew's apologetics. William Harper in *The Pro-Slavery Argument* (Charleston: Walker, Richards and Company, 1852), pp. 2–3.

[24] Holmes, "Chastel," p. 29.

[25] George Frederick Holmes, "Ancient Slavery," *De Bow's Review*, XIX (November and December 1855), 559–60.

and the pursuit of science could be profitably mixed. Comparative historical studies might enable the present generation to purge from the institution the dross of outmoded custom.[26] Perhaps the fault lay not in slavery as such, but in weaknesses that could be remedied. In any event, the commitment of the Western world to the ideal of science made such an objective examination of slavery mandatory. Facts had to be established—no easy job in itself—and specific problems carefully delineated. This Holmes saw as his immediate task, and in accomplishing it, in preparing the way for some future scientifically sound resolution of the slavery problem, he was also advancing the interests of the South: interests that threatened to be surrendered virtually by default as long as southerners were content to allow abolitionists to write the commonly accepted history of slavery, substituting for science their "hasty compilations, patched together without discrimination, enriched by the idle stories and copious misrepresentations of trashy newspapers, but illuminated by neither philosophy nor learning, and unredeemed by either intelligence or sincerity."[27] An objective history of slavery such as he wanted, Holmes knew, was necessarily a work of time. In the meantime "every interest, every . . . sect" must have its voice—and that of the South must not be the least among them. When all have been heard, perhaps "a general concurrence may be attained," but, he warned, "that concurrence will be unfavorable, perhaps, ruinous to the slave-holding communities, unless they, too, find a voice for the expression of their views, and examine and interpret for themselves the series of facts wrested from their true sense to their discomfiture." As things stood, the abolitionists had "proceeded in their indictment of slave-holders like honest Dogberry: 'Masters, it is proved already that you are little better than false knaves; and it will go near to be thought so shortly.'" Pro-slavery writers, equally guilty of neglecting a scientific historical approach (although there had been historical writing enough), all too often had merely entered a "plea of confession and avoidance."[28] Propaganda from either side was not what was needed.

Any defense of slavery, if it was to be intelligible, had to rest upon an explicit definition of slavery. Holmes was critical of most of the commonly received definitions because of their legalistic indifference to the impact of historical change on the institution. Slavery, he held, had always existed, but it had not always and everywhere been the same. Its familiar aspects, those which people would immediately

---

[26] *Ibid.*, p. 635. [Holmes], "Universities," p. 449.
[27] Holmes, "Ancient Slavery," pp. 560–61.
[28] *Ibid.*, pp. 560, 562.

settle on as the basis of a definition, were quite variable and consequently it was fallacious to attempt to define slavery by the usage of any one time or place.[29] If slavery were to be defined at all, the definition had to be limited to its essence alone. To illustrate, Holmes quoted the definition of slavery put forth by the seventeenth-century French jurisconsult, Jean Domat: "The slave is one who is under the power of a master and belongs to him, so that his master may sell him and dispose of his person, his industry, and the fruits of his labor, without his having the power to make anything, have anything, or acquire anything which shall not belong to his master." A priori definitions such as this, Holmes argued, which attempted a universally valid statement of the circumstances of slavery were invariably unhistorical. Domat's definition was contrary to practice in the Roman Empire where the master's power of life and death was restricted, in ancient Athens where a slave could buy his own freedom or force a cruel master to sell him, and in the American South where Negroes frequently hired themselves out and made money.[30] That the last was a matter of custom rather than of law underscored Holmes's point: slavery could never be understood or characterized by consulting only law books. The reality of slavery, past and present, was a matter of life, of history, and not merely a matter of law.[31]

This would seem to leave Holmes with the conclusion that slavery was an institution that could be described as it had existed during any given historical era, but one that could not be defined by a generalization valid in all eras. He insisted, however, that bondage did possess an universality which could be captured in a definition. The essence of slavery, he thought, was not to be found in the material condition of the bondman, in his rights or his legal status; the essence of slavery existed in the relation between master and slave. An "accurate view of slavery," he wrote, would be to "regard it as continuous and involuntary dependence and service, leaving the degree of dependence and its form, and the character and extent of the service undefined, as these vary with the varying moods of masters, and the fluctuating conditions of society." Slavery, then, essentially involved "undefined

[29] The difficulty of defining such an amorphous institution as slavery is appreciated by Davis, *Problem of Slavery*, pp. 30, 31–35, 246. See also W. W. Buckland, *The Law of Slavery: the Condition of the Slave in Private Law from Augustus to Justinian* (Cambridge: Cambridge University Press, 1908), pp. 1–8.

[30] [Holmes], "Observations," p. 195.

[31] Interestingly, the modern Tannenbaum school of slavery historiography has been criticized for relying too much on the letter of the law and not enough on actual practice. See Davis, *Problem of Slavery*, p. 225n and, more recently, Carl Degler, "Slavery in Brazil and the United States: An Essay in Comparative History," *American Historical Review* (April 1970), 1006–07.

and continuous" service which could not be legally limited by the will of the slave. Historical factors, Holmes believed,

circumstances, and degrees of civilization, the comparative density and the proportions of the population, the amount and the distribution of capital, may vary the forms [of the relationship]. But [when] enforced by law, it is termed slavery—if enforced by custom . . . it may be called merely service,—but in its real essence, it is no less continuous, involuntary, and unlimited dependence, consequently no less slavery.[32]

The idea of slavery as an involuntary dependent relationship as well as a legally sanctioned condition of bondage, which can be found in a number of pro-slavery writers, led logically to the attacks on the capitalistic free labor system which Holmes and others, and especially George Fitzhugh, leveled against the North in the 1850s. A worker, they said, whom necessity forced to labor on terms dictated by his employer, who has no real choice in the nature of his work, and who was denied a union to enable him to change the terms of his employment, was just as much a slave as any Negro toiling in an Alabama cotton field. Free labor in the factories of the North and, even more so, of Europe was covert slavery with all of its evils and none of its benefits. Fitzhugh drew the obvious conclusion and advocated the enslavement of the European working class (though in a milder form than American Negroes knew) for in Europe the sufferings of labor had reached a maximum degree of inhumanity.[33] Holmes never went so far. Unlike Fitzhugh, he was not interested in completely discrediting free society as a system but in defending the propriety of slave holding and, once he had a clear idea of what slavery was, he turned to this more compelling problem.[34]

When Holmes first took up the issue, southerners had had some success convincing people outside the South that Negro bondage was economically necessary because of the world-wide importance of the cotton crop and that it was politically and socially desirable because of the unassimilability of the Negroes, but even the most sympathetic doughface or cotton-whig had trouble accepting the growing southern contention that Negro slavery was just. It was this weak spot which he judged to have been left in the southern armor by Calhoun, Harper, Dew and other apologists that Holmes hoped to reenforce.[35] If the world could be persuaded that slavery

[32] [Holmes], "Observations," p. 195.
[33] Fitzhugh, *Sociology for the South*, pp. 94–95.
[34] Holmes, "Fitzhugh's Sociology," p. 190; [Holmes], "Slavery and Freedom," p. 86.
[35] [Holmes], "Observations," p. 193.

was just under some circumstances and in some historical periods, then the moral propriety of American Negro slavery could be more accurately evaluated. Holmes did not attempt to show—nor did he believe—that slavery was always right; rather he argued that it was not always wrong. In Holmes's opinion, there were two ways to convince any rational man of this. One was the natural law argument put forth in its classic form by Aristotle. The second, a related argument, was a moral corollary of the popular belief in human progress and in the mission of America.

The main thesis for slavery had been laid down by Aristotle in the *Politics*: " 'Nature has clearly designed some men for freedom and others for slavery,—and with respect to the latter, slavery is both just and beneficial.' " Holmes acknowledged that the harshness of this observation made it offensive to the modern libertarian temper, but it was no less true for that. The reasoning behind it as a general principle had never been refuted and, in the nineteenth century, it still stood "firm as a rock unshaken by the vain assaults continually directed against it."[36] Holmes, however, could not accept Aristotle's position without some modification. The dictum as it stood implied that the justice of slavery was determined solely by differences between human beings and was not influenced by other factors. He, on the other hand, believed that slavery could be unjust even in cases where the man held in bondage was a "natural" slave.

The institutions and customs which Holmes thought to be natural for man, that is in accord with natural law, were not to be discovered by speculation—a persistent error in the nineteenth century—but by the study of history. "The only mode of determining what is natural, and what is unnatural in Social and Political Philosophy," Holmes wrote, "is to discover what things are habitually attached to Political or Social Organization, in the various stages of its development."[37] Holmes was almost saying that whatever was, is right. But not quite. Unlike some proslavery writers he did not argue that slavery was right simply because it had always existed. He based his case on history but not on such simple history as that. Nor was he merely proposing a shallow utilitarian relativism: that the "right" institutions are those that do the job. He offered, instead, a means of determining what was in accord with the design of Providence and what was not. Here, as elsewhere, his view of historical development is predicated on the idea of a reigning Providential order. He recognized that while some human institutions or principles of association were universal because society could not exist without them, there were

---

[36] *Ibid.*, pp. 193–94. [Holmes], "Slavery and Freedom," p. 75.
[37] [Holmes], "Observations," p. 196.

others which were legitimate only when they served a necessary historical function; and, while they might survive beyond the time in which they originated, they no longer enjoyed the sanction of natural law when their usefulness had ended. The dependency of some men on others, in which Holmes recognized the essence of slavery and which Aristotle thought distinguished master from slave, was a universally and necessary condition of human society.[38] But, unlike Aristotle, Holmes did not conclude from this that slavery was also universally proper; chattel slavery, on the contrary, was in his second category. In was an institution that was natural and just only under certain circumstances. What were the circumstances? There were two. Slavery was just under natural law when the welfare of a given Society depended on it and when the improvement or permanent supervision of an inferior race required it.

This left the slaveholder with little to disturb his conscience for it would take no great casuistical ability to justify oneself under these broad and general sanctions. Negro slavery had obvious economic importance to the modern world. Its function as a brake on the rate of social changes in the South was no less important. And men, whatever their race, could always stand improvement. Nor was it easy, if one accepted Holmes's line of argument, to find sound reasons for opposing slavery. Brutalization of slaves was no argument against it. Individual masters might abuse their wards, but this gave no grounds for abolishing slavery as its enemies mistakenly imagined. One might as reasonably suggest doing away with the family or marriage because parents sometimes abuse their children and husbands their wives. All three institutions were natural and good.[39] But Holmes did not intend for the sanction implied in the comparison to be exact. Slavery, unlike the family and marriage, was not a universal necessity. And it was just "only so long as it . . . advances the interests of the slave concurrently with the interests of the master." This he found in accord with "the great law of social morals and social wisdom . . . that all men are created for each other; but no man, no class, no race is created for the particular and separate interest of another man, another class, or another race. If selfishness in the individual is sin, it is vice, and blindness, and fatal folly in society."[40] The master class, of course, by virtue of its advanced state, would be the judge of how well the interest of the slave was served.

As a Christian Holmes could not be satisfied with a defense of slavery that rested its case only on the authority of Aristotle and the

[38] *Ibid.*, pp. 194–96.
[39] Holmes, "Ancient Slavery," pp. 566–67.
[40] [Holmes], "Slavery and Freedom," p. 88.

doctrines of natural law. Powerful though these arguments were, he knew that the light of nature was a weak and sometimes a false guide. While, unlike so many southerners, he did not find confirmation in scripture for the enslavement of Negroes specifically, it seemed clear that the Christian revelation sanctioned the institution of slavery generally, and once this was accepted reason could work out the proper limitations on its practice. Holmes found this general sanction in those passages customarily cited by other pro-slavery writers: God's approval of the slave system among the Patriarchs of the Old Testament and Paul's assurances to slaves that conversion to Christianity did not release them from their obligations to their masters.[41] Merging divine approval with his own conclusions based on natural law Holmes reasoned that slavery was not contrary to the Gospel unless those held in bondage were capable of exercising their freedom in a wise and civilized way. The history of Haiti and other alledgedly abortive attempts to allow the slaves liberty showed him that Negroes had not yet reached a state of maturity in which they could be trusted to govern themselves. "When the African slave," he decided, "is prepared to take advantage of and improve by our modern civilization, if manumitted, then it would be contrary to the spirit of the Gospel to prolong the state of servitude."[42] But not before. How they were to learn self-government while in a state of dependent servitude he did not explain.

An important part of Holmes's defense of Negro bondage rested on the claim that black men were benefited by association with whites. How, then, did he justify the enslavement of persons of the same race, as in antiquity? This was no problem. Equals in race might be enslaved justly to discipline them, to introduce them to a higher level of culture, or, to save them from their vices when their own civilization was in decline.[43] Thus the Romans could quite rightly enslave the wild Germans, the backward Gauls and Iberians, the degenerate Greeks. Nonetheless, Holmes had to recognize that most moderns, whatever their opinion about Negro slavery, looked on ancient slavery as an evil.

In response to this attitude, he determined to show that ancient slavery, whatever its shortcomings, had not been the cause of the decline of classic civilization as had been so often alleged by authorities from Montesquieu to Guizot and as was contended by such in-

41 [Holmes], "Observations," p. 196. MS vol. 1802, p. 374. The passages in the New Testament cited by Holmes were 1 Timothy VI: 1–5 and 1 Cor. VII: 20–24.
42 [Holmes], "Observations," p. 197.
43 Holmes, "Ancient Slavery," pp. 570–71.

fluential histories as Henri Wallon's *Histoire de l'esclavage dans l'antiquité* (1847) and most recently in an article "in a contemporary review by a learned professor at the north."[44] On the contrary, said Holmes, the glories of Greece and Rome could not have existed without it. It had not "rendered labor disreputable, and thereby degraded the citizens and impoverished the state." Contempt for manual labor was a mark of high civilization and would exist whether or not slavery was present. It had not "displaced free laborers, and destroyed the population, the industry, and the agriculture of the ancient world." Slavery, in fact, flourishes only where the free laboring population is inadequate. It was the land hunger of the rich that drove the yeomen off their farms and into the cities and the dole which kept them there that destroyed the economy of the ancient world. Slavery, Holmes argued, merely filled the labor vacuum so created. Nor did slavery sap the vitality of the ancient world and lead to the decline and fall of Rome. It was not slavery but the "decay of public and private virtues" and "the increase of wealth, luxury, and rapacity" that accomplished the destruction of the ancient world. To be sure, these vices might, and did, lead to an evil abuse of slavery, but slavery was not their cause.[45] As moderns should know, they could exist all too easily in the absence of slavery.

With his belief that slavery could be unnatural and wrong as well as natural and right, Holmes recognized that a demonstration of the propriety of ancient bondage did not constitute a defense of American Negro slavery.[46] No, the justice of the enslavement of the Negro had to stand or fall alone. But the general sanctions of philosophy, history, and scripture, as he and others worked them out, coupled with his acceptance of the conventional southern belief in the near-universality of the benevolent master ever attentive to the improvement of his wards, gave Holmes confidence that it stood.[47] But even though he yielded place to no man in his defense of it, he did not believe it would stand forever.

Ancient slavery had been historically necessary; and because it was necessary, it was also morally right and natural. Indeed, to call slavery a necessary evil was for Holmes a contradiction in terms.

[44] *Ibid.*, pp. 563–64, 572–73. The identity of the "learned professor" has not been discovered.

[45] *Ibid.*, pp. 572–621. The relation of slavery to the ancient world is still a subject of debate. Holmes's position finds some modern defenders. See, for instance, the essays collected in M. I. Finley, ed., *Slavery in Classical Antiquity: Views and Controversies* (Cambridge: Heffer & Sons, [1960]).

[46] Holmes, "Ancient Slavery," pp. 569–70.

[47] [Holmes], "Uncle Tom's Cabin," p. 729.

When slavery was truly necessary—as in the South—it could never be wrong though admittedly it might contain abuses. When it lost this historical necessity, when it no longer served a socially useful purpose, it would die out in accordance with the laws governing the development of society. This was what Holmes expected eventually to happen to American Negro slavery. Given his belief in the racial inferiority of Negroes, however, it is doubtful that he expected the great mass of blacks in the South to advance in civilization to the point where their emancipation would clearly be the course of justice. He anticipated, instead, that southern society would eventually reach a stage of economic development and population density that would make chattel slavery no longer advantageous to the whites. Consequently, when faced with forceful abolition as a result of the Civil War, he wrote in his diary: "It would have been better if it could have died out slowly by the progress of events and the change of interests." But, he added, "It must go more rapidly now—and bring much misery to both black and white by its extinction."[48]

In order to encompass fully Holmes's thinking on the slavery question, and to understand his second argument for slavery, that it was humanitary and progressive, it is necessary to recall that in his historical writing of the early 1840s he gave great importance to the element of race. And for him, as for many other historians of mid-century, race continued to be one of the determining forces in world history.[49] Holmes's notion of race would not satisfy a modern critic, but it was a common-sense one for his time. First of all, by race he designated the obvious major groupings conventionally based on skin color: white, black, yellow, red. By race he also meant any group which was culturally distinct: for instance, Latins, Germans, Slavs, Arabs, and so forth. Hence, caucasian Europeans constituted a "race" but within this there were also English, French and German "races."

The importance of race was primary to a correct understanding of history. "It is a remarkable phenomenon," he wrote, "attested by every page of history, and so strongly confirmed that it may be regarded as the law of the succession of nations, that every great change of civilized dominion is attended and produced by a coincident change of race." Furthermore, the tide of history was irreversible;

[48] MS vol. 1791, February 24, 1862. Also G. F. Holmes to Tom Taylor, January 6, 1845, Holmes papers, D.

[49] Herbst, *German Historical School*, p. 7. Calcott, *History in the United States*, pp. 167–171. Levin, *History as Romantic Art*, ch. 6. M. Seliger, "Race Thinking During the Restoration," *Journal of the History of Ideas*, IXX (April 1958), 273–82. Thomas F. Gosset, *Race: the History of an Idea in America* (Dallas: Southern Methodist University Press, 1963), pp. 87–98.

one race, having had its day, was never again given the chance to lead.[50] If to the Marxist the pivot of history was the class struggle, for Holmes it was the race struggle. But all races were not equal in the struggle. Some would never bare the torch of progress while others would each have their turn advancing the fortunes of humanity. The less gifted would at best struggle along in the flickering light cast by the brilliance of the more able. At worst, the lesser races would be destroyed in the struggle.

Conquest, extension, appropriation, assimilation, and even the extermination of inferior races has been and must be the course pursued in the development of civilization. Woe may be unto those by whom the offence comes, when there is a real offence—but such is unquestionably the plan prescribed for the progressive amelioration of the world.[51]

Holmes saw the culture of all societies as aggressive, proselytizing, and expansive. Each sought to transform neighboring groups in accord with its own image; each obeyed a command of nature to erase the alien. Hence there arose the drive toward conquest that had characterized the great nations of the past and was no less characteristic of those of the present. "It is a fixed law of society, or at least of history," he wrote, "that every type of civilization aspires after universality, and that an unrealized tendency to unity brings, more or less imperfectly, together into one system contemporary nations of like social grade and development." In this way the races of Europe had been molded into a single force: they had evolved a common civilization; the balance-of-power conception of international relations had made possible a serviceable political unity; and colonialism had turned Europe outward to spread its culture over the earth.[52]

But if race was the secret of the success of some nations, it was also the cause of the failure of others. In 1844 Holmes wrote a long essay on the dismal future apparently in store for the American Indian. The red men were a race doomed by their inability to adjust to the changing demands of an advancing order. "If . . . they cannot alter their condition and live as civilized men," he concluded, "they must pay the penalty entailed upon them by their nature, and must give way to other races."[53] A similar fate he thought probably awaited all primitive people; the experience of the Indians seemed illustrative of an historical law: keep up or die. This was a hard doctrine and Holmes warned it should not be allowed to smother compassion for

---

[50] Holmes, "Races of Europe," pp. 538–39.
[51] Holmes, "Old and New Worlds," p. 529.
[52] *Ibid*., pp. 522–26.
[53] [Holmes], "North American Indians," p. 133.

those whom nature had condemned. They should be saved if possible; but there seemed to be only two ways to save them: amalgamation or enslavement. Needless to say, the former had little to recommend it to Holmes; the latter seemed far better suited to the purposes of Providence.

In 1856 he took the Papuans of New Guinea as a test case for the thesis that primitive peoples could be most humanely dealt with by making slaves of them. The natives of Papua were too dangerous to be let alone—they were pirates—and too savage to tame through the efforts of missionaries; it was very doubtful that they could ever civilize themselves. But, fortunately for them, and for the outside world, they improved marvelously under slavery, showing a much greater aptitude for this mode of instruction than did the white races. Regrettably, the necessary means to this end was the slave trade which, Holmes admitted, was barbarous; but the only alternative to it—continued savagery and murder—he thought much worse.[54] Humanity, therefore, supported his contention: civilized slavery was preferable to the free but wild life of the backward races. This, then, was the argument based on the moral imperative of a faith in progress. Slavery was the only way to deal mercifully with the wretched of the earth.

It followed easily from such considerations that American Negro slavery was the most proper and just form of bondage yet known to mankind. The evidences of history, from the inscriptions of ancient Egypt on, demonstrated that the Negro had always been a slave. He was a slave by custom and by nature: "the virtues of the Negro are the virtues of slavery," Holmes proclaimed, "and become vices when his condition is changed."[55] While there might be a reasonable doubt about the justice of some forms of slavery, there could be none about Negro servitude. In a case where the enslaved race was "confessedly the lowest type of humanity" Holmes found the humanitarian and supervisory function of it unquestionable.[56] Nor could anyone seriously challenge the economic need for Negro bondage: cotton undergirded Western civilization. In Holmes's view, then, black men fit admirably both of the requirements of natural law: white civilization needed them and they needed white civilization.

But this suggests a paradox. To be just without ambiguity slavery must perform both historical functions simultaneously. It must serve the interests of both master and man. What would be the case if—and

---

[54] [George Frederick Holmes], "The Papuans—Negritos," *Quarterly Review of the Methodist Episcopal Church, South,* X (October 1856), 493–507.

[55] [Holmes], "Observations," p. 200.

[56] Holmes, "Ancient Slavery," pp. 570–71.

this would seem to be what Holmes anticipated for the South—if the master class lost its need for the slaves before the slaves lost their need for the masters. Under his scheme, to free the slaves while they needed tutelage would be wrong; conversely, to keep them in bondage, even for their good, when the interests of society were harmed by it would also be wrong. The difficulty was that while Holmes's justification of Negro slavery assumed a static society in the south, his expectations for the future of the region assumed a dynamic one. To be sure, slavery was there to act as a brake; but such a brake would only slow, it would not stop. Eventually the interests of the slaveholders and slaves would diverge. What then would be the just course? Abolition? The slaves need guidance. Bondage? Society needs free labor. Was Holmes aware of this future dilemma? There is no sign of it. But, then, he seems to have had a weakness for inherently unstable solutions.

Not all of Holmes's efforts in defense of the peculiar institution were devoted to historical and philosophical discourses. In 1852 he answered an appeal from the editor of the *Southern Literary Messenger* to write a review a Harriet Beecher Stowe's *Uncle Tom's Cabin*: "hot as hell-fire, blasting and searing the reputation of the vile wretch in petticoats who could write such a volume."[57] Holmes's belief in the wisdom of scientific candor about the treatment of slaves in the South weakened in the face of an assault like *Uncle Tom's Cabin*. In his review he protested that Mrs. Stowe's calumnies were the fruit of ignorance, distortion, and malice and contrary to the experience of every southerner. He wavered, however, between patriotism and objectivity and in his closing remarks admitted that her charges could not be "utterly" denied, although the instances of cruelty she recorded were far from typical. When Mrs. Stowe published her *Key to Uncle Tom's Cabin* defending herself against such criticism and citing her sources, Holmes had recovered his composure sufficiently to acknowledge the substantial truth of her stories: such things did occasionally happen. Indeed, he could tell worse if he chose. But the accuracy of her volume was not the issue, armies of indignant southrons to the contrary notwithstanding. As he emphasized in his initial review and repeated in his essay on the *Key*, the real danger of the novel was the thesis that "any organization of society . . . which can by possibility result in such instances of individual misery, or generate such examples of individual cruelty as are exhibited in this fiction, must be criminal in itself, a violation of all the laws of Nature and of God, and ought to be universally con-

[57] J. R. Thompson to G. F. Holmes, August 24, 1852, vol. I, Holmes papers, LC.

demned, and consequently immediately abolished." This idea, Holmes asserted, was "absolutely fatal to a human society" of any kind—or, at least, of any kind possible to man given his present nature.[58] It was no surprise to him that *Uncle Tom's Cabin* proved so popular with those deluded men who were universally rising up in rebellion against the laws of God and man.

Holmes also contributed to the South's cause through his support of George Fitzhugh's attempt to turn the still defensive positive good argument into an offensive and carry the war to the enemy by attacking the very idea of a "free society." Holmes had hoped that the furor over *Uncle Tom's Cabin* would be followed by a period of quiet reaction in which a calm discussion of slavery would be possible. By 1854, when Fitzhugh published *Sociology for the South*, he had begun to lose that hope; but it was still possible that Fitzhugh, by stirring the South to the offensive, could provoke an equally candid, even if more abusive, debate.[59]

Fitzhugh's emphasis on the failure of free society, though overdrawn in Holmes's judgment, was congenial to him, complementing as it did his own thesis that abolitionism was basically a hypocritical diversionary movement and that the disruptions currently rampaging in the North and in Europe were the effects of the extreme libertarian philosophies dominant there. But he found *Sociology for the South* lacking in serious ways. Its basic flaw was an indifference to the role of social law in molding societies and to the importance of social science as an instrument of reform. For Fitzhugh, social science seemed to be little more than a stick for beating the North. Having no adequate grasp of his subject, he easily made mistakes. He was wrong in lauding slave labor as just and free labor as unjust without sufficient qualification. He was wrong in blaming the failure of free societies almost solely on the free labor system; societies were never so simplistic in their operation. He was wrong in underestimating the force of moral and intellectual errors. The free communities of the North and Europe were, Holmes thought, being destroyed more by greed and selfishness, which evils were encouraged by the dogmas of individualism and egalitarianism, than by the condition of freedom. Free society need not always fail; he believed that, in certain stages of civilization, the concentrations of population and industry required it. But it would fail "in conjunction with free competition and the rabid pursuit of gain" which produced an indifference to the fate of the worker. At times Fitzhugh seemed aware of the importance of

58 [Holmes], "Uncle Tom's Cabin," pp. 726–28, 730. [Holmes], "Key," pp. 323–25.
59 Holmes, "Fitzhugh's Sociology," pp. 180, 187–88.

ideas but he was too prone to simply embrace the opposite of the doctrine he denounced. Hence he made the mistake of condemning political economy in its entirety when, as Holmes had pointed out, the evils it had created were the result of an abuse of the discipline rather than of its proper use.

As unwelcome as anything was Fitzhugh's attack on the southern traditions of agriculture and free trade. Too exclusively an agricultural economy, he felt, had hurt the South. The remedy lay in economic diversification: manufacturing, commerce, and the growth of towns. This accomplished, the South would become self-sufficient and her civilization would bloom. Holmes thought not. Salvation for the South did not lay in "imitating, aping, borrowing and rivalling" the North in a desire to grow rich quickly. There were already too many boosters in the South and Fitzhugh's program would, if followed, rapidly turn the South into a copy of the North. Since capitalistic enterprise required free labor the end of slavery would follow and with its going would come all the ills of free society. Southerners, he went on, had not themselves learned the lesson they were trying to teach the rest of the world: that slow gradual social change was the *sine qua non* of social tranquility, and slavery was the best guarantor of gradual social development.[60]

And yet, despite Fitzhugh's shortcomings, there was considerable truth in his message. Free societies had

unquestionably failed, they have not produced the permanent or general blessings anticipated from them, they have produced overwhelming social disaster, multiplied indefinitely the woes and the vices of the poor, threatened all society and government and national existence in those communities, and announced a future so dark that little more than its gloom and spectral shapes can be distinctly recognized."[61]

Fitzhugh was right also in his insistence on the ubiquity of slavery. It was a persistent institution. In free societies where men had attempted to abolish it by simply outlawing it, it merely changed its name and continued on. It could not be abolished save by the slow and natural processes of social and economic change, and totally ended in all forms and essences throughout the earth—never.[62]

Holmes's fundamental differences with Fitzhugh are significant. He did not see the universal enslavement doctrines of *Sociology for the South* and *Cannibals All!* as "the logical outcome of the slave-

---

[60] *Ibid.*, pp. 187–88, 190–91. [Holmes], "Free Societies," pp. 131–36. [Holmes], "Working Classes," p. 203. Fitzhugh, *Sociology*, pp. 81, 118, 155–56, 183.

[61] [Holmes], "Free Societies," pp. 136–37.

[62] Holmes, "Ancient Slavery," pp. 564–66.

holders' philosophy." His own natural law argument, which geared the justice of slavery to variable conditions, was opposed to such a conclusion. For Holmes the South was fortunate to have a means of escaping the engulfing social dissolution; but her advantage was not for export. Social science, not re-instituted slavery, was to solve the problems of free society. This means that if Eugene Genovese is correct in his interpretation of Fitzhugh and the world view of the Old South, Holmes was a bourgeois interloper in a pre-capitalistic society.[63] Despite the fact that at times (as in his aversion to industrializing the South) he stood closer to the planter-cavalier ideal than even Fitzhugh, he was in the South but not completely of it. His sights were set beyond and his concern was with the fate of bourgeois civilization as a whole. Modern revolt and reform, of which the abolitionist crusade was merely the most immediate part to confront Holmes, proved to him that the future of this civilization was tied up with the future of Christianity. They were both under attack by the same forces.

In his work on slavery Holmes tried to demonstrate what he had argued in other contexts as well: that social problems could only be solved by a true social science. Neither he nor anyone else had been able to construct and apply such a science, but if the laws of society held the secret to reform, his appointment to the University of Virginia gave him another opportunity to discover them. Unfortunately, the world would not wait. Holmes's work on slavery was neither dogmatic nor final and was intended to clear the air for discussion, not to end it. But the time for talking had passed.

63 Genovese, *World Slaveholders Made*, part II, passim.

VIII In the Groves of Academe
1857-1897

IN THE autumn of 1857 Holmes left the mountains for the University of Virginia. His hopes were high, but he did not find there the anticipated end to his trials. During the hectic September in which he left Burke's Garden he busied himself trying to get his crops in without loss, hiring an overseer for Tanglewood, and settling as many of his local debts as he could. Shortage of money forced him to leave several works of history, philosophy, and reference from his library with the local doctor. Finally, late in the month, and after deciding to leave the children temporarily in the Garden, Holmes and Lavalette set out on an extended nine-day journey to Charlottesville.[1]

They arrived to find poor accommodations and the town in a great uproar because of a bank suspension. Not long after, the general confusion coinciding with Holmes's advent was enhanced by a typhoid epidemic at the University which eventually provoked student demonstrations and a few desertions. The harried Holmes was forced to give his "introductory address" on the morning following his arrival but, mercifully, it was another week before classes began. Disappointingly few students enrolled in his courses at first, and he found himself "very much exhausted" by the unaccustomed effort of lecturing. Unable to find a suitable place to live, he finally settled in a very unsatisfactory boarding house: "a gun twice fired off below my window to-night," he wrote in his diary, "This is the fourth since Lav left fired at, from, or near our Boarding House." Meanwhile, Lavalette, who was pregnant again and hated boarding house life, returned to the mountains to get the children; she was to stay almost the entire winter.[2]

The first several months that Holmes spent at the University were an agony of loneliness and frustration. The despairs of that unfortunate winter began in late November when Brewster, the new overseer at Tanglewood, asked permission to leave the farm because Lavalette would not permit the slaves to do his laundry and cooking.

[1] MS vol. 1791, September 1857.
[2] *Ibid.*, October and November 1857; February 4, 1858. Letitia Preston Lewis to Nicketti Johnston, June 24, 1858, typed copy in possession of N. Floyd Holmes.

Holmes had no choice but to consent even though he believed that with Brewster went the last possibility that Tanglewood would show a profit. He later discovered that his overseer had taken it upon himself to sell two of Holmes's favorite steers and, by one means or another, had lost his employer about a thousand dollars. But even with that the course of his economic misfortune was not ended. After Brewster's departure, Lavalette decided to stay on for awhile and, with the help of a Mr. Johnston, put Tanglewood in order. Her husband was despondent over this development. "Poor Lav," he sorrowed, "she has been breaking her heart in efforts to do the best she could, and to arrange everything economically and profitably . . . and yet I fear that two or three thousand dollars will hardly cover the losses occasioned by her prudent management." Lavalette also decided to leave the slaves on Tanglewood without an overseer. This was risky and foolish, Holmes thought, for they would certainly produce nothing but expense and disorder. Nor was that all. "The grain and stock I left behind was worth about $3000," he worried. "Will there be $1000 worth of it left next summer? But, poor Lav meant and acted for the best—and this is a full excuse for me, and as usual entirely satisfactory for herself." Sarcasm, however, could not fully relieve his feelings. A bill of indictment seemed in order. "She made me leave the Garden and go to Jeffersonville—ruin. She made me give up the management of Tanglewood to herself and Ed—ruin again—scarcely relieved by five years labour. Now she has made me give up everything to herself and Mr. Johnston." As in the past, Holmes saw no prospect but defeat coming out of his wife's enterprises. One cannot believe, however, that Holmes's continuing difficulties were all Lavalette's fault. Maryanne knew her son and, in 1860, when he considered selling Tanglewood, she exploded to Ed,

The very place you had by both energy of mind & body been making into a valuable farm! I can not comprehend him—he is continually changing his plans. The professorship at 4 or 5 hundred [pounds] a year, with proper management he ought to have laid by the half of it. Long since he had said his professorship would soon relieve him of all pecuniary difficulties, and now he seems to be worse off than ever!

Quite apart from the worry of financial loss, the absence of his family hurt Holmes's studies and lecturing; and this, in time, raised the fear that his one-year trial appointment would not be made permanent. In his diary, he bitterly accused Lav of being careless of time and thoughtless. He was convinced that, in view of her belief that she could do nothing wrong and his absolute lack of influence over her, if he should fail at the University, she would never understand or accept her part in it. But as the winter passed, so did a large part of his grief, and by mid-February Lav and the children had returned from the mountains.[3]

Life in Charlottesville during Lavalette's absence did little to discourage Holmes's increasing pessimism. With his family far away, his social life took on the monotony of occasional suppers with other faculty members. One evening, though, he departed from his routine and attended a local soirée.

Went to a party at Mrs. Carrington's, [he wrote in his diary] ignorant that it was to be one. My first party in Charlottesville!—and I hope my last—for it was utterly intolerable. . . . It is strange to me to see persons & families who condemn dancing as profane and immoral sanctioning such a style of dress as is certainly indecent. All that prevents the excitement of improper desires is the stronger excitement of disgust. . . . I am sick of the age, and dismayed at the prospects of the future.[4]

Holmes found little in the microcosm of Charlottesville to challenge his interpretation of the course being followed by the great world outside. As time passed it became increasingly improbable that his experiences at the University of Virginia would modify the forebodings which he had experienced during the years of his rustication.

In so far as can be determined, Holmes spent the few years between his arrival in Charlottesville and the eruption of the Civil War in the uneventful but busy routine of academic life.[5] In his initial enthusiasm he had not overestimated the scope of his new opportunity. His position was truly desirable. The University of Virginia was easily the finest institution of its kind in the South, with high academic standards and a superior faculty. Among Holmes's colleagues were the pioneer philologists Gessner Harrison and Maximilian Schele De Vere, the excellent classicist Basil Gildersleeve, and William H. McGuffey who created the *Eclectic Reader* series. Holmes's school was one of the smallest among the liberal arts,[6] but lecturing on history twice weekly and once on literature he soon be-

[3] MS vol. 1791, January 10, 1853, November 12 and December 29, 1857, January 18, 28 and February 1, 13, 1858. Maryanne Holmes to Edward A. Holmes, December 12, 1860.

[4] MS vol. 1791, January 15, 1858.

[5] There is a break in the Holmes diary from June 29, 1858, when he ceased keeping it "without reason or excuse," to February 9, 1862. While there is no surviving G. F. Holmes correspondence for this period, Maryanne passed on his complaints of overwork to Ed. Maryanne Holmes to Edward A. Holmes, April 10, 1860, Buchanan, *Holmes Family History*, p. 62.

[6] For the enrollment in all schools for 1857–1861 see *Catalogue of the University of Virginia. Forty-third Session 1866–67* (Richmond: [University of Virginia], 1867), p. 19.

came known as one of the University's best teachers. One who heard him recalled the experience years later:

I remember with great distinctness the profound and favorable impression which his lectures made, especially upon the better and more mature students. . . . The lectures were well attended, and certain of them (those on Tennyson, Shakespeare, and the like), used to attract large crowds of students, not members of the class; and during the war gentlemen and ladies in considerable numbers used to go up from Charlottesville to hear his most famous lectures. He was wonderfully fluent, his vocabulary choice and elegant and his manner dignified. His encyclopaedic information was also a source of surprise and admiration to the older men.

Holmes himself so enjoyed his performance that he sometimes ran as much as an hour over the allotted time without being aware of it.[7]

But there had been things in his mind other than teaching and scholarship when he decided to go to Charlottesville. An improvement in his financial condition seemed certain. At a time when the typical professorial salary in the United States was about one thousand dollars a year, professors at the University of Virginia were among the best paid in the country with a maximum remuneration of two thousand two hundred fifty dollars. During his first year Holmes was allowed to add all of the fees of his school until his total salary reached twenty-five hundred dollars. But even this new affluence proved insufficient. He had not been in Charlottesville two months before he had drawn over two thousand dollars of his first year's salary. The continuous grumbling among the faculty about the expense of living in Charlottesville during the years just prior to the Civil War suggests that he did not find there the debt-free life he sought.[8]

None the less, in his position at the University of Virginia Holmes had the raw materials for a new, productive, and—in so far as was possible to one of his temperament—a happy life. But the storm that he had feared and had sought to prevent soon broke over the country and brought him new afflictions.

For Holmes the Civil War was the culmination of the dangerous social conditions which he had seen spreading in the North and against which he had warned during the 1850s. "When the war was only in prospect," he wrote in 1862, "I characterized it as a crusade

<hr />

[7] W. R. Abbot in William M. Thornton, "The Letter Book of George Frederick Holmes," *Alumni Bulletin of the University of Virginia*, V (August 1898), 41–42. MS vol. 1791, February 15, 1862.

[8] BVM, June 29, 1857. Bruce, *University of Virginia*, III, 99–101. MS vol. 1791, October 10 and November 4, 1857.

of anarchy, corruption, and agrarianism."[9] The attack on the South was something akin to a war against heretics: in this case heretics unwilling to embrace the values of the nineteenth century. Although never politically active, Holmes had always been a convinced States' Rights man, an admirer of John C. Calhoun, and an opponent of the protective tariff.[10] Not surprisingly then, like most of the faculty at Charlottesville, he favored secession—at first. But in private, if not publicly, he soon became what the Southern press contemptuously dubbed a "croaker," a "Cassandra in breeches" who bemoaned the war and predicted its inevitable loss.[11] By the end of 1862 he knew that the overthrow of the South could not be prevented and that a forced reunion of the nation was unavoidable. But even as the war continued, he hoped that the United States might emerge from it "reformed, regenerated, matured, with the characteristics of an established civilization."[12]

That he saw justice in the Southern cause is certain, for he felt keenly the betrayal he detected in the conduct of both public officials and private citizens. In February of 1862, he declared in his diary

I am . . . sick of the boastful pretensions and hollow professions of multitudes of Southern patriots. . . . The fact is that the Southern cause has been lost by the incompetency of the leaders, the corruption of the officials and the vices of the people. Misplaced ambition, desire of pay and plunder, love of notoriety, hope of popularity, the pride of 'a little brief authority,' greed, rapacity, drinking, gambling, dissipation have gradually usurped the place of principle.

He was disgusted by the "vice & immorality" that he found in Richmond and by the polite but contemptuous rebuff which greeted his efforts to persuade the Confederate authorities to establish a commission to advise the government on financial policy, taxation, logistics, and war production in the light of historical experience. The crude empiricism of Secretary of the Treasury Christopher Memminger who replied that nations could learn little or nothing from the past infuriated him. That most southerners did not share this skepticism toward the value of history was no comfort for they, in turn, failed

[9] MS vol. 1791, December 5, 1862.

[10] G. F. Holmes to J. D. Pope, August 20, 1844, MS vol. 1808. G. F. Holmes to Edward Nicholson, September 25, 1844, *ibid.* Holmes to Lieber, April 14, 1847. Holmes to Lavalette Holmes, March 1, 1847.

[11] For faculty sentiment see John S. Patton, *Jefferson, Cabell and the University of Virginia* (New York: Neale Publishing Company, 1906), pp. 199, 202. For croakerism see J. C. Andrews, "The Confederate Press and Public Morale," *Journal of Southern History,* XXXII (November 1966), 452.

[12] MS vol. 1791, February 24 and November 29, 1862; October 30, 1864.

to understand what they accepted. After Lee's surrender, Holmes characterized the South's struggle for independence as an effort dominated by mythology, by "an apish imitation of the imagined actions of former times as gathered from trashy historians, 4th of July orations, Abbott's Napoleon and Macaulay's England. From History and former experience," he lamented, "our people, politicians, and governors have learnt farces and charades, not statesmanship and wisdom."[13]

The general effect of the Civil War on the colleges and universities of the South was to close them down and devour their students. The University of Mississippi closed in 1861 when virtually the entire student body marched off to war; South Carolina College, Franklin College in Georgia, and Louisiana State Seminary suspended teaching in 1863. A few schools, on the other hand, were able to continue in spite of severely reduced resources and depleted enrollment and faculties. The University of Virginia was one of them.

The faculty and the Board of Visitors agreed that it would be unwise to close the University during the war. The danger of damage to the buildings and grounds if the campus were left vacant was as clear as the probable difficulty of reorganization following a complete and lengthy cessation of normal activity. It was this concern for the continuing operation of the school that prompted the unsuccessful and rather unpatriotic opposition of the faculty and the Board to the use of some of the buildings as hospitals by the Confederate forces in the summer of 1862. In spite of occasional disruptions, however, the University continued to function normally throughout the war, and was not completely bare of students even when the Federal forces passed through Charlottesville in the spring of 1865. At that time the school narrowly escaped looting, but the cooperation of the Federal commanders in supplying guards prevented any serious theft.[14]

When the war began the number of students enrolled fell dramatically from over six hundred in 1860 to sixty-six in 1861 and to forty-six the following year. Attendance in 1863 and 1864 was fifty and fifty-five respectively. Holmes was among the professors hardest hit by the decline in students and, of course, the accompanying reduction of income from fees. He had one hundred eight students in 1860, but the following year only eight. In 1862 this small number fell to three. He picked up two new students in the next two years but had no students at all enrolled in his literature class in 1864.[15] As

---

13 *Ibid.*, February 18, 1862, November 14, 18, 1863, April 18, 1865.
14 Bruce, *University of Virginia*, III, 312–15, 331–40.
15 *Catalogue, 1866–7.* p. 19. Student roll on MS vol. 1810, Holmes papers, D.

elsewhere, the initial and deepest cut in the student population resulted from the early mass withdrawals in order to enlist, but later
in the war conscription also took its toll in spite of a struggle by the
colleges to have students exempted.[16]

The University suffered not only from a sharp decline in enrollment but also from the financial chaos which engulfed the entire
Confederacy. A remorseless rise in prices produced a steady drop in
the purchasing power of faculty salaries. In the blackest days of the
war an economy-minded Board of Visitors worsened things by
cutting salaries to as little as $500.00. Holmes wondered how one was
expected to survive when soap was $4.55 a cake and "a pair of panta-
loons" cost $100.00.[17]

The ranks of the faculty also were thinned by the war. Several
professors volunteered and served on active duty, while those left
behind carried on the work of the school by taking over the teaching
responsibilities of their absent colleagues. These stay-at-homes organized a "reserve" unit so as to not be completely left out. The unit
was formed very early in the war under the command of Professor
Schele de Vere who had had some military training in Prussia during
his youth. This force was later described by one of its members,
Professor Francis H. Smith.

Wisely for a time the company performed its evolutions in a private room;
but, later on, grew bold enough to appear on the Lawn, to the boundless
amusement of the better drilled students. Armed with old-fashioned flint-
lock muskets of antiquated pattern, gotten from a revolutionary residue
long kept in the State arsenal at Lexington, which they held at all inclina-
tions to the vertical, they presented the most wonderful variety of movements for each word of command. It was too much for human composure
to see the pairs of optics converged upon Mr. Schele, when he gave the
sharp, convulsive command, 'Attention, Squat,' as it sounded to us. Unfortunately for the Confederacy, this squad, calculated to be so formidable
to its foes, was never called to the field.[18]

Neither the fact that Holmes was a British subject nor that he was
blind in one eye and shortsighted in the other reduced his willingness
to defend Virginia's soil if the need arose. In the spring of 1863, as
Federal forces neared Charlottesville, he got his chance and as a member of the home guard was called out to defend the city. He bravely
went forth equipped with a double barreled shotgun and newly-

[16] Faculty Minutes, University of Virginia, 1860–1861, University of Virginia
Library, Charlottesville, Virginia, passim; hereinafter cited as FM. Also see MS
vol. 1791, January 30, 1864.
[17] FM, October 29, 1863, December 1, 1865. MS vol. 1791, October 8, 1863.
[18] Quoted in Bruce, *University of Virginia*, III, 279–80.

soled shoes which hurt his feet. He and his companions encountered
no Yankees, but a rotten stump full of "long black ants" was a source
of concern when the time came to encamp. The home guardsmen
burned down their tent in an attempt to get rid of the ants, and
Holmes was forced to spend the night in the open. All he got for his
trouble was a cold. Later, he remarked that it was fortunate that he
and his fellow warriors were not attacked, "for, besides the scantiness
of our numbers, and the total want of order, discipline, or knowledge,
it was subsequently proved that we had only seven rounds of powder
for the three cannons—no wadding, and only a little scrap iron for
shrapnel."[19]

The war's eventual impact on Holmes as a teacher and a scholar
was disastrous, though he responded to the initial crisis energetically
enough. Just before hostilities began, Holmes conceived the project
of collecting and depositing at the University for the use of future
historians all public documents dealing with the origins of the war.
The University appropriated one hundred dollars as a special library
fund for the purchase of newspapers and other materials and appointed a committee headed by Holmes to oversee the project.[20]
Copies of a broadside explaining the purpose of the collection were
sent to various officials, North and South, asking for contributions of
public documents for the proposed archive. Only one acknowledge-
ment was received—from Simon Cameron, Lincoln's first Secretary
of War—and no contributions from anyone. Holmes's enterprise died
of indifference before it was well underway.[21] This outcome was
prophetic. As the war progressed, Holmes found it more and more
difficult to find within himself any enthusiasm for scholarship and
teaching despite the fact that his shrunken classes left him with increased leisure. Concern for his family absent in Burke's Garden and
the discouragement of lecturing to his meager classes (the crowds of
gentlemen and ladies from Charlottesville apparently disappeared
early in the war) combined to wear him down. He suffered from the
conviction that his teaching had become "laborious, and most unin-
teresting;" while "literary studies," as he wrote during the dismal
winter of 1863, "appear unseemly frivolities when life, liberty, fortune, and subsistence are all hazarded—and often sacrificed."[22]

Lavalette and the children had left Charlottesville for the moun-

[19] MS vol. 1791, February 14, 1862, May 5, 1863.
[20] FM, March 1, 1861.
[21] Harry Clemons, *The University of Virginia Library, 1825–1950* (Charlottesville: University of Virginia Press, 1954), pp. 39–40. A copy of the broadside may
be seen in the Broadside Collection, Duke University Library.
[22] MS vol. 1791, November 10, 1863, May 3, 1864.

tains and Tanglewood soon after the war began. There was little in Tazewell County to attract the enemy—or so Holmes thought—and there they would have a secure food supply and be relatively safe from the danger of slave insurrections should any grow out of the excitement of the war.[23] But, as it turned out, unexpected Federal troop movements in the western part of the state caused him a great deal of anxiety.

His worries were multiplied by Ed's decision to enlist in the army. This, in effect, abandoned the family to any marauders who might pass by. Holmes had pleaded with his brother to stay out of the conflict on the grounds of his British citizenship, and their mother added her advice to "not get involved" and "stay out of all scrapes," but Ed volunteered anyway and was commissioned a first lieutenant of infantry in John Buchanan Floyd's command. Holmes's bitterness increased when Ed's clothes were stolen in Tennessee and he had to re-outfit him at his own expense. Ever since his arrival in America Ed had been nothing but a burden, Holmes ungenerously wrote home to England. "There is a waywardness and a recklessness about him, accompanied with a continual jealousy and suspicion which prevents his doing anything for himself or anybody else." Though, he hoped, "He may make it up yet."[24]

Holmes's anticipation about the safety of Tanglewood was basically sound. There were several Federal raids into the county but no occupation; and his family, while frequently frightened and anxious and twice pillaged by the enemy, was not harmed. In the summer of 1862 a "hostile band of cavalry" camped for one night on the edge of the farm but moved on without incident.[25] The following year, in July, General John Toland and a thousand Federal cavalry came through Tazewell on a raid to Wytheville. They destroyed a few houses in the county and burned a storehouse in Burke's Garden, and were followed in August by a small force of raiders out to disrupt communications in the county. When Holmes went home for Christmas in 1863 he found that during these operations Federal cavalry had plundered Tanglewood but had left enough food and other supplies to keep the family from hardship. General W. W. Averill's main force of 2,500 troopers came through the following spring intent on destroying the lead and salt mines in the area and cutting the railroad at Wytheville. This time a foraging party under

[23] *Ibid.*, February 17 and November 23, 1862.
[24] Buchanan, *Holmes Family History*, pp. 75–76. G. F. Holmes to Charlotte Isabella Holmes, November 23, 1863, Holmes papers, D. Maryanne Holmes to Edward A. Holmes, April 10, 1860 and April 15, 1861.
[25] Holmes to Charlotte Isabella Holmes, November 23, 1863.

a "polite colonel" deprived Lavalette of no more than a cake of sugar. The largest action was an assault on the Preston Salt Works in nearby Smyth County by 5,000 men under General S. G. Burbridge in the fall of 1864 but these troops only passed through Tazewell and avoided the vicinity of Tanglewood completely.[26]

The exposure of his family to Federal attack and Ed's absence forced Holmes to make several dangerous trips to Tanglewood. In the fall of 1863, even though worried almost to desperation, he was able to comfort himself with the knowledge that the family had provisions enough for the coming year.[27] In the spring Lavalette shattered what assurance may have remained after his Christmas visit. Nearly all the lambs and much of the other livestock had died during the winter: "a loss of nearly $5000 at the prices ruling here," he mourned. A week later she wrote again: another cow had died, twenty hogs were gone, and the farm would be out of both feed and bread by mid-summer. Holmes began feverish but futile attempts to get money from England and considered speculating in what commodities and gold he could scrape together. In a few days another letter arrived: two Negro slaves were dead; and, among the stock sixteen head of cattle and forty hogs had been lost. He could stay in Charlottesville no longer.

Boarding the train for Lynchburg, he headed west only to be turned back because of the threat of a Federal advance into the area as a result of Grant's new offensive. Three days later he tried again and this time, in spite of delays because of landslides and the fear of raiding parties, the train made it as far as Salem where it stopped. Holmes spent three days with a friend at Big Lick close by and, when rail travel resumed, went on to New River. There he found a freight train and journeyed in a boxcar to Dublin where he was unable to get food or shelter until someone mistook him for a preacher. The next morning he went on to Wytheville where he found the tavern closed and the town almost deserted; it was impossible even to hire a horse. By luck he caught a ride in an ambulance on its was to Tazewell. Once there he borrowed a horse and finally made his way to the farm where, to his surprise, he found Ed home on leave but "broken down and suffering from the army scratches."

Lavalette had not exaggerated. The family's supplies were almost gone and the stock continued to die from disease and the lack of proper feed. To worsen things, Confederate cavalry had recently destroyed their oats and corn. Although it was almost impossible to

---

[26] Pendleton, *Tazewell County*, pp. 613–31. MS vol. 1791, January 1, 1864. MS vol. 1792, summary of a trip to Tanglewood in May, 1864.

[27] Holmes to Charlotte Isabella Holmes, November 23, 1863.

buy supplies, Holmes gathered enough grain to feed the family until July when the year's yield of beans and potatoes were ready. They then lived on beans, potatoes and mutton until fall. But a poor harvest at summer's end made the prospect for the coming winter even grimmer than that just passed.

In August, Ed, who by then had given the "army scratches" to everyone in the family, left to return to the army; but only to be captured in September and to spend the remaining months of the war in the United States military prison at Johnson's Island in Lake Erie. Holmes himself tried to return to the University twice during the summer of 1864 but was not able to travel far because of the destruction of bridges and railroads. At last, in October, after a hard and apprehensive but relatively peaceful summer, he was able to get away and to take fifteen-year-old Letty with him so that she might go to school in Charlottesville.[28]

Things went better on the farm that winter than anyone had reason to expect. Lavalette wrote in January that all was well. The "army scratches" were still there and the county was in confusion owing to recent raids but she was optimistic enough to suggest a visit to the University at the end of the month. Holmes knew there was little chance that she would come, but her desire for a reunion on their wedding anniversary was so intense that he decided to make another trip west.

After providing Letty with a list of relatives and friends in Virginia, the North, and England, and leaving her in the care of her school mistress, he set out by rail for Wytheville and this time arrived without incident. But it was necessary to go the rest of the way on horseback. Holmes suffered miserably from the bitter cold. His horse, frightened by the body of a dead cow, once threw him into the snow; he was forced to spend the night in a deserted fireless house; his ears were frostbitten and his breath froze on his glasses causing him to wander from the road and lose his way. But finally, "sick, sore, and fatigued," he reached Tanglewood to be welcomed by a grateful wife and, of course, the "army scratches."[29]

In time the fighting ended, but the events surrounding its ending were as terrifying to Holmes as the events attending it. He early had become convinced that the war would eventually cause such severe convulsions in the northern states that a military dictatorship there could be the only result. When Lincoln was assassinated, he was sure

[28] MS vol. 1791, April 13, 20, 21, and May 7, 1864. MS vol. 1792, summary of the summer of 1864. For Ed's capture see Buchanan, *Holmes Family History*, pp. 76–77.
[29] MS vol. 1792, January 21, 24, 1865 and summary of the trip.

his murder was the first step to that end for the entire country. The President's death, the "greatest and most unanticipated tragedy of modern years," he expected to so disrupt society, so "benumb the hands of rulers," so "destroy the faith and confidence of men," so "overwhelm the finances, crush industry, disseminate terror and distrust and . . . let loose all the furies of agrarianism and anarchy," that dictatorship would be the only way to hold the reunited nation together.[30]

Fortunately, his prophecies did not come true. He quietly took the amnesty oath in May, attempted to mend his fences by assuring his acquaintances in the North that "as an Englishman" he had not taken part in the war, and brought his family home to the University. When Ed returned to live on Tanglewood life resumed the routine uneventfulness of the prewar years. But life was not easy. The University only slowly recovered from the effects of war. More than six months after the end of hostilities the salaries of the professors were still suspended. "I am prostrated," Holmes wrote to McClintock, "though not crushed. . . . My family are almost bare, my furniture of all sorts worn out or destroyed. My means of subsistence inadequate to our support, my expenses greatly increased for the moment, my receipts exceedingly limited. I have almost to start life anew."[31]

Though never a steady churchgoer, Holmes had begun attending Episcopal services in Charlottesville and the gatherings at the University Chapel with reasonable regularity when he arrived in 1857. This was, of course, an outward sign of the great need for Christianity which had engulfed him. The war years brought his faith to the peak of its fervor. His personal helplessness in the face of his family's insecurity forced him to draw on what he soon discovered to be inadequate spiritual resources. Tied to his duties in Charlottesville and confronted with Lavalette's letters, his only alternatives were prayer or mental collapse. "I am impotent to save," he despaired in his diary, "I am powerless to help—and must trust them to the mercies of a tender and beneficent Providence." But he knew that the ends of Providence were not always served in ways acceptable to men and could draw little comfort from his trust. This dismayed him. "Why can I have no more faith?," he cried, "no greater reliance on God?—no sincerer resignation to say 'not my will, but thine, oh Lord, be done?'—Strengthen me, oh my God!"[32]

[30] MS vol. 1792, November 29, 1862, April 21, 1865.

[31] *Ibid.*, May 16, 1865. Buchanan, *Holmes Family History*, p. 64. Holmes to McClintock, November 17, 1865.

[32] MS vol. 1791, April 14, 1862 et passim.

The shallowness of his faith was not his only spiritual concern during that terrible time. Catholicism continued to haunt him. During the war he confessed to having "long suspected" that the influence of Protestantism lay at the heart of the modern revolt against Christianity. In spite of his attempts to "repel such suspicion," he was seized by the frightening idea that Protestantism with its emphasis on private judgment was itself "the mark of the Beast spoken of in the Apocalypse." If this were true, then the agonies of the nineteenth century were but the just penalty "for the rejection of spiritual authority," for the "cannonization" of intellect, for the rejection of the "sentiment of reverence" and the "habit of obedience." Protestantism stood "absolutely condemned by the decree of Heaven written in the course of history; and Catholicism . . . absolutely sanctioned."[33]

Such reflections lent urgency to the religious meditations which became a part of each day's activity towards the war's end. By the spring of 1865 Holmes had arrived at the most orthodox period of his life. But this had not been accomplished by reflection alone. In the winter of 1862 his favorite daughter, Coralie, became ill with diptheria and died while he was on his way across the state to be at her side. Coralie's loss brought him more than sorrow; it brought a challenge. " 'Tell Pa to be a Catholic, and come to God, where I shall be,' " was the message she left behind for her absent father. Sometime later Holmes recalled, " 'There is something fearful as well as overpoweringly tender in her dying words, 'I shall see Pa, but Pa will not see me.' This must be my constant care. God grant me grace to follow whither she has gone."[34]

His attempt to follow Coralie led him into the twisting paths of mystical speculation: an area into which he ventured reluctantly. But personal grief again prepared the way before him. Just as the pain caused by the death of his first son had increased the appeal of Christianity, so now the "mystery of the Incarnation," the possibility of a union of human and divine natures in one person, was clarified by the life and death of Coralie. Soon his mind was crowded with "new and unexpected manifestations and evidences of the divine scheme" and confused by "many far-reaching and hazardous speculations." Holmes was half afraid of this new spiritual vitality. "God grant that I may not be deluding and bewildering myself," he wrote. "God grant that these apparent illustrations of the Divine Order in the work of grace and redemption may not lead me into fatal error."[35]

[33] *Ibid.*, November 16, 1862.

[34] *Ibid.*, March 17, 1864, undated entry preceding that for March 8, 1863. MS vol. 1792, January 7, 1865.

[35] MS vol. 1791, March 9, 1864. MS vol. 1803, March 4, 1864.

As part of his meditations Holmes began keeping a notebook devoted to an investigation of "Practical Religion and Theology" in order better to seek "the attainment of a religious habit of mind and heart." The project was completely orthodox in both letter and spirit and, unlike the religious notes of his youth, betrayed not the least tincture of rationalism or skepticism. The short essays, which dealt with various Christian doctrines, were neither profound nor systematic. Their author's assumptions and his conclusions were those of contemporary piety. He even became more tolerant of natural theology (though this indulgence lapsed after the war).

The important thing about these ruminations, however, was not their content; but that, like the Philosophy of Faith earlier (and which was, of course, still a fundamental part of his thought), they avoided the question of the historical truth of important Christian beliefs. Man's natural reason, Holmes was certain, could know nothing of God unless enlightened by revelation. And the acceptance of revelation was an act of faith; just as its rejection was an act of will. He did not explore the possibility of a theism grounded in reason and independent of biblical revelation. Nor did he raise the question of the historical reliability of scriptural testimony even if only to answer it affirmatively.[36] Holmes still had sufficient faith to find safety in the age-old fortress of believers, *credo quia absurdum est*:

> There are mysteries [he wrote] in all religions: in all there must be mysteries. In that religion which is pure and true there will be the most and the greatest mysteries, in consequence of its very purity and truth. Religion is the lively acceptance by faith; not dim apprehension by the understanding, looking 'as through a glass darkly'—of things supernatural, lying beyond knowledge and comprehension.[37]

Stimulated by this stronger faith, Holmes turned once more to the question which had preoccupied him since his first speculations in the 1840s. More eager now than ever before to witness a new instauration, he found the postwar world fully as rich in indications as previous decades had been that the end of the present age was approaching. He sang his old song with renewed energy. "A fever of anarchy and revolution" he found raging "in the veins of society." He saw governments maintaining themselves by force alone; the masses of the world becoming increasingly impatient of authority and more devoted to "license and caprice;" despotism and ochlocracy the only political alternatives with the sanction of history behind them; and civilization, as it existed in the nineteenth century, able to survive

---

[36] MS vol. 1840, pp. 11–25. MS vol. 1803, pp. 23–24, 485.
[37] MS vol. 1840.

neither. The struggle for supremacy between these two political forces would in time produce such conflicts as would destroy existing institutions and clear the ground for a new and unexperienced order of society. Staggering economic changes portended the same end. A ruthless capitalism was grinding out its own nemesis as class hatred enveloped society and the natural resources of the earth were sacrificed to personal enrichment. Unquestioning religious belief, always the bastion of faith, was rapidly dying. The Christian church as it had existed for centuries was simply falling to pieces. Holmes found "such an implacable and hopeless antagonism in the developments of society" and in the turmoils of philosophy and religion that he was sure it must be obvious that "no solution of these fatal dissensions is discernable."[38]

In like vein and closer to home, he recognized that the Civil War marked the end not only of the Old South but signified the victory in America of those same forces which he had watched rending Europe before 1861. The political and military verdict of the conflict was only one phase of the much greater revolution. In the South as elsewhere the former state of things was gone beyond any hope of recall. It became indisputable with the destruction of slavery and the planter aristocracy that the forces he had opposed were going to win. In more confident moments in the years immediately following Appomattox, his reaction was one of accommodation. "We must," he told those reluctant to accept the new state of things,

recast our practical philosophy to make it harmonize with altered necessities. We cannot do this by feeding upon the past, and renewing a dissipated dream. We must turn, though with no credulous ear, to those whose whole habit of thought is diverse from our own, but more accordant with the changed systems under which we have to live and work.[39]

But he did not, of course, accept all aspects of the new order with enthusiasm. He submitted from necessity, as one submits to the operation of unyielding force, not from approval.

In addition to his general apprehension about the future of western society, Holmes worried particularly about the vulgarization of culture, which development seemed especially a compulsion of the American mind and an inseparable part of American democracy.

---

[38] George Frederick Holmes, "Aspects of the Hour," *De Bow's Review*, III, n.s. (April 1867), 337–50. See also George Frederick Holmes, "Influences of Commerce and Finance in Determing the Revolutions of Fortune in the History of Nations," *ibid.*, I, n. s. (April 1866), 464–65.

[39] [George Frederick Holmes], "Carey on Reconstruction," *ibid.*, V, n.s. (May 1868), 582–84, 586. See also Holmes to McClintock, January 19, 1866.

Unless this tendency to admire the tawdry and to rest satisfied with the shallow could be modified he was sure that the country would be poorly prepared to deal with the challenges to come.

In "Americanisms," an essay devoted to American literature, he considered this problem at length.[40] While dissenting from the patriotic faith that the United States was *the* land of the future, Holmes had no doubt that it was *a* land of the future and would in time produce a culture and a literature congenial with the ethos of the nation. Unfortunately, the democratic traditions of American life seemed to be against quality. "Our prejudices, our judgment, our common sense are repugnant to . . . those influences which tend to foster a learned class, devoting life-long energies to study and research." There was no aristocracy or established clergy in America to accept as its special responsibility the cultivation of learning and art. As a result the national taste was "worse than none at all;" it was "an inherently vicious taste" with an unerring instinct for the cheap, the commonplace, the violent. The intellectual efforts of Americans were inevitably second-rate. Walt Whitman, whom Holmes thought to be the most gifted American poet of the postwar period, made poems profusely and automatically "as other machinery turns out paper collars." George Bancroft, "our typical historian," looked impartially on "American fact and American fiction" and used both indifferently. Ralph Waldo Emerson " 'the great American philosopher' (and the only one, thank Heaven!)" concealed the banality of his argument beneath a brilliant style, but even this Holmes found frequently ungrammatical and "neglectful of rhythm." The inferiority of the American intellect reflected the growing vulgarity of American life. Both were the products of national vanity and of a self-bemused democracy which put its faith in thin utilitarian popular education and found its reward in cultural anarchy. They were the result of

our crazy ambition to be peculiar and notorious at all hazards, and our proclivity to make the leveling instinct of democracy the one single law of social culture as well as political life. Under these influences we cut ourselves adrift from the lessons and fruits of experiences elsewhere; we grew not only impatient of study and control, but came to scorn all but short-cuts, and we fancied the slightest thing we did at our ease to be better than the best products of the most zealous labor of all others.

At heart Americans nurse a profound contempt for intellect: "we are confessedly not bookish ourselves, and we make a merit of it. . . . We teach our youth to despise learning and culture" as interfering

---

[40] [George Frederick Holmes], "Americanisms: A Study of Words and Manners," *Southern Review*, IX (April–July 1871), 290–319, 529–60.

with the real business of life. As a result, the leisure class in America, which should be a reservoir of wisdom and public service, is not "able to correct our evils," but is "only competent to give them greater force and poignancy."

To some extent, this jeremiad against a democratic culture born in the Jacksonian era and maturing in the "Gilded Age" was a manifestation of Holmes's sense of British superiority; just as it was, at the same time, a last parting shot from the patrician South. And it certainly sprang to no little degree from his own feeling of frustration and alienation as an intellectual. But beneath this there was something more. There was the fear that the shortcomings of democratic civilization were not peculiar to the United States but were prophetic of that social destiny towards which the entire West was moving.

In the face of such dolorous prospects, men could hardly be blamed if they folded their hands in despair or retreated into nihilism. Holmes, however, took neither course. The "analogies of the past," which he had studied so carefully, permitted him to continue to believe what he had before the war: that "the human race is now entering into the agonies of a universal dissolution preparatory to a universal transmutation." Men may have lost control of events but that was no reason for despair. Helpless though they might be, their way was clear: "We have nothing more to do than to observe, to wonder, to adore, and to submit;" for, he rejoiced, "a new birth of time is at hand; a new cycle of ages is preparing to unroll itself."[41]

The remaining years of Holmes's life were not happy ones. He remained pursued by debts and subject to professional and academic frustrations. Perhaps he could have better endured these if his children had not burdened him with additional grief and disappointment. Everything taken together was too much, and his spirit was eventually completely broken. Only his oldest child, poor Mary Anne, and his youngest daughter, Isabel, gave him no trouble; in fact, he leaned increasingly on Isabel for comfort in his old age. But for years Holmes thought Letty to be a constant trial, and his relations with the two boys Henry and Fred were stormy.

When he had had Letty all to himself in Charlottesville during the war he had found her almost unmanageable. Condemning her as "willful," and lacking in "candor and openness," he reflected that these were also Lavalette's faults, but, he added, "there is nothing sly or indirect about her Mother, as there appears to be about herself."[42] Letty never married and later joined Henry in some of his

---

[41] Holmes, "Aspects of the Hour," pp. 351–52.
[42] MS vol. 1792, April 30, 1865.

expensive and ill-fated enterprises. Not until the last decade of her father's life did she, in his estimate, begin "to come right."[43]

The rift between Holmes and his two sons was wider. The evidence here is somewhat one-sided and meager for much of it comes from his brief and sporadically kept diaries. Yet the tone of Holmes's remarks leaves little doubt that tension was everpresent. In the boys' defense, it must be said that Holmes was probably not an easy father to live with. When a man became upset if his twenty-six-year-old son stayed out late at night, and instituted such a strict code of behavior for a son in college that it allowed "no *visiting* except one young lady . . . , no going to town after dark . . . , [and] no time for recreation except 1½ [hours]," it is not surprising that his sons rebelled or that his relatives thought him a tyrant.[44]

Holmes's disciplinary severity was very likely in part a compensa-for his disappointment that neither of his sons chose a life of scholarship with its long hours of demanding work. This disappointment grew with each passing year as Henry and Fred moved farther and farther away from the things which their father loved.[45] It was understandable that they did so. Both boys had been raised in the rustic environment of Burke's Garden and because of the war and their father's poverty had not had the education they needed to follow him in a literary life.[46] One might also wonder what effect Holmes's never-ending struggles had on their own choices. Nevertheless, when they reached college age Fred and Henry were both enrolled in classes at the University of Virginia: Henry as a medical student in 1875 and Fred in Latin and his father's courses in history and literature two years later.[47]

Although Henry was practicing medicine when, in 1893, he was

[43] MS vol. 1795, June 15, 1874, Holmes papers, D. MS vol. 1797, February 28, 1884, *ibid*. MS vol. 1799, December 14, 1887, *ibid*.

[44] MS vol. 1796, May 16, 21 and June 19, 1881, *ibid*.; loose sheet in back of *ibid*., dated December 1, 1876. Edward Holmes to Mrs. E. A. Holmes, November 17, 1895, Buchanan, *Holmes Family History*, p. 97.

[45] In his will Holmes regretted that he had no child to whom he could leave his library. Typed copy of last will and testament, Holmes papers, D.

[46] On their lack of education see Holmes to Charlotte Isabella Holmes, November 23, 1863.

[47] *University of Virginia Decennial Catalogue of Visitors, Faculty, Officers and Students, 1874–1884* (Richmond: [University of Virginia], 1889), p. 44. *Catalogue of the Officers and Students of the University of Virginia, Fifty-Six Session, 1879–80* (Richmond: [University of Virginia], 1880), p. 10. *Catalogue of the Officers and Students of the University of Virginia, Fifty-Fifth Session, 1878–9* (Richmond: [University of Virginia], 1879), p. 10. Henry also attended Georgetown University and the University of Maryland, memoir of N. Floyd Holmes in possession of N. Floyd Holmes.

killed by a train near Altavista, Virginia while going to a patient,[48] he apparently mixed medicine with other business for several years after he left the University in 1881. Why he did so is a mystery. Did this reflect his own choice or was it the result of pressure from his father? One cannot say. In any event, Holmes became closely involved financially in Henry's activities and his diary reflects several years of impatient standing on the sidelines watching his son.

In 1874, before Henry began his medical education, he had gone west to Iowa to make his fortune and had taken Letty with him. Their venture failed and Letty returned home. Henry went on to Kansas and Missouri, but in that depression year he could not find work and actually came close to starving. At length, Holmes sent him money to enable him to return home. When Henry left school in 1881 the same story was repeated in Texas, though without Letty's participation. After returning to Tazewell, Henry practiced medicine, married in 1883, and, after a brief return to Texas as a physician, went to Florida to continue his practice and to grow oranges. Again he took Letty and Holmes once more gave financial help. Three years of growing oranges must have been enough, for Henry appears in Holmes's diary as a citrus fruit farmer for the last time in December 1887. Had he determined to give all his time to medicine? Perhaps so, but it was without his father's blessing. In August, 1888, Holmes wrote to the dependable Isabel:

Henry's mulishness, perversity, blindness and folly, are giving me great worry and anxiety, even more than Fred's exhibition of the like virtues occasion. Each of the boys has independence in sight, if steady, patient, and able to turn to account such aid as I may give them from time to time, and which would increase with their profitable employment of it. Henry is disposed once more to throw away all that has been done or learnt, or begun in the past. Of course, such a procedure destroys entirely my ability to give further help, or countenance.

With an occasional trip home Henry remained in Florida until 1891 when he returned to Virginia with his family only to lose his life two years later. Shortly before his own death Holmes decided that he had been too harsh with his older son,[49] but by that time Henry was beyond the reach of reconciliation.

Holmes's relationship with Fred was cut from the same cloth. Two years after his younger son began classes at Charlottesville the humili-

[48] Buchanan, *Holmes Family History*, p. 87.

[49] MS vols. 1795, 1796, 1797, 1798, passim; MS vol. 1799, December 31, 1887, Holmes papers, D. Memoir of N. Floyd Holmes in possession of N. Floyd Holmes. G. F. Holmes to Isabel Holmes, August 8, 1888, Holmes papers, D. N. Floyd Holmes to the author, December 12, 1964, in possession of the author.

ated father stayed away from the faculty meeting which expelled
Fred for being rowdy in the Public Hall during services one Sunday
evening.[50] Like Henry, Fred was a wanderer causing Holmes expense
and worry. His travels were extensive: Brazil, Texas, a tour of duty
in the United States Navy, a short time in Florida with Henry. ("No
man escapes his cares or his duties," Holmes remarked in his diary
when Fred returned from the orange groves.) Eventually Fred settled down to farm in Tazewell and to practice law but Holmes never
lost his feeling of apprehension nor his disappointment.[51]

For a time Holmes could share his sorrows with Lavalette. "Greater
difficulties," he once wrote to her, "are gathering round our age,
but, I trust, we may draw still more closely together, and that God,
in his mercy, may give you health and strength, and accord us a few
years of rest and peace and hope for our poor, blundering, and misguided children."[52] But this support was removed by her death in
August, 1887. Shortly before this he had privately poured out his
misery on a scrap of paper that was subsequently saved with his other
papers.

Pelted with duns like a snow storm. Harassed with insufficient means and
overwhelmed with anxieties. Alarmed and uncertain about the subsistence
and future support of my children—without intelligence of the hazards
and calamities present and in prospect—disappointed and degraded in heart
and mind—disgraced before the public, yet feeling my life still indispensa-
ble to my divided and discordant family, having none to consult, none to
help, because compelled to absolute [silence?], as speech of mine would
revive or aggravate the discredit of my children, I live in impotent agony,
worse than any form of speedy death could be.[53]

Now, with Lavalette gone, life crowded in on the old man.

The story of final alienation is told in his will. Holmes left his
property and money to his daughters, and nothing but a desk to Fred,
remarking pointedly that he and Henry had each received "a pro-
portinate share of my receipts" during their father's life. Holmes
named Isabel's husband, William H. Perkinson, as his executor because "the actions of my children have for years precluded me from
having such intimacies as would authorize me to claim from any one

50 FM, July 1, 1879. BVM, July 3, 1879.

51 MS vols. 1796 passim; 1799, October 17, 1887 et passim. N. Floyd Holmes
to the author, July 18, 1969, in possession of the author. MS vol. 1800, passim,
Holmes papers, D.

52 G. F. Holmes to Lavalette Holmes, October 20 [no year], Holmes papers, D.
The handwriting would indicate the 1880s or late 1870s.

53 Fragment dated December 14, 1886, Holmes papers, D.

services in life, in death, or after death."[54] The years of persistent and nagging disappointment had taken their toll.

As a professor Holmes was a very different person from the worry-racked father whom his family knew. The "tall, lean and lank" figure of "Daddy Holmes, the walking Encyclopaedia" was a familiar sight on the University campus for forty years. His indifference to dress—"as to both fit and fashion," his moderate eccentricities, and his erudition made him an object of legend. Many apochryphal tales of his vast learning surrounded Holmes; one may serve as an example of the rest. He had, so the story goes, a difference of opinion with one of his colleagues about a point which fell within the specialty of the other professor. The latter, seeking authoritative judgement, wrote to the "president" of an English university. That scholar referred his correspondent to a definitive treatment of the question " 'written by a man named Holmes, who, I think, holds a professorship at your University.' " A variant of this anecdote has the question one of international law and William Gladstone as the English authority but the result praising Holmes's knowledge is the same. Some students found Holmes distant, but others thought him kind, sympathetic, and generous.[55] That few of his students seemed to be aware of the silent torments of his life testifies both to his resilience and to his pathetic isolation and loneliness.

Holmes's academic responsibility was the School of History and Literature, to which was added rhetoric in 1867 and political economy in 1868.[56] In 1882, when a new School of English Literature was created, he lost literature and rhetoric and was thereafter known as the Professor of Historical Science. In this capacity he taught two classes: "General History," and "Political Economy and the Science of Society."[57] In 1890 he turned "General History" over to an adjunct professor and concentrated on the "Science of Society" which included political economy but which was devoted primarily to the study of the laws governing the origin, growth, and decay of civilizations.[58] This course was his pet and in teaching it he became one of

[54] Holmes will, pp. 1–6.

[55] "Death of Professor Holmes," *Alumni Bulletin of the University of Virginia*, IV (November 1897), 86. Robinson, "George Frederick Holmes," p. 73. David M. R. Culbreth, *The University of Virginia, Memories of Her Student-Life and Professors* (New York: Neale Publishing Company, 1908), p. 408.

[56] BVM, June 26, 1867 and June 27, 1868.

[57] *Catalogue of the Officers and Students of the University of Virginia, Fifty-Ninth Session, 1882–3* (Richmond: [University of Virginia], 1883), p. 27.

[58] BVM, February 9, 1889. *University of Virginia Catalogue of Session 1891–92* (Richmond: [University of Virginia], [1892]), pp. 12–13.

the first in the United States to put what came to be called sociology into the classroom.

Holmes introduced the science of society into the University of Virginia curriculum against a background of increasing academic interest in the subject. From the antebellum days when the Associationists, Fourieristes, Owenites, and other Utopian reformers had hoped to discover in the laws governing the development of society a key to the realization of their dreams, there had been a steadily growing interest in the scientific study of society among American intellectuals. Symptomatic of this was the founding of the American Social Science Association (in imitation of its British counterpart) in 1865. Dominated by moderate reformers and academics, the Association marked a move away from the "crank"-ridden earlier social science movement toward a more sober and methodologically scientific discipline. In time tensions within the Association brought about its dissolution into a number of more specialized organizations and, in 1889, its unifying function was taken over by the American Academy of Political and Social Science to which Holmes belonged. One of the interests of the American Social Science Association was the promotion of social science courses in the nation's colleges. This, plus a growing awareness of the need for a more sophisticated public awareness of the causes of modern social problems, lead to a considerable rise in the number of such courses during the last decades of the nineteenth century.[59]

The social science that Holmes taught at Charlottesville lacked the originality of his pre-war speculations in the philosophy of history. He now used the standard authorities of the time: Spencer, Maine, Tylor, Lubbock and others; his topical division conventionally covered pre-history, barbarism and civilization, and analyzed such social institutions as the family and property. As a result, his course, though a pioneering one, contained little that was novel. Finding the religious implications of certain aspects of the new science too hazardous, he cautiously refused to employ a Darwinian evolutionary scheme of historical development, and pointedly emphasized to his students that the science of society was too recent a discipline to permit hasty speculations about the origins of man and society. Instead he presented his data in a classification based on logical relationships rather than chronological ones.[60] Nor was he

[59] Bernard, *Origins of American Sociology*, pp. 527–29, 611–13, 656. *Annals of the American Academy of Political and Social Science*, I (1890), 46 of supplement.

[60] Holmes, *Science of Society*, chapters I, IV and VI.

any more receptive to the work of Karl Marx who as well as any other might have been that "heresiarch" of Socialism and Bacon of social science whose appearance Holmes had forecast in the forties. He read *Capital* twice in the 1880s—once in English and once in German—and had enough interest in Marx to notice his death in 1883, but as early as 1866 Holmes had rejected economic determinism as an adequate view of the processes of history. He acknowledged the importance of commerce and finance in history and considered their operation an element too much neglected by historians; but his teacher in such things was Heeren rather than Marx. Admittedly, economic and political power might transfer from class to class, but its passage from nation to nation and from race to race he found more important.[61] Then too, for Holmes, history always contained a realm of spirit which was not to be subordinated to any type of materialism whether historical or scientific.

To assist his class he published privately in 1883 a syllabus of his lectures entitled *The Science of Society*. This little book has been pointed to as one of the first treatises in social science written in America.[62] It was hardly that. In reality it was no more than an outline, a study guide, and a very sketchy one, and passed unnoticed by contemporary specialists. But the book was not aimed at scholars. It, like the course, was conceived and written to show the young men at the University the numerous portents of a new world order which their professor saw in the present and in the past and to bring home to them the message that the world was changing, changing drastically, and that if they were wise they would learn how and why and would change with it.

Throughout his long career Holmes kept the skill as a teacher that he had shown when he first came to Charlottesville. He remained an entertaining lecturer and his peculiarities endeared him to his students. His penchant for accidental punning, which he considered more an affliction than an accomplishment, often caused the class to break into applause.[63] And his absent-minded habit of rolling his handkerchief on the dusty desk and frequently wiping his face with it left him "pretty well smeared" when his lecture was over.[64] He

---

[61] *Ibid.*, chapter XIV; Holmes, "Influence of Commerce," passim. MS vol. 1803, p. 549 et passim.

[62] Bernard, *Origins of American Sociology*, p. 235. The Bernards, of course, realized the book's limitations.

[63] George Fawcett, "Student Life at the University in the Seventies," *University of Virginia Alumni News*, XXVII (March 1939), 110.

[64] Edward H. Green, "Sixty Years Ago," *ibid.*, XXI (March 1933), 126.

sometimes became so engrossed in his subject that he was oblivious to the very presence of the class and the roar of disorder would gradually rise until it penetrated his consciousness. Then, one of his students remembered, he "would . . . pause, scan the room from over his spectacles, only thereafter to receive perfect respect and order. Thus . . . we happily knew how far to go."[65] His method of teaching was purely didactic. Lectures were the "chief thing" and the class was conducted with a minimum of student participation.[66] "Old Holmes," wrote Matthew F. Maury, who found his class "exceedingly entertaining," "rarely calls on anyone, being too full of his theories and fancies, the full benefit of all of which he affords us through successive 'Extra Lectures' on Fridays." Of all his professors, young Maury liked "Old Holmes" the best.

I know old Holmes best, [he wrote] and can talk to him best, and know that he likes me, and altogether we have a good time; why, when I stood my special for Hist. & Lit, I took an easy chair, and he took an easy chair, we exchanged a few words on nothingnesses and then we had a pleasant little chat about Eng. Hist, and Eng. People, and Eng. Geography; now and then he asked me a question, and I would ask him one, and when it was over I felt more as if I had been conversing with an old friend, than standing an Examination under a far famed Professor of the University of Va.[67]

The attitude of students toward Holmes probably was closely connected with their ability and interest in history. When answering Herbert B. Adams' questionnaire on history instruction in 1887 he replied to the question, "what methods have been abandoned as unprofitable?" curtly: "the endeavor to teach history to those who have no capacity for it."[68] Maury was a good student; others were not. Holmes did not concern himself with the latter. All together, though, his existence must have seemed idyllic to his students, but as he grew older even academic life became a source of defeat.

The Board of Visitors of the University were capable of highhanded action and in the 1890s Holmes became a victim of this. Nor was he the only victim. In 1896 Professor James M. Garnett awoke

[65] Culbreth, *University of Virginia*, p. 410.

[66] Questionnaire in Herbert B. Adams, *The Study of History in American Colleges and Universities* (Washington, D. C.: Government Printing Office, 1887), p. 274.

[67] M. F. Maury to R. L. Maury, October 13 and December 19, 1881, Richard Launcelot Maury Papers, Duke University Library, Durham, North Carolina.

[68] Adams, *Study of History*, p. 275.

one morning to discover that the chair of English literature, which he had occupied since 1882, had been abolished. An angry letter from the amazed Garnett demanding an explanation received only the brief reply that the Board intended their action to be no reflection on him.[69] Holmes fared somewhat better than this but did not escape the same indignity which Garnett experienced.

The trouble began in 1889 when the Board decided that the School of Historical Science was becoming too much for one man to handle. Consequently, they elected Richard Heath Dabney of the University of Indiana as adjunct professor of history at an annual salary of $1500. But, as the chair of historical science had only $3500 appropriated for faculty salary, it was necessary to reduce Holmes's income to $2000 to provide a salary for Dabney. No protest from Holmes survives but one may assume that he was not pleased. In 1893 Dabney's salary was raised to $1800 but Holmes still could expect only $2,000. The full catastrophe came in 1896. The previous year, the Rotunda had burned and the University was forced into a second mortgage to raise funds for extensive repairs; even with that, it operated in the red during 1896–97. The money-conscious Board resolved "that the salary of Prof. Geo. Frederick Holmes be reduced from $2000 to $1000." It was represented to the Board by its Executive Committee that Holmes had agreed to the reduction. Holmes soon notified them that not only had he not agreed, he had not even known that the move was contemplated. Like Garnett he wanted to know why. Were there charges of misconduct or incompetency? If so, he wanted to hear them. If not, he added bitterly, what changes would there be in his duties—if any? Upon reconsideration, the Board decided to offer the old man $1500 a year. He took it, of course. What choice had he? This episode severely damaged Holmes's strained finances (his children's needs had already forced him to liquidate his insurance) and was humiliating as well. He could interpret it in no other terms than as a vote of little confidence: "my 'miserable taking off' " he called it. Holmes was scarcely in his grave before Dabney was elevated to his professorship at a full salary of $3000 per year.[70]

The resentment which this experience added to the last year of his life may be imagined, but it was only an additional weight to

[69] James M. Garnett to the Board of Visitors, June 16, 1896, in BVM, June 16, 1896.

[70] BVM, February 9, 1889, June 15, 1896, October 2, 1896, December 10, 1897. Bruce, *University of Virginia*, IV, 273, 373. G. F. Holmes to the Board of Visitors, June 25, 1896, Holmes papers, D. Holmes will, p. 5. Fragment of a letter, G. F. Holmes to an unknown party, June 27, 1896, Holmes papers, D.

bear. He had long before reaped a full harvest of disappointment. In 1874 he had written on the flyleaf of his diary:

I renew my desire and request that should death over take me during the year, as it may well come and be welcome, there may be no Faculty or other Resolutions in regard to my sorrowful and struggling career. My soul holds these well meant hypocrises in utter abhorance. Let there be comparative silence. What I am and what I have tried to be God knows— and my only hope and trust are in 'the multitude of his mercies.'

The pervading despair of his last years was echoed a few years later in a letter to Isabel: "All the springs of life with me are broken, and the works run feebly, and may at any time run down, and move no more. There is little cause for regret in this. My work is ended, without being done—and the heart has gone out of me."[71]

A growing conviction of failure during the postwar years, however, did not stop his pen. He continued to write, but his efforts were nothing like the earlier out-pouring. Writings reflecting his religious concern were fewer and much less ambitious than earlier. Some were never published. For a few years after the war his essays continued to appear in *De Bow's Review*; thereafter his only outlets were the *Southern Review* (which failed in 1873 owing him two hundred dollars)[72] and the *Southern Magazine*. He was unable to renew his connection with the *Methodist Review*, and, though their pages were opened to him, apparently never wrote for the *Nation* and the *North American Review*.[73]

Increasingly his time was devoted to teaching at Charlottesville and at other institutions, among them Georgetown University and the Peabody Institute in Baltimore; to his public lecturing (he moved on the Chautauqua circuit); to his widely used series of school grammars and readers; and to his successful and conciliatory history of the United States which he wrote to help erase the animosity between North and South.[74] He also wrote some forty-six articles on philosophy and history for John McClintock's twelve-volume *Cyclopaedia of Biblical, Theological, and Ecclesiastical Literature*.[75] These

[71] MS vol. 1795, G. F. Holmes to Isabel Holmes, August 22, 1880, Holmes papers, D.

[72] MS vol. 1794, May 5 and August 23, 1873, Holmes papers, D.

[73] Holmes to McClintock, November 17, 1865 and January 19, 1866.

[74] G. F. Holmes to J. Randolph Tucker, November 17, 1866, Tucker Family Papers, Southern Historical Collection, University of North Carolina, Chapel Hill, North Carolina. George Frederick Holmes, *A School History of the United States of America* (New York: University Publishing Company, 1871), pp. 3, 329. For the series of grammars and readers, see bibliography. For the significance of his school history see Van Tassel, *Recording America's Past*, pp. 156–57.

[75] See bibliography.

various activities brought him a moderate fame which won him notice in the *Encyclopaedia Britannica* as an "American educator" and an honorary degree—Doctor of Civil Law—from his old school, Durham University.[76]

But this success was only ashes in his mouth. He was often admired by his students for his modesty. One of them remembered that he had once called Holmes "Doctor" knowing that he disliked the title "professor." " 'You needn't mind the "Doctor," either,' " his teacher remarked, " 'the circus clown and the patent medicine man, the dancing master, are Professors, and I will leave them the dignity of the title; while the "Doctor" had best be kept for the M.D.'s. Just plain Mr. Holmes, please.' "[77] In 1890 he refused to "stand and deliver" his life for a projected biographical encyclopedia on the grounds that he objected to being pinned like a bug in a display case.[78] But was this genuine modesty? Or was it rather the irritated rejection of an unwelcome notoriety which only underscored his failure to realize his lifelong desire to be one of the founders of a science of history? Life had not been kind to that aspiration. First, Comte had chilled his initial efforts; then poverty, frustration, and war had worked against him. A multitude of intellectual interests led him into innumerable byways and scattered his energies. "It has always been my misfortune," he wrote to a friend in 1887, "to be beset by swarms of pestilent thoughts too multitudinous to be mastered, too vague to be defined, and by accidentally acquired information too various and unsystematic to be reduced to form."[79] In view of this unfulfilled ambition, the quiet despair which gradually spread over the last decades of his life seems justified. But the full story of his defeat was not contained in that disappointment. Running through these years there was also the final episodes of his struggle with modernity.

[76] *Encyclopaedia Britannica*, 9th ed., Supplement III, 673. *The Times* (London), June 25, 1891.

[77] Robinson, "George Frederick Holmes," p. 74.

[78] With characteristic ambivalence, however, he closed an indigant letter of refusal with the information that the facts of his life could be found in the *Britannica*. G. F. Holmes to James Roberts Gilmore, October [no date], 1890, Holmes papers, D.

[79] G. F. Holmes to John Mercer Patton, April 30, 1887, Holmes papers, D.

IX "Overwhelmed with Honest Doubts"

The afterglow of the intense personal piety of the Civil War years left Holmes decidedly unreceptive to substantial changes in his beliefs. His first reaction to an age whose intellectual life was dominated by Charles Darwin was to choose not to play by the currently fashionable rules. This meant that the years just after the war and through the seventies were a time in which he withdrew into the protective realm of faith and left modern ideas to the consideration of those who thought they could profit from them. A man with Holmes's commitment to learning, however, found the indefinite continuation of such a self-imposed exile difficult. Not surprisingly, then, the decade of the 1880s was a time of return and confrontation. But it was a confrontation which was to end in his capitulation to those tendencies in modern thought which he had opposed for so long. The last years of his life were devoted to determining what, if anything, could be salvaged from the wreck of his former beliefs.

Under the spell of orthodoxy the fideism latent in the Philosophy of Faith came to the fore during the immediate postwar years. The religious half of the faith-reason dualism now openly enjoyed the superiority which it had long tended to exercise in fact. Holmes's initial rejection of Darwinian evolution was not the result of a careful inspection of the epistemological questions involved, as one might have expected, but was simply a flat refusal to believe such an idea even if sanctioned by all the authority of science. His religion told him differently. This rebellion against science on a scientific matter constituted the first obvious breakdown of the Philosophy of Faith. Never before had he rejected so completely a respectable scientific opinion. Always he had sweetened his skepticism with faint praise. But his reaction to evolution clearly revealed the flaw which would prevent his scheme of reconciliation from working. Later, when Holmes began to change his mind about the probable truth of evolution and other modern ideas, the same process was repeated the other way: religious dogmas were rejected not for theological reasons but because they were incompatible with science. The source of this instability, as noted earlier, was contradictory and overlapping authority; a difficulty which was apparent in his first formulation but which Holmes failed to recognize. Consequently, he clung to the Philosophy of Faith to the end, still believing in its effectiveness despite the fact that his religion, which was so strong in the immediate post Civil War period, had, by the end of his life, apparently become little more than a faith in faith, a religion of sentiment virtually devoid of any dogmatic content; and this was so largely because of the unresolved conflict of authority between faith and reason. Far from reconciling Christianity and science, the Philosophy of Faith simply allowed Holmes to be pulled this way or that depending on which persuasion was dominant in his mind.

His unsuccessful attempt to flee the intellectual life of his time, however, was not prompted by his religious views alone. It was encouraged by his disappointed realization that the renewal of philosophy which he had heralded before the war would not be accomplished as readily as he had hoped. Holmes could scarcely avoid suspecting that the increasing enthusiasm for Darwinian evolution among his contemporaries was an inescapable consequence of a failure in philosophical reform. If men no longer thought soundly, what could one expect but the current advocacy of wild and preposterous ideas. The seeds of skepticism and sophistry sown by Hume in the previous century he saw now bearing abundant fruit in the work of "Darwin, Huxley, Mill, and of nearly all of the infidel writers of the present day."[1]

Not now, no more than in the fifties, did Holmes think his contemporaries short on mental power; the opposite, if anything, was true. But ingenuity was not enough. Discussing the condition of modern philosophy in *De Bow's Review* just after the war, Holmes found the explanation of the century's philosophical failure not so much in a lack of ability as in a lack of sound originality: a tendency to be novel in error but merely to repeat truths already established. The founder of Positivism, for instance, had more than his share of personal vagaries, but in most of what was sound in his thought Comte had been anticipated by Aristotle, Kant, and a host of lesser lights. More recently, Herbert Spencer had equalled Comte in brilliance, if not in eccentricity, but had no more authentic originality. Holmes would not deny Spencer a claim to novelty in building his system, but he found "very little that is distinctively new in principles" in it and what appeared to be new could be found in the work of Comte or someone else. Holmes expected that in no long while both the Synthetic and the Positive philosophies would lose what hold they had on men's attention and give way to other (although

---

[1] [Holmes], "Hume's Philosophy," 92n.

perhaps equally delusive) doctrines.[2] He no longer had hope of better things from Scotland, where the philosophy of Hamilton, from which he had once expected so much, lay dead, the victim of betrayal by Germanizing epigoni, the critical assaults of Mill, and the master's own inanition.[3] Of the Germans nothing need be said. The only Teutonic thinker in whom Holmes showed any interest after the war was Hermann Lotze, and he was dismissed in the late eighties as well-intentioned but a dealer in the same "vapory idealism" as the rest of his nation.[4] Confronted with this philosophical bankruptcy and forced to admit more candidly than ever before that contemporary science and Christianity seemed at hopeless odds, Holmes saw no alternative to the Philosophy of Faith if the two were to be reconciled.[5]

The scientific views which Holmes was interested in reconciling with his religion in the years just after the war were not the products of Darwinism, as he did not yet take that challenge seriously. Rather, they were the science-inspired philosophies of the Comtians and other positivists who shared a skepticism about the genuiness of religious knowledge. For Holmes the reconciliation of science and religion was still a question of epistemology just as it had been in the fifties. It had not yet become a problem seriously complicated by scientific and historical facts incompatible with traditional Christianity. Evolution, which might have made it so, he dismissed as merely a revival of an ancient error. Though ignorant of Darwin's work, he re-read Lucretius and decided that surely the British natualist could offer no improvement on the imaginative speculations in *De Rerum Natura*.[6] Among moderns, Comte himself had rejected Lamarckian evolution and a prescient Kant had destroyed the philosophical foundations upon which would be erected such immediate precursors of Darwin as Robert Chambers' *Vestiges of the Natural History of Creation*.[7] With these two authorities on his side, Holmes found it easy to persuade himself that Darwin's theory was not worth investigating. Consequently, he paid little attention to evolution dur-

[2] George Frederick Holmes, "Modern Philosophical Systems," *De Bow's Review*, I, n.s. (March 1866), pp. 225-32.

[3] Holmes to Thornwell, August 8, 1856, for his early distrust of Hamilton's followers; for his later disillusionment with Hamilton himself see George Frederick Holmes, "Sir William Hamilton," *Cyclopaedia of Biblical, Theological, and Ecclesiastical Literature*, IV, 48.

[4] George Frederick Holmes, "Recent Phases of Scepticism," *Cyclopaedia*, XII, 823.

[5] George Frederick Holmes, "Faith and Reason," *Cyclopaedia*, III, 464-67. George Frederick Holmes, "Pierre Gassendi," *ibid.*, III, 746-48.

[6] MS vol. 1833, Holmes papers, D.

[7] [Holmes], "Auguste Comte and Positivism," p. 134n.

ing these years except to mock it. His *Index Rerum* for the late 1860s contains only a single reference to it (and that to a refutation) and in one of his few published acknowledgments of the theory's existence he grouped it with "clairvoyance, table-turning, . . . and planchette" as one of the transient fads of the age.[8]

Ridicule could not satisfy him indefinitely, however; and his commitment to historical science gradually forced him to give reluctant attention to the theory which was rapidly becoming a major assumption of so many historians. He did not surrender easily. It is tempting to think that to some degree the flood of readers and grammars, the traveling here and there to lecture, the work in literature and philology were attempts to evade the problem through activity: a busyness that reflected his growing uneasiness and his disinclination to wrestle with the implications of Darwinism. If so, it was no use. In addition, his own writings in the mid-seventies hint of a drifting away from the deep piety of the war years. And with that went his main defense against modernity. He no longer experienced the emotional, almost mystical, faith he had had then. He still admired those who possessed it, but now found himself pitying some of the delusive forms it took.[9] Though his interest in Anglicanism was to be renewed later, in the seventies he fell once again into his youthful laxness in attending church.[10] As his religious absorptions lessened with the decrease of acute crisis in his life, he became more susceptible to the influence of new ideas. That the society he had sought to preserve was destroyed may itself have helped to take the edge off his will to resist the intrusions of heterodoxy. But whatever the reasons, his guard was slowly lowered, and during the 1880s the consequences of this became evident.

The revolution worked by historical scholarship and the theory of evolution in the nineteenth century was most radical in its view of origins: the origins of man, of civilization, of moral and religious ideas. Once this revolution had taken effective hold, it was no longer possible to draw a clear line separating man and his works from nature. The new theory taught that the mental and emotional attributes of human beings, as well as their bodies, were not the products of a special creation or of a unique human nature but were refinements of beginnings made among non-human ancestors. In its various

[8] MS vol. 1806. George Frederick Holmes, "Pleas for Astrology," *Southern Magazine*, VI (October 1873), 427.

[9] [George Frederick Holmes], "Armageddon," *Southern Review*, XII, (January 1873), 133, 141, 155.

[10] Culbreth, *University of Virginia*, p. 411. On the flyleaf of his diary for 1885, Holmes expressed his devotion to the Church of England. See MS vol. 1798.

forms, human culture was but another stage in a long and gradual process of development. Civilization was but another means of adapting to one's environment; it was the scion of an unimaginably ancient line, unrecognizable in its beginnings and having its ultimate origin among brutes more animal than human. Like many others who found themselves in this new universe of ideas, Holmes thought this startling view of the human past confusing and alarming. He spent the last two decades of his life exploring its implications, at last accepting as much of it as he saw he must.

Once he had felt the full impact of this revolution, its effect on Holmes's religious beliefs was shattering. But here, as with Positivism, it was not so much contradictions that shook him, not facts which his faith could not accommodate—though these played their part and their importance should not be minimized. Rather it was a new way of thinking, or, to be more accurate, an accustomed way of thinking made clear. Not until he was confronted with the stimulus of evolutionary thinking with its emphasis on qualitative development did Holmes begin to realize fully what it meant to think historically, to see the possible relativism concealed in the view of historical development which he had himself advocated ever since his early enthusiasm for Vico and his work on Herder and Schlegel: a view which saw history as a series of distinctive cultures. Now he began to understand the serious consequences for traditional Christianity in historically recreating as singular and exclusive mental experiences the world views of different civilizations. The combination of myths, faiths, beliefs, and institutions developed in one age in response to unique circumstances could not easily be those of another which organized its existence around different principles and assumptions and faced different exigencies. Evolution, then, was not merely a source of unwelcome ideas; it was also a catalyst to his own thinking just as Positivism had been. Comte's philosophy had opened his eyes to the implications of his empiricism, and now Darwinism brought into focus for him the true challenge of the historical revolution in nineteenth-century thought.

It was a portent of things to come that the first article which Holmes published after the war dealt with the origin of human language. He decided that the investigations of modern philologists were inconclusive and left the subject as mysterious as they had found it.[11] His discussion, however, foreshadowed two problems which were to be central to his later religious dilemma. The first of

---

[11] George Frederick Holmes, "Language: Its Sources, Changes and Philosophy," *De Bow's Review*, I, n.s. (January 1866), 34–35.

these had to do with historical data; in this case, those involved in the genesis of language. As Holmes pointed out, there were at present few facts to work with regarding the beginning of language; the potential problem, however, was there. Later he would be very concerned with new and disturbing facts about the origins of men and civilization, of religion and Christianity. The second was a question of theory: how could the qualitative innovations needed for the rise of language or civilization happen at all? How was it possible for such necessary characteristics of civilization as intelligible speech—certainly an extraordinary innovation—to begin spontaneously? Could such a thing occur without an intervening miracle? It seemed clear to Holmes that a race of men which could not speak could never spontaneously begin to speak given ever so much time. The difference between dumbness and speech was a difference in kind not of degree.

No amplification of the years of the world—no relegation of the transaction to the gloom of an unfathomable antiquity removes or diminishes the difficulty of conceiving the original formation of language. This remains the same whether it be supposed to have happened four thousand years ago, or twenty thousand, or a hundred thousand, or a million.[12]

This difficulty with the origin of language could be easily extended to civilization: could a race of savages ever spontaneously become civilized? In both cases one had to account for the appearance in history of astonishing novelties. How did they originate? Given the seeming nature of things, how could they originate?

Holmes did not suggest solving this second problem by calling in divine intervention. That was no suitable solution for science. But science apparently could offer nothing better. To speak of gradual development, as some were doing, would not solve the problem any more than long stretches of time would solve it. Everyone knew, of course, that as far back as history could be traced men were found improving their knowledge of how to domesticate wild beasts, to till the soil, to build shelters, to use fire, smelt metals and so forth, just as they were found using language. But improvement was not origination. "The consideration of the process of development is unavailing," he wrote, "it reflects very little light on the causes or modes of the primitive commencement." Language, (and, by implication, arts

---

[12] *Ibid.*, p. 33. Holmes here follows the thought—and even the language—of the famous German linguistic scholar Baron Christian Bunsen. The Orientalist, F. Max Müller, who quoted Bunsen on the origin of language in his Presidential Address to the Anthropology Section of the British Association for the Advancement of Science in 1891, found the qualitative leap still an insurmountable problem. *Nature*, September 3, 1891, pp. 428-35.

and sciences) could develop in degree through a "regular and un-
broken tradition," but how could a man who was ignorant of the
very idea of speech begin to speak; how could he know what speaking
was before he spoke?[13] To a mind locked in a static Aristotelian
world of immutable forms and essences the conundrum seemed
insolvable.[14]

Holmes's difficulty in visualizing the occurrence of changes in
kind is important. It goes far toward explaining the set of his mind
on the eve of his encounter with evolution. His inability to believe
that innovations in kind could result from gradual changes in degree
was the same difficulty that advocates of the immutability of species
had with Darwin's theory. By no process observable in nature, they
argued, could a species of animal become other than what it was.
Variations from the parent form, even though they admittedly occurred, always reverted to the original type which was permanent.
Holmes, like these naturalists, was philosophically predisposed to
reject a major thesis of both Charles Darwin's biology and Sir Charles
Lyell's geology: that processes of development like those observable
in the present or detectable in the immediate past could completely
account for all natural conditions and changes in the past and, in the
case of Darwin's theory, arrange plants and animals on genetically
connected scales showing development through eons of time. Nor
could he accept the same reasoning applied to human history. Man,
he wrote several years after his article on language, "can never become more than he had a latent potency in the beginning of becoming."[15] If he had been in capacity a mere savage, he could never
have become civilized unaided.

Actually Holmes's thinking about origins had changed very little
from what it had been in the early 1840s when he, like so many others
at that time, accepted the doctrine recently revived by Archbishop
Richard Whately that contemporary savages represented not, as
some said, the early stages of human social evolution but a degeneration from a previous civilized state and that the primeval condition
of man had not been savagery but civilization. In his article on the
North American Indians (1844) Holmes, like Whately, had argued
that historians knew of no people "among whom civilization was or

[13] *Ibid.*, p. 32, 34–35.

[14] For an able discussion of Darwin's escape from the "essentialistic" pre-
suppositions of nineteenth-century science see Michael T. Ghiselin, *The Triumph of the Darwinian Method* (Berkeley: University of California Press,
1969).

[15] [George Frederick Holmes], "Primitive Law," *Forum*, III (April 1875),
238–39.

has been spontaneous," that the myths of all nations indicated a foreign source for the beginnings of their culture, that the ultimate origin of civilization must be, to history at least, a "sealed page."[16] It was a sealed page because the most the historian could discover about it was its development after Noah's flood. That ancient worthy had brought out of the ark "the arts and civilization of the ante-diluvian world, such as they were," and succeeding races made what they could of this legacy. Some degenerated into savages and others, more gifted, established the foundations of later kingdoms and empires. All civilizations, Holmes concluded, require civilized antecedents.[17] The infinite regress this involves is arresting but is not to the point. The significant thing is that Holmes apparently preferred logical paradox to nonsense. And to him it would have been nonsensical to talk of civilization coming out of utter savagery. The article on language and certain passages in his *Science of Society* in the same vein show that he continued to think about origins in this way through the seventies and even into the early eighties.[18] His delayed grappling with Darwinism was certainly a major cause for this. But his idea, formed years earlier, that racial character was virtually fixed in some races perhaps also played a part. If racial aptitudes, especially in the so-called lower (and for Holmes more genetically pure) races, were virtually immutable, then the idea of savages spontaneously developing into civilized men presented the same difficulty as man evolving from an ancestor among the lower animals. Both required qualitative innovations of almost miraculous dimensions.

Holmes, as a good Baconian, knew that the solution of these difficult questions required facts. And, to his eventual confusion, facts soon came in overwhelming number as new areas of investigation

[16] [Holmes], "North American Indians," pp. 147–48. Richard Whately, *Introductory Lectures on Political Economy*, 2nd ed. (London: B. Fellowes, 1832), pp. 106–71. A follower of Whately, W. Cooke Taylor, published in 1840 his *Natural History of Society* which Holmes read and continued to use even in the seventies and early eighties. For the popularity of the degeneration hypothesis in the eighteenth century see Margaret T. Hodgen, *Early Anthropology in the Sixteenth and Seventeenth Centuries* (Philadelphia: University of Pennsylvania Press, [1964], pp. 379–81. In 1867 there was still sufficient interest in the theory for Sir John Lubbock's paper against Whately, given at the Dundee meeting of the British Association, to attract considerable public attention. See *The Times* (London), September 11, 1867, p. 10 and Margaret T. Hodgen, *The Doctrine of Survivals* (London: Allenson, 1936), p. 31; also Burrow, *Evolution and Society*, p. 274; and Andrew Dickson White, *A History of the Warfare of Science with Theology in Christendom* (New York: D. Appleton and Company, 1898), I, 304–09 for a brief sketch and bibliography.

[17] [Holmes], "Schlegel's Philosophy," pp. 289–90.

[18] Holmes, *Science of Society*, chapters VI and VII.

came to his attention. He was not able to escape the challenge by abstaining from reading Darwin; there were others equally subversive of his beliefs though less notorious than the English naturalist. This he gradually discovered as he read widely in anthropology, prehistoric archaeology, comparative mythology, and other fields.[19] The requirements of Baconian induction temporarily enabled him to avoid a crisis by urging caution and advising against premature conclusions. It was necessary, he told his students, not only to have all the facts but to see each subject area against a background of all the others so that an accurate idea of their interrelations could be formed. Only then might conclusions safely be drawn.

The Science of Social Development [he said] is not designed to promote any theories of wild innovation, but rather to encourage a prudent hesitancy and conservative restraint, till all the agencies are clearly apprehended in their nature and tendency, and all the conditions of each problem are understood in their relation to the coincident system at any time.

To do otherwise, to jump to conclusions, would lead one into vapory delusions similar to those of Herder, Hegel, Schlegel, and others which the world was fortunately beginning to forget.[20]

But wise as this counsel might be, men insisted on drawing conclusions. And as time passed it became increasingly difficult for one who believed in science as Holmes did to dismiss the acknowledged leaders in the new disciplines as fools. Once he accepted their serious purpose, the implications of what they were saying could not be avoided. During the 1880s a farreaching reorientation was accomplished in Holmes's mind.

Two developments were crucial in this transformation. First, his reading lifted a curtain on an unknown and mysterious human past of heretofore unimagined antiquity and overwhelmed him with facts and authoritative argument about it. Three of the leaders in the new sciences, whose works he read, Sir John Lubbock, Sir William Boyd Dawkins, and Sir Edward Burnett Tylor, were in agreement on several critical points: that the primeval condition of man had been savagery, that the emergence and growth of civilization had been the result of a slow development over long reaches of time, and that Charles Darwin's theory of evolution was correct.[21] Unlike Comte

---

[19] [George Frederick Holmes], MS "Historical Science: Introductory Lecture," p. 8, Holmes papers, D. The MS dates from around 1880.

[20] *Ibid.*, pp. 5–9.

[21] The works read by Holmes relevant here were: Sir Edward Burnett Tylor, *Anthropology: An Introduction to the Study of Man and Civilization* (New York: D. Appleton and Company, 1889); Sir John Lubbock, *Pre-Historic Times*

and Spencer, these men were not armchair theorists. As a Baconian, Holmes must have been greatly impressed by Lubbock's and Dawkins' patient collecting of information in the field; just as he must have been given pause by Tylor's assertion that the new anthropology was predicated on the evolution of man from savage and sub-human beginnings.[22] Holmes had long boasted that Christian intellectuals could meet scientific skepticism on its own ground and beat it with its own weapons.[23] Now, given the new body of knowledge, this seemed to him less certain.

The impact on Holmes of the ideas of these writers, the three mentioned and others, was increased by the absence or virtual absence from the work of many of them of that militant hostility toward religion so characteristic of earlier skepticism. He could stand off open "infidelity" but scientific authority mixed with a desire to be reasonably accommodating about difficulties between religious doctrine and science was something else. Lubbock, for one, thought that the disquieting findings on the antiquity of man would in time be absorbed into the Christian view of things just as those of astronomy and geology had been earlier, and professed surprise that "the great principle of Natural Selection . . . which . . . teaches us humility for the past, faith in the present, and hope for the future, should have been regarded as opposed to the principles of Christianity or the interests of true religion."[24] Science like this, decked out in vague pieties or prudently silent about religious implications letting the reader draw his own conclusions, was seductive.

When Holmes turned to scientific writers of more traditional or, at least, of dissenting views for support in his own faith the results were disappointing. One of the most prestigious opponents of the dominant views of the evolutionists concerning the origin of man and his primitive condition was the respected Canadian geologist, Sir John William Dawson. Dawson ventured into popularized science to combat "that materialistic infidelity, which, by robbing nature of the spiritual element, and of its presiding Divinity, makes science dry, barren, and repulsive, diminishes its educational value, and even

---

as *Illustrated by Ancient Remains and the Manners and Customs of Modern Savages* (London: Williams and Norgate, 1865) and *The Origin of Civilization and the Primitive Condition of Man* (London: Longmans, Green & Company, 1870); Sir William Boyd Dawkins, *Early Man in Britain and His Place in the Tertiary Period* (London: Macmillan and Company, 1880). For his extensive reading of similar books during these years see his reading lists in MS vols. 1836, 1837, 1838, Holmes papers, D.

[22] Tylor, *Anthropology*, pp. v–vi.
[23] [Holmes], "Vestiges," p. 248.
[24] Lubbock, *Pre-Historic Times*, pp. viii–ix, 481–82.

renders it less efficient for purposes of practical research."[25] Mixing his science with liberal amounts of Paleyan natural theology, Dawson argued for the recent appearance of man on the earth—six to eight thousand years ago was all he would allow—and denied that the first men were savages. Nor did he see any truth in Darwin's *Descent of Man*: man was and always had been *homo sapiens*.[26] Dawson's voice was a strong one and must have given Holmes temporary comfort. But other voices were no less worthy and they told a different tale. And even Dawson gave some grudging credence to Natural Selection. It might, he conceded, have played a small part in the development of some species among the lower animals.[27] The ranks of the opposition, then, seemed to waver. If Dawson held firm on the primeval condition and age of man and weakened on evolution, the French naturalist, Armand de Quatrefages, though skeptical about evolution, conceded the savagery of early man and located his first appearance in the miocene epoch, which was far earlier than most evolutionists would have dared to believe.[28] Two other writers in this camp whom Holmes respected, John Tulloch, a prominent Scottish theologian, and Joseph J. Murphy, Irish essayist and poet, blew their trumpets with as uncertain a sound as Dawson and Quatrefages. Tulloch would not oppose evolution as such but did feel that, perhaps, too much emphasis had been placed on Natural Selection.[29] Murphy, like Holmes, was historically oriented and cautious in social theory; he was one of the few from whose work Holmes copied out lengthy extracts and made extensive notes. He stood uncompromisingly for religion, but endorsed evolution fully. He insisted, however, that Darwinian mechanisms could not account for it and that a theistic view of the process was the only tenable one.[30] Just as the conciliatory appeals of Lubbock reached out toward religion, so the theistic evolution supported by Murphy sought to make the new science spiritually acceptable if not orthodox. The effort made by

[25] Sir John William Dawson, *The Story of the Earth and Man* (New York: Harper and Brothers, 1873), pp. vii–viii.

[26] *Ibid.*, pp. 2–3, 293–94, 372. Sir John William Dawson, *Fossil Men and Their Modern Representatives* (London: Hodder and Staughton, 1880), pp. 4–5, 246, 249.

[27] Dawson, *Story of Earth*, pp. 77–78, 79, 321–22, 341–42.

[28] Armand de Quatrefages, *The Human Species* (New York: D. Appleton and Company, 1881), pp. 93–95, 151–52, 242–43.

[29] John Tulloch, *Modern Theories in Philosophy and Religion* (London: Blackwood and Sons, 1884), pp. 145–46, 155–56.

[30] Joseph John Murphy, *Habit and Intelligence, In Their Connexion With the Laws of Matter and Force* (London: Macmillan and Company, 1869), I, 13, 130f, 206f.

some scientists to avoid unduly embarrassing religion, then, plus the continuing controversy over human origins in which an authoritative majority opinion was clearly forming in favor of the evolution of both man and civilization from primitive beginnings, had a deep effect on Holmes's hesitant and uncertain intellectual struggle.

The second step in the transformation of Holmes's mind was his gradual understanding of the importance of the historical dimension in the conflict between science and religion. At this point, frankly, one must conjecture. Holmes left no record of an experienced change in his thinking, a change that must have been subtle and almost imperceptible since it was not entirely novel but rather was a dawning awareness of the implication of ideas he had long held. And yet, something of the sort suggested here must have happened in view of what eventually followed in Holmes's thinking.

Years earlier, in defending Christianity against its friends the natural theologians, Holmes had pointed out that arguments based on analogy and inference could demonstrate, if valid, a compelling degree of probability and were worthy of acceptance even though lacking the force of an absolute proof.[31] His intention had been to oppose the confusion of the two and to argue that the rationalistic proofs of natural theology, being of the former kind, were at best merely confirmatory of revelation; they could never have the logical precision to stand as absolute proofs. This being so, they could never replace the certainty of revelation nor rival the compelling mathematical demonstrations of natural science. But analogical and inferential arguments were exactly the sort employed by the new historical sciences of biology and geology and by history. Holmes himself had used them in his early speculations in the forties. The new anthropology, comparative mythology, and similar disciplines all assumed, as Holmes had, the existence of laws of social evolution which made possible the employment of analogies to clarify the past. Present day cultures at a certain point on the scale of social development could be enlightening about similar cultures in the past. The astonishing discoveries of biologists and geologists rested on inference, on what was, in effect, the evaluation of historical evidence and the imaginative reconstruction of the past. Once he grasped the identity of this mode of reasoning with his own and realized that he had admitted its force there was no escaping accepting the new sciences. Holmes could object to nothing on theoretical grounds. In brief, he was caught. As soon as he realized what had been implicit in his argument all along but never fully appreciated by him: that

---

[31] [Holmes], "Butler's Analogy," pp. 219–21, 227–28.

the province of science under the terms of the Philosophy of Faith must include the past equally with the present and the timeless realm of mathematical truth, he had no choice but to accept, in principle at least, the picture of the past being created by science. But it was a picture greatly at variance with the historical teaching of traditional Christianity. A new area of potential conflict was thereby opened up to him, for it was no longer possible to dismiss these theories as illegitimate intrusions into the realm of religion.

By the end of the 1880s Holmes's total resistance to evolution had given way somewhat before the combined strength of new information, scientific authority, and historical thinking. Prodded by the enthusiasm around him, he had finally read some of Darwin's work and had come to a partial acceptance of his theories. The books seemingly had been lying idle since 1874 when he received "Darwin's works" as a gift; it was not until the late eighties that his notebooks began to contain any indication that he was reading them. Even then only *The Descent of Man* and *The Expression of the Emotions in Man and Animals* are mentioned.[32] Strangely, there is no evidence that he ever read *The Origin of Species*, an omission that may not be without significance. Holmes had serious reservations about evolution which were never removed but which might have been lessened by a close study of the *Origin*. He was willing to believe that alterations in species might occur as a result of the operation of Natural Selection. One might in this way get different species of horses, but they would always be horses. Unlimited development resulting in evolution on the generic level he denounced in the 1891 edition of McClintock's encyclopedia as a "worse hallucination than alchemy."[33] But it was not the biological aspects of evolution that disturbed him most. Rather he objected to the "arrogant and unwarrantable assumptions" of many advocates of the new theory. Evolution, he charged, "presents itself as an adequate and exclusive theory of the universe." Like the Positivists earlier, the evolutionists seemed determined to rid the world of religion. But, Holmes asked, "What necessarily preceded all germs and processes of Evolution, and communicated the impulse and prescribed the law and process of development? . . . The everlasting enigma of matter and of life remains impenetrable."[34]

A Christianized evolution might, of course, overcome this difficulty and Holmes returned again and again to the idea that there was no

[32] MS vol. 1795, October 8, 1874. MS vol. 1837, pp. 77, 92, 117.

[33] Holmes, "Scepticism," pp. 821–22. George Frederick Holmes, "Positivism," *ibid.*, VIII, 439.

[34] MS vol. 1838, p. 114.

necessary incompatibility between evolution and Christianity. "All the facts," he wrote shortly before his death,

not the conjectures and inferences of Evolutionism[,] may be accepted without the doctrine of Evolution being directly antagonistic to that of creation. The process of Evolution, even the variable and in some degree optional character of development may be due to the plastic force inserted into the elementary 'initia' by the Creator. The whole scheme of existence will then be rendered intelligible—instead of issuing from clouds and darkness without illuminating ray. . . . There is no necessary conjunction of Evolution and Agnosticism.[35]

In fact, he suggested, the Darwinian doctrine of adaptive variations might have its uses in natural theology as evidence of intelligent design in nature: "Behind the stimulation of surroundings and the responsive activity of the organism, there is something higher and more important to be considered—the form of the adaptation, the impulse of the surroundings, and the capacity of the subject to create changes." All was evidence of a "Divine implantation of the germs of an elastic progressive development."[36] It should not escape notice, however, that in this conciliation Holmes had abandoned the straightforward version of creation given in scripture, and his Christianity threatened to become no more than theism.

Along with a partial acceptance of biological evolution Holmes was gradually brought to acknowledge that savagery might well have been the earliest human condition. In the *Science of Society* he had rejected this position, attributing it to the tendency of "recent science" to reach "premature conclusions" rather than to engage in "the cautious examination and careful determination of perplexing facts."[37] He had admitted, however, that the evidence brought forward from the "bone caves" to support this thesis was "striking," but had declined to be convinced by it.[38] Instead, he had pushed the question aside and organized his exposition logically rather than chronologically. As he used the phrase, primitive man meant "the least

[35] *Ibid.*, p. 444.

[36] *Ibid.*, p. 446. [George Frederick Holmes], MS "What is Man?," pp. 10–13, Holmes papers, D. It is interesting to wonder if Holmes was influenced in his late conversion to evolution by the surrender of that doughty opponent of Darwin, the Duke of Argyll. The views expressed by Holmes are very like those of the Duke. See George Douglas Campbell, Duke of Argyll, *Organic Evolution Cross-examined or, Some Suggestions on the Great Secret of Biology* (London: John Murray, 1898). The book was published earlier as essays in *The Nineteenth Century* which Holmes read regularly.

[37] Holmes, *Science of Society*, Chapter VI, section 3.

[38] *Ibid.*, Chapter IV, section 10–11.

developed state of Man," not "the most ancient and primitive condition of Man."[39] At times though, the doubts expressed in *Science of Society* might seem mere caviling. He granted that the human residents of the "bone caves" were "anterior to all historical record," that they were "anterior to the earliest history or legend in the localities where they have been found, for they had left no memory behind them. Some of them," he went on, "must be more ancient than any history, as they have been found in India and Egypt, yet they were utterly unknown to the literature of those countries."[40] And yet, in the face of strong probability, he still held that the question of man's primeval condition could not be even tentatively resolved. Was he really as undecided in his mind as he claimed, or was his professed skepticism partly for his own spiritual comfort and to protect the supposed sensibilities of his students? At any rate, before a decade had passed, he had become less convinced of the reasonableness of his doubts. Though still refusing to accept the savagery of man's original state as proved, he was willing to treat the idea as a possibility; and his lack of resolution on the question was mirrored in a new uncertainty about his older belief. "What is Man?," his last essay on the subject, was marked by a hesitant evasiveness and a failure to take a clear stand one way or the other.

In fairness to Holmes it should be said that advocates of the new anthropology were not always as certain of the strength of their position as their popular pronouncements frequently indicated. Tylor, for example, in a candid address before the Anthropological Section of the British Association in 1879, admitted that the evidence produced by prehistoric archaeology from the river drifts of the Somme valley supporting the tremendous antiquity and savage condition of early man might not survive the criticisms being leveled against it by scientific skeptics. He assured his audience, however, that the new doctrine did not depend entirely on this data and that other arguments were available if needed. Nor was the evidence from the "bone caves" free of ambiguity. Boyd Dawkins, one of Britain's leading prehistorians, found it disturbingly incompatible with the received evolutionary idea of mind and material culture advancing *pari passu* when evidence began to appear that cavemen had possessed religious sentiments somewhat higher than they should have had. The Somme valley evidence withstood its attackers, of course, and the theory governing the reconstruction of human evolution was modified to absorb the indications of religion and art among cave dwellers without abandon-

[39] *Ibid.*, Chapter VI, section 4.
[40] *Ibid.*, Chapter VI, section 2.

ing their savagery. But the disquiet among the scientists was enough to make Holmes's doubts something more than mere obstinacy. Had they been but that, he would not have changed his mind.[41]

The religious implications of an acceptance of the possibility that the first men had been no more advanced than the wild beasts around them would have been great. Unfortunately, we cannot be assured that Holmes appreciated them. Here again his silence forces us to conjecture and to suggest rather than demonstrate what went on in his mind. While Holmes never accepted evolution so fully as to give man an ancestor among the lower animals and continued to believe that man was a special creation of God—"Darwin, and Wallace, and Huxley may make him only the elder brother of the ape, the baboon, and the gorilla," he sneered, "but these are merely the vagaries of aberrant science"[42]—his indecision about man's original state presented him with the possibility that man might have been created a near brute. He clearly felt there was a great deal of evidence to support the idea of the savagery of early man. This, if true, he would have found hard to reconcile with his old beliefs in a pure primitive revelation and a golden age before true religion was replaced by the many superstitions of the heathen. As he learned from Tylor and Sir James Frazer, the inspired nature of the Christian tradition had itself become suspect by the survival in it of what seemed to be only thinly disguised savage cults and superstitions. Frazer's article on Totemism in the *Encyclopaedia Britannica*, which Holmes read, could easily have suggested to him analogies between certain elements of the Judeo-Christian tradition and primitive religion: dietary prohibitions, ritual death and resurrection, even mention of a god who died for his people. Tylor remarked in his *Anthropology* that "looking closely into the thoughts, arts, and habits of any nation, the student finds everywhere the remains of older states of things out of which they arose."[43] Thus an element of theological confusion could easily have been introduced into his thinking by this inexplicable creation of a brute-man, and Holmes left theologically disoriented, less sure of the purity or of the continuing relevance of the Christian revelation, and more capable of quietly abandoning it piecemeal.

Evolution and its far-ranging implications was not the only solvent working on Holmes's faith during the last years. His interest in

[41] Sir Edward Burnett Tylor in *Nature*, August 28, 1879, p. 414; Sir William Boyd Dawkins, *Cave Hunting, Researches on the Evidences of Cave Respecting the Early Inhabitants of Europe* (London, 1874), pp. 19–21, 243–47, 255–58.

[42] MS "What is Man?," p. 6.

[43] MS vol. 1838. Sir James G. Frazer, "Totemism," *Encyclopaedia Britannica*, 9th ed., XXIII, 467–76. Tylor, *Anthropology*, p. 15.

mythology had been constant since the 1840s and was ultimately a more serious challenge to his orthodoxy than Darwin's theories. Though not persuaded by them, during the fifties he had paid close attention to the interpretations of myth offered by George Grote in his *History of Greece* and by D. F. Strauss's *Das Leben Jesu* and had made eleven pages of notes on the latter's work in his notebooks.[44] He had found himself compelled to admit the strength of Strauss's argument in support of his thesis that the Gospels were largely the product of mythmaking by the early Christian community. In its rationalism and anti-supernaturalism *Das Leben Jesu* was, he felt, closely allied to Positivism and, like that philosophy, peculiarly attuned to the general intellectual temper of modernity.[45] Grote's treatment of the Greek myths as the product of a mythopoeic mentality different from that of the later more sophisticated Greeks (and of moderns) intrigued Holmes. Already familiar with this idea from his reading of Vico, he took extensive notes on it and readily connected it with Strauss's work.[46] Pursuing his own biblical studies at the same time, he had noted that curiously similar ideas, customs and religious usages, occurred in the New Testament and in classical literature.[47]

After the war, and even during the period in which he refused to read Darwin, he continued these studies, and, in addition, began to read widely in the writings of the students of comparative religion.[48] From time to time he came upon things that puzzled and worried him: parallels in classical and early Christian religious ideas, similarities between Hebrew and pagan myths where there was no question of influence, many religions other than Christianity claiming divine inspiration and incarnation;[49] but his encounter with myth, though it might raise questions about the uniqueness of Christianity, did not become dangerous to his belief until he fitted it into an evolutionary framework. Then he had a much more serious problem: how could the faith of men living in an earlier age and forming their beliefs in accord with a different and less advanced constellation of ideas than his own, be his faith?

The acceptance of the principle of evolution, of the possible initial savagery of man, and the recognition of the important role played

44 MS vols. 1792; 1803, p. 330f.

45 MS vol. 1792. [Holmes], "Morell's Philosophy," p. 387. [Holmes], "Black Arts," pp. 201–02, 206–07.

46 MS vol. 1802, pp. 3–4.

47 MS vol. 1803, passim.

48 MS vol. 1793, November 30, 1872. MS vol. 1833, "index."

49 [George Frederick Holmes], MS "The Elsmere Problem," pp. 28–33, 34–35, Holmes papers, D.

by mythic thinking in the formation of religions forced Holmes to modify his earlier incredulity about qualitative innovations in history. He had to acknowledge that not only had there been an historical progression of human society, of arts, of sciences and institutions (which, of course, he had never denied), but that these changes may have started from beginnings which he had hitherto thought to be too incredibly primitive; and, furthermore, that there had also been a similar progression of ideas. Contrary to his earlier beliefs, the intellectual history of mankind now seemed to him to have been not merely a story of increasing knowledge and enlightenment, but a series of changing and incompatible world views, of contradictory paradigms of the possible and the significant. This raised the question which became the basic cause of his capitulation: the question of the credibility of the record of events and their explanations given by men living in climates of opinion alien to his own. Holmes had been verging on a full encounter with this problem of the acceptability of beliefs arising out of world views different from his for sometime. It was latent in Vico's philosophy and in Comte's Law of the Three Stages. It had been implicit in his own historical thinking since the forties. It lurked not only in his early work in comparative history but especially in the formula for intellectual progress which he had worked out as part of his investigation into the causes of major instaurations. In those essays he had touched on ideas closely analogous to the changing paradigms and disjunctive innovations required by the new evolutionary view of intellectual history. The advances in logic which Holmes had described created basic changes in thinking which were suggestively similar to changes in paradigms in their reorganizing effects on society and subsequent thought. In this, as in other ways, he had carefully prepared the way for his own undoing. The problem was now focused sharply for him by Mrs. Humphrey Ward's controversial novel, *Robert Elsmere*.

Robert Elsmere, which was published in 1888, created a scandal in Christian circles. Through it many who had no more than heard of the higher criticism nor directly encountered any form of modern skepticism, who would never have read a treatise but who might read a novel, had their faith challenged for the first time. It was not a pleasant experience and the book soon became notorious. Its fame had been unwisely enlarged, Holmes thought, "by injudicious antagonism, and by the misplaced denunciations of the clergy." It had been attacked "as a herd of mad cattle attack a red rag," blindly and mindlessly. Even William Gladstone's attempt to answer Mrs. Ward in the pages of the *Nineteenth Century*, in which he had defended the credibility of the New Testament miracles, had denied the thesis that a mythic world view had clouded the thought of antiquity, and had cast doubt on the idea that Christianity might be effectively modernized, had fallen short. Holmes acknowledged the justice of his criticisms of the novel as literature, but added that that was "the only part of his essay that merits acceptance."[50] Such a response by Christians was a mistake, he felt, for the book undertook to teach no "systematic heresy;" rather, its significance lay in its reflecting the religious "doubt and yearnings, now besieging all sincere and reflecting minds, clerical, ecclesiastical, and lay." To ignore this was to close one's eyes to the demanding realities of the present religious situation. Great changes in Christianity were underway and they were being accomplished by those who no longer found orthodoxy satisfying. "Earnest natures," Holmes wrote, "overwhelmed at once with honest doubts" could not and should not be silenced by thunder from the pulpit.[51]

Elsmere, a young clergyman in the Church of England, had found his undoer in Squire Wendover, a gruff landowner who was also one of England's most famous skeptics. The Squire was a very learned and urbane scholar and had been for more than thirty years laboring on a history of testimony, a study of the changing paradigms of human belief. Elsmere lost his faith when the Squire demonstrated to him that since he did not share the world paradigm of the authors of the Gospels—a supernatural view of nature including miracles, demons and so forth—he could not rationally accept their narratives as historically true. The credibility of testimony, said the Squire, depended upon one's acceptance of the assumptions underlying it. The paradigmatic assumptions of first-century Palestine were not those of nineteenth-century England.

Squire Wendover had little to tell Holmes that he had not already encountered in Strauss, Grote, Vico, and Comte; so the effect of Mrs. Ward's book on him was not what it often was on others. It was not so much a shock as a stimulus: the novel's explicit formulation of the problem and the popular controversy which followed caused him to pull things together. The same was perhaps true of two other books which he read soon after *Robert Elsmere* appeared. These were Tito Vignoli's *Myth and Science*, a work with overtones of the theories of Strauss and Comte, and Ernest Renan's naturalistic *Life of Jesus*, written in a more popular vein than Strauss's earlier study and

[50] William E. Gladstone, " 'Robert Elsmere' and the Battle of Belief," *Nineteenth Century*, XXIII (May 1888), 766–88. [Holmes], MS "Elsmere Problem," p. 2.
[51] [Holmes], MS "Elsmere Problem," pp. 2–3, 9–10.

even more notorious among the faithful.[52] Both of these books may have quickened Holmes's interest in myth and raised his apprehensions about its presence in the Christian religion. That Renan's work influenced his thinking about the historical origins of Christianity is sure.[53] But he read more than he wrote now, and what he wrote was seldom published. Increasingly, he kept his musings to himself; perhaps to spare pain to those around him; perhaps from his own uncertainty and weariness. But, whatever the cause, the effect was to reduce the possibility of knowing fully the thoughts of his last years.

It is clear, however, that the problem of incompatible paradigms was the decisive one for Holmes. Like Elsmere, once he had grasped the dilemma it was not possible to avoid the conclusion that Christianity as he had always accepted it was no longer believable. But if his faith in orthodoxy was shaken, his faith in the Philosophy of Faith was not. Agnosticism, into which drifted so many of his contemporaries who reached similar conclusions about Christianity, he condemned as philosophically contemptible and morally pernicious. It made even less sense than atheism for its advocates "admitted the reality of what they exclude from consideration and from rational inquiry": the realm of divinity and faith. They merely passed it by "with a flippant sneer" as being unknowable. Agnosticism was the "substitution of . . . nescience for . . . knowledge."[54] The only reply one could give to agnosticism and other forms of skepticism was " 'I believe where I do not know' " which answer, of course, men of science would scorn. But this was only because they "fail to perceive that all their observations and conclusions rests upon like undemonstrated and undemonstrable faith."[55] This was the old argument, and, ostensibly, the Philosophy of Faith held firm.

His statements of his perennial doctrine in this new crisis, however, were strikingly modified. It is not surprising to find him calling for "the interpretation of science in accordance with Christianity"; that is simply the old primacy asserted once again. But what is one to think of the insistence that Christianity be interpreted "in accordance with science" or that religion "must be interpreted and accepted, so as to be in entire harmony with all other intellectual movements [for] larger comprehensions will require modified expositions"? To be

[52] Holmes's reading lists indicate that all three books were read after 1888. MS vol. 1838, passim.
[53] [George Frederick Holmes], MS "The Development of Christianity," MS vol. 1840.
[54] Holmes, "Scepticism," p. 822. [Holmes], MS "Elsmere Problem," p. 41.
[55] [Holmes], MS "Elsmere Problem," p. 14.

sure, Holmes added that "the essential Faith may be preserved the same."[56] But might it? And what was the essential faith? It was no longer "Christianity as rigidly preached in the churches"; for that Christianity must fall before the criticisms of Squire Wendover. Nor was there any safety in obscurantism: a "belief that requires to be blindly and virulently maintained is already unsettled and transmuted, in the minds of its advocates, pastors and congregations." A "modified interpretation" of Christianity was urgent.[57] What Holmes would not countenance when he originally formulated the Philosophy of Faith, tampering with the accepted doctrines of the Church, he was now prepared to do to save "the essential Faith." There was no real choice, of course. "In the progress of the world," he wrote, "it is impossible to stand still; it is hopeless to return upon our steps towards the trusting Faith and its innocent acceptance which characterized the early years, before doubts, born of wider knowledge, began to fester in the mind." If new interpretations "consonant with the altered sphere of knowledge and range of thought" were not achieved "the Old Faith would become an empty shell and a vain ceremonial. It is not," he added firmly, "a question of whether this transfiguration is right or wrong: it is inevitable."[58]

What new interpretations did Holmes have in mind? The "instructive and remarkable volumes" of Renan[59] and those of other students of the historical development of Christian doctrine had led him to reject both the authority of the church and the historic creeds as guides to an authentic Christianity. The history of the creeds—their dubious origins and late appearances—seemed to him "inconsistent with positive inspiration" and the development of other doctrines over the centuries was clouded by a possible contamination by influences outside the faith.[60] For reasons made clear by Squire Wendover, the faith of the original Christians was no better standard of truth. How, then, did Holmes propose to meet the problem of paradigms? By a form of syncretism. All religions, he decided, rest on faith and so must be "in their original impulse, of God." They all teach morality; they all are formed to accord "with the conditions, intellectual, social, political etc. of the peoples by which they are held." All religions, therefore, are "agencies of Providence, in the government of His Creation." The gradation of religions ranking from the lowest to the

---

[56] *Ibid.*, pp. 5–6, 50, 52.

[57] *Ibid.*, p. 5.

[58] *Ibid.*, pp. 50–51.

[59] His reference is to the *Origins of Christianity* of which the *Life of Jesus* is one volume.

[60] [Holmes], MS "The Development of Christianity."

most sophisticated and ranging widely in both time and space, he thought, formed a training school of the spirit.[61] In this scheme each age would necessarily have its own faith; a faith providentially attuned to its special needs, and which not only could not but should not be that of another.

And so Holmes solved his problem. But in solving it he had abandoned almost everything he had set out to defend forty years before. In this sense, although perhaps only in this sense, he had failed. Holmes, of course, did not see his solution as a failure. After all, the Philosophy of Faith seemed to work as well as it ever had; it allowed him to preserve the "essential faith." Only now that part of his faith which had before been provided by orthodox dogma was now determined indirectly by what science would permit him to believe. He still spoke of Providence, God, and Faith. In fact, some of his statements from his last writings taken out of context would sound as orthodox as any he ever made, but this was semblance. The orthodoxy was only verbal: a pouring of new wine into old bottles. His beliefs were no longer grounded in an authoritative tradition of church or scripture. The articles of his personal religious creed were no longer dogmas so much as they were hypotheses held provisionally until the advance of science should make them untenable for him. His final position, then, was one of acquiescence in that dismantling of traditional Christianity which he had so long opposed; a nascent Modernism remarkably close to the Germanic "tinkering" he had so long despised; a sincere and painful groping after a faith believable in his own time, a faith compatible with the paradigm produced by modern knowledge. His long struggle with the nineteenth century, which had engendered over the years such a large body of writing and which finished amid jottings and notes and a few manuscript essays, had ended in defeat. Of all the ironies in his life, this, perhaps, was the greatest of all: his warning that the intellectualism of his time would destroy orthodox Christianity was realized in his own religious transformation. But the final and, in view of his extensive writing, most cruel irony of his career is found in his obituary in the *American Historical Review*. There one learns that Professor Holmes "published little, but was of note as a teacher."[62] In that area of learning where he had labored for over fifty years he was almost completely unknown.

[61] [George Frederick Holmes], MS "In Re Elsmere," pp. 40–42, Holmes papers, D. The syncretistic scheme presented here was suggested in a briefer form in "The Elsmere Problem" but only as a possible solution. In "In Re Elsmere" it is set forth without qualification or apology.

[62] *American Historical Review*, III (January 1898), 392.

Death finally freed him from an existence he had come to hate. His health began to fail; a cataract formed on his remaining good eye; and in 1896 he fell in class and broke three ribs.[63] Though well enough to spend the summer at Tanglewood where he sat on the porch, rocked, and talked of the old days, he was too feeble in the autumn to resume teaching.[64] He fell ill and after several weeks lapsed into a coma. He died on November 4, 1897 without regaining consciousness and was buried beside Lavalette at Sweet Springs, West Virginia.

[63] Memoir of N. Floyd Holmes in possession of N. Floyd Holmes.
[64] N. Floyd Holmes to the author, December 12, 1964.

Select Bibliography

This bibliography is divided into four parts: manuscript collections utilized in writing the book, the publications of George Frederick Holmes, primary sources, and secondary sources. The sections devoted to primary and secondary sources list only those works cited or of special interest. No attempt has been made to provide a bibliography of works related to Holmes's milieu such as the history of the South or the intellectual history of the nineteenth century as these are readily available elsewhere.

A. Manuscript Collections.

Albert Taylor Bledsoe Papers, Library of Congress, Washington, D. C.

James Barbour Papers, University of Virginia Library, Charlottesville, Virginia.

Board of Trustees Minutes, Mississippi Collection, University of Mississippi, University, Mississippi.

Board of Visitors Minutes, University of Virginia Library, Charlottesville, Virginia.

Faculty Minutes, University of Virginia Library, Charlottesville, Virginia.

George Frederick Holmes Papers, Duke University Library, Durham, North Carolina.

George Frederick Holmes Papers, Library of Congress, Washington, D. C.

George Frederick Holmes Papers, Swem Library, College of William and Mary, Williamsburg, Virginia.

George Frederick Holmes Papers, University of Virginia Library, Charlottesville, Virginia.

Johnston-McMullin Family Papers, Duke University Library, Durham, North Carolina.

John McClintock Papers, Emory University Library, Atlanta, Georgia.

Richard Launcelot Maury Papers, Duke University Library, Durham, North Carolina.

William Gilmore Simms Papers, Library of Congress, Washington, D. C.

James Henley Thornwell Papers, South Caroliniana Library, University of South Carolina, Columbia, South Carolina.

Tucker Family Papers, Southern Historical Collection, University of North Carolina, Chapel Hill, North Carolina.

John Tyler Papers, Library of Congress, Washington, D. C.

Isabel Holmes Perkinson Williamson Papers, Duke University, Durham, North Carolina.

William and Mary College Papers, Swem Library, College of William and Mary, Williamsburg, Virginia.

B. PUBLICATIONS OF GEORGE FREDERICK HOLMES.

Articles of doubtful authorship, though mentioned in the notes, are omitted.

[Holmes, George Frederick]. "Amram; the Seeker of Oblivion," *Southern Literary Messenger*, V (November 1839), 734–41.

————. "Outlines of an Essay on the Causes Which Have Contributed to Produce the Peculiar Excellence of Ancient Literature," *Family Companion*, I (October and November 1841), 56–58; 112–20.

[————]. "Abou Hassan, the Recluse of the Mountain: an Allegory," *Southern Literary Messenger*, VII (November 1841), 754–58.

[————]. "Bulwer's Zanoni," *Southern Quarterly Review*, II (July 1842), 178–87.

[————]. "Whewell on the Inductive Sciences," *Southern Quarterly Review*, II (July 1842), 193–231.

[————]. "History of Literature," *Southern Quarterly Review*, II (October 1842), 472–517.

[————]. "Anthon's Classical Dictionary," *Southern Quarterly Review*, III (January 1843), 109–42.

[————]. "Percival Keene," *Southern Quarterly Review*, III (January 1843), 236–44.

[————]. "Leverett's Latin Lexicon." *Southern Quarterly Review*, III (January 1843), 248–52.

[————]. "On Slavery and Christianity," *Southern Quarterly Review*, III (January 1843), 252–56.

[————]. "A Day on Cooper River," *Southern Quarterly Review*, III (January 1843), 256–58.

[————]. "The Wonders of the World," *Southern Quarterly Review*, III (January 1843), 259–60.

[————]. "Schlegel's Philosophy of History," *Southern Quarterly Review*, III (April 1843), 263–317.

[————]. "Inda, and Other Poems," *Southern Quarterly Review*, III (April 1843), 367–88.

————. "A Day in the Woods of Lower Canada," *Magnolia*, II (February 1843), 120–25.

[———]. "Lays of Ancient Rome," *Southern Quarterly Review*, IV (July 1843), 76–81.

[———]. "Bulwer's Last of the Barons," *Southern Quarterly Review*, IV (July 1843), 215–35.

[———]. "Noctes Ambrosianae," *Southern Quarterly Review*, IV (July 1843), 238–41.

[———]. "History of the Reformation," *Southern Quarterly Review*, IV (October 1843), 514–15.

[———]. "The North American Indians," *Southern Quarterly Review*, V (January 1844), 118–56.

[———]. "Herder's Philosophy of History," *Southern Quarterly Review*, V (April 1844), 265–311.

[———]. "Brande's Encyclopedia," *Southern Quarterly Review*, VI (July 1844), 264–65.

[———]. "Anthon's Greek Prosody," *Southern Quarterly Review*, VI (July 1844), 247–50.

[———]. "Rome and the Romans," *Southern Quarterly Review*, VI (October 1844), 269–306.

[———]. "The Heretic of Lajetchnikoff," *Southern Quarterly Review*, VI (October 1844), 343–52.

[———]. "Spalding's Review of D'Aubigné," *Southern Quarterly Review*, VI (October 1844), 446–53.

[———]. "The History of Rome," *Southern Quarterly Review*, VI (October 1844), 521–23.

[———]. "A New Spirit of the Age," *Southern Quarterly Review*, VI (October 1844), 524–25.

———. "The Present State of Letters," *Southern Literary Messenger*, X (July, September, November 1844), 410–14, 538–42, 673–78, XI (March 1845), 172–77.

After the initial essay, the title of the series changes to "The Present Condition of Letters."

[———]. "Life and Writings of Rabelais," *Southern Quarterly Review*, VII (January 1845), 124–52.

[———]. "Mrs. Gray's History of Etruria," *Southern Quarterly Review*, VII (January 1845), 211–19.

[———]. "Ante-Roman Races of Italy," *Southern Quarterly Review*, VII (April 1845), 261–99.

———. *Address Delivered Before the Beaufort District Society*. Columbia, S. C.: A. S. Johnson, 1845.

[———]. "Coningsby, or The New Generation," *Southern Quarterly Review*, VIII (October 1845), 513–16.

[————]. "The Wandering Jew," *Southern Quarterly Review*, IX (January 1846), 73–114.

[————]. "Writings of Hugh Swinton Legare," *Southern Quarterly Review*, IX (April 1846), 321–61.

[————]. "History of the Christian Church," *Southern Quarterly Review*, IX (April 1846), 541–43.

[————]. "Life and Writings of Hugh Swinton Legare," *Southern Literary Messenger*, XII (April 1846), 252–54.

[————]. "Roman History," *Southern Literary Messenger*, XII (August 1846), 507–12.

[————]. "Munford's Homer," *Southern Quarterly Review*, X (July 1846), 1–45.

[————]. "Thimm's Book," *Southern Quarterly Review*, XI (January 1847), 90–105.

[————]. "Athens and the Athenians," *Southern Quarterly Review*, XI (April 1847), 273–321.

[————]. "Mr. Wintrysides—A Character," *Southern Literary Messenger*, XIV (June 1848), 383–84.

[————]. "On the Importance of the Social Sciences in the Present Day," *Southern Literary Messenger*, XV (February 1849), 77–80.

————. *Inaugural Address Delivered on Occasion of the Opening of the University of the State of Mississippi, November 6, 1848*. Memphis, Tenn.: Franklin, 1849.

[————]. "Life and Times of Pericles," *Southern Literary Messenger*, XVI (February 1850), 65–82.

[————]. "Observations on a Passage in the Politics of Aristotle Relative to Slavery," *Southern Literary Messenger*, XVI (April 1850), 193–205.

[————]. "John C. Calhoun," *Southern Literary Messenger*, XVI (May 1850), 301–03.

[————]. "Origin and History of the High Court of Chancery," *Southern Literary Messenger*, XVI (May 1850), 303–15.

[————]. "Morell's Philosophy of the Nineteenth Century," *Southern Literary Messenger*, XVI (July 1850), 385–96.

[————]. "General Zachary Taylor," *Southern Literary Messenger*, XVI (September 1850), 530–33.

[————]. "California Gold and European Revolution," *Southern Quarterly Review*, I, n.s. (July 1850), 273–313.

[————]. "Latter-Day Pamphlets," *Southern Quarterly Review*, II, n.s. (November 1850), 313–56.

[————]. "Antonina," *Southern Literary Messenger*, XVII (February 1851), 104–10.

[————]. "Cimon and Pericles," *Southern Quarterly Review*, III, n.s. (April 1851), 339–75.

―――. "Philosophy and Faith," *Methodist Quarterly Review*, III (April 1851), 185–218.

[―――]. "The Athenian Orators," *Southern Quarterly Review*, IV, n.s. (1851), 352–89.

[―――]. "Greeley on Reforms," *Southern Literary Messenger*, XVII (May 1851), 257–80.

[―――]. "The Nineteenth Century," *Southern Literary Messenger*, XVII (August 1851), 457–67.

[―――]. "Faith and Science–Comte's Positive Philosophy," *Methodist Quarterly Review*, IV (January and April 1852), 9–37; 169–99.

[―――]. "Instauratio Nova–Auguste Comte," *Methodist Quarterly Review*, IV (July 1852), 329–60.

[―――]. "Uncle Tom's Cabin," *Southern Literary Messenger*, XVIII (December 1852), 721–31.

[―――]. "Vestiges of Civilization," *Methodist Quarterly Review*, V (April 1853), 213–49.

[―――]. "The Bacon of the Nineteenth Century," *Methodist Quarterly Review*, V (July and October 1853), 329–54; 489–513.

[―――]. "Sir William Hamilton's Discussions," *Southern Quarterly Review*, VIII, n.s. (October 1853), 289–337.

―――. "The Caesars," *Quarterly Review of the Methodist Episcopal Church, South*, VII (July 1853), 363–90.

[―――]. "A Key to Uncle Tom's Cabin," *Southern Literary Messenger*, XIX (June 1853), 321–30.

[―――]. "Spiritual Manifestations," *Southern Literary Messenger*, XIX (July 1853), 385–95.

[―――]. "Tennyson's Poems," *Southern Literary Messenger*, XIX (November 1853), 649–58.

―――. "The Ascetical Devotions of Pascal's Late Years," *Quarterly Review of the Methodist Episcopal Church, South*, VIII (January 1854), 29–32.

[―――]. "Butler's Analogy," *Quarterly Review of the Methodist Episcopal Church, South*, VIII (April 1854), 214–48.

[―――]. "Revival of the Black Arts," *Methodist Quarterly Review*, VI (April 1854), 191–213.

[―――]. "The Positive Religion; or, Religion of Humanity," *Methodist Quarterly Review*, VI (July 1854), 329–59.

[―――]. "The Sibylline Oracles," *Methodist Quarterly Review*, VI (October 1854), 489–526.

[―――]. "Universities and Colleges," *Southern Literary Messenger*, XX (August, October and November 1854), 449–60; 577–90; 641–52.

[―――]. "Louis Napoleon and Augustus Caesar," *Southern Quarterly Review*, X, n.s. (July 1854), 1–37.

[————]. "Auguste Comte and Positivism," *North British Review*, XXI (May 1854), 128–53.

[————]. "Mrs. Somerville's Physical Geography," *Quarterly Review of the Methodist Episcopal Church, South*, VIII (October 1854), 513–40.

[————]. "The Blunders of Hallam," *Southern Quarterly Review*, XI, n.s. (January 1855), 46–87.

————. "Greece and Its History," *Quarterly Review of the Methodist Episcopal Church, South*, IX (January 1855), 38–61

————. "Fitzhugh's Sociology for the South," *Quarterly Review of the Methodist Episcopal Church, South*, IX (April 1855), 180–201.

————. "Baskerville's Poetry of Germany," *Quarterly Review of the Methodist Episcopal Church, South*, IX (July 1855), 345–70.

————. "The Races of Europe," *Quarterly Review of the Methodist Episcopal Church, South*, IX (October 1855), 514–43.

[————]. "The History of the Working Classes," *Southern Literary Messenger*, XXI (April 1855), 193–203.

[————]. "Failure of Free Societies," *Southern Literary Messenger*, XXI (March 1855), 129–41.

[————]. "Niebuhr," *Methodist Quarterly Review*, VII (October 1855), 530–57.

————. "Ancient Slavery," *De Bow's Review*, XIX (November and December 1855), 559–78; 617–37.

[————]. "Remains of Latin Tragedy," *Methodist Quarterly Review*, VIII (January 1856), 76–106.

[————]. "Alchemy and the Alchemists," *Methodist Quarterly Review*, VIII (July 1856), 468–86.

[————]. "Blakey's History of Logic," *Methodist Quarterly Review*, VIII (October 1856), 505–37.

————. "Chastel on Charity," *Quarterly Review of the Methodist Episcopal Church, South*, X (January 1856), 28–50.

[————]. "Spencer's Social Statics," *A Quarterly Review of the Methodist Episcopal Church, South*, X (April 1856), 185–218.

[————]. "Gibbon's Decline and Fall," *Quarterly Review of the Methodist Episcopal Church, South*, X (July 1856), 321–47.

[————]. "The Papuans-Negritos," *Quarterly Review of the Methodist Episcopal Church, South*, X (October 1856), 481–507.

————. "Relations of the Old and the New Worlds," *De Bow's Review*, XX (May 1856), 521–40.

————. "Gold and Silver Mines," *De Bow's Review*, XXI (July 1856), 30–57.

————. "Effects of the Increase of Gold Throughout the World," *De Bow's Review*, XXI (August 1856), 103–21.

————. "Bledsoe on Liberty and Slavery," *De Bow's Review*, XXI (August 1856), 132–47.

————. "Population and Capital," *De Bow's Review*, XXI (September 1856), 217–32.

[————]. "Slavery and Freedom," *Southern Quarterly Review*, I, n.s. (April 1856), 62–95.

[————]. "Greek in the Middle Ages," *Southern Quarterly Review*, I, n.s. (August 1856), 219–48.

[————]. "Speculation and Trade," *Southern Quarterly Review*, II, n.s. (November 1856), 1–35.

[————]. "Grote's History of Greece," *Southern Quarterly Review*, II, n.s. (November 1856), 89–124.

[————]. "Motley's Dutch Republic," *Southern Quarterly Review*, II, n.s. (February 1857), 427–55.

[————]. "Remains of Sir William Hamilton," *Methodist Quarterly Review*, IX (January 1857), 9–34.

[————]. "Philosophy of Sir William Hamilton," *Methodist Quarterly Review*, IX (April 1857), 175–201.

————. "Theory of Political Individualism," *De Bow's Review*, XXII (February 1857), 133–49.

————. "Capital and Labor," *De Bow's Review*, XXII (March 1857), 249–65.

[————]. "Friar Bacon and Lord Bacon," *Methodist Quarterly Review*, X (January and April 1858), 5–27; 173–87.

————. "The Virginia Colony, or the Relation of the English Colonial Settlements in America to the General History of the Civilized World, *Virginia Historical Reporter*, II (1860), pt. 1.

————. "Language: Its Sources, Changes and Philosophy," *De Bow's Review*, I, n.s. (January 1866), 25–35.

————. "Modern Philosophical Systems," *De Bow's Review*, I, n.s. (March 1866), 225–38.

————. "Influences of Commerce and Finance in Determining the Revolutions of Fortune in the History of Nations," *De Bow's Review*, I, n.s. (April and May 1866), 337–52; 449–65.

———— (ed.). *The Southern Pictorial Primer, or First-Fifth Reader.* Southern University Series. New York: Richardson and Company, [1866].

———— (ed.). *The Southern Elementary Spelling-book For Schools and Families.* Southern University Series. New York: Richardson and Company, [1866].

———— (ed.). *Holmes' Pictorial Primer, for Home or School.* Southern University Series. New York: Richardson and Company, 1867.

————. "Milton's Domestic Life—His Ethics of Divorce," *De Bow's Review*, III, n.s. (January and February 1867), 12–24; 113–25.

————. "Aspects of the Hour," *De Bow's Review*, III, n.s. (April and May 1867), 337–52.

————. "Early History of the East India Trade—The Arabs Before Mahomet," *De Bow's Review*, IV, n.s. (October 1867), 273–86.

[————]. "Recent Histories of Julius Caesar," *Southern Review*, I (April 1867), 383–412.

————. *An Elementary Grammar of the English Language.* New York: Richardson and Company, 1868.

————. "Who Wrote Shakespeare?," *De Bow's Review*, V, n.s. (February 1868), 113–34.

————. "Recent Biographies of Lord Bacon," *De Bow's Review*, V, n.s. (April 1868), 396–411.

————. "Carey on Reconstruction," *De Bow's Review*, V, n.s. (May 1868), 582–95.

————. "Auguste Comte," II, 448–51; "Rene Descartes," II, 752–56; "Juan Donoso-Cortes," II, 864–65; "Eleatic School," III, 119–22; "Elizabeth," III, 161–63; "Empiricism," III, 182–84; "Epicurean Philosophy," III, 257–59; "Faith and Reason," III, 464–67; "Marsilius Ficinus," III, 545–46; "Fief—Feudalism," III, 547–51; "Pierre Gassendi," III, 746–48; "Robert Grosseteste," III, 1013–17; "Sir William Hamilton," IV, 48–51; "David Hartley, IV, 91–92; "David Hume," IV, 400–03; "Immanuel Kant," V, 11–17; "Knighthood," V, 127–32; "Gottfried Wilhelm, Baron von Leibnitz," V, 332–37; "John Locke," V, 477–480; "Nicholas Malebranche," V, 680–83; "John Milton," IV, 281–86; "Nostradamus," VII, 196–99; "William of Occam," VII, 285–89; "Philosophy," VIII, 124–27; "Plato," VIII, 272–82; "Platonic Philosophy," VIII, 282–89; "Georgius Pletho," VIII, 291–92; "Plotinus," VIII, 294–99; "Melchior de Polignac," VIII, 350–54; "Positivism," 437–40; "Pythagoras," VIII, 826–30; "Realism," VIII, 940–43; "Holy Roman Empire," IX, 92–96; "Scholasticism," IX, 422–26; "John Scotus (Erigena)," IX, 459–62; "Lucius Annaeus Seneca," IX, 525–28; "Socrates," IX, 847–54; "Benedict de Spinoza," IX, 934–40; "Stoic Philosophy," IX, 1032–36; "Stoics," IX, 1037–41; "Georgius Syncellus," X, 84–85; "Synesius," X, 88–91; Byzantine Historians," XI, 714–16; "Cause," XI, 851–54; "Anna Comnena," XII, 52–54; "Recent Phases of Scepticism," XII, 819–25. *Cyclopaedia of Biblical, Theological, and Ecclesiastical Literature.* John McClintock and James Strong, eds. 12 vols. New York: Harper and Brothers, 1868–1891.

———— (ed.). *Holmes' First* [-Sixth] *Reader.* 6 vols. University Series. New York: University Publishing Company, [1870]–1872.

————. *A Grammar of the English Language.* New York: University Publishing Company, [1871].

————. *A School History of the United States of America, from the*

Earliest Discoveries to the Year 1870. New York: University Publishing Company, 1871.

[————]. "Americanisms: A Study of Words and Manners," *Southern Review*, IX (April and July 1871), 290–319; 529–60.

[————]. "Hume's Philosophy," *Southern Review*, XI (July and October 1872), 92–120; 309–36.

[————]. "Pleas for Astrology," *Southern Magazine*, VI (October 1873), 420–27.

————. "Popular Prophecies," *Southern Magazine*, VI (November 1873), 543–52.

[————]. "Armageddon," *Southern Review*, XII (January 1873), 128–59.

[————]. "The Sibyls and Their Oracles," *Southern Magazine*, VII (February 1874), 159–66.

————. "Joachim, Abbot of Flora," *Southern Magazine*, VII (October 1874), 393–404.

————. "Merlin," *Southern Magazine*, VII (June 1874), 627–37.

————. "Joachim and Joachimites," *Southern Magazine*, VIII (November 1874), 517–29.

————. "The Civil Law," *Forum*, I (January and April 1874), 34–65; 320–55, II (July and October 1874), 71–101; 217–48.

————. "Primitive Law," *Forum*, III (April and July 1875), 230–71; 401–25.

————. "Nostradamus," *Southern Magazine*, IX (January 1875), 24–38.

————. "Dr. John Dee and Sir Edward Kelly," *Southern Magazine*, IX (April 1875), 373–88.

————. "The Eastern Question and the Berlin Treaty," *Southern Review*, XXV (January 1879), 47–87.

————. *The Science of Society*. [Charlottesville, Va.]: Miller School Print, 1883.

————. *New School History of the United States*. New York: University Publishing Company, 1883 and 1886.

————. "Professor John Millington, M. D." *William and Mary Quarterly*, III, 2nd s. (January 1923), 23–35.

C. PRIMARY SOURCES.

Adams, Herbert B. *The Study of History in American Colleges and Universities*. Washington, D. C.: Government Printing Office, 1887.

American Historical Review, III (January 1898), 392.

Andrews, Stephen Pearl. *Science of Society*. New York: W. J. Baner, 1851.

Annals of the American Academy of Political and Social Science. I, (1890).

Anthon, Charles. *A Classical Dictionary*. New York: Harper and Brothers, 1841.

Argyll, George Douglas Campbell, Duke of. *Organic Evolution Cross-examined or, Some Suggestions on the Great Secret of Biology*. London: John Murray, 1898.

Buchanan, Mary Hull, ed. *Holmes Family History*. Published privately, 1960.

Catalogue of the University of Virginia. Richmond, Va. and Baltimore: [University of Virginia], 1856–1893.

Comte, Auguste. *Cours de philosophie positive*. 6 vols. Paris: Borrani et Droz, 1835–1852.

————. *Système de politique positive*. 4 vols. Paris: Cariliau-Goeury and V. Dalmont, 1851–1854.

————. *A General View of Positivism*. Trans. by J. H. Bridges. London: Truebner and Company, 1865.

————. *The Positive Philosophy of Auguste Comte*. Freely trans. and abridged by Harriet Martineau. London: J. Chapman, 1853.

Cousin, Victor. *Cours de l'histoire de la philosophie: introduction à l'histoire de la philosophie*. Nouvelle ed. Paris: Didier, 1841.

Culbreth, David M. R. *The University of Virginia, Memories of Her Student-Life and Professors*. New York: Neale Publishing Company, 1908.

Darwin, Charles R. *The Descent of Man and Selection in Relation to Sex*. London: J. Murray, 1871.

————. *The Expression of the Emotions in Man and Animals*. London: J. Murray, 1872.

Dawkins, Sir William Boyd. *Cave Hunting, Researches on the Evidence of Caves Respecting the Early Inhabitants of Europe*. London: Macmillan, 1874.

————. *Early Man in Britain and His Place in the Tertiary Period*. London: Macmillan and Company, 1880.

Dawson, Sir John William. *The Story of the Earth and Man*. New York: Harper and Brothers, 1873.

————. *Fossil Men and Their Modern Representatives*. London: Hodder and Staughton, 1880.

"Death of Professor Holmes," *Alumni Bulletin of the University of Virginia*, IV (November 1897), 86–87.

Emerson, Ralph Waldo. *The Complete Works of Ralph Waldo Emerson*. Centenary Edition. 12 vols. Boston: Houghton Mifflin Company, n.d.

Fawcett, George. "Student Life at the University in the Seventies," *University of Virginia Alumni News*, XXVII (March 1939), 109–11.

Fisher, Richard S. *Statistical Gazetteer of the United States*. New York: J. H. Colton and Company, 1857.

Fitzhugh, George. *Sociology for the South, or, the Failure of Free Society*. Richmond: A. Morris, 1854.

———. *Cannibals All! or, Slaves Without Masters*. Richmond: A. Morris, 1857.

Frazer, Sir James George. "Totemism," *Encyclopaedia Britannica*. 9th ed. vol. XXIII.

Gladstone, William E. " 'Robert Elsmere' and the Battle of Belief," *Nineteenth Century*, XXIII (May 1888), 766–88.

Green, Edward H. "Sixty Years Ago," *University of Virginia Alumni News*, XXI (March 1933), 125–27.

Grote, George. *A History of Greece*. 12 vols. London: J. Murray, 1846–1856.

Guizot, François Pierre G. *History of Civilization in Europe*. New York: American Publishers Corporation, n.d.

Haskel, Daniel and J. Calvin Smith. *Descriptive and Statistical Gazetteer of the United States*. New York: Sherman and Smith, 1844.

Hegel, Georg Wilhelm Fredrich. *The Philosophy of History*. Trans. by J. Sibree. New York: Dover Publications, Inc., [1956].

Herder, Johan Gottlieb von. *Outlines of a Philosophy of the History of Man*. Trans. by T. O. Churchill. 2 vols. 2nd ed. London: J. Johnson, 1803.

Jamison, David F. "Progress of Civilization," *Southern Quarterly Review*, III (January 1843), 1–17; IV (October 1843), 157–78.

[———]. "The French Revolution," *Southern Quarterly Review*, V (April 1844), 1–102.

[———]. "Lamartines Histoire des Girondins," *Southern Quarterly Review*, XVI (October 1849–50), 53–76.

———. *The Life and Times of Bertrand de Guesclin, a History of the Fourteenth Century*. 2 vols. Charleston, S. C.: J. Russell, 1864.

Lubbock, Sir John, Baron Avebury. *Pre-Historic Times as Illustrated by Ancient Remains and the Manners and Customs of Modern Savages*. London: Williams and Norgate, 1865.

———. *The Origin of Civilisation and the Primitive Condition of Man*. London: Longmans, Green and Company, 1870.

McClintock, John. "Horace Binney Wallace," *Methodist Quarterly Review*, VI (January 1854), 132–42.

[McCord, Louisa]. "Slavery and Political Economy," *De Bow's Review*, XXI (October and November 1856), 331–49, 443–67.

Michelet, Jules. *Introduction à l'histoire universelle*. 2nd ed. Paris: Librairie classique, 1834.

―――. *History of the Roman Republic.* Trans. by William Hazlitt. New York: D. Appleton and Company, 1847.

Mill, John Stuart. *The Positive Philosophy of Auguste Comte.* New York: Henry Holt and Company, 1887.

Minor, Benjamin Blake. "Some Further Notes Relating to Dr. G. F. Holmes; Munford's Homer, etc." *Alumni Bulletin of the University of Virginia,* V (November 1898), 74–79.

Morell, J. D. *An Historical and Critical View of the Speculative Philosophy of Europe in the Nineteenth Century.* New York: Robert Carter and Brothers, 1849.

Murphy, Joseph John. *Habit and Intelligence In Their Connexion With the Laws of Matter and Force.* 2 vols. London: Macmillan and Company, 1869.

National Intelligencer, February 27, 1843.

Nature, August 28, 1879; September 3, 1891.

New York Herald, November 22, 1839.

New York Times, November 5, 1897.

[O'Connell, James]. *Vestiges of Civilization: or, The Aetiology of History, Religious, Aesthetical, Political, and Philosophical.* New York: H. Bailliere, 1851.

Palmer, B. M. *The Life and Letters of James Henley Thornwell, D. D., LL. D.* Richmond: Whittet and Shepperson, 1875.

Pope, James E. "Reminiscences of Dr. George Frederick Holmes," *University of Mississippi Magazine,* XX (December 1895), 2–6.

Pro-Slavery Argument. Charleston: Walker and Richards and Company, 1852.

Quatrefages, Armand de. *The Human Species.* New York: D. Appleton and Company, 1881.

Renan, Ernest. *Histoire des origins du christianisme.* 7 vols. Paris: Michel Lévy Frères, 1863–1899.

Richmond Enquirer, 1847–1860.

Richmond Examiner, 1854.

Schlegel, Friedrich von. *The Philosophy of History.* Trans. by J. B. Robertson. London: Saunders and Otley, 1835.

―――. *Lectures on the History of Literature, Ancient and Modern.* Trans. by J. G. Lockhart. New York: Langley, 1841.

Simms, William Gilmore. *The Geography of South Carolina.* Charleston: Babcock and Company, 1843.

―――. *The Letters of William Gilmore Simms.* Ed. by Mary C. S. Oliphant *et al.* 5 vols. Columbia: University of South Carolina Press, 1952.

"Southern Quarterly Review," *United States Catholic Magazine and Monthly Review,* IV (February 1845), 103–08.

"Southern Quarterly Review," *United States Catholic Miscellany,* October 19, 26, November 16, 1844, pp. 118–19, 126–27, 150.

Spencer, Herbert. *Social Statics.* New York: D. Appleton and Company, 1883.

Statistics of the United States of America as Collected and Returned by the Marshals of the Several Judicial Districts Under the Thirteenth Section of the Act for Taking the Sixth Census; Corrected at the Department of State. June 1, 1840. Washington, D. C.: Blair and Rives, 1841.

Strauss, David F. *The Life of Jesus.* Trans. by Marian Evans. London: 1846.

Taylor, W. Cooke. *The Natural History of Society.* 2 vols. London: Longman, 1840.

Thompson, Jacob. *Address Delivered on Occasion of the Opening of the University of the State of Mississippi, in Behalf of the Board of Trustees, November 6, 1848.* Memphis, Tenn.: Franklin, 1849.

Thornton, William M. "The Letter Book of George Frederick Holmes," *Alumni Bulletin of the University of Virginia,* V (August 1898), 31–42.

The Times (London), September 11, 1867; June 25, 1891.

Tulloch, John. *Modern Theories in Philosophy and Religion.* London: Blackwood and Sons, 1884.

Tylor, Sir Edward Burnett. *Anthropology, An Introduction to the Study of Man and Civilization.* New York: D. Appleton and Company, 1889.

United States Census Office. *Seventh Census of the United States, 1850.* Washington, D. C., n.p., 1853.

———. *Eighth Census of the United States: Population.* Washington: Government Printing Office, 1864.

University of Virginia Decennial Catalogue of Visitors, Faculty, Officers and Students, 1874–1884. Richmond: [University of Virginia], 1889.

Vico, Giambattista. *Oeuvres choisies de Vico.* Trans. by Jules Michelet. Paris: Flammarion, n.d.

———. *The New Science of Giambattista Vico.* Trans. by Thomas Goddard Bergin and Max Harold Fisch. Abridged ed. Garden City, N. Y.: Doubleday and Company, [1961].

Vignoli, Tito. *Myth and Science: An Essay.* New York: D. Appleton and Company, 1882.

Waddel, John N. *Memorials of Academic Life: being an Historical Sketch of the Waddel Family, Identified Through Three Generations with the History of Higher Education in the South and Southwest.* Richmond: Presbyterian Committee of Publication, 1891.

Wallace, Horace Binney. *Art, Scenery and Philosophy in Europe.* Philadelphia: Herman Hooker, 1855.

Wallon, Henri. *Histoire de l'esclavage dans l'antiquité.* 3 vols. Paris: Dezobry, 1847.

Ward, Mrs. Humphry. *Robert Elsmere.* London: Macmillan and Company, 1888.

Waterton, Charles. *Wanderings in Sounth America, the North-West of the United States, and the Antilles, In the Years 1812, 1816, 1820, and 1824.* New ed. London: Macmillan and Company, 1879.

Whately, Richard. *Introductory Lectures on Political Economy.* 2nd ed. London: B. Fellowes, 1832.

Whewell, William. *History of the Inductive Sciences.* London: J. W. Parker, 1837.

D. SECONDARY SOURCES.

Acton, H. B. "Comte's Positivism and the Science of Society," *Philosophy,* XXVI (October 1951), 291–310.

Adams, Herbert B. *Thomas Jefferson and the University of Virginia.* Washington, D. C.: Government Printing Office, 1888.

Ambler, Charles H. "Life of John Floyd," *John P. Branch Historical Papers of Randolph-Macon College,* V (June 1918), 5–117.

Andrews, J. C. "The Confederate Press and Public Morale," *Journal of Southern History,* XXXII (November 1966), 445–65.

Bartlett, Irving H. "Bushnell, Cousin and Comprehensive Christianity," *Journal of Religion,* XXXVII (April 1957), 99–104.

Bernard, L. L. and Jessie Bernard. *Origins of American Sociology: the Social Science Movement in the United States.* New York: Thomas Y. Crowell Company, [1943].

Bertelson, David. *The Lazy South.* New York: Oxford University Press, 1967.

Betts, Leonidas. "George Frederick Holmes: Nineteenth-Century Virginia Educator," *Virginia Magazine of History and Biography,* LXXVI (October 1968), 472–84.

Brown, Jerry Wayne. *The Rise of Biblical Criticism in America, 1800–1870: The New England Scholars.* Middletown: Wesleyan University Press, [1969].

Bruce, Philip Alexander. *History of the University of Virginia, 1819–1919.* 5 vols. New York: Macmillan and Company, 1921.

Buckland, W. W. *The Roman Law of Slavery: The Condition of the Slave in Private Law from Augustus to Justinian.* Cambridge: Cambridge University Press, 1908.

Burrow, J. S. *Evolution and Society: A Study in Victorian Social Theory.* Cambridge: Cambridge University Press, 1968.

Bury, J. B. *The Idea of Progress: An Inquiry Into Its Origin and Growth.* New York: Dover Publications, Inc. [1932].

Cabaniss, James Allen. *A History of the University of Mississippi.* University, Mississippi: The University of Mississippi, 1949.

Callcott, George H. *History in the United States: Its Practice and Purpose.* Baltimore: Johns Hopkins Press, [1970].

Clemons, Harry. *The University of Virginia Library, 1825–1950.* Charlottesville: University of Virginia Press, 1954.

Cornuz, Jeanlouis. *Jules Michelet, Un Aspect de la Penseé Religîeuse au XIXe Siècle.* Genève: Librairie E. Droz, 1955.

Crooks, George Richard. *Life and Letters of the Rev. John McClintock.* New York: Nelson and Phillips, 1876.

Crowson, E. T. "George Frederick Holmes," *Virginia Cavalcade*, XVII (Spring 1968), 19–29.

———. "George Frederick Holmes and Auguste Comte," *Mississippi Quarterly*, XXII (Winter 1968–69), 59–70.

Daniels, George H. *American Science in the Age of Jackson.* New York: Columbia University Press, 1968.

Davis, David Brion. "The Emergence of Immediatism in British and American Antislavery Thought," *Mississippi Valley Historical Review*, XLIX (September 1962), 209–30.

———. *The Problem of Slavery in Western Culture.* Ithaca: Cornell University Press, 1966.

Degler, Carl. "Slavery in Brazil and the United States: An Essay in Comparative History," *American Historical Review*, LXXV (April 1970), 1004–28.

Dorfman, Joseph Henry. *The Economic Mind in American Civilization, 1606–1933.* 5 vols. New York: Viking Press, 1946–1959.

Easton, Loyd. *Hegel's First American Followers.* [Athens, Ohio]: Ohio University Press, 1966.

Eaton, Clement. *The Growth of Southern Civilization, 1790–1860.* New York: Harper and Brothers, [1961].

Ekirch, Arthur A., Jr. *The Idea of Progress in America, 1815–1860.* New York: Columbia University Press, 1944.

Forbes, Duncan. *The Liberal Anglican Idea of History.* Cambridge: Cambridge University Press, 1952.

Fowler, Joseph Thomas. *Durham University, Earlier Foundations and Present Colleges.* London: F. E. Robinson and Company, 1904.

Freehling, William W. *Prelude to Civil War: The Nullification Controversy in South Carolina, 1816–1836.* New York: Harper & Row, [1966].

Freidel, Frank. *Francis Lieber: Nineteenth-Century Liberal*. Baton Rouge: Louisiana State University Press, [1947].

Gates, Paul W. *The Farmer's Age; Agriculture, 1815–1860*. New York: Holt, Rinehart and Winston, [1960].

Genovese, Eugene D. *The Political Economy of Slavery: Studies in the Economy & Society of the Slave South*. New York: Pantheon Books, [1965].

———. *The World the Slaveholders Made: Two Essays in Interpretation*. New York: Pantheon Books, [1969].

Ghiselin, Michael T. *The Triumph of the Darwinian Method*. Berkeley: University of California Press, 1969.

Gillespie, Neal C. "The Spiritual Odyssey of George Frederick Holmes: A Study of Religious Conservatism in the Old South," *Journal of Southern History*, XXXII (August 1966), 291–307.

———. "George Frederick Holmes and the Philosophy of History," *South Atlantic Quarterly*, LXVII (Summer 1968), 486–98.

———. "Ole Miss: A New Look at Her First President," *Journal of Mississippi History*, XXX (November 1968), 275–90.

——— and Gerald H. Davis. "Auguste Comte: Four Lost Letters to America," *Journal of the History of Philosophy*, VIII (January 1970), 49–63.

Gooch, George Peabody. *History and Historians in the Nineteenth Century*. Boston: Beacon Press, [1959].

Gossett, Thomas F. *Race: the History of an Idea in America*. Dallas, Texas: Southern Methodist University Press, 1963.

Haac, Oscar A. *Les Principes inspirateurs de Michelet: sensibilité et philosophie de l'histoire*. New Haven: Yale University Press, 1951.

Hartz, Louis. *The Liberal Tradition in America*. New York: Harcourt, Brace and World, [1955].

Hawkins, Richmond Laurin. *Auguste Comte and the United States, 1816–1853*. Cambridge: Harvard University Press, 1936.

———. *Positivism in the United States, 1853–1861*. Cambridge: Harvard University Press, 1938.

Herbst, Jurgen. *The German Historical School in American Scholarship*. Ithaca: Cornell University Press, [1965].

History of the College of William and Mary From Its Foundation, 1660 to 1874. Richmond: J. W. Randolph and English, 1874.

Hodgen, Margaret T. *The Doctrine of Survivals*. London: Allenson, 1936.

———. *Early Anthropology in the Sixteenth and Seventeenth Centuries*. Philadelphia: University of Pennsylvania Press, [1964].

Hollis, Daniel Walker. *University of South Carolina*. 2 vols. Columbia: University of South Carolina Press, 1951.

"Holmes, George Frederick," *Appleton's Cyclopaedia of American Biography*. 6 vols. New York: D. Appleton and Company, 1887–1889.

"Holmes, George Frederick," *Encyclopaedia Brittanica*. 30 vols., 9th ed. New York: Henry G. Allen Company, 1889.

"Holmes, George Frederick," *National Cyclopaedia of American Biography*. 57 vols., New York: James T. White and Company, 1893–

House, Floyd Nelson. *The Development of Sociology*. New York: McGraw-Hill, 1936.

Hubbell, Jay B. *The South in American Literature, 1607–1900*. Durham: Duke University Press, 1954.

Jenkins, William Sumner. *Pro-slavery Thought in the Old South*. Chapel Hill: University of North Carolina Press, 1935.

Jordan, Winthrop D. *White Over Black*: *American Attitudes Toward the Negro, 1550–1812*. Chapel Hill: University of North Carolina Press, [1968].

Lange, Victor. "Frederich Schlegel's Literary Criticism," *Comparative Literature*, VII (Fall 1955), 289–305.

Levi, Albert William. "The Idea of Socrates: The Philosophic Hero in the Nineteenth Century," *Journal of the History of Ideas*, XVII (January 1956), 89–108.

Levin, David. *History as Romantic Art*. Palo Alto: Stanford University Press, 1959.

Levy-Bruhl, Lucien. *The Philosophy of Auguste Comte*. Trans. by Kathleen de Beaumont-Klein. New York: G. P. Putnam's Sons, 1903.

Longton, William Henry. "Some Aspects of Intellectual Activity in Ante-Bellum South Carolina, 1830–1860: An Introductory Study." Unpublished Ph. D. dissertation, University of North Carolina, Chapel Hill, North Carolina, 1969.

McKitrick, Eric L., ed. *Slavery Defended*: *the Views of the Old South*. Englewood Cliffs, N. J.: Prentice-Hall, [1963].

Manierre, William R. "A Southern Response to Mrs. Stowe: Two Letters of John R. Thompson," *Virginia Magazine of History and Biography*, LXIX (January 1961), 83–92.

Manuel, Frank Edward. *The Prophets of Paris*. Cambridge: Harvard University Press, 1962.

Merk, Frederick. *Manifest Destiny and Mission in American History*. New York: A. Knopf, 1963.

Meyers, Marvin. *The Jacksonian Persuasion*: *Politics and Belief*. Palo Alto: Stanford University Press, 1957.

Mitchell, Samuel Chiles. "George Frederick Holmes," *Dictionary of American Biography*. 24 vols. New York: Charles Scribners Sons, 1928–

Mott, Frank Luther. *A History of American Magazines*. 3 vols. New York: D. Appleton and Company, 1930–1938.

Muirhead, J. H. "How Hegel Came to America," *Philosophical Review*, XXXVII (May 1928), 226–240.

Passmore, John. *A Hundred Years of Philosophy*. London: George Duckworth and Company, [1957].

Patton, John S. *Jefferson, Cabell and the University of Virginia*. New York: Neale Publishing Company, 1906.

Pendleton, William C. *History of Tazewell County and Southwest Virginia, 1748–1920*. Richmond: n.p., 1920.

Pfleiderer, Otto. *The Development of Theology in Germany Since Kant and Its Progress in Great Britain Since 1825*. Trans. by J. Frederick Smith. London: Swan Sonnenschein and Company, 1890.

Pochmann, Henry A. *German Culture in America: Philosophical and Literary Influences, 1600–1900*. Madison: University of Wisconsin Press, 1961.

Potter, David M. "Depletion and Renewal in Southern History," Edgar T. Thompson, ed., *Perspectives on the South: Agenda for Research*. Durham: Duke University Press, 1967.

Riley, Isaac Woodbridge. *American Thought from Puritanism to Pragmatism and Beyond*. New York: Henry Holt and Company, 1923.

Robinson, John. "Sunderland Worthies, No. 3: George Frederick Holmes, D. C. L.," *Library Circular: A Quarterly Guide and Catalogue for Readers at Sunderland Public Library*, No. 5 (1900), 70–75.

Rogers, Arthur Kenyon. *English and American Philosophy Since 1800*. New York: Macmillan and Company, 1928.

Rossiter, Clinton. *Conservatism in America*. 2nd ed. New York: Vintage Books, [1962].

Ryan, Frank Winkler, Jr. "The Southern Quarterly Review, 1842–1857, A Study in Thought and Opinion in the Old South." Unpublished Ph. D. dissertation, University of North Carolina, Chapel Hill, North Carolina, 1956.

Seliger, M. "Race Thinking During the Restoration," *Journal of the History of Ideas*, IXX (April 1958), 273–82.

Seth, James. *English Philosophers and Schools of Philosophy*. London: J. M. Dent and Son, 1929.

Shepherd, Henry E. "George Frederick Holmes," *Library of Southern Literature*, 16 vols. Atlanta, Ga.: Martin and Hoyt Company, 1907–1913.

Simon, W. M. *European Positivism in the Nineteenth Century: An Essay in Intellectual History*. Ithaca: Cornell University Press, [1963].

Smith, Wilson. *Professors and Public Ethics: Studies of Northern Moral Philosophers before the Civil War*. Ithaca: Cornell University Press, [1956].

Somkin, Fred. *Unquiet Eagle: Memory and Desire in the Idea of American Freedom, 1815–1860.* Ithaca: Cornell University Press, [1967].

Stern, Madeline B. *The Pantarch: A Biography of Stephen Pearl Andrews.* Austin: University of Texas Press, [1968].

Taylor, William R. *Cavalier and Yankee: The Old South and American National Character.* New York: George Braziller, 1961.

Thompson, James Westfall. *A History of Historical Writing.* 2 vols. New York: Macmillan and Company, 1942.

Van Tassel, David D. *Recording America's Past: An Interpretation of the Development of Historical Studies in America, 1607–1884.* Chicago: University of Chicago Press, [1960].

Von Hofe, Harold. "Frederick Schlegel and the New World," *PMLA,* LXXVI (March 1961), 63–67.

Wade, John Donald. *Augustus Baldwin Longstreet.* New York: Macmillan and Company, 1924.

White, Andrew Dickson. *A History of the Warfare of Science with Theology in Christendom.* 2 vols. New York: D. Appleton and Company, 1898.

Wish, Harvey. "George Frederick Holmes and the Genesis of American Sociology," *American Journal of Sociology,* XLVI (March 1941), 698–707.

———. "Stephen Pearl Andrews, American Pioneer Sociologist," *Social Forces,* XIX (May 1941), 477–82.

———. "George Frederick Holmes and Southern Periodical Literature," *Journal of Southern History,* VII (August 1941), 343–56.

———. *George Fitzhugh, Propagandist of the Old South.* Baton Rouge: Louisiana State University Press, 1943.

Index

Abelard, Peter, 134, 136, 138
Abolitionism, 178–79, 182
Adams, Herbert B., 222
Agnosticism, 245
Allen, Joseph Henry, 124
American Academy of Political and Social Science, 220
American Historical Review, 247
American Social Science Association, 220
Andrews, Steven Pearl, 174, 175
Anthon, Charles, 69–70
Aquinas, Thomas, 80, 104, 129
Argyll, George Douglas Campbell, Duke of, 239n
Aristotle, 80, 102, 112–13, 134–36, 138, 147, 173, 188–89, 227

Bacon, Sir Francis, 109, 112, 115, 134, 136, 138, 160, 169; influence on Holmes, 13, 49, 67, 69, 113
Baconianism, 50, 57, 233–34
Bancroft, George, 55, 214
Beard, Charles A., 161
Bennett, James Gordon, 17
Bertelson, David, 162
Biblical criticism, 43–44, 116–17, 119–20, 242
Bledsoe, Albert Taylor, 33, 34, 37, 89–90
Boole, George, 139
Bowen, Francis, 57
Breckinridge, Robert J., 46
British Guiana, 4, 5, 6
Brownson, Orestes A., 123
Burckhardt, Jacob, 61–62
Burke's Garden, 26, 39, 81, 82, 87, 88 , 199, 206, 216
Byron, George Gordon, Lord, 16, 77

Cabet, Etienne, 166
Calhoun, John C., 183, 187, 203

Canada, 7–8
Cameron, Simon, 206
Capitalism, 152, 154
Carlyle, Thomas, 58
Cavan, 82, 83
Chambers, Robert, 146, 228
Channing, William Henry, 123
Charlottesville Advocate, 91
Chateaubriand, Viscount de, 103
Christian, John B., 28–29, 30
Christian apologetics, 117–19
Christian Observer, 46
Civil War, 202–10, 213
Coleridge, Samuel Taylor, 58
College reform, 34–38
Comte, Auguste, 77, 87, 92, 123–24, 137, 139, 152, 156, 157, 166, 225, 227, 228, 230, 234, 238, 243; *see also* Holmes, George Frederick and
Condorcet, Marquis de, 143
Cooper, Thomas, 44, 51
Cousin, Victor, 52, 54, 58, 66, 110, 127, 147; *see also* Eclecticism
Cowan, James, 3, 5, 42
Cudworth, Ralph, 45

Dabney, Richard H., 223
Darwin, Charles, *see* Darwinism
Darwinism, 220, 226–39
D'Aubigné, Jean Henri Merle, 45
Dawkins, Sir William Boyd, 234, 240
Dawson, Sir John William, 235–36
De Bow, James D. B., 93, 160
De Bow's Review, 15, 93, 224, 227
Degenerationism, 232–33, 239–41
De Maistre, Joseph, 103–4, 123
Demerara, British Guiana, 4, 5, 180
Democracy, 12, 154, 164–65, 214–15
De Morgan, Augustus, 139
Dew, Thomas R., 22, 23, 24, 28, 183, 187
De Wette, Wilhelm L., 52

Domat, Jean, 186
Dorfman, Joseph, 171n
Durham University, 3, 5, 42, 225

Eclecticism, 52, 54, 109, 110
Edgar, Henry, 174
Eleatic philosophy, 134, 136
Emerson, Ralph Waldo, 76, 92n, 156, 214
Empiricism, *see* Holmes, George Frederick, empiricism and crypto-positivism
Everett, Edward, 14
Evolution, *see* Darwinism

Fitzhugh, George, 172–77, 181, 187, 196–98
Floyd, Benjamin Rush, 18, 175
Floyd, George, 18, 23, 29
Floyd, John, 18
Floyd, John Buchanan, 18, 82, 90, 207
Floyd, Letitia Preston, 18, 82
Floyd, William Preston, 18, 23
Fourier, Charles, 166
Fraser, Alexander Campbell, 98
Frazer, Sir James, 241

Garnett, James M., 222–23
Genovese, Eugene, 162, 163, 198
Gibbon, Edward, 12, 59
Gildersleeve, Basil, 90, 201
Gillespie, William Mitchell, 124
Gladstone, William, 219, 243
Grange School, The, 3, 5, 42
Greeley, Horace, 167, 168
Grote, George, 59, 242, 244
Guizot, F. P. G., 11, 52, 54, 63, 190

Haiti, 190
Hamilton, Sir William, 57, 87, 92, 96, 137n, 138, 228; *see also* Realism, Scottish
Hammond, James H., 183
Harper, William, 23, 183, 184, 187
Harrison, Gessner, 201
Hartz, Louis, 171n
Heeren, Arnold, 55, 221
Hegel, G. W. F., 54, 56, 58, 62, 80, 120, 139, 234
Herder, Johann G. von, 53, 61, 63–65, 71, 230, 234

Historiography, British, 59; French, 52–60; German, 54–59
Holmes, Annamaria, 3, 4, 20
Holmes, Charlotte, 5
Holmes, Coralie, 81, 211
Holmes, Edward A., 5, 6, 20, 83, 85–86, 88, 97, 99, 181, 200, 207, 208, 210
Holmes, Eliza Lavalette Floyd, 18–21, 23, 24, 37, 82, 180, 199–201, 206, 208, 210, 215, 218, 249
Holmes, Frederick Lawrence, 81, 215, 216, 218
Holmes, George Frederick: academic career, 20–23, 82, 88–91, 201–2, 204–5, 206, 219–25; attitude toward North, 8, 32, 108; attitude toward South, 12, 163, 197, 203–4; childhood in England, 5–6, 13; at College of William and Mary, 23–31; and Comte, 50, 70, 75, 79, 80, 85, 96, 98, 100, 102, 105, 108, 110–11, 114, 122, 124–33, 137–38, 140–45, 148, 230, 242; domestic life, 21, 26, 75, 83–84, 199–201, 215–19; early religious views, 42–49, 50–51, 62, 66–67, 70, 143; empiricism and crypto-positivism, 49–52, 75, 77, 109; influence of father, 6–7; late religious views, 229, 235, 241, 243–47; leaves England, 3; legal career, 9–10, 20, 23, 29, 87–88; literary career, 12–18, 84–87, 91–99, 224–25; marries, 18–20; newspaper career, 82–83; not a citizen of United States, 91; Philosophy of Faith, 110–17, 119, 120, 212, 226–27, 228, 237–38, 245, 247; philosophy of history, 12, 22, 25, 40–41, 52–75, 99–101, 103, 133–37, 139–40, 230, 234; political views, 24, 203; poverty, 10, 19, 84–86, 93, 98, 141–42, 202, 218; president of University of Mississippi, 9, 30–38, 81, 108; and reform of logic, 109, 137, 139; religious orthodoxy, 51–52, 80, 101–3, 104–7, 111–12, 114–15, 119–22, 150, 152, 210–12; social criticism, 40–41, 75–79, 92, 101–2, 108–9, 138–39, 151–77, 212–15; at University of Virginia, 89–91, 199–225
Holmes, Henry Hendon, 81, 215–16, 217, 218
Holmes, John Floyd, 26, 75, 103, 211

Holmes, Joseph Henry Hendon, 4, 5, 6, 7, 180
Holmes, Letitia, 81, 209, 215, 217
Holmes, Mary Anne, 37, 75, 215
Holmes, Maryanne, 3, 4, 5, 6, 12, 19–20, 82–83, 85, 88, 97, 99, 180, 200, 207
Horne, Thomas Hartwell, 43
Hume, David, 49, 59, 98, 104–6, 139, 227
Huxley, Thomas Henry, 227, 241

Idealism, 109; German, 51–52, 54, 56–58, 79–80, 109–10, 112–13

Jamison, David Flavel, 22, 23, 25, 30, 39, 48, 82–83, 84, 88–89; influence on Holmes, 11–12, 45, 53
Jeffersonville, Virginia, 82
Johnston, Nicketti Floyd, 18–19

Kant, Immanuel, 51, 54, 56, 79–88, 113, 227, 228

Lacordaire, Jean B. H., 104
Lawrence, John G., 8
Lewes, George Henry, 123
Lewis, Letitia Preston Floyd, 18–19, 22, 47
Lewis, William S., 18
Lieber, Francis, 20, 23, 24, 160
Lincoln, Abraham, 209
Littré, Emile, 123–24, 148
Longstreet, Augustus Baldwin, 32, 37
Lotze, Hermann, 228
Lubbock, Sir John, Baron Avebury, 220, 233n, 234, 235, 236
Lyell, Sir Charles, 232

Macauley, Thomas B., 59, 204
McCandlish, Robert, 29, 30
McClintock, John, 87, 88, 95, 98, 102, 132, 141, 144, 146, 147–48, 149, 180–81, 210, 224, 238
McCord, D. J., 48
McCord, Louisa Cheves, 160–61
McGuffey, William H., 201
Maine, Sir Henry S., 220
Manifest Destiny, 179–80
Marx, Karl, 221
Mathews, Cornelius, 14, 17

Maury, Matthew F., 222
Memminger, Christopher, 203
Metaphysics, 51, 79–80, 92, 103, 105, 108–9, 112, 129–32
Methodist Quarterly Review (New York), 93, 97, 224
Mill, John Stuart, 57, 77, 97, 123, 132, 137, 139, 143n, 184, 227, 228
Millington, John, 26, 28, 30, 33
Michelet, Jules, 52, 53, 54, 58, 59–60, 61, 62, 63, 66, 67, 71, 72, 103, 152
Minnigerode, Charles, 26–27
Minor, Benjamin B., 8
Minor, William G., 8, 9, 17
Mississippi, University of, 9, 30–38, 81, 108
Montesquieu, Baron de, 65, 66, 190
Motley, John L., 55
Murphy, Joseph J., 236
Mythology, 68–70, 102, 230, 241–42, 244–45

Nation, 224
National Intelligencer, 17, 90
Nativism, 9, 20, 22, 28, 47
Natural theology, 118–19, 212, 237
Negroes, 71, 81, 180, 187, 192; *see also* Slavery
Niebuhr, Barthold, 11, 55, 67, 68, 71, 72, 87
North American Review, 14, 224
North British Review, 98, 104, 106
Norton, Andrews, 57, 117n

O'Connell, James, 145–48
Orangeburg, South Carolina, 11, 12, 18, 20
Owen, Robert, 166
Ozanam, Frederic, 104

Paine, Thomas, 120
Parker, Theodore, 123
Peachy, A. C., 26–27, 30
Pemberton, Elizabeth, 3, 5, 6, 12
Pemberton, George, 6
Pemberton, Stephen, 4
Perkinson, William H., 218
Phillips, Wendell, 174
Philosophy of Faith, *see* Holmes, George Frederick

Philosophy of history, *see* Holmes, George Frederick
Planter-cavalier ideal, 35, 161–63, 198
Plato, 135
Platonism, 80, 135
Political economy, 158–61
Pope, James E., 37n
Positive Philosophy, *see* Comte, Auguste; Holmes, George Frederick, and Comte
Positivists, American, 145–50
Prescott, William H., 55
Preston, William C., 22, 23
Proslavery argument, 24, 96–97, 178–98
Proudhon, Pierre Joseph, 139, 157, 160, 166

Quarterly Review of the Methodist Episcopal Church, South, 93
Quartrefages, Armand de, 236

Racialism, 70–72, 192–95, 233
Ranke, Leopold von, 55
Realism, Scottish, 49, 57, 77, 99, 109, 113, 228
Renan, Ernest, 244–46
Richie, William F., 24
Richmond College, 10, 12, 21, 88
Richmond Examiner, 83
Ripley, George, 123
Robert Elsmere, 243–44
Roman Catholicism, 20, 45–47, 80, 102–4, 211

Saint-Simon, Henri de, 123, 166
Santayana, George, 115
Saunders, Robert, 25, 27, 30, 86
Savigny, F. K. von, 55
Schele De Vere, Maximilian, 201, 205
Schelling, F. W. J. von, 56
Schlegel, Frederick von, 53, 63–64, 65, 68, 74–75, 103, 230, 234
Schleiermacher, Friedrich, 52, 56
Simms, William Gilmore, 11, 12, 16, 17–18, 22–23, 76, 88, 92n, 94, 154, 183; influence on Holmes, 77
Slavery, 81, 162–63, 180–81, 194–95; *see also* Negroes; Proslavery argument

Smith, Francis H., 205
Social science, 78–79, 156–57, 171–72, 220–21
Socialism, 108, 136, 166–67
Socrates, 134
Sophists, Greek, 134
South Carolina College, 20, 22, 88–89
Southern Literary Messenger, 8, 15–17, 76, 93, 109, 125, 141, 176, 195
Southern Magazine, 224
Southern Quarterly Review, 12, 14–15, 45, 46, 74, 92–93, 93–95, 102, 160
Southern Review, 224
Southwestern Advocate, 82
Spalding, M. J., 45–46
Sparks, Jared, 55
Spencer, Herbert, 92, 158, 164, 165, 168, 171, 174, 220, 227, 234
Spiritualism, 138, 140
Sterling, Hutchinson, 57
Stowe, Harriet Beecher, 195
Strauss, David F., 70, 102, 110, 117, 120, 139, 242, 244

Tanglewood, 83, 199–200, 207–8, 209–10, 248
Tannenbaum, Frank, 186n
Taylor, W. Cooke, 233n
Tazewell County, 180, 207, 208, 217
Thierry Augustin, 71
Thirlwall, Connop, 59, 72
Thomism, 104
Thompson, Jacob, 31–32
Thompson, John R., 141, 195
Thornwell, James H., 14, 15, 46, 90, 91, 94, 102, 160
Thorpe, Charles, 42
Toynbee, Arnold J., 62
Tucker, Nathaniel Beverly, 29, 30
Tullock, John, 236
Turner, Nat, rebellion of, 183
Tyler, John, 23, 28
Tyler, Samuel, 57, 101, 181
Tylor, Sir Edward Burnett, 220, 234, 240, 241

Uncle Tom's Cabin, 195–96
United States Catholic Magazine, 46
United States Catholic Miscellany, 47

Vico, Giambattista, 63, 65–66, 143, 242–
  43; influence on Holmes, 59, 61, 67,
  68, 133, 230
Vignoli, Tito, 244
Virginia, University of, 89–91, 199–225
Voltaire (François-Marie Arouet), 61

Waddel, John, 32–33, 34, 36
Wallace, Alfred Russel, 241
Wallace, Horace Benney, 148–50
Wallon, Henri, 191
Walterboro, South Carolina, 10–11
Ward, Mrs. Humphrey, 243
Warren, Josiah, 174
Welling, James C., 90
Westminster Review, 97–98

Whately, Richard, 232, 233n
Whedon, Daniel D., 95, 98
Whewell, William, 41
Whitaker, Daniel K., 14, 45–46
White, W. Thomas, 17
Whitman, Walt, 214
Wilkinson, E. C., 32, 34, 38
William and Mary, College of, 23–31
Williamson, Isabel Holmes Perkinson,
  81, 215, 217, 218, 224
Winckelmann, Johann J., 61
Wise, Henry A., 96
Wolf, Friedrich August, 68

Zeno of Elea, 134